A Certain Scientific Railgun

Vol. 7

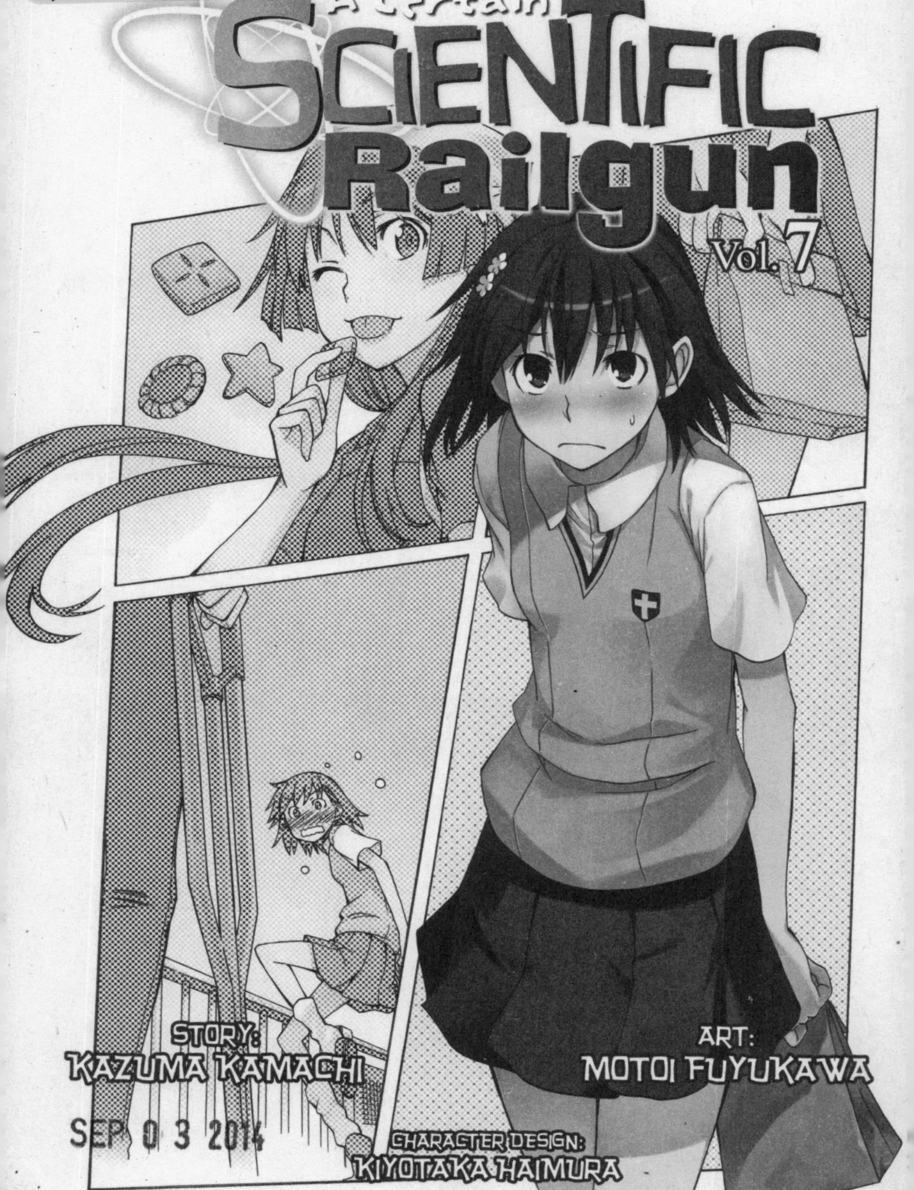

STORY:
KAZUMA KAMACHI

ART:
MOTOI FUYUKAWA

CHARACTER DESIGN:
KIYOTAKA HAIMURA

A Certain SCIENTIFIC Railgun

VOLUME 7

story by **Kazuma Kamachi**

art by **Motoi Fuyukawa**

Character Design **Kiyotaka Haimura**

STAFF CREDITS

translation	**Nan Rymer**
adaptation	**Maggie Danger**
lettering	**Roland Amago**
layout	**Bambi Eloriaga-Amago**
cover design	**Nicky Lim**
copy editor	**Shanti Whitesides**
assistant editor	**Alexis Roberts**
editor	**Jason DeAngelis**
publisher	**Seven Seas Entertainment**

A CERTAIN SCIENTIFIC RAILGUN VOL. 7
Copyright © 2011 Kazuma Kamachi / Motoi Fuyukawa
First published in 2011 by ASCII MEDIA WORKS, Tokyo, Japan.
English translation rights arranged with ASCII MEDIA WORKS.

ISBN: 978-1-937867-21-8

Printed in Canada

First Printing: April 2013

10 9 8 7 6 5 4 3 2 1

FOLLOW US ONLINE: www.gomanga.com

READING DIRECTIONS

This book reads from *right to left*, Japanese style.
If this is your first time reading manga, you start
reading from the top right panel on each page and
take it from there. If you get lost, just follow the
numbered diagram here. It may seem backwards
at first, but you'll get the hang of it! Have fun!!

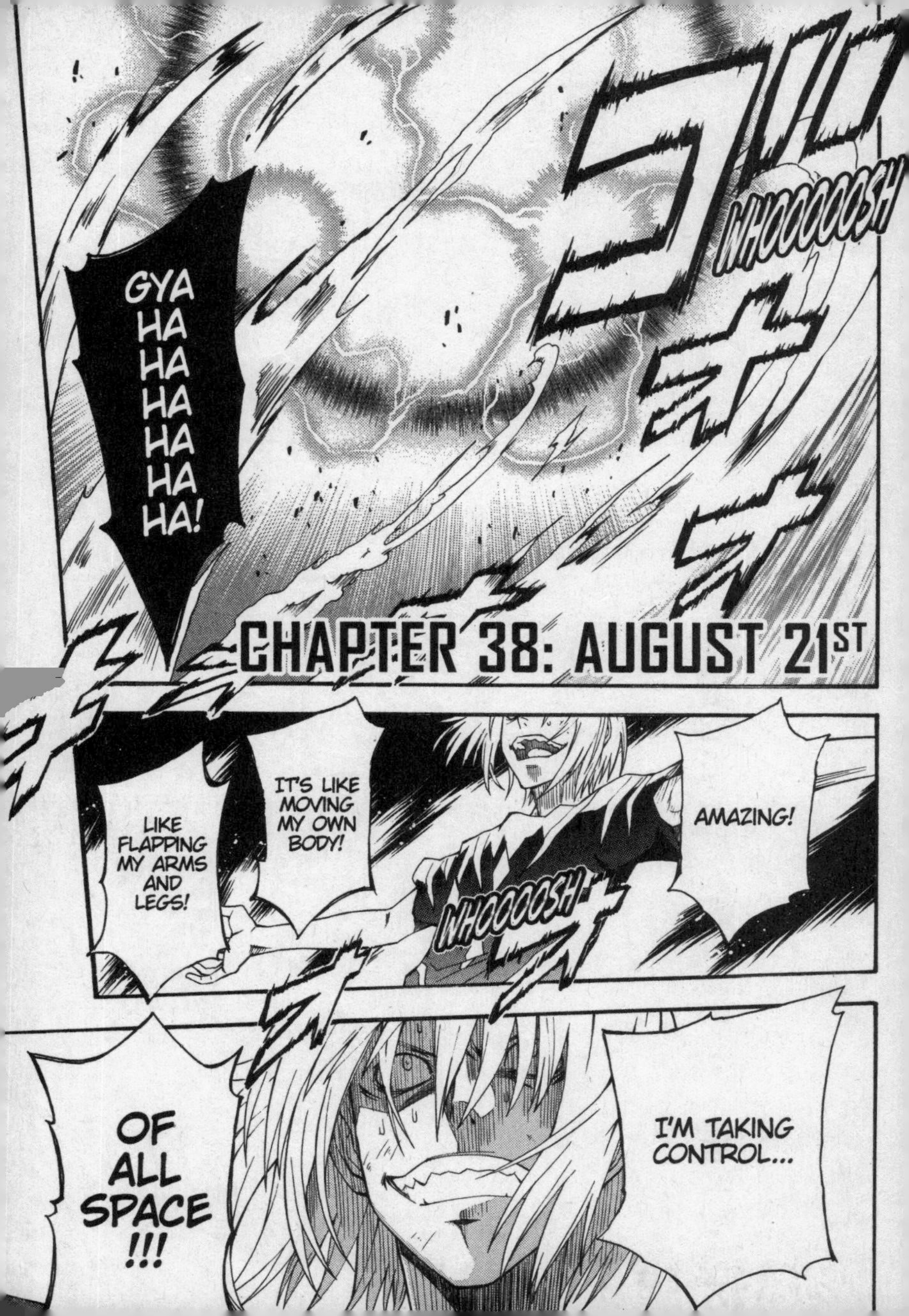
WHOOOOOSH
GYA HA HA HA HA HA HA HA!
CHAPTER 38: AUGUST 21ST
AMAZING!
IT'S LIKE MOVING MY OWN BODY!
LIKE FLAPPING MY ARMS AND LEGS!
WHOOOOSH
I'M TAKING CONTROL...
OF ALL SPACE!!!

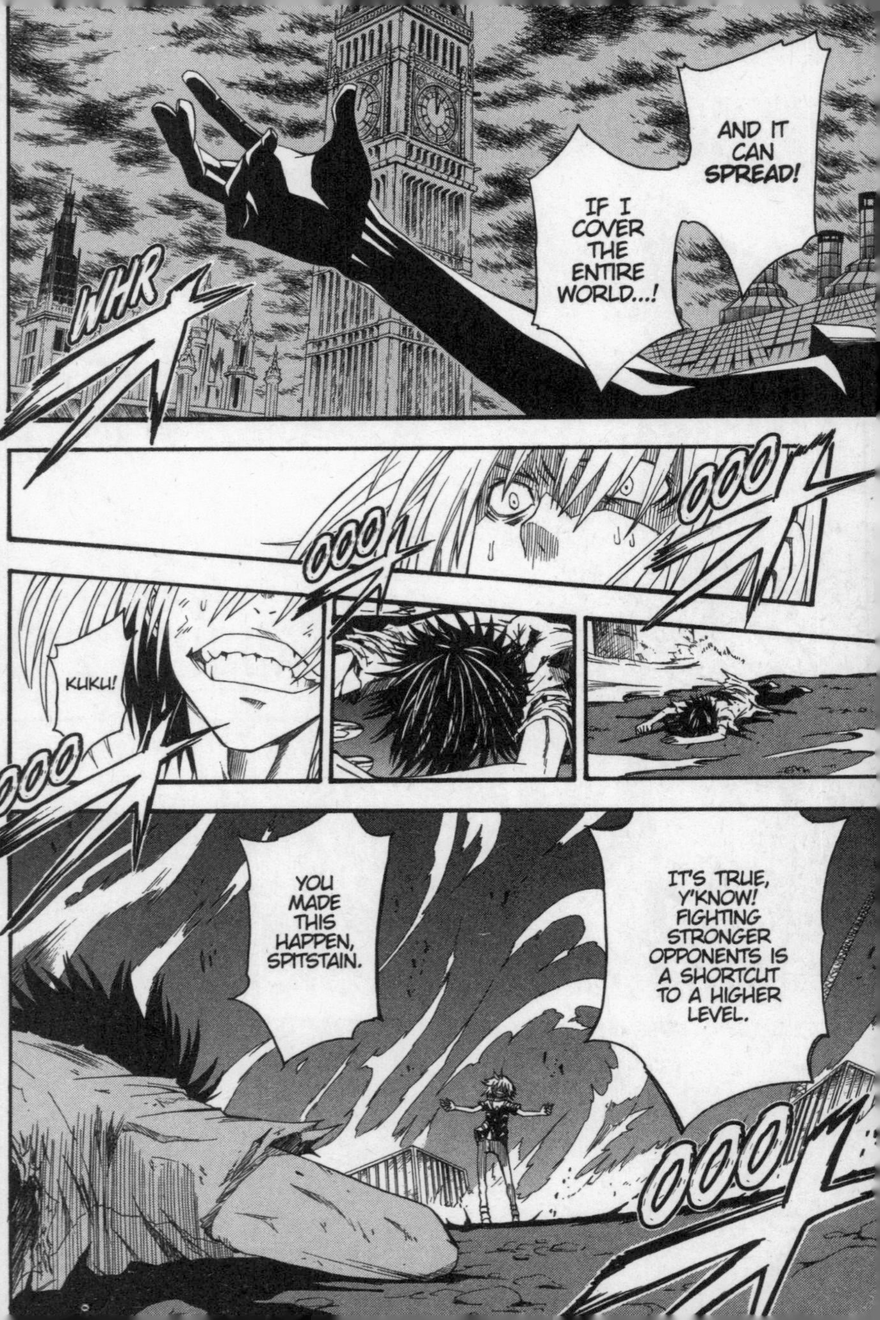
AND IT CAN SPREAD!
IF I COVER THE ENTIRE WORLD...!
WHR
OOO
OOO
OOO
KUKU!
IT'S TRUE, Y'KNOW! FIGHTING STRONGER OPPONENTS IS A SHORTCUT TO A HIGHER LEVEL.
YOU MADE THIS HAPPEN, SPITSTAIN.
OOO

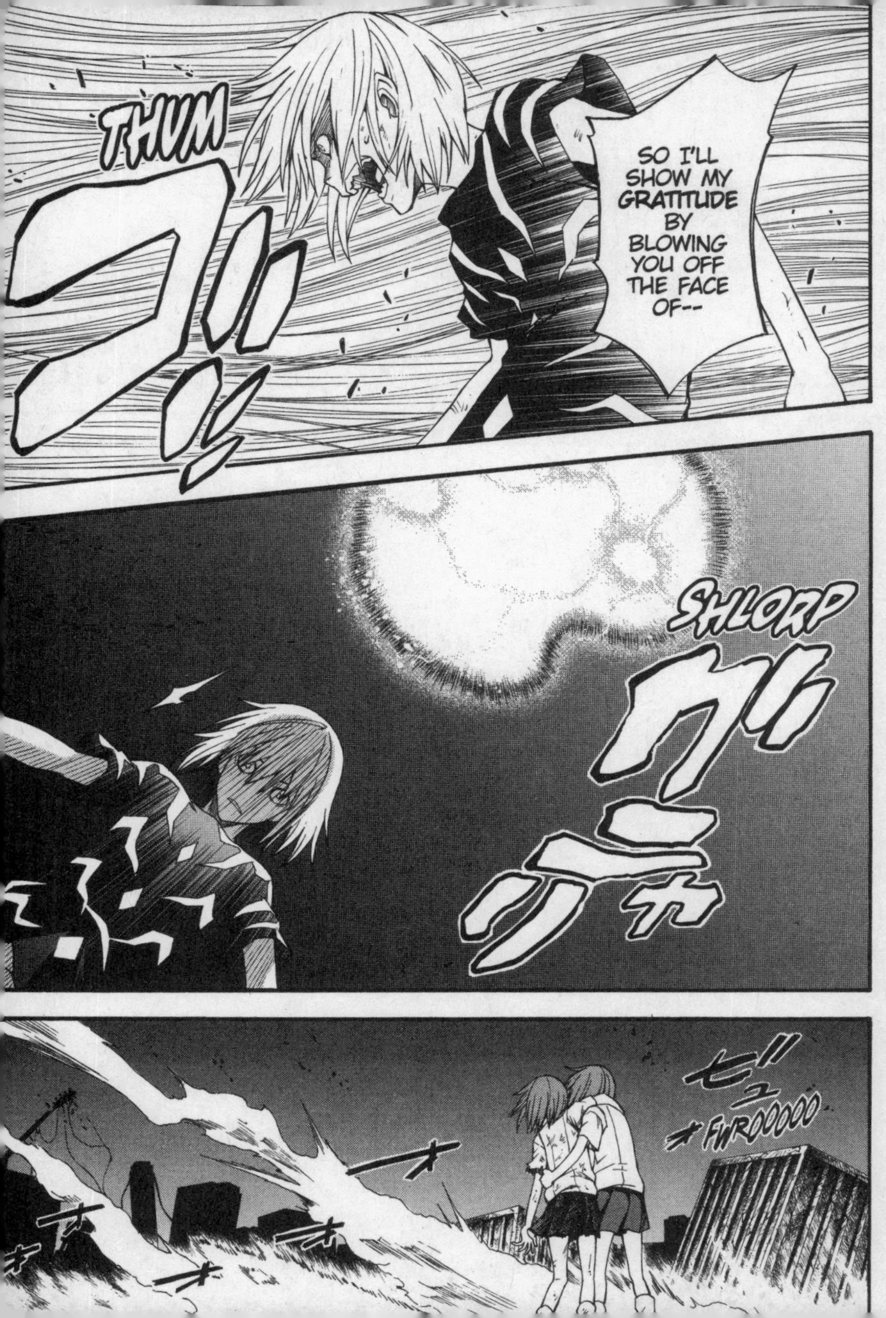
SO I'LL SHOW MY GRATITUDE BY BLOWING YOU OFF THE FACE OF--
THUM
SHLORP
FWROOOOO

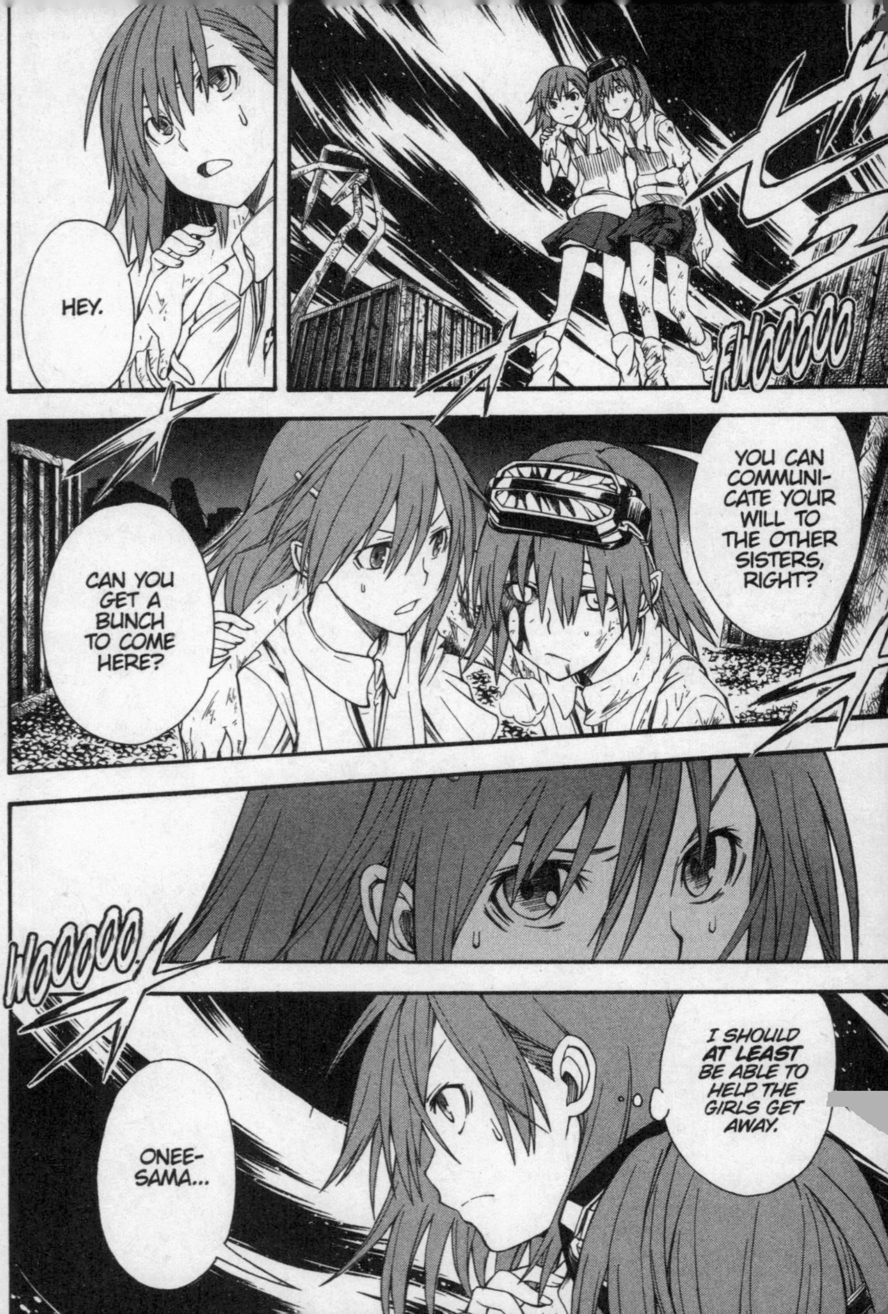
FWOOOOO
HEY.
YOU CAN COMMUNICATE YOUR WILL TO THE OTHER SISTERS, RIGHT?
CAN YOU GET A BUNCH TO COME HERE?
WOOOOO
I SHOULD AT LEAST BE ABLE TO HELP THE GIRLS GET AWAY.
ONEE-SAMA...

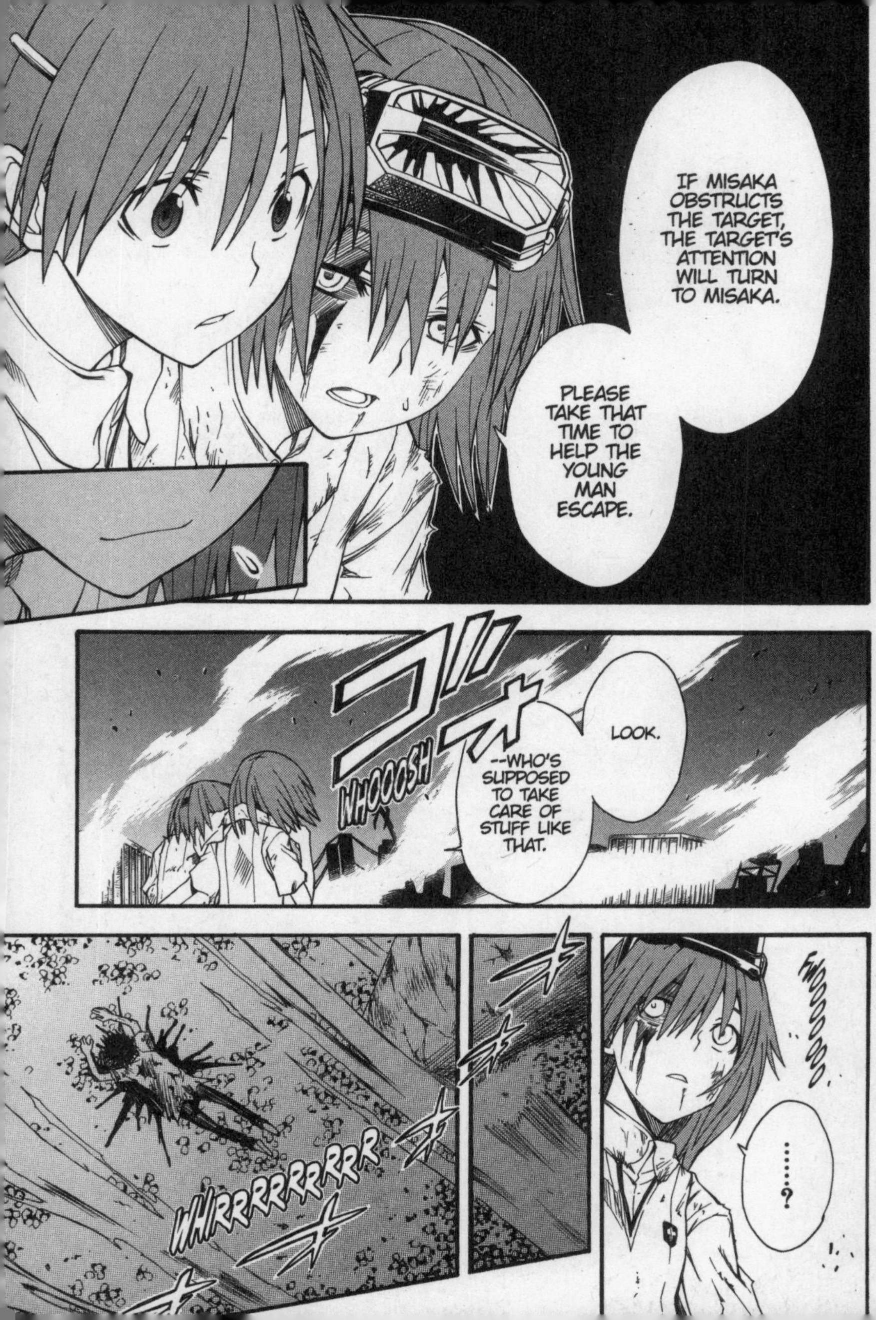
IF MISAKA OBSTRUCTS THE TARGET, THE TARGET'S ATTENTION WILL TURN TO MISAKA.
PLEASE TAKE THAT TIME TO HELP THE YOUNG MAN ESCAPE.
WHOOOSH
LOOK.
--WHO'S SUPPOSED TO TAKE CARE OF STUFF LIKE THAT.
......?
WHIRRRRRRRRR

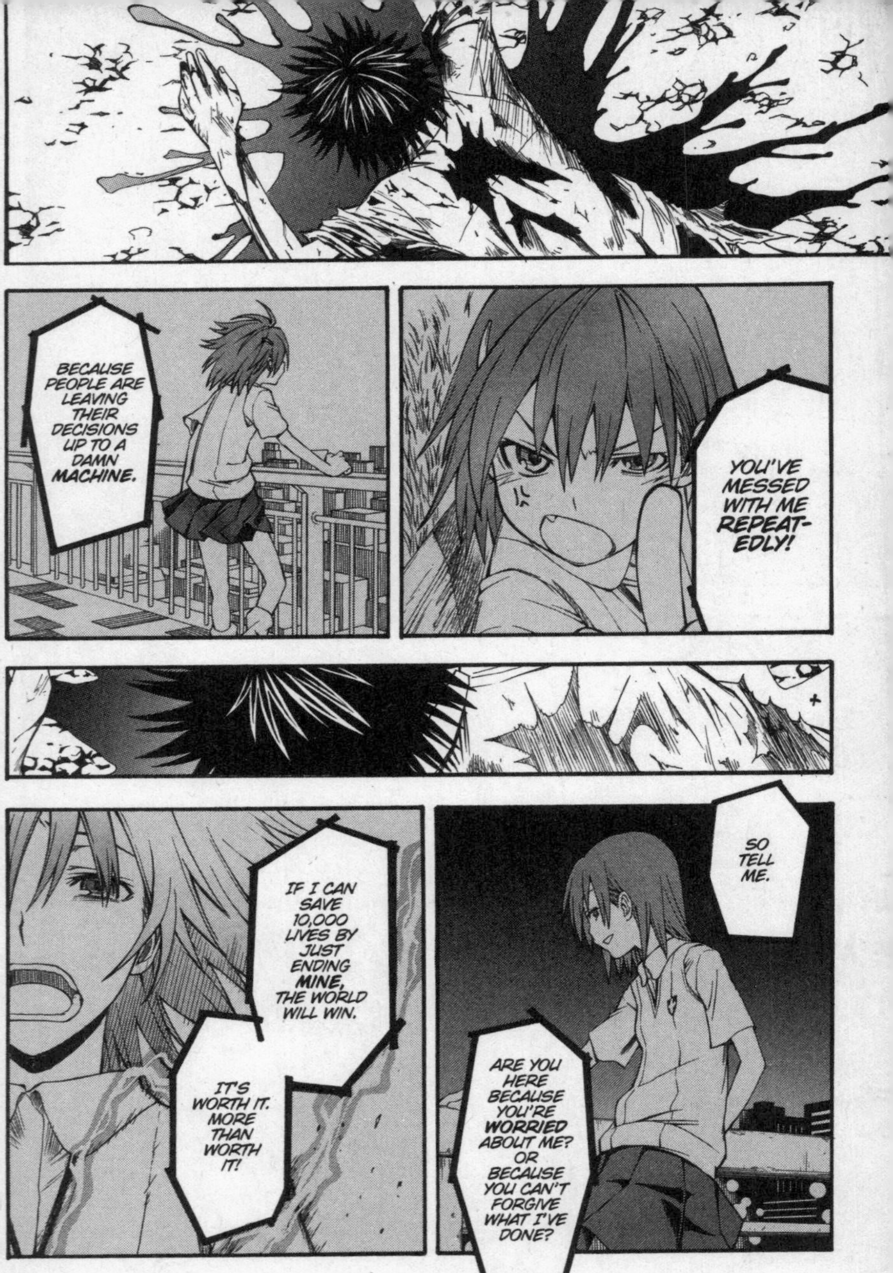
YOU'VE MESSED WITH ME REPEATEDLY!
BECAUSE PEOPLE ARE LEAVING THEIR DECISIONS UP TO A DAMN MACHINE.
SO TELL ME.
ARE YOU HERE BECAUSE YOU'RE WORRIED ABOUT ME? OR BECAUSE YOU CAN'T FORGIVE WHAT I'VE DONE?
IF I CAN SAVE 10,000 LIVES BY JUST ENDING MINE, THE WORLD WILL WIN.
IT'S WORTH IT. MORE THAN WORTH IT!

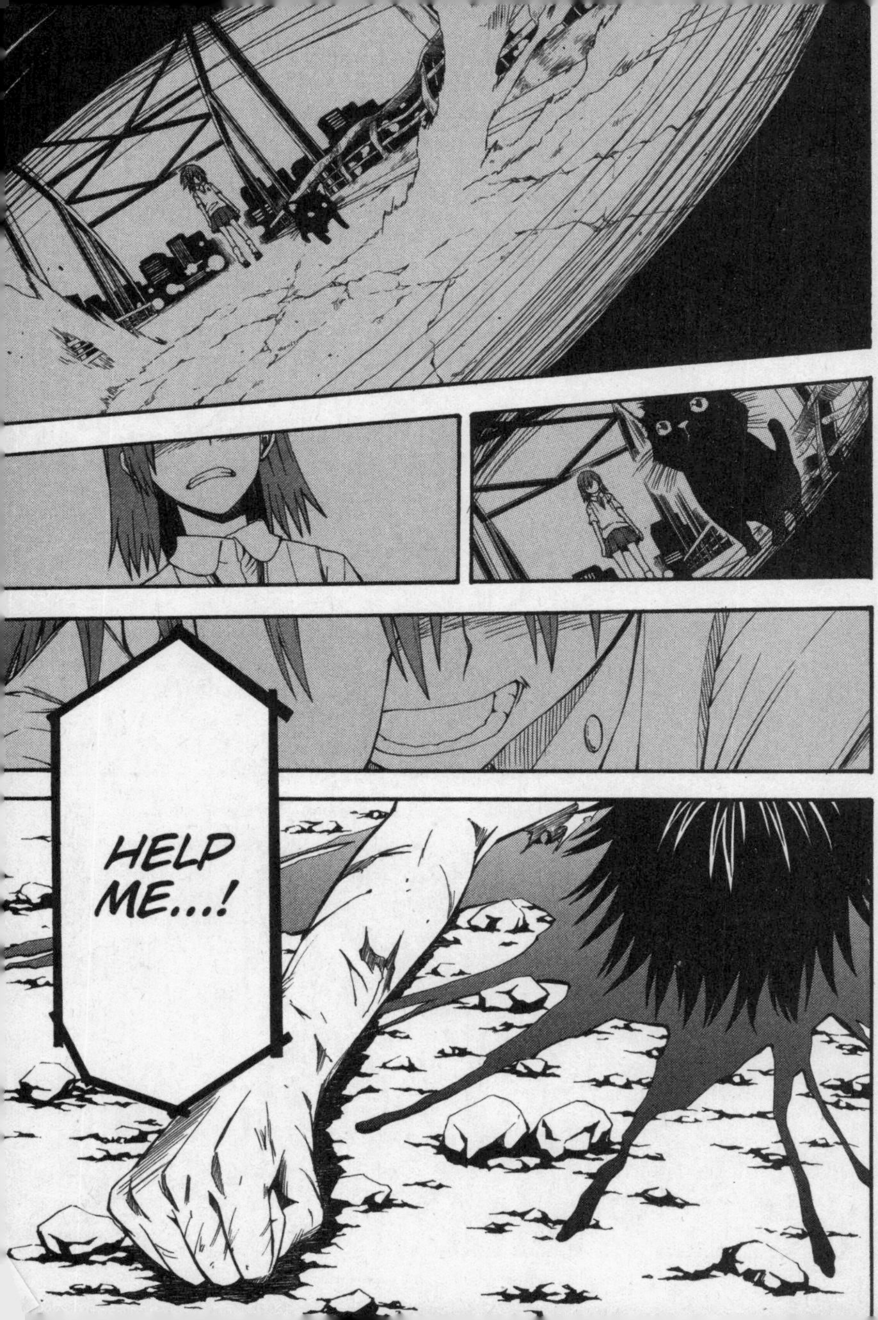
HELP ME...!

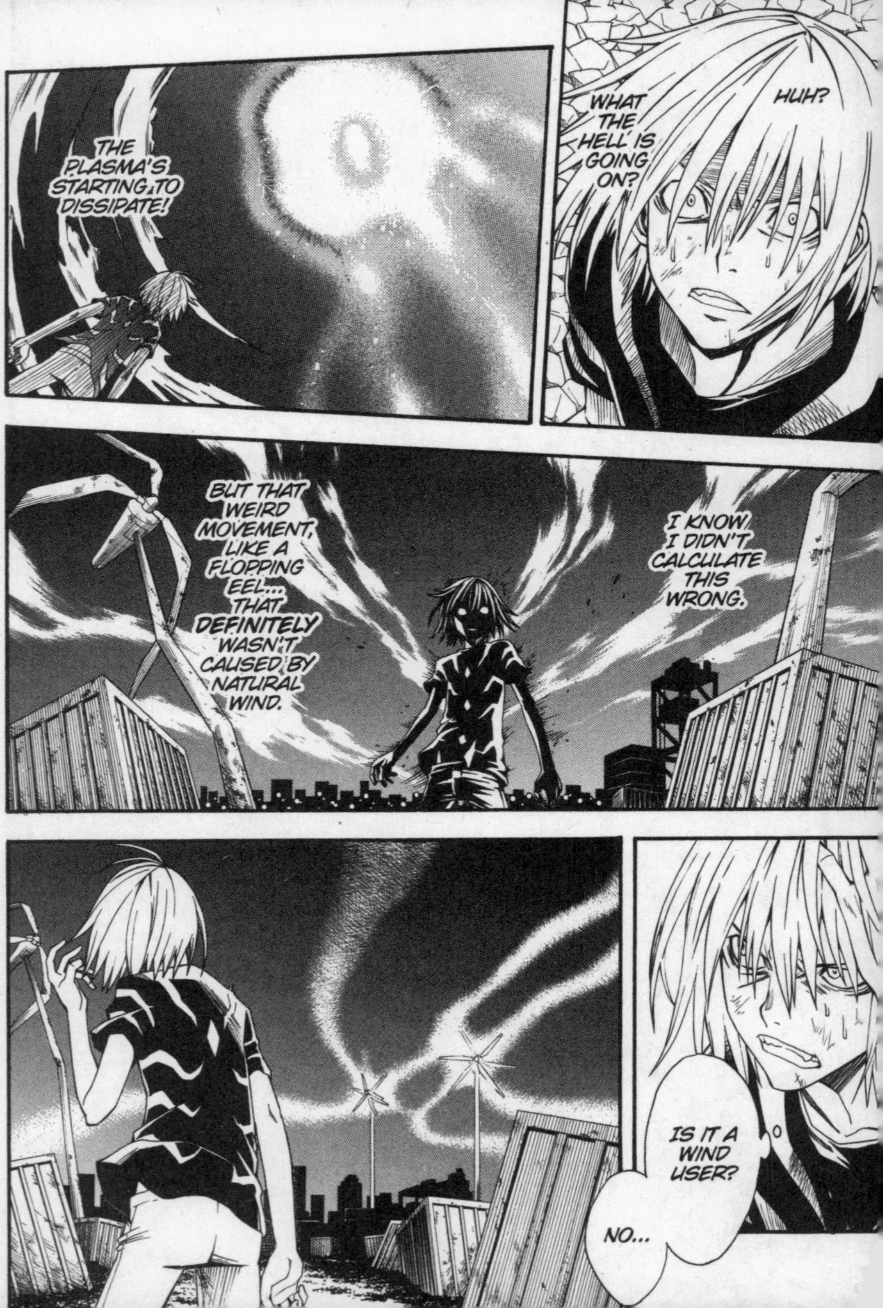
HUH?
WHAT THE HELL IS GOING ON?
THE PLASMA'S STARTING TO DISSIPATE!
I KNOW I DIDN'T CALCULATE THIS WRONG.
BUT THAT WEIRD MOVEMENT, LIKE A FLOPPING EEL... THAT DEFINITELY WASN'T CAUSED BY NATURAL WIND.
IS IT A WIND USER?
NO...

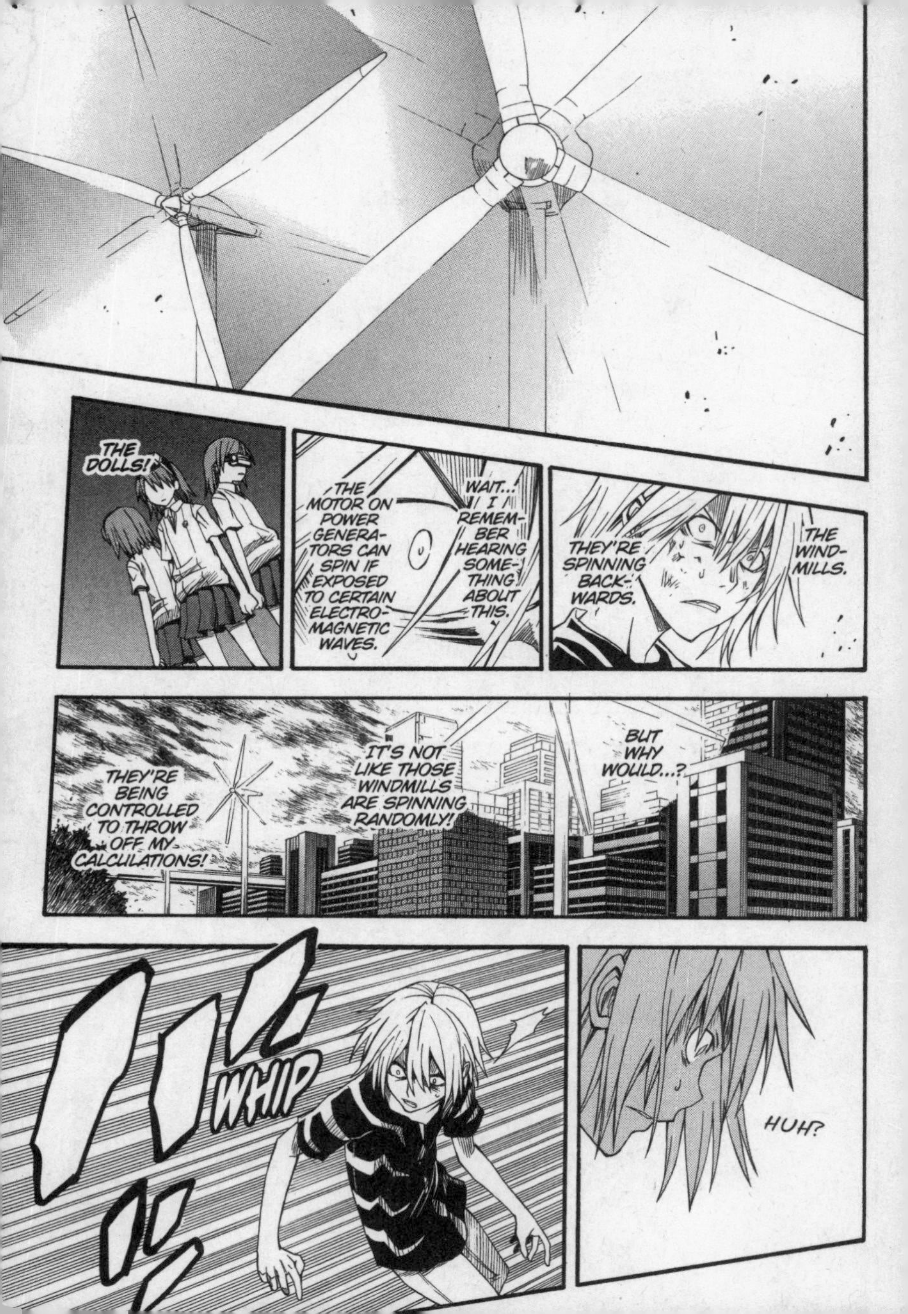
THE WINDMILLS.
THEY'RE SPINNING BACKWARDS.
WAIT... I REMEMBER HEARING SOMETHING ABOUT THIS.
THE MOTOR ON POWER GENERATORS CAN SPIN IF EXPOSED TO CERTAIN ELECTROMAGNETIC WAVES.
THE DOLLS!
BUT WHY WOULD...?
IT'S NOT LIKE THOSE WINDMILLS ARE SPINNING RANDOMLY!
THEY'RE BEING CONTROLLED TO THROW OFF MY CALCULATIONS!
HUH?
WHIP

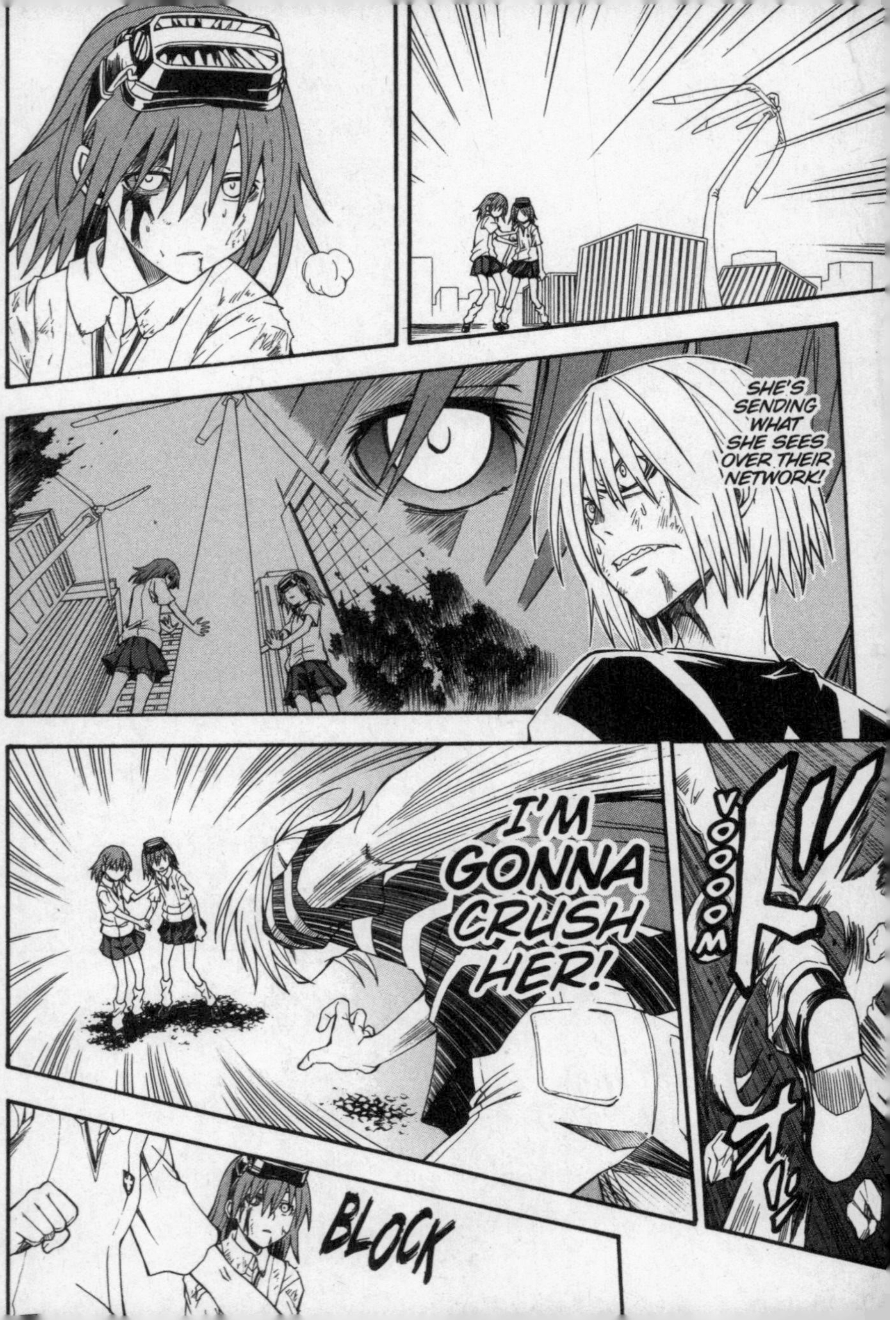
SHE'S SENDING WHAT SHE SEES OVER THEIR NETWORK!
VOOOOOM
I'M GONNA CRUSH HER!
BLOCK

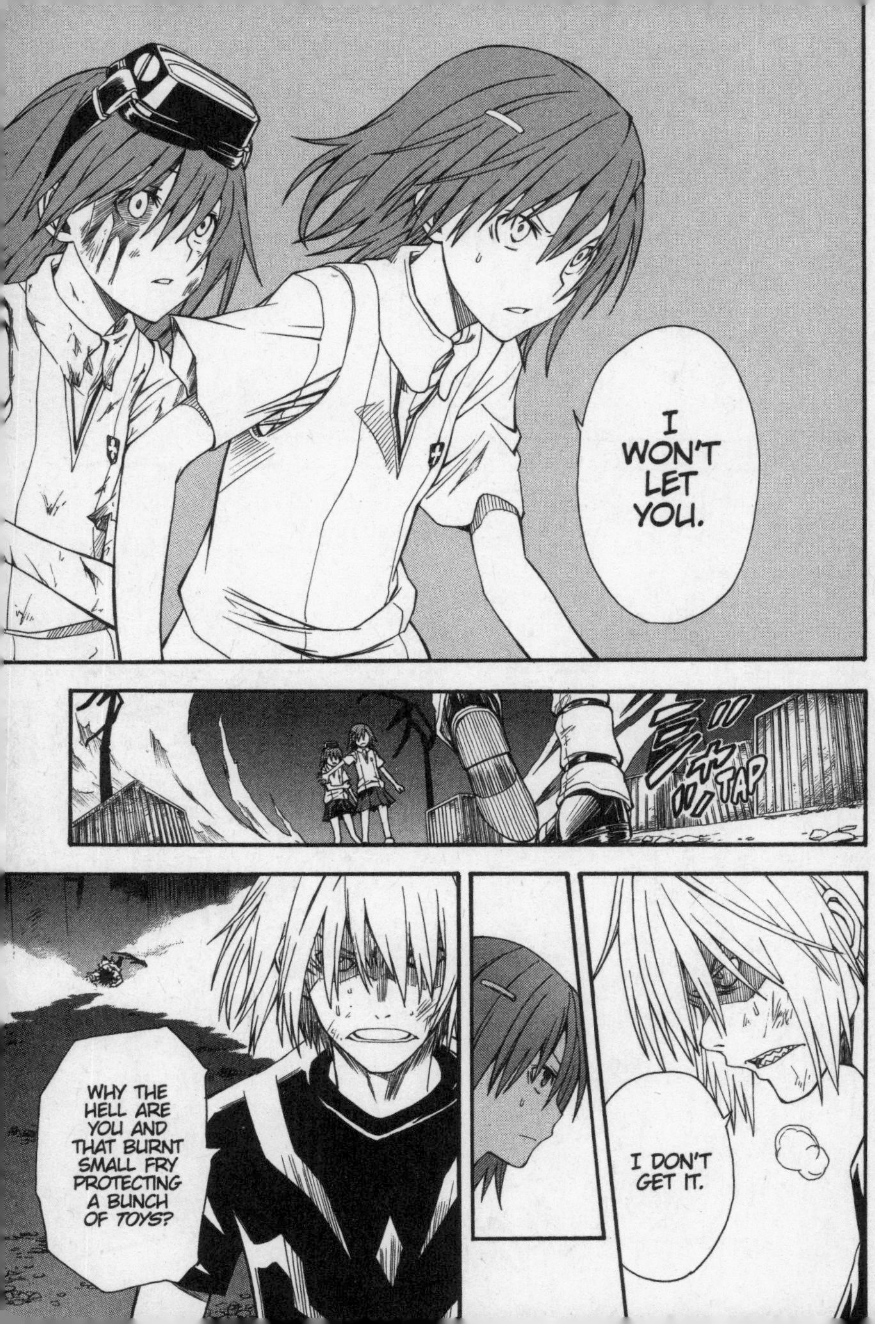
I WON'T LET YOU.
TAP
I DON'T GET IT.
WHY THE HELL ARE YOU AND THAT BURNT SMALL FRY PROTECTING A BUNCH OF TOYS?

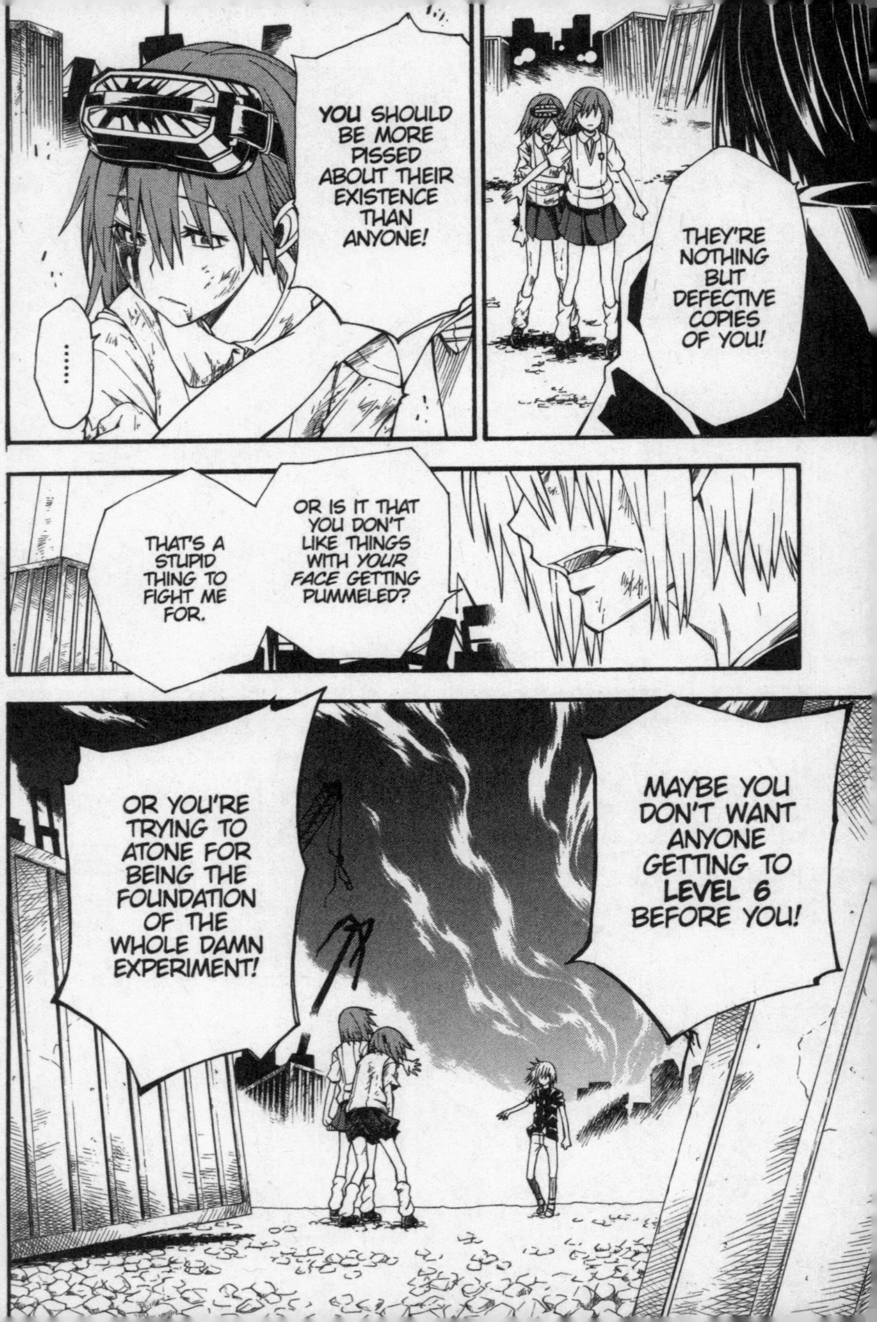
THEY'RE NOTHING BUT DEFECTIVE COPIES OF YOU!
YOU SHOULD BE MORE PISSED ABOUT THEIR EXISTENCE THAN ANYONE!
......
OR IS IT THAT YOU DON'T LIKE THINGS WITH *YOUR FACE* GETTING PUMMELED?
THAT'S A STUPID THING TO FIGHT ME FOR.
MAYBE YOU DON'T WANT ANYONE GETTING TO LEVEL 6 BEFORE YOU!
OR YOU'RE TRYING TO ATONE FOR BEING THE FOUNDATION OF THE WHOLE DAMN EXPERIMENT!

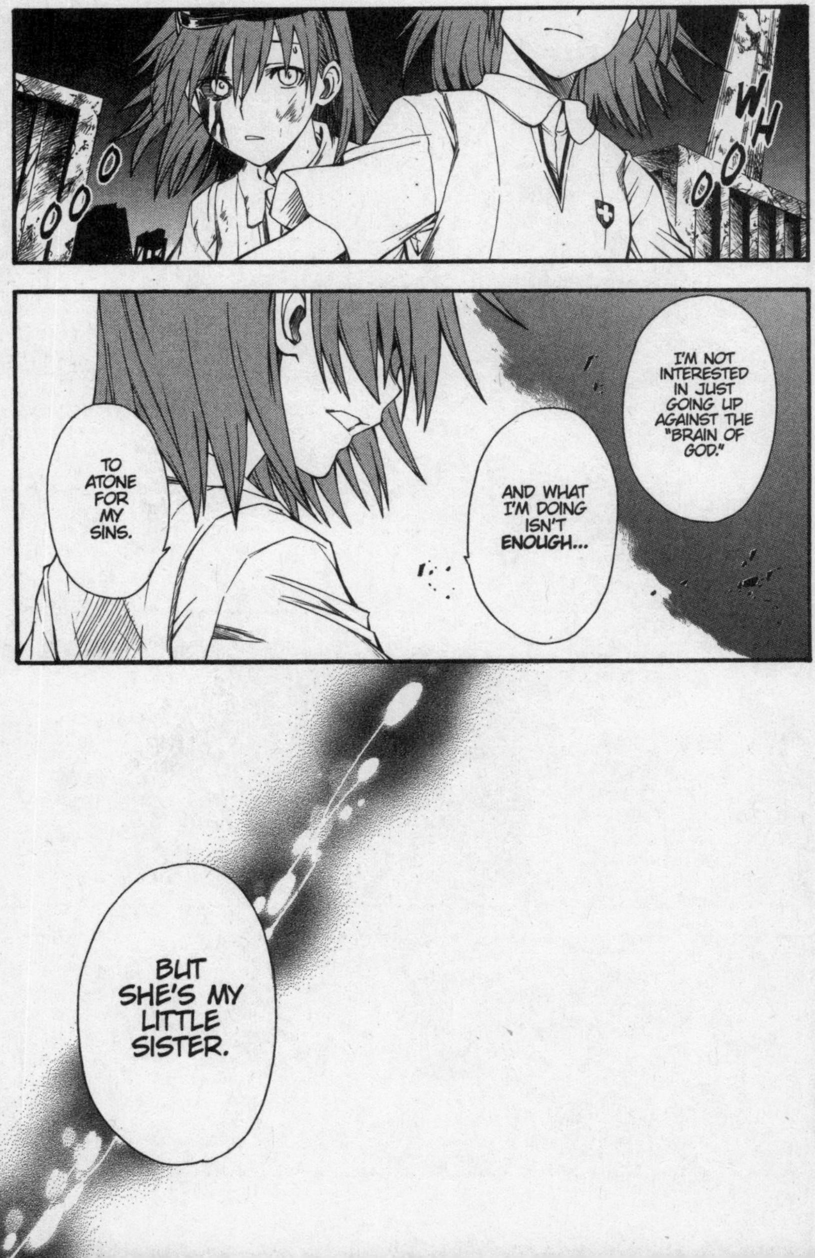
WHOO
OOOO
I'M NOT INTERESTED IN JUST GOING UP AGAINST THE "BRAIN OF GOD."
AND WHAT I'M DOING ISN'T ENOUGH...
TO ATONE FOR MY SINS.
BUT SHE'S MY LITTLE SISTER.

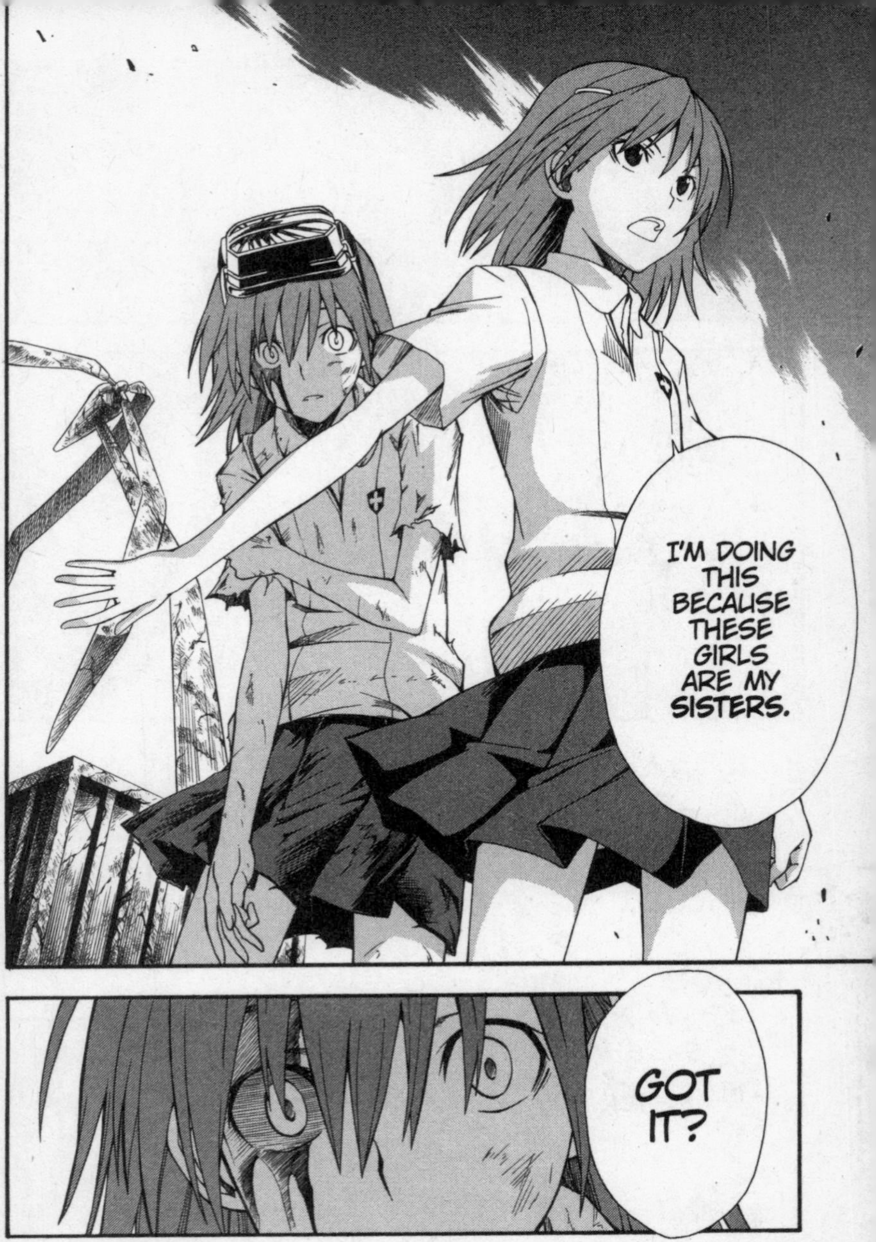
I'M DOING THIS BECAUSE THESE GIRLS ARE MY SISTERS.
GOT IT?

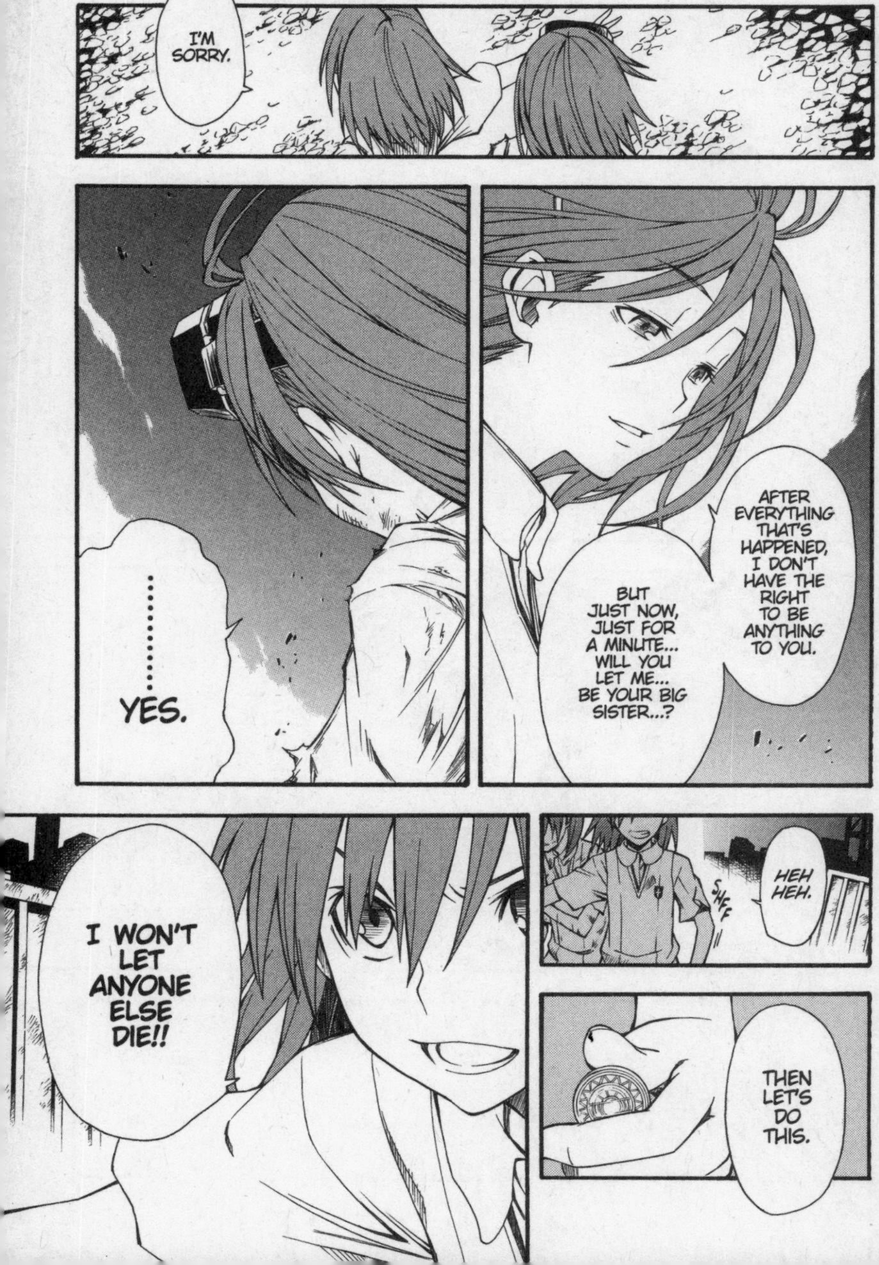
I'M SORRY.
AFTER EVERYTHING THAT'S HAPPENED, I DON'T HAVE THE RIGHT TO BE ANYTHING TO YOU.
BUT JUST NOW, JUST FOR A MINUTE... WILL YOU LET ME... BE YOUR BIG SISTER...?
......YES.
HEH HEH.
SHFF
THEN LET'S DO THIS.
I WON'T LET ANYONE ELSE DIE!!

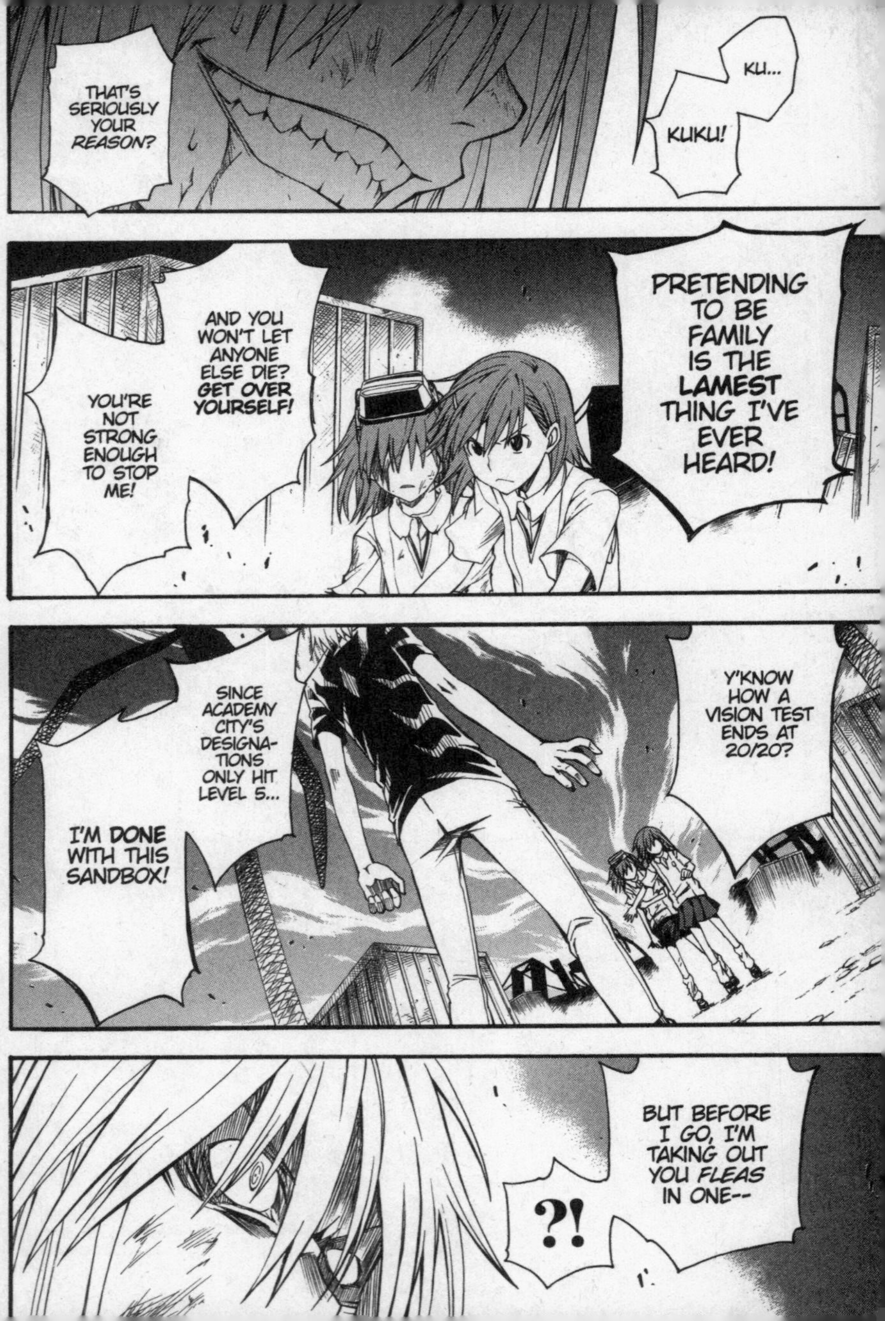
KU...
KUKU!
THAT'S SERIOUSLY YOUR *REASON*?
PRETENDING TO BE FAMILY IS THE **LAMEST** THING I'VE EVER HEARD!
AND YOU WON'T LET ANYONE ELSE DIE? **GET OVER YOURSELF!**
YOU'RE NOT STRONG ENOUGH TO STOP ME!
Y'KNOW HOW A VISION TEST ENDS AT 20/20?
SINCE ACADEMY CITY'S DESIGNATIONS ONLY HIT LEVEL 5...
I'M **DONE** WITH THIS SANDBOX!
BUT BEFORE I GO, I'M TAKING OUT YOU *FLEAS* IN ONE--
?!

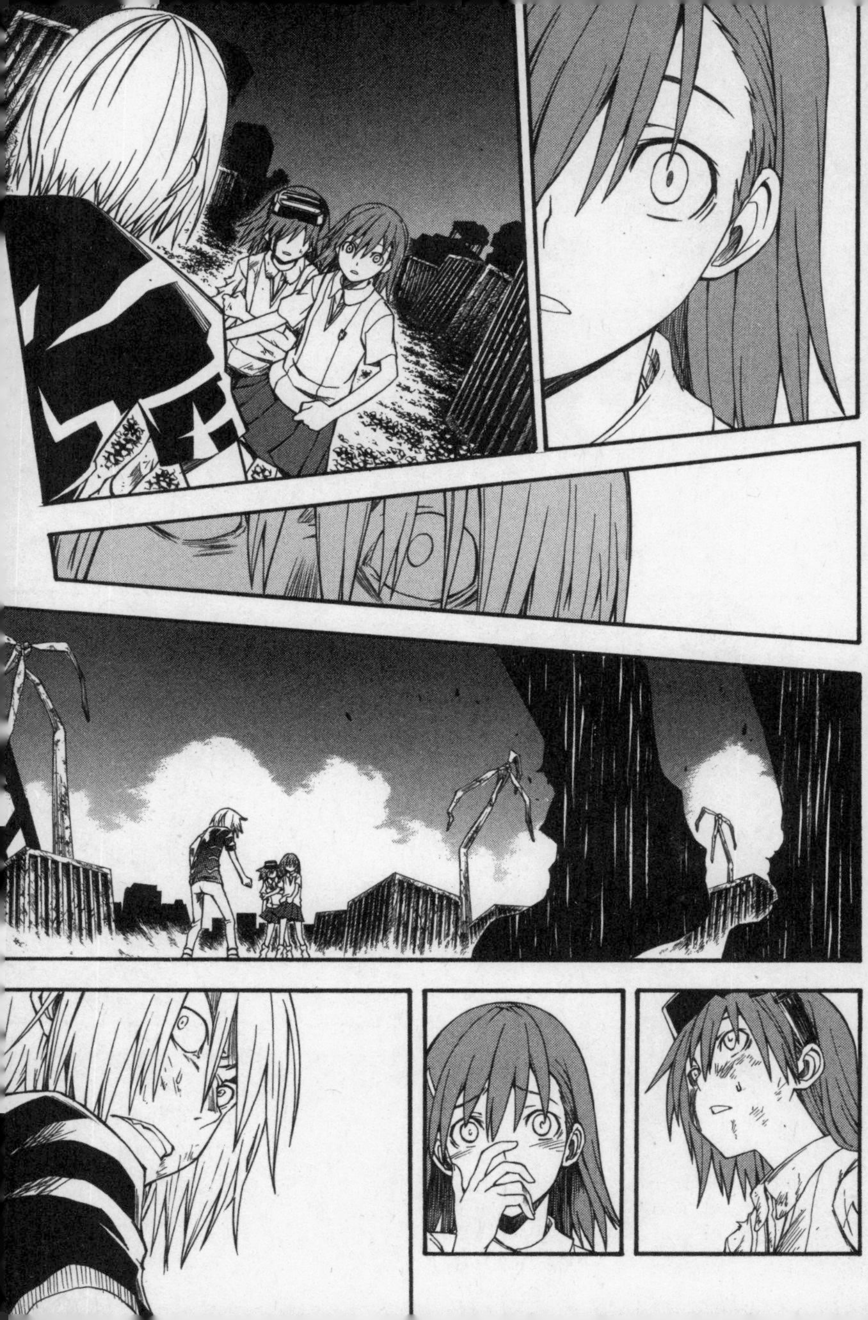

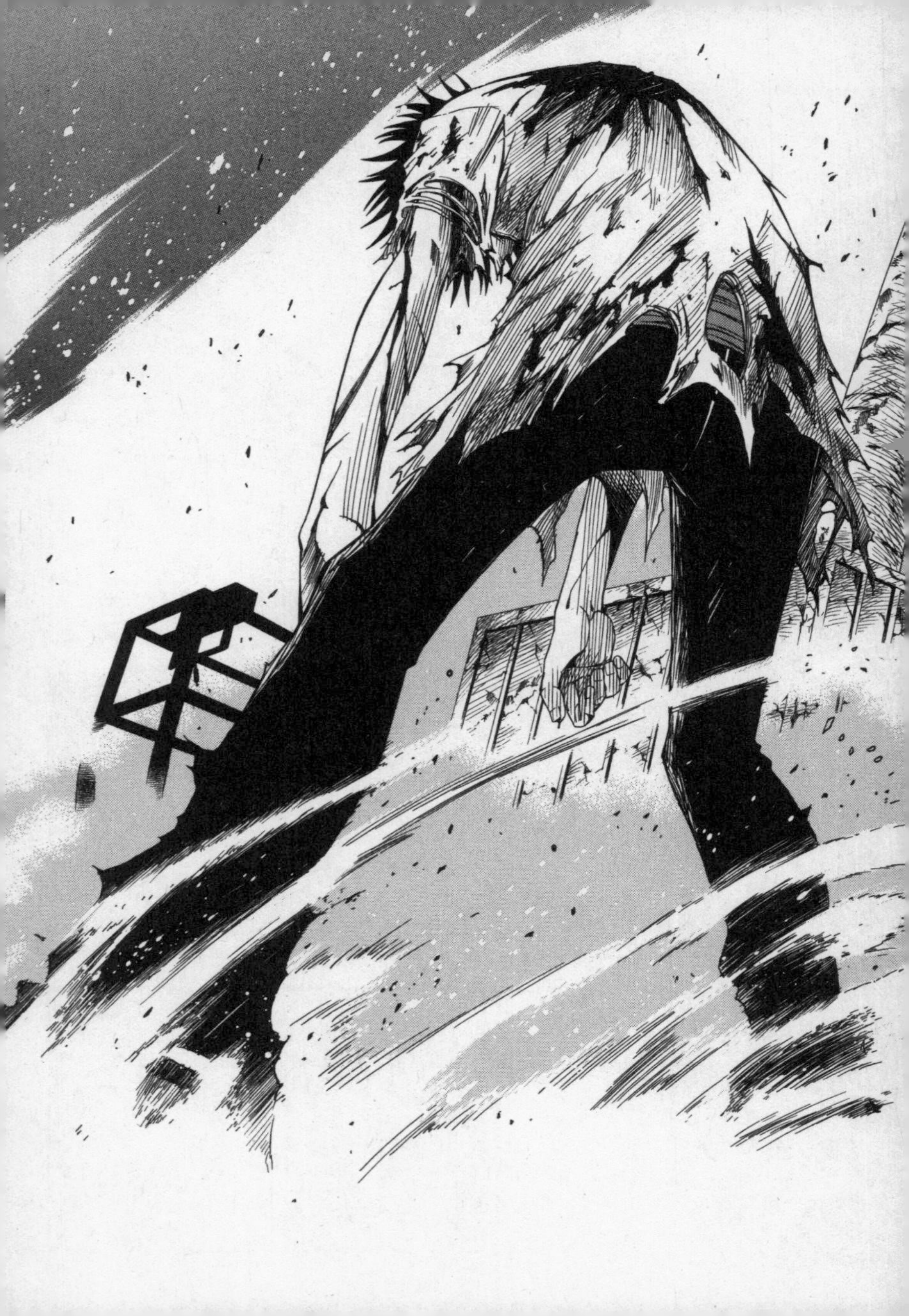

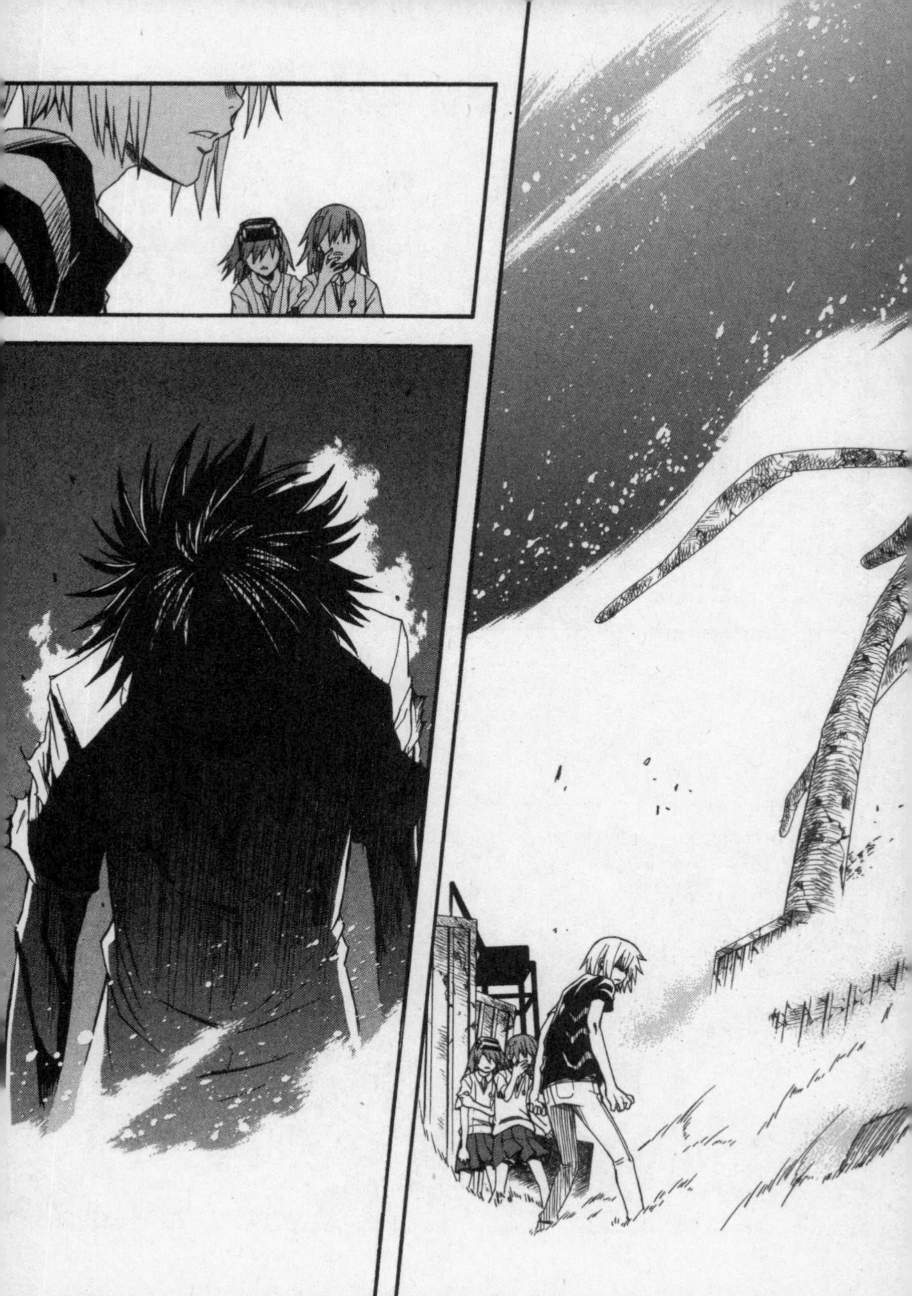

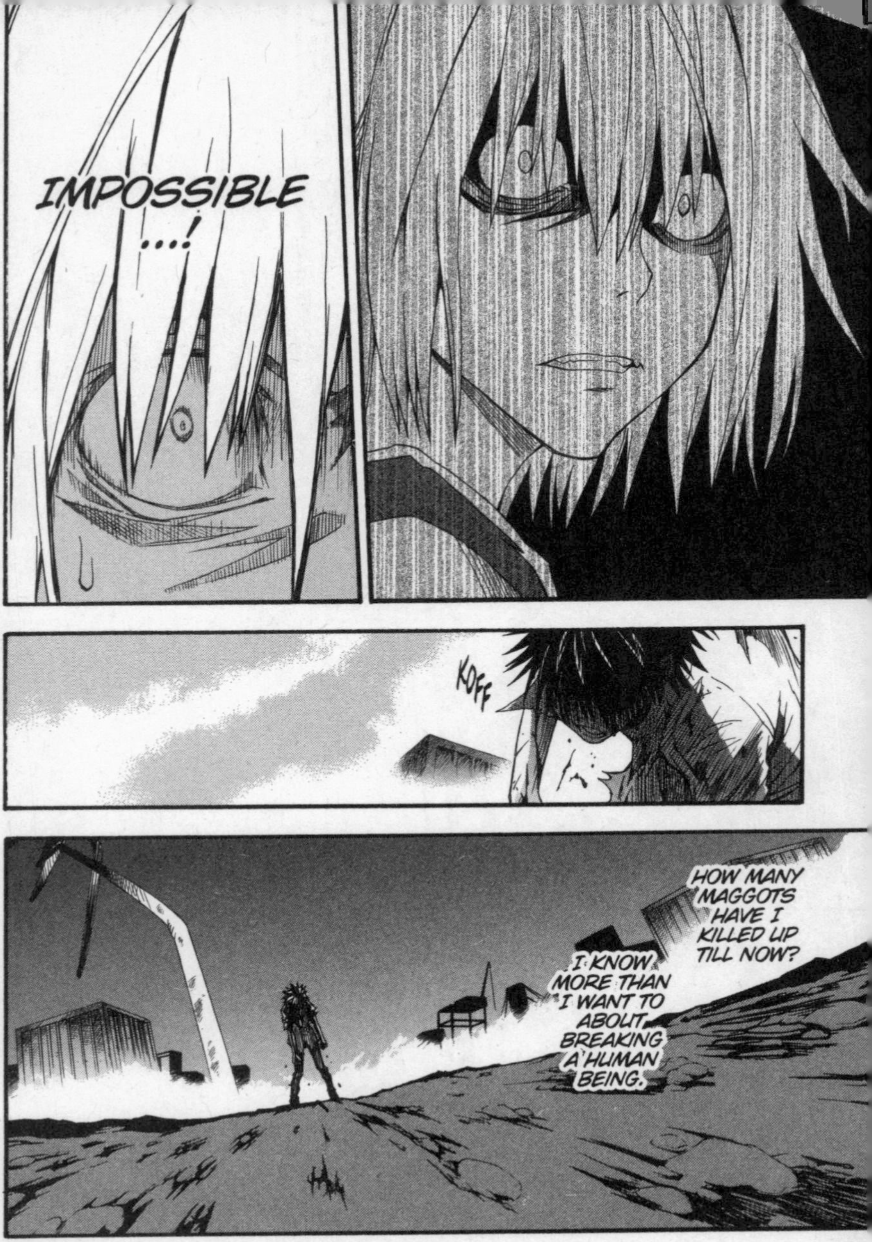
IMPOSSIBLE ...!
KOFF
HOW MANY MAGGOTS HAVE I KILLED UP TILL NOW?
I KNOW MORE THAN I WANT TO ABOUT BREAKING A HUMAN BEING.

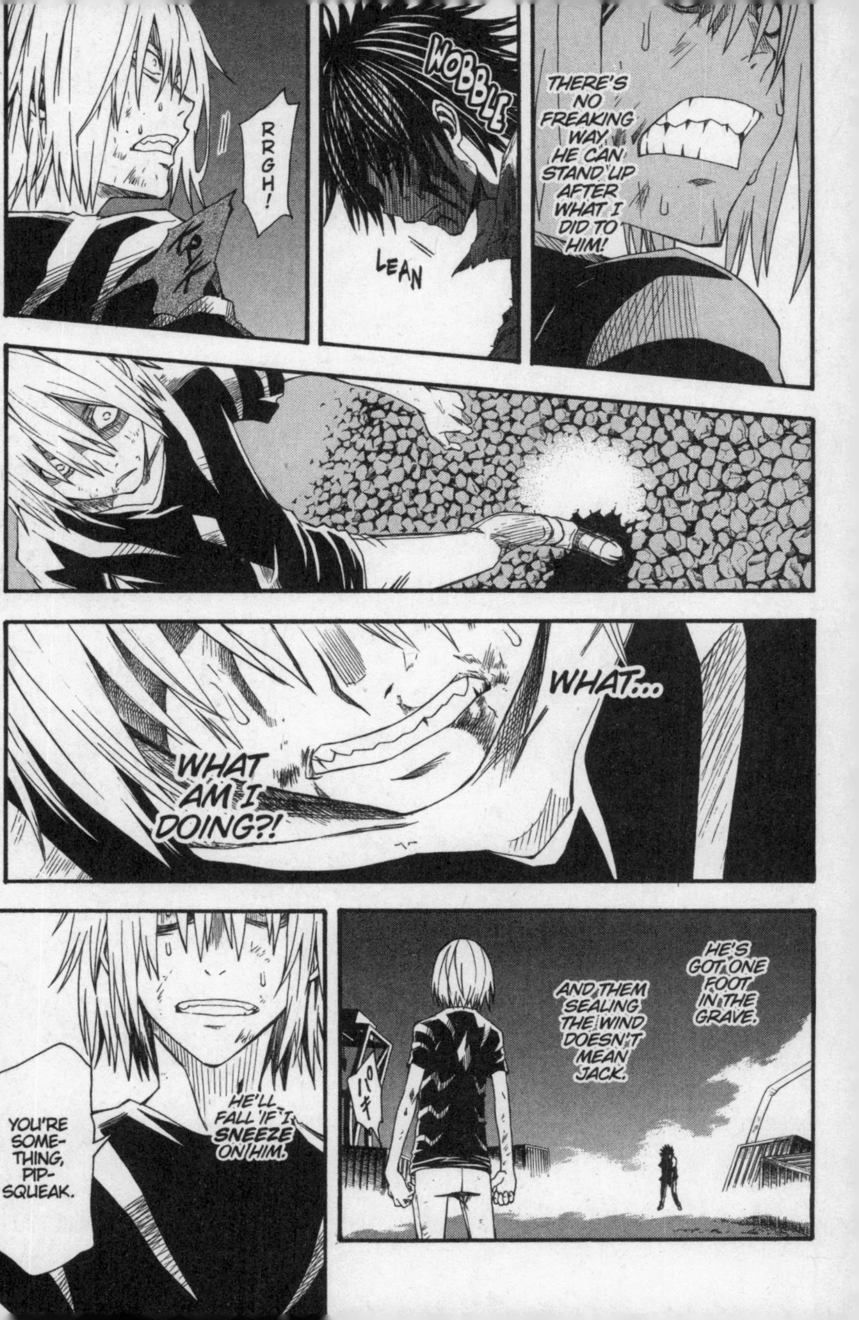
THERE'S NO FREAKING WAY HE CAN STAND UP AFTER WHAT I DID TO HIM!
WOBBLE
LEAN
RRGH!
KRIK
WHAT...
WHAT AM I DOING?!
HE'S GOT ONE FOOT IN THE GRAVE.
AND THEM SEALING THE WIND DOESN'T MEAN JACK.
パキ
HE'LL FALL IF I SNEEZE ON HIM.
YOU'RE SOME-THING, PIP-SQUEAK.

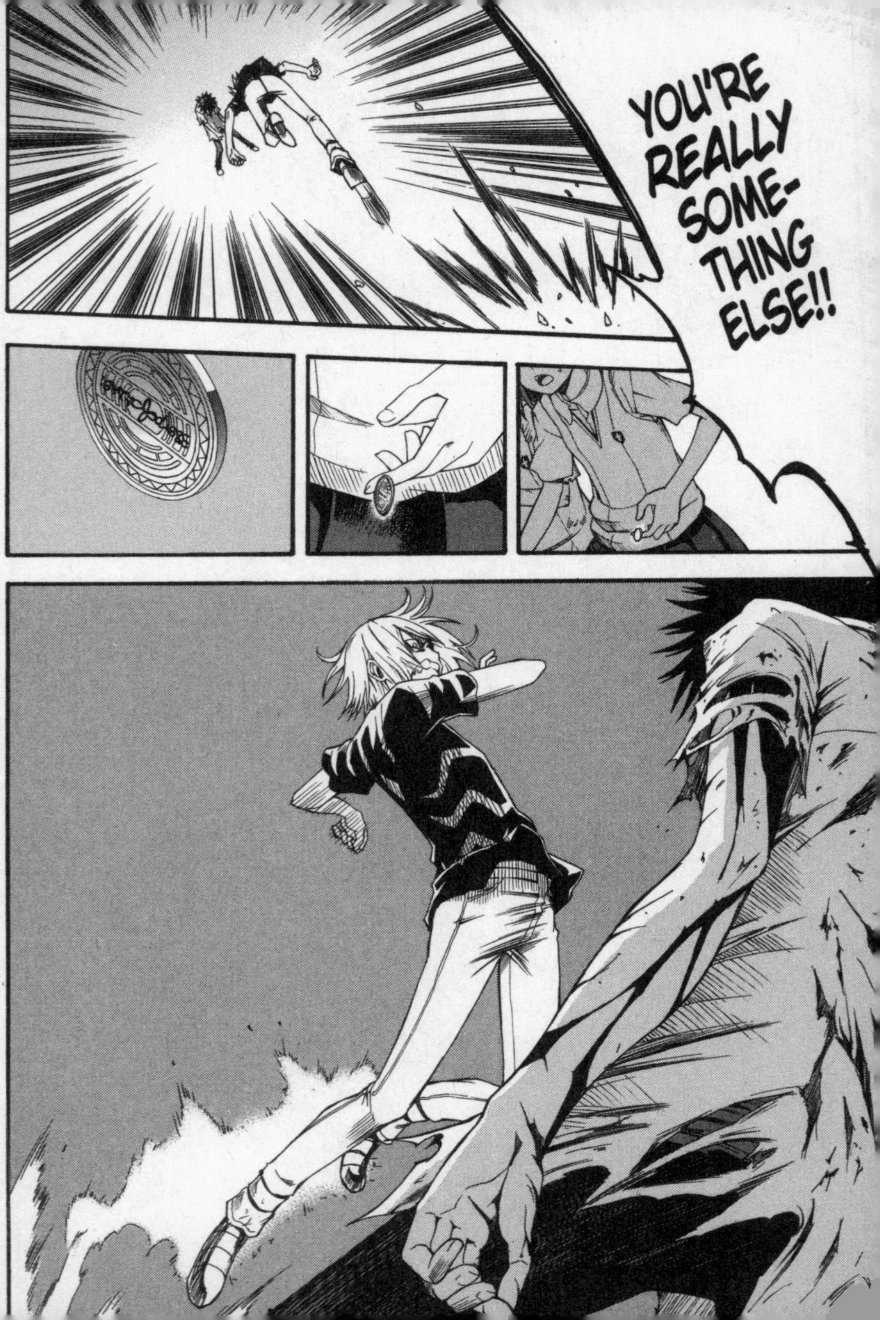
YOU'RE REALLY SOME-THING ELSE!!

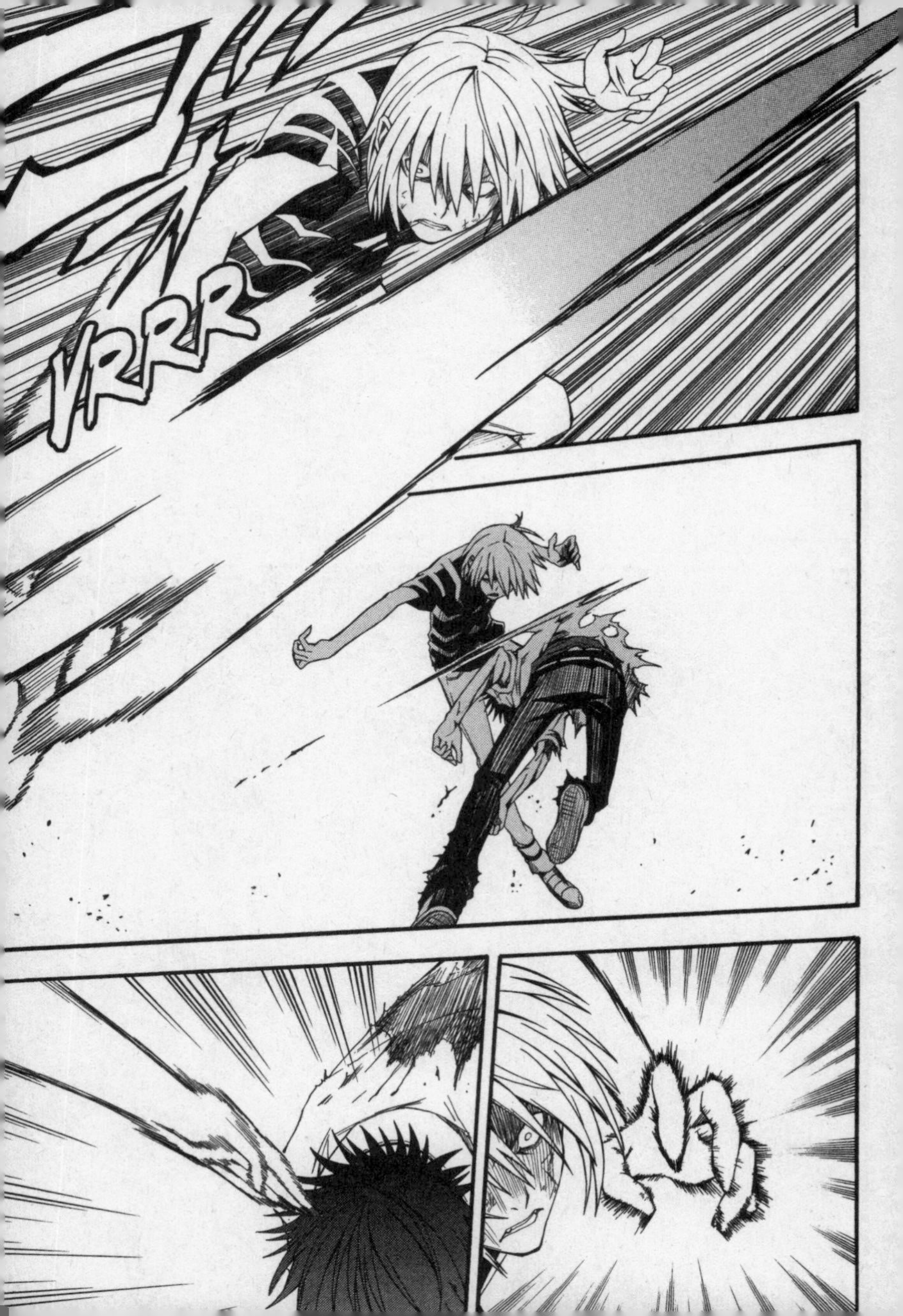
VRRR

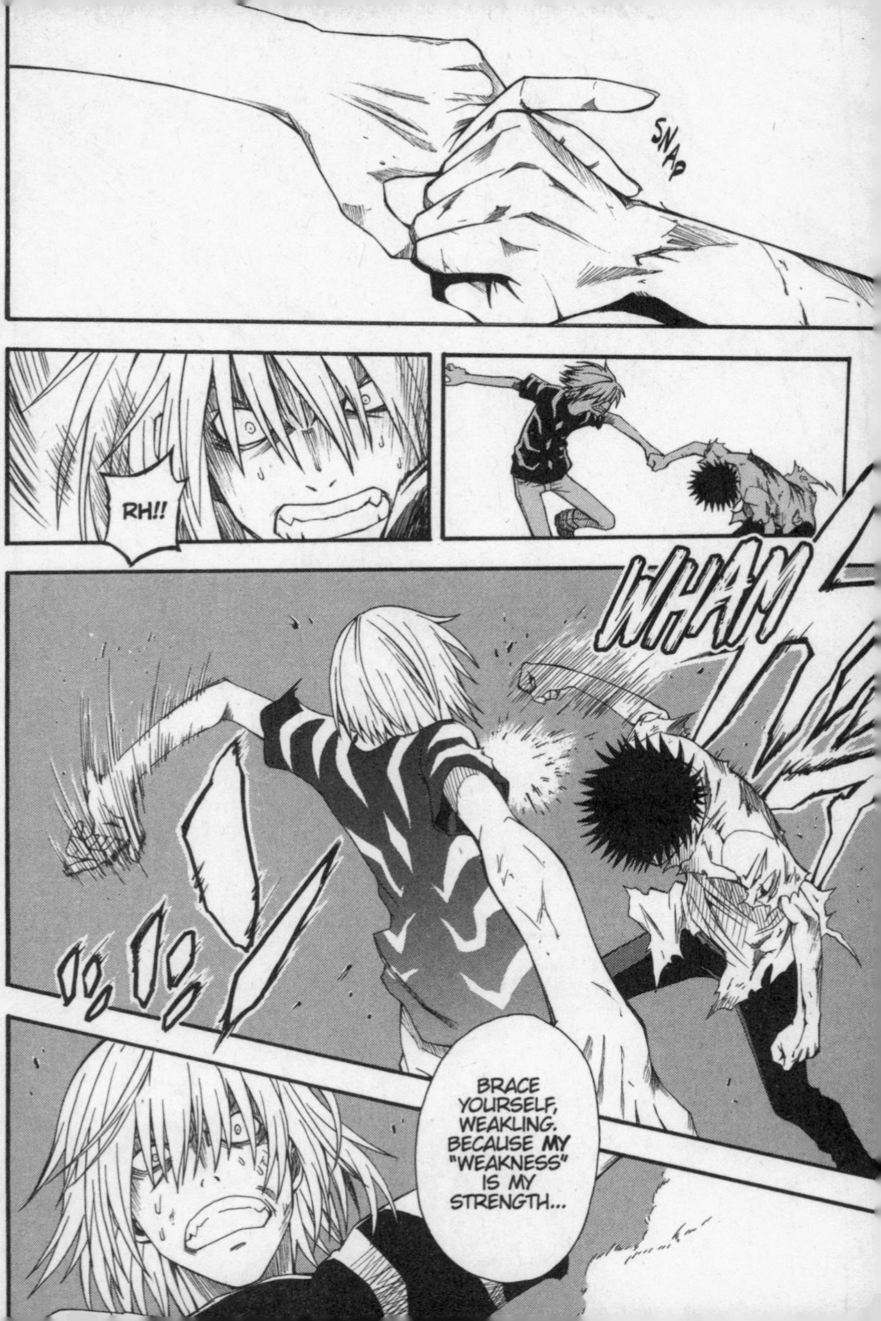
SNAP
RH!!
WHAM
BRACE YOURSELF, WEAKLING. BECAUSE MY "WEAKNESS" IS MY STRENGTH...

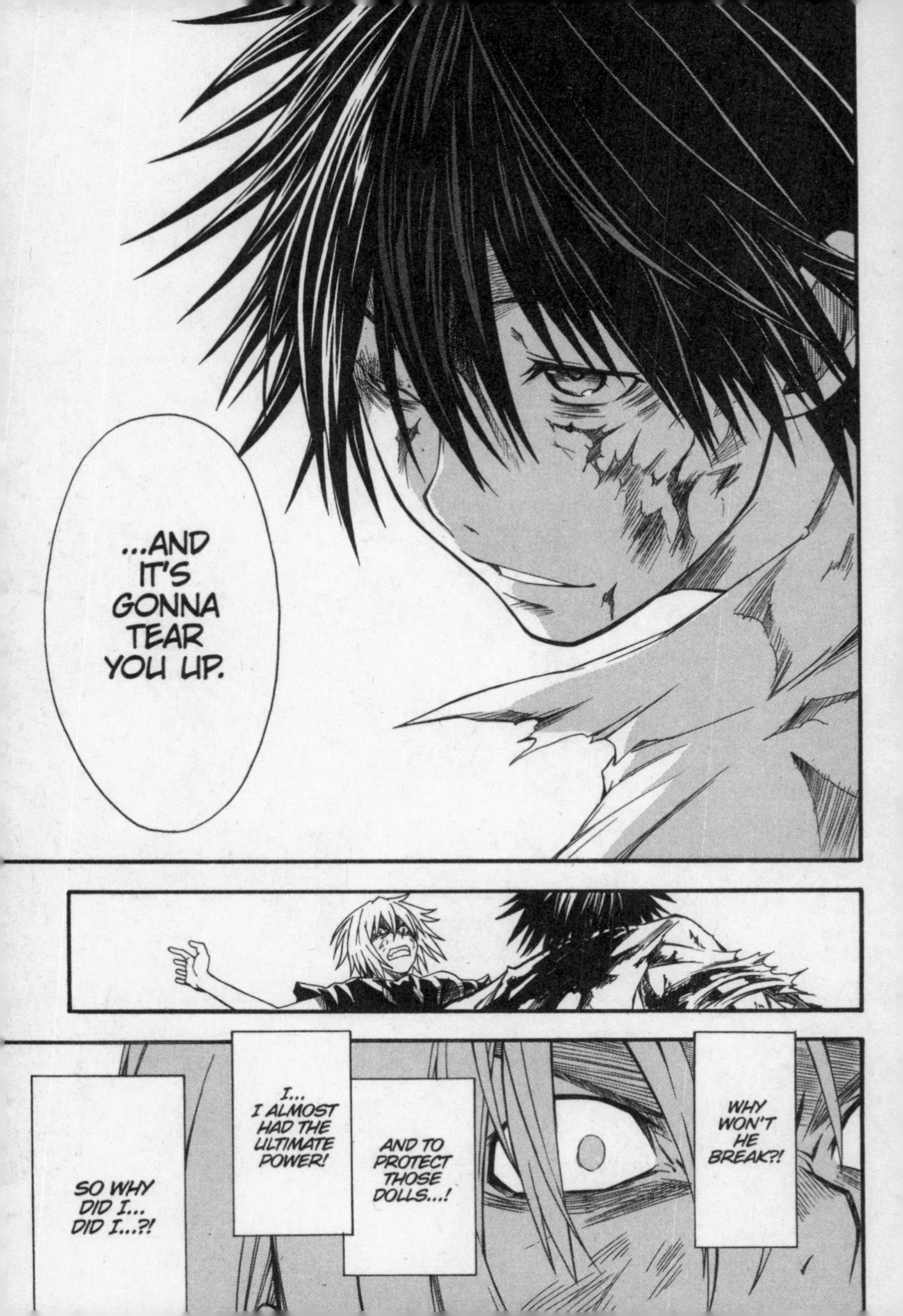
...AND IT'S GONNA TEAR YOU UP.
WHY WON'T HE BREAK?!
I... I ALMOST HAD THE ULTIMATE POWER!
AND TO PROTECT THOSE DOLLS...!
SO WHY DID I... DID I...?!

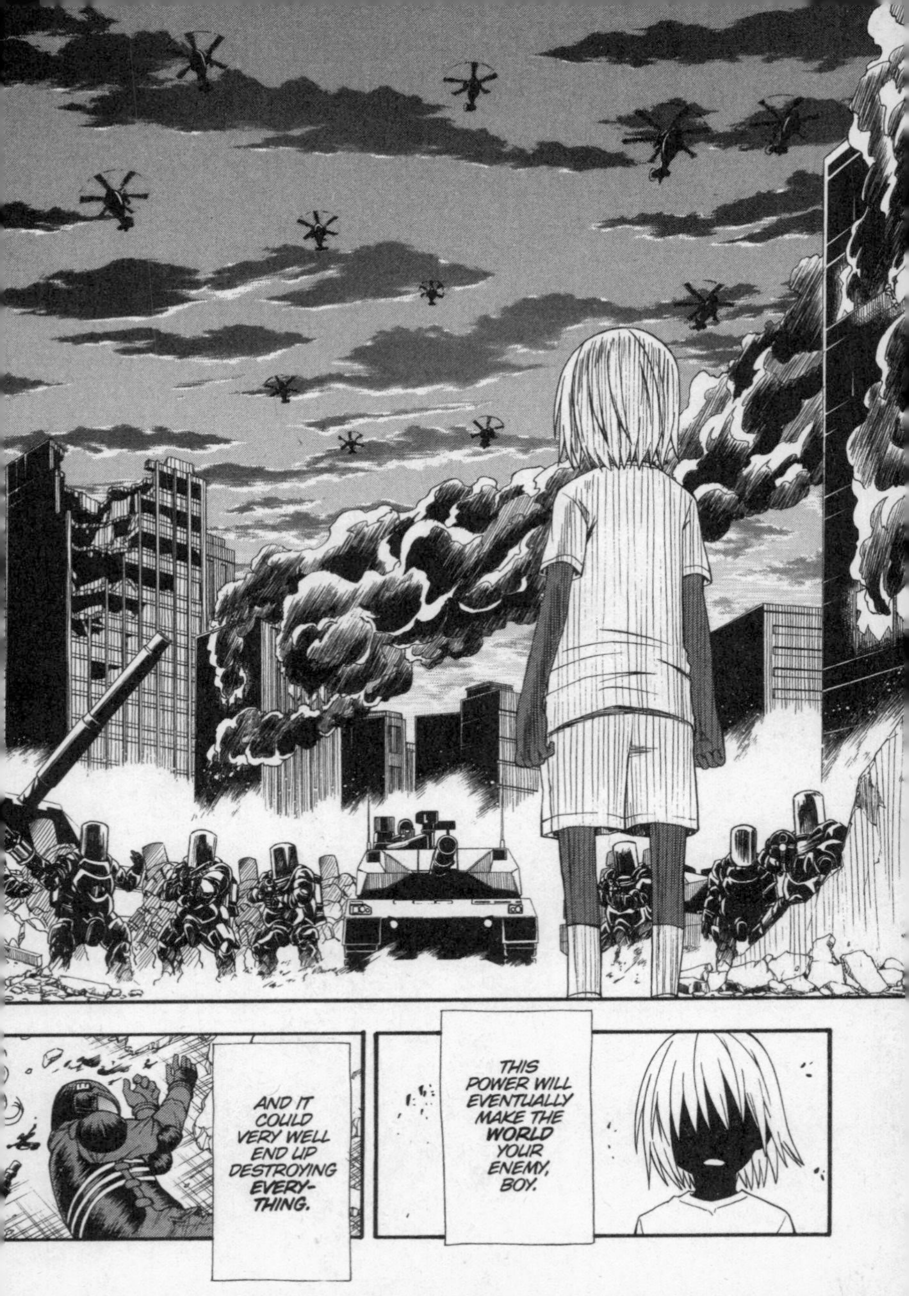
THIS POWER WILL EVENTUALLY MAKE THE WORLD YOUR ENEMY, BOY.
AND IT COULD VERY WELL END UP DESTROYING EVERY-THING.

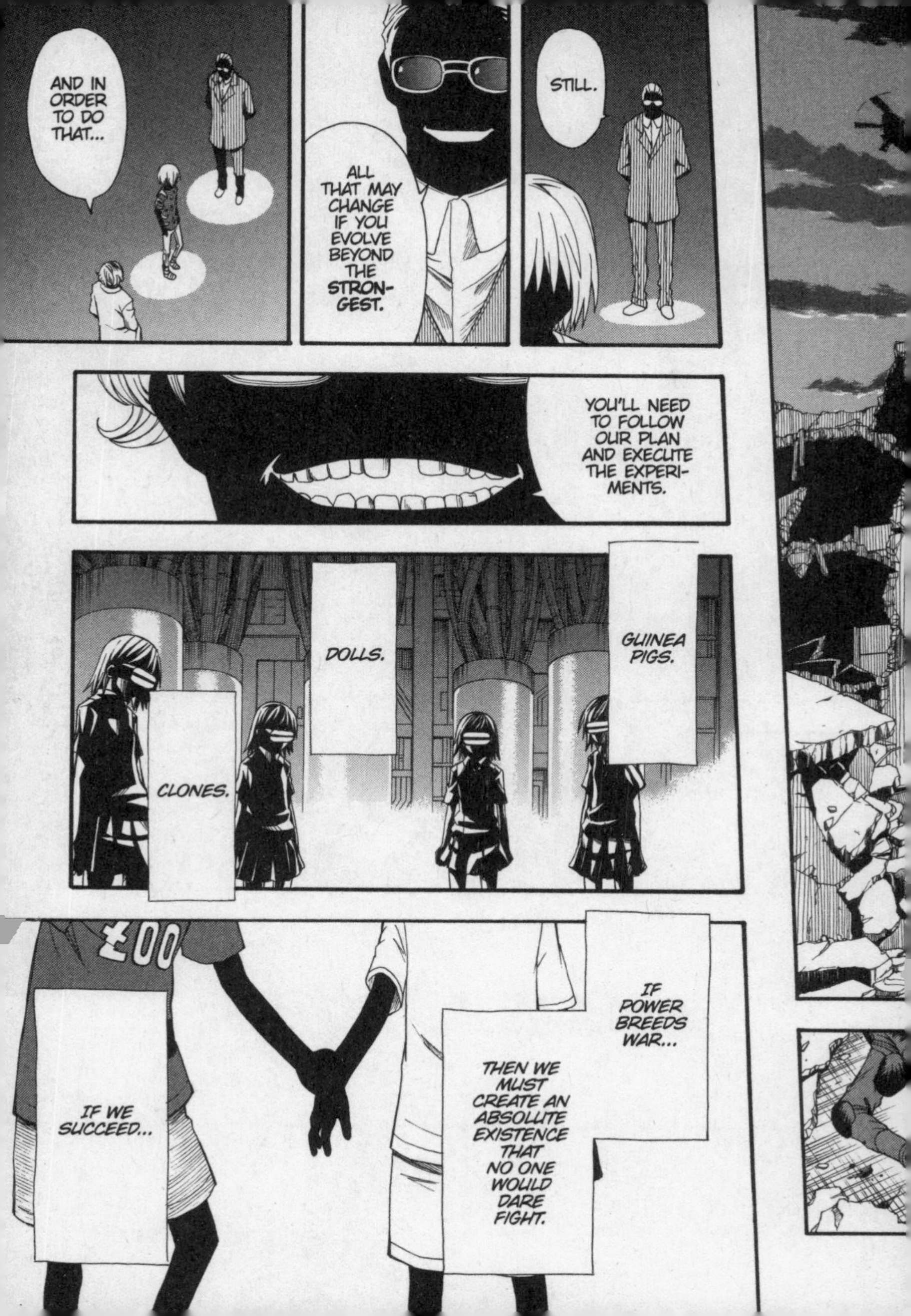
STILL.
ALL THAT MAY CHANGE IF YOU EVOLVE BEYOND THE STRONGEST.
AND IN ORDER TO DO THAT...
YOU'LL NEED TO FOLLOW OUR PLAN AND EXECUTE THE EXPERIMENTS.
GUINEA PIGS.
DOLLS.
CLONES.
IF POWER BREEDS WAR...
THEN WE MUST CREATE AN ABSOLUTE EXISTENCE THAT NO ONE WOULD DARE FIGHT.
IF WE SUCCEED...

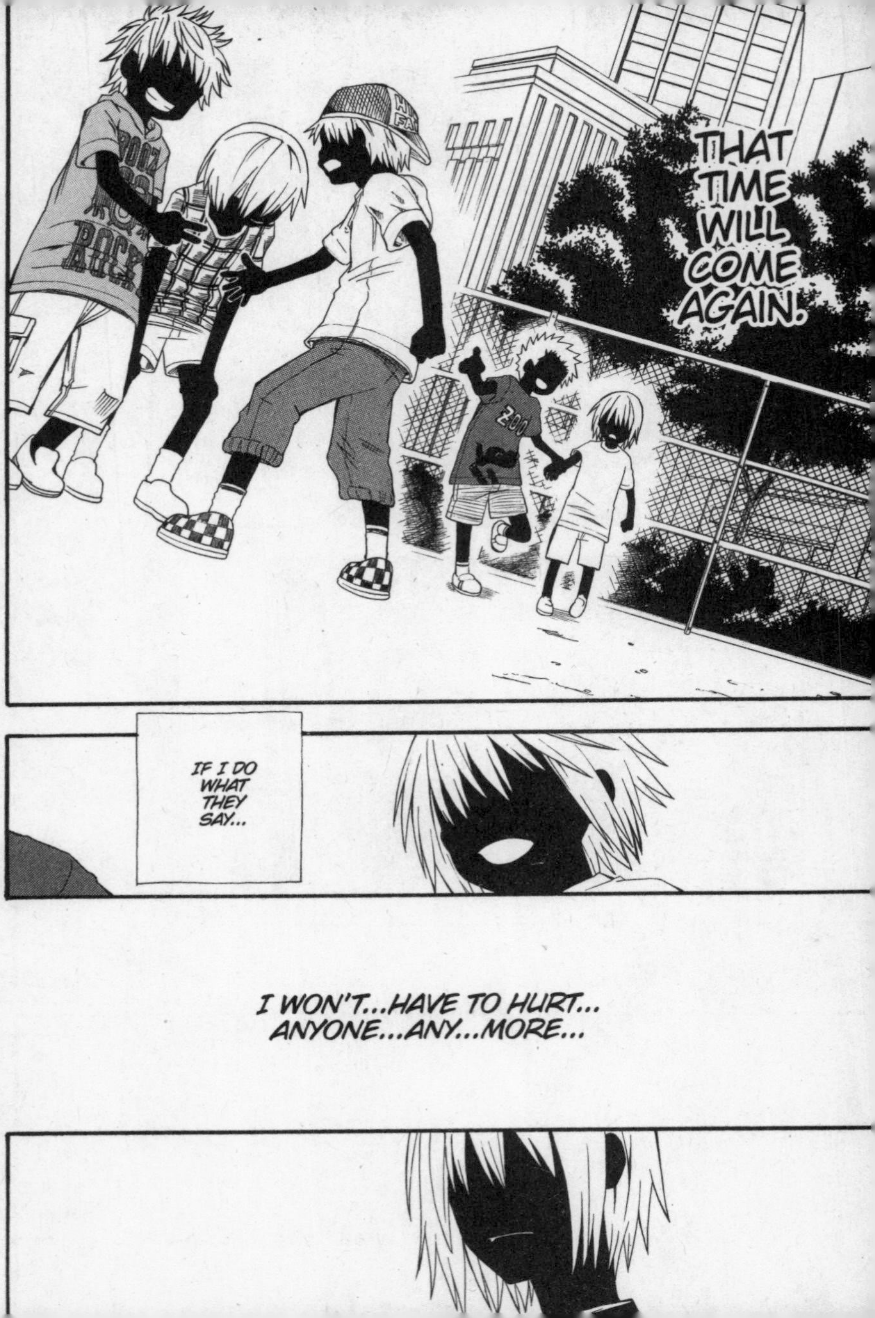
THAT TIME WILL COME AGAIN.
IF I DO WHAT THEY SAY...
I WON'T...HAVE TO HURT... ANYONE...ANY...MORE...

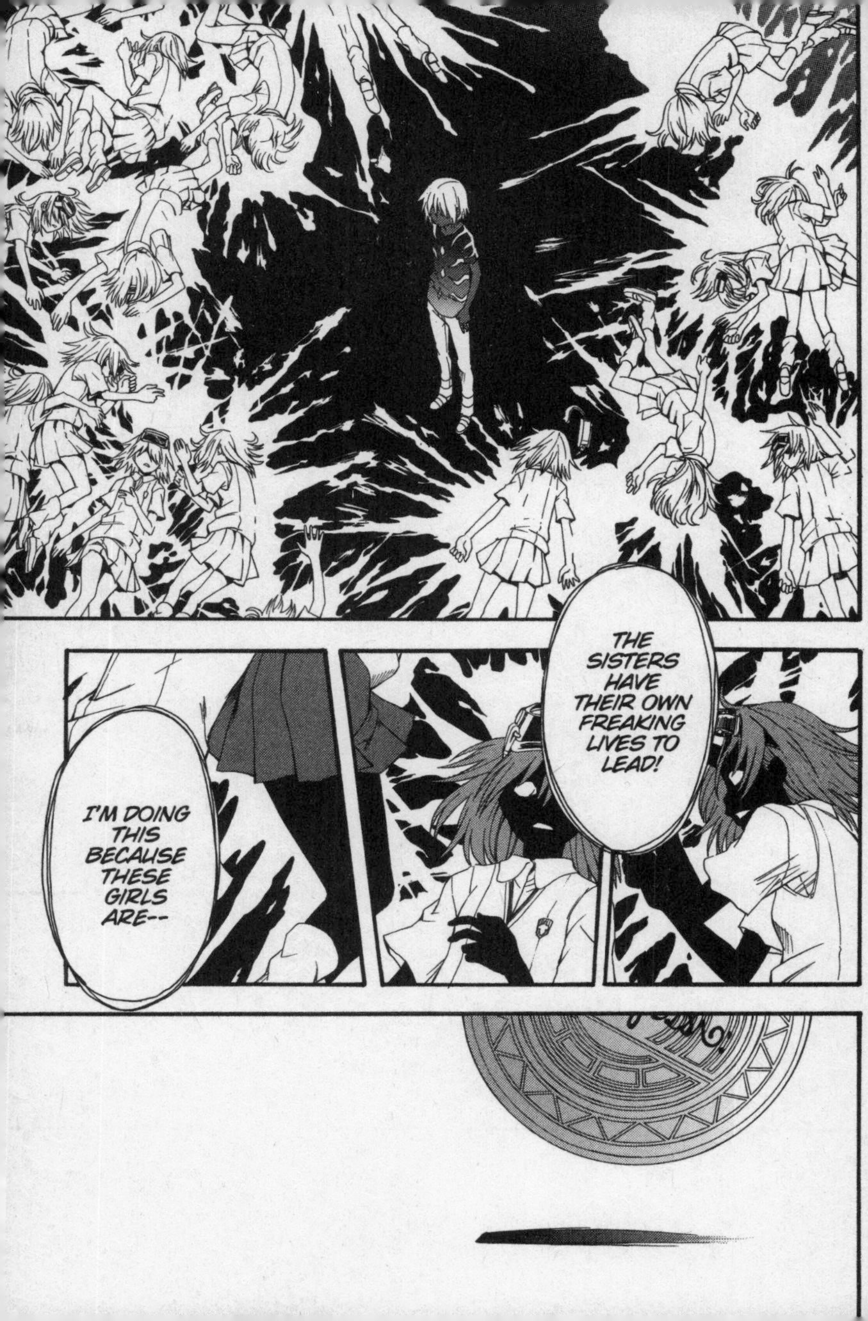
THE SISTERS HAVE THEIR OWN FREAKING LIVES TO LEAD!
I'M DOING THIS BECAUSE THESE GIRLS ARE--

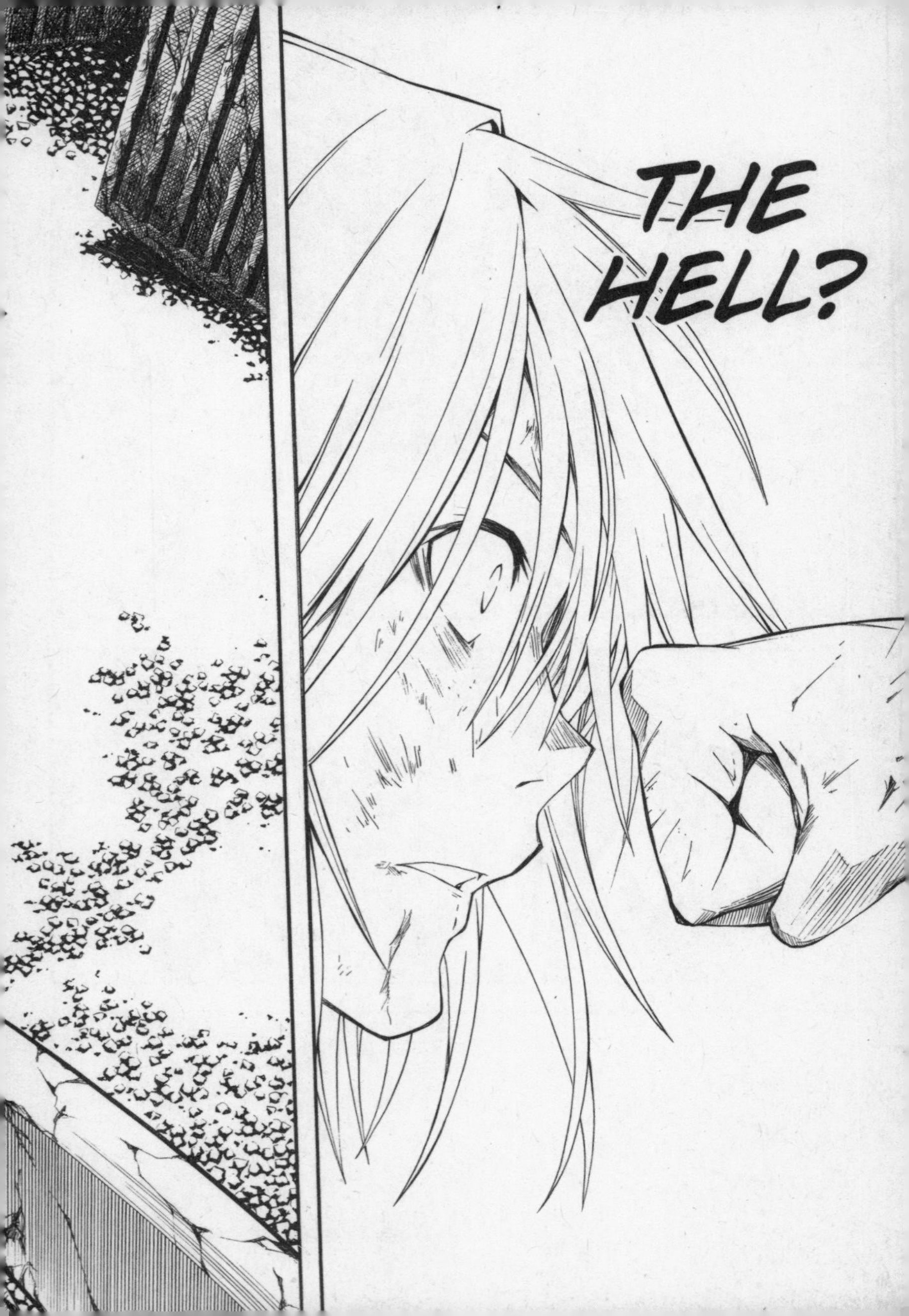
THE HELL?

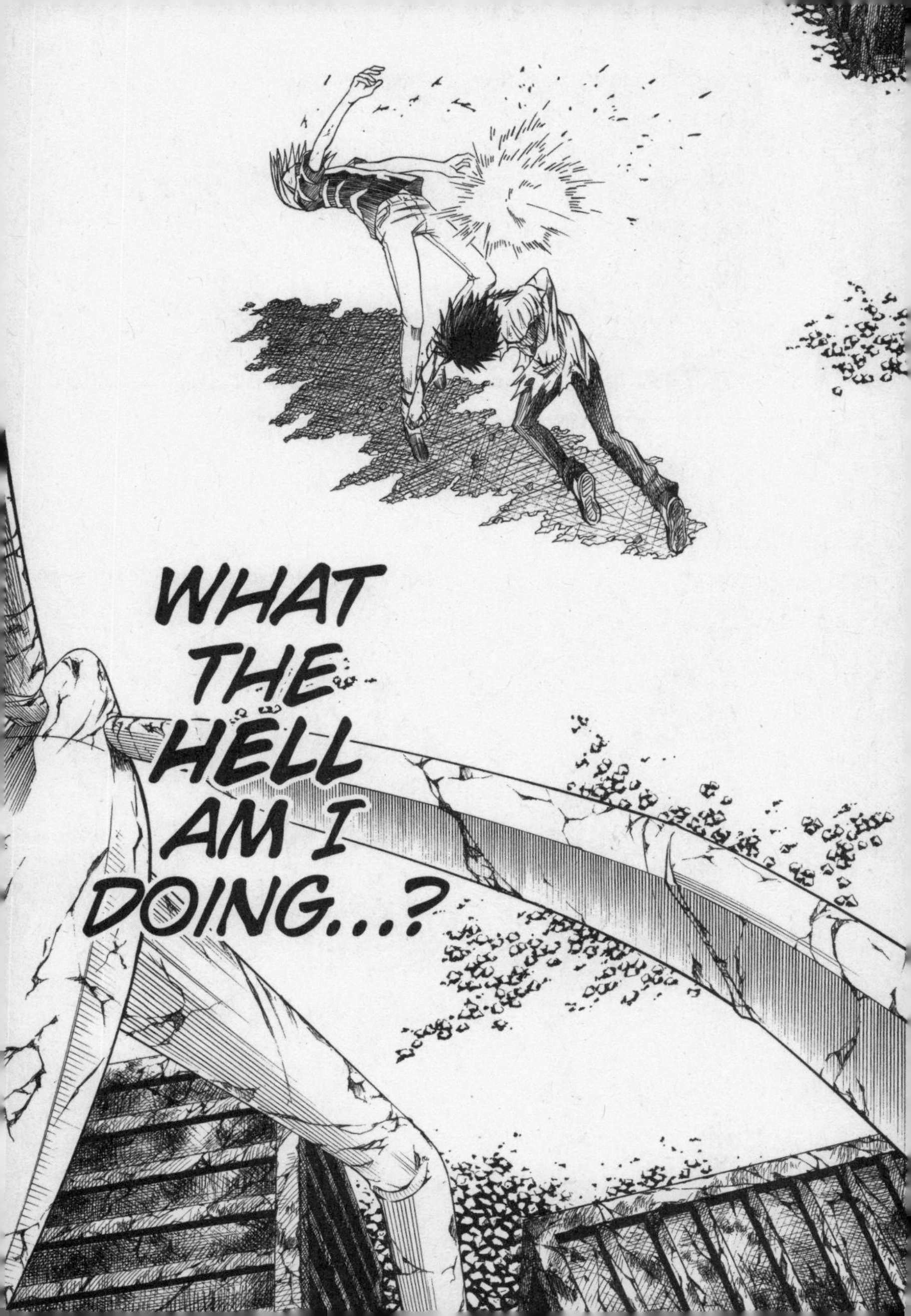
WHAT THE HELL AM I DOING...?

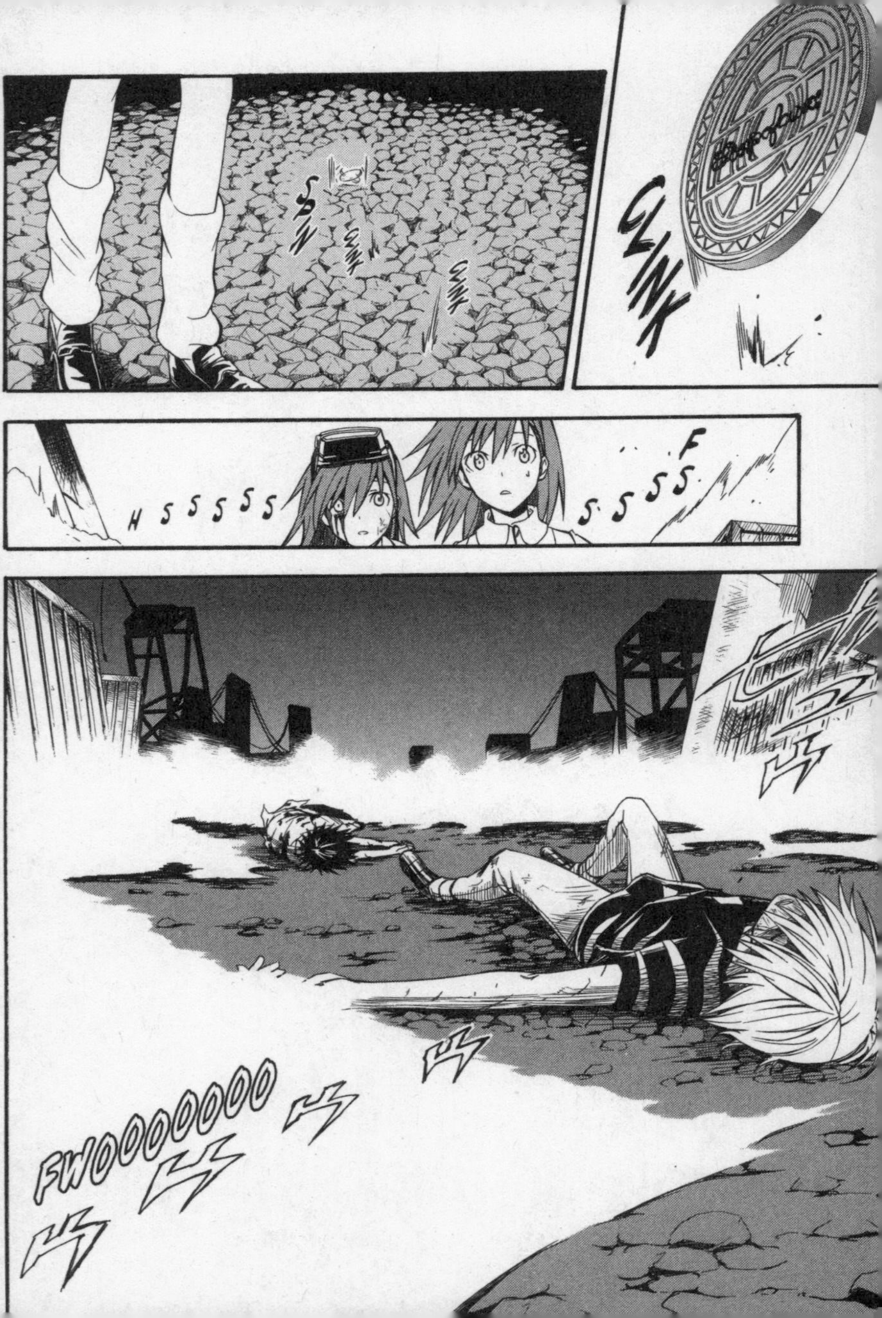
CLINK
CLINK
CLINK
SPIN
FSSSSS
HSSSSS
FWOOOOOOO

A Certain SCIENTIFIC Railgun

A Certain Sisters' Promise

IF MISAKA OBSTRUCTS THE TARGET, THE TARGET'S ATTENTION WILL TURN TO MISAKA.
PLEASE TAKE THAT TIME TO HELP THE YOUNG MAN ESCAPE...
!!
NO NO, PLEASE ALLOW UNIT 10039 THAT HONOR.
FWIP
SHOOP
NO NO, LEAVE THIS TO UNIT 10777.
UNIT 13577 WOULD BE BEST.
CLAMOR CLAMOR
E-EASY, GUYS!
FRET
UNIT 19090 MAKES A BID.
I'M THE BIG SISTER, SO *I'LL* DO IT-- OKAY?!
MISAKA BELIEVES YOU SHOULD LEAVE THIS TO 10854.
ARGUE ARGUE
FRET
BY ALL MEANS.
HEEEEY!
MOTION

CHAPTER 39: AUGUST 22ND

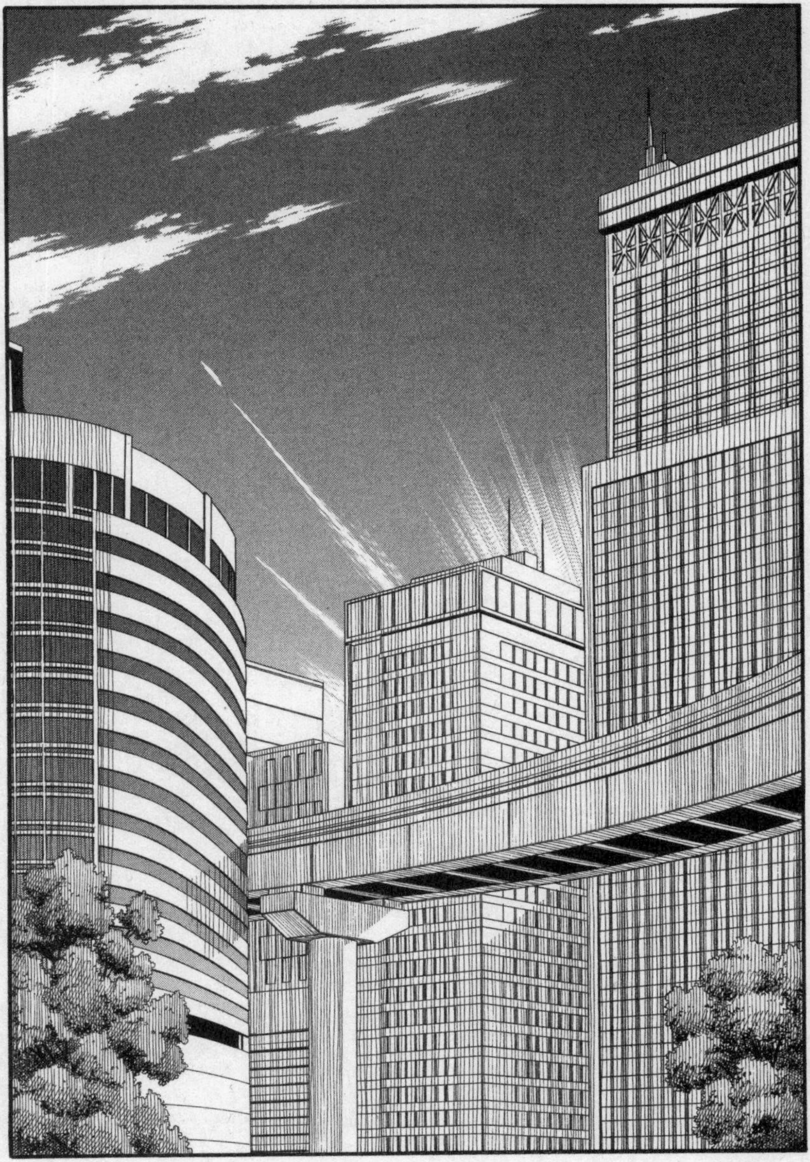

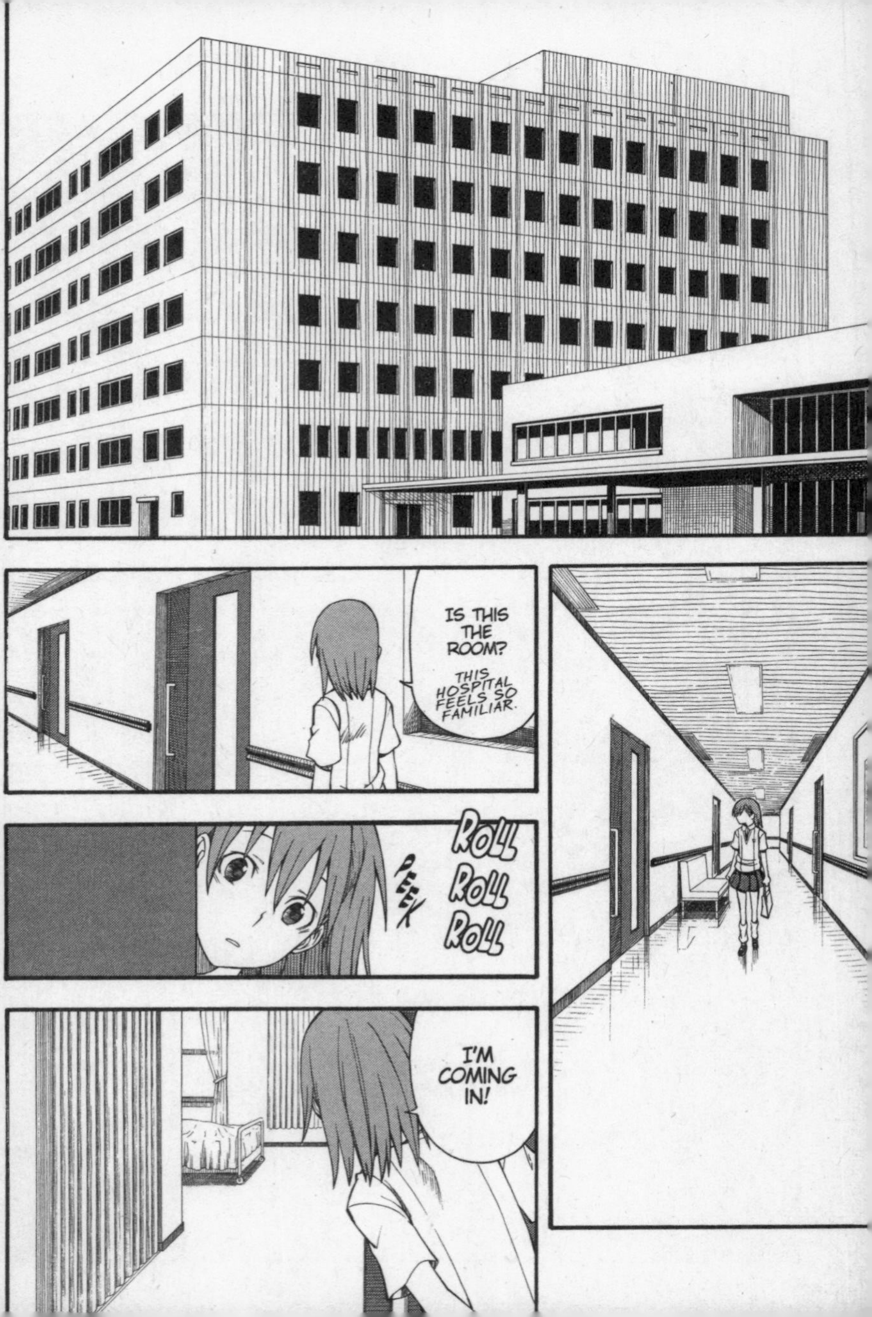
IS THIS THE ROOM?
THIS HOSPITAL FEELS SO FAMILIAR.
ROLL ROLL ROLL
PEEK
I'M COMING IN!

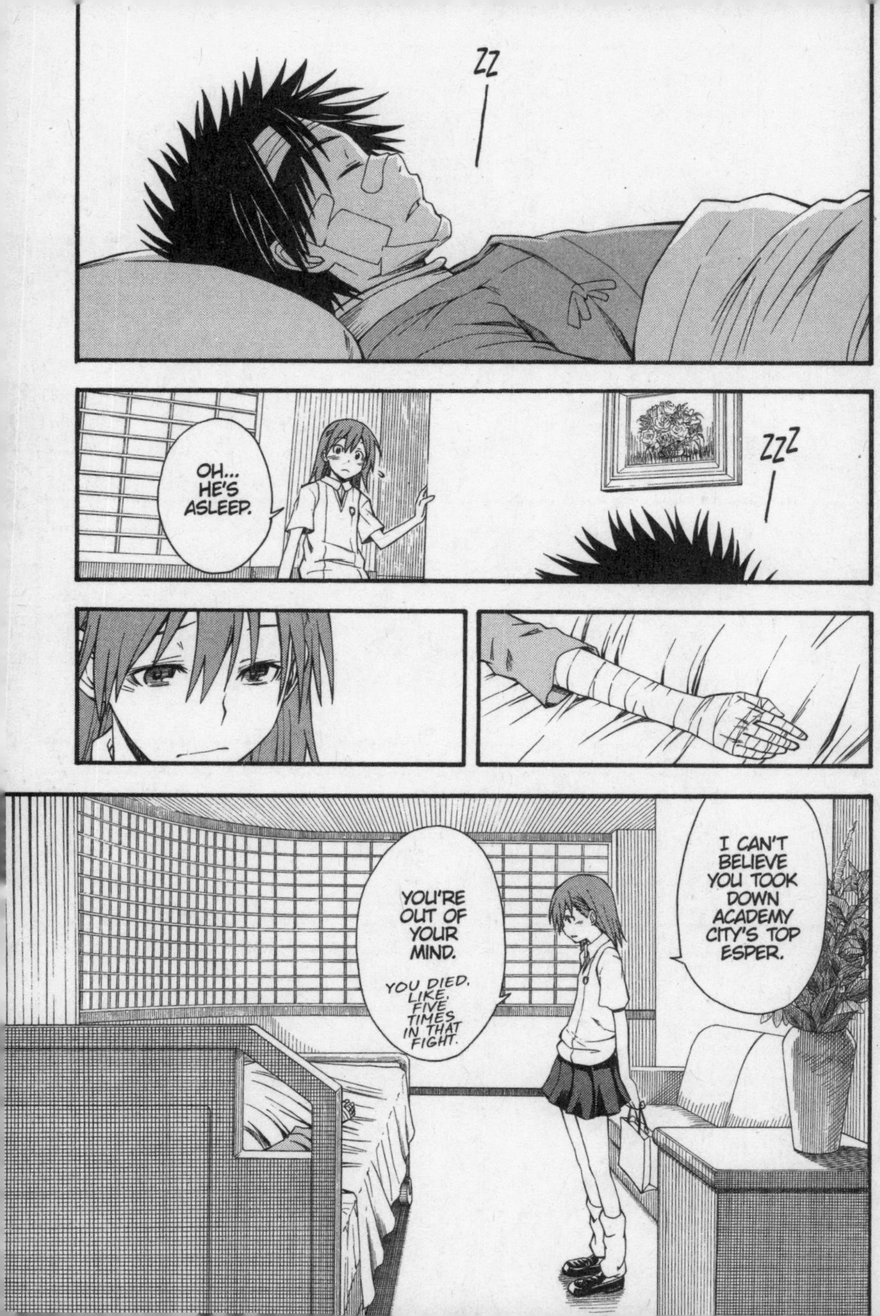
ZZ
ZZZ
OH... HE'S ASLEEP.
I CAN'T BELIEVE YOU TOOK DOWN ACADEMY CITY'S TOP ESPER.
YOU'RE OUT OF YOUR MIND.
YOU DIED, LIKE, FIVE TIMES IN THAT FIGHT.

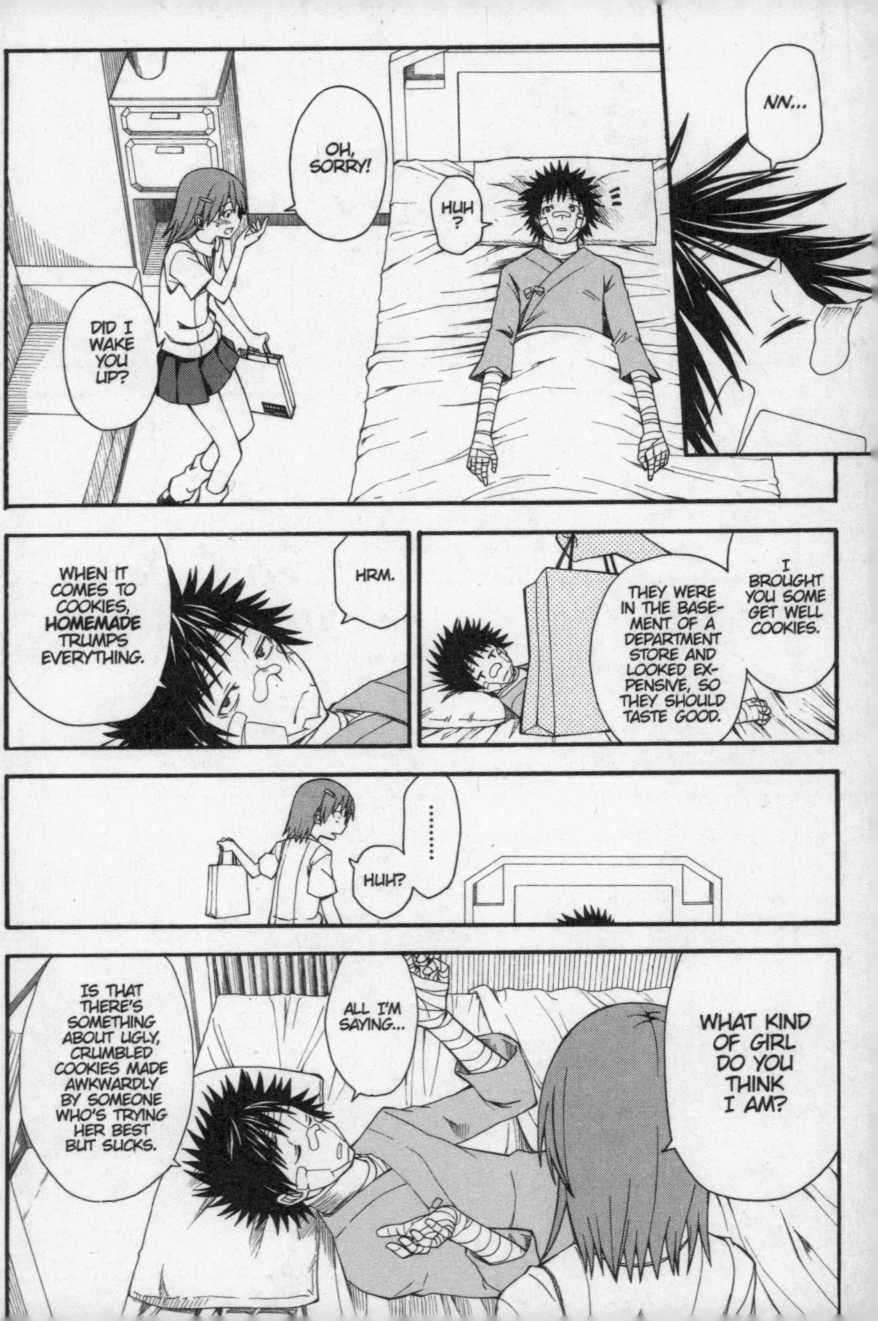
NN...
HUH ?
OH, SORRY!
DID I WAKE YOU UP?
I BROUGHT YOU SOME GET WELL COOKIES.
THEY WERE IN THE BASEMENT OF A DEPARTMENT STORE AND LOOKED EXPENSIVE, SO THEY SHOULD TASTE GOOD.
HRM.
WHEN IT COMES TO COOKIES, HOMEMADE TRUMPS EVERYTHING.
....
HUH?
WHAT KIND OF GIRL DO YOU THINK I AM?
ALL I'M SAYING...
IS THAT THERE'S SOMETHING ABOUT UGLY, CRUMBLED COOKIES MADE AWKWARDLY BY SOMEONE WHO'S TRYING HER BEST BUT SUCKS.

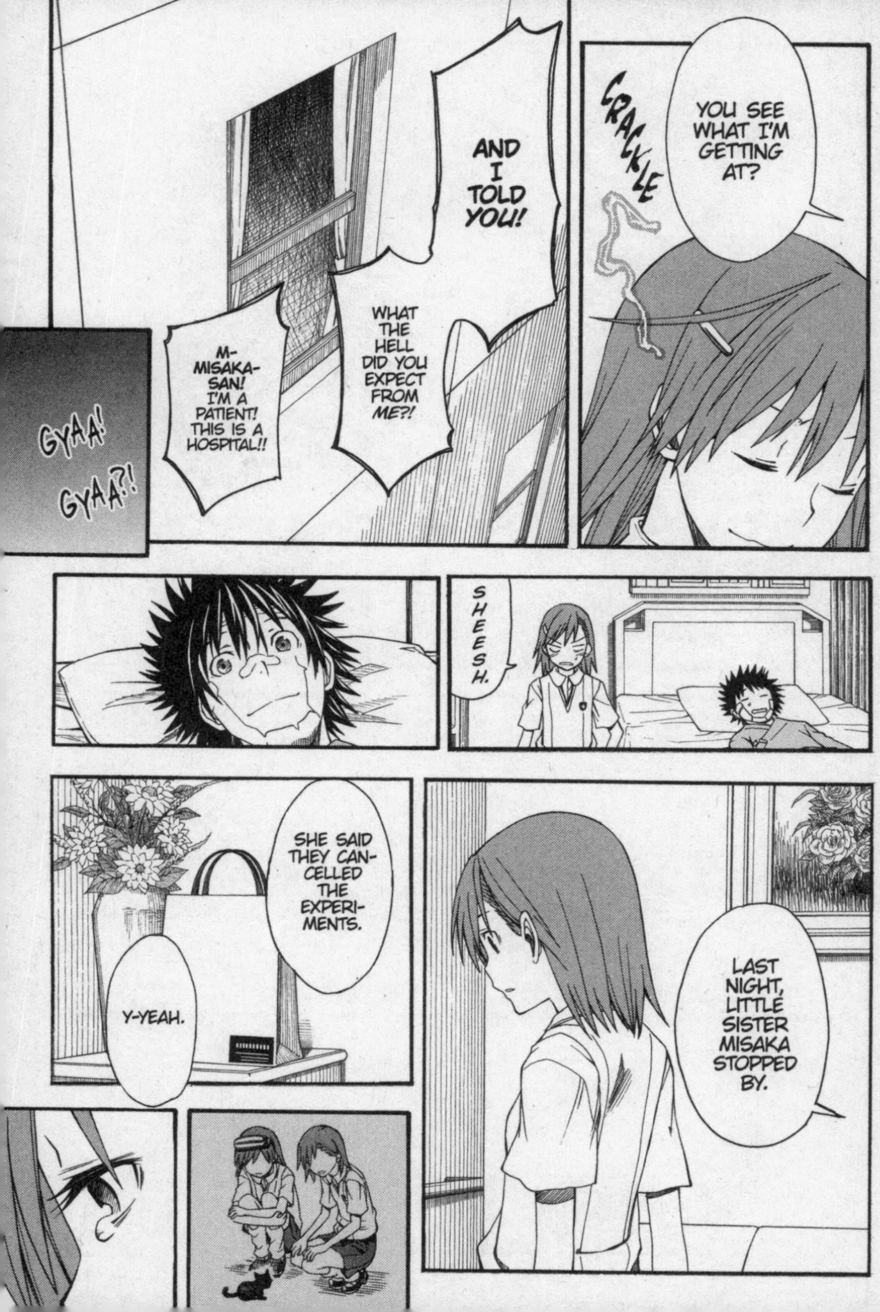
YOU SEE WHAT I'M GETTING AT?
CRACKLE
AND I TOLD YOU!
WHAT THE HELL DID YOU EXPECT FROM ME?!
M-MISAKA-SAN! I'M A PATIENT! THIS IS A HOSPITAL!!
GYAA! GYAA?!
SHEESH.
LAST NIGHT, LITTLE SISTER MISAKA STOPPED BY.
SHE SAID THEY CAN-CELLED THE EXPERI-MENTS.
Y-YEAH.

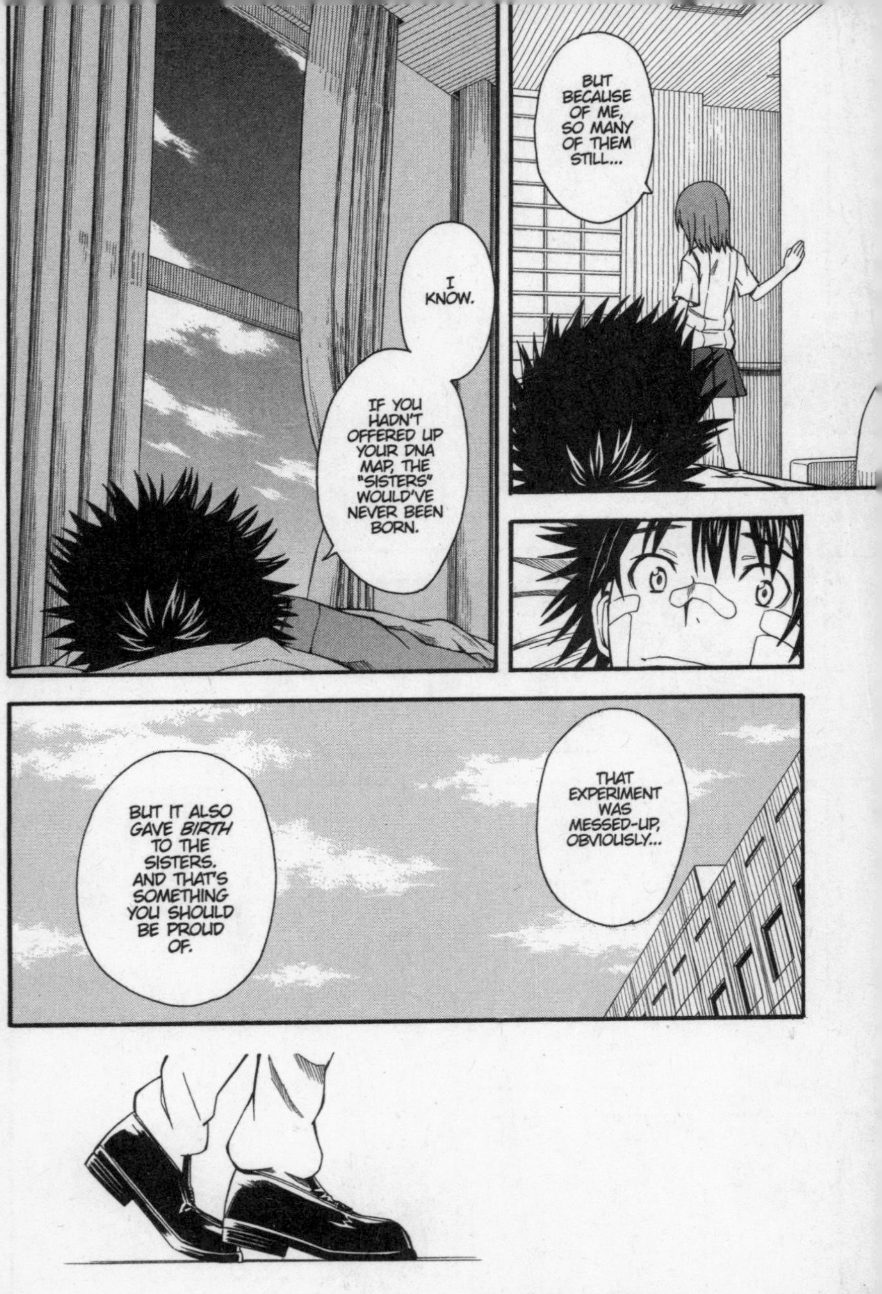
BUT BECAUSE OF ME, SO MANY OF THEM STILL...
I KNOW.
IF YOU HADN'T OFFERED UP YOUR DNA MAP, THE "SISTERS" WOULD'VE NEVER BEEN BORN.
THAT EXPERIMENT WAS MESSED-UP, OBVIOUSLY...
BUT IT ALSO GAVE *BIRTH* TO THE SISTERS. AND THAT'S SOMETHING YOU SHOULD BE PROUD OF.

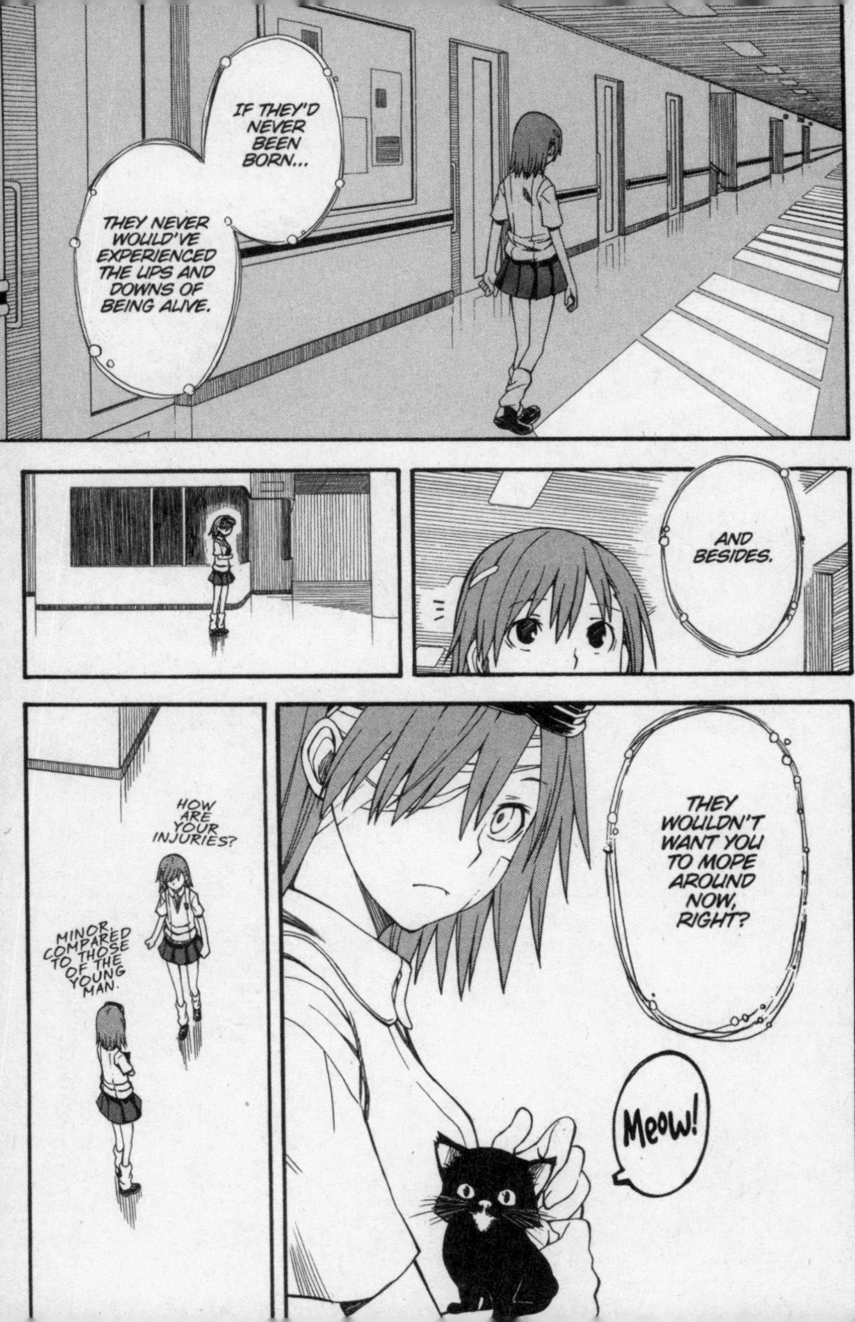
IF THEY'D NEVER BEEN BORN...
THEY NEVER WOULD'VE EXPERIENCED THE UPS AND DOWNS OF BEING ALIVE.
AND BESIDES.
THEY WOULDN'T WANT YOU TO MOPE AROUND NOW, RIGHT?
Meow!
HOW ARE YOUR INJURIES?
MINOR, COMPARED TO THOSE OF THE YOUNG MAN.

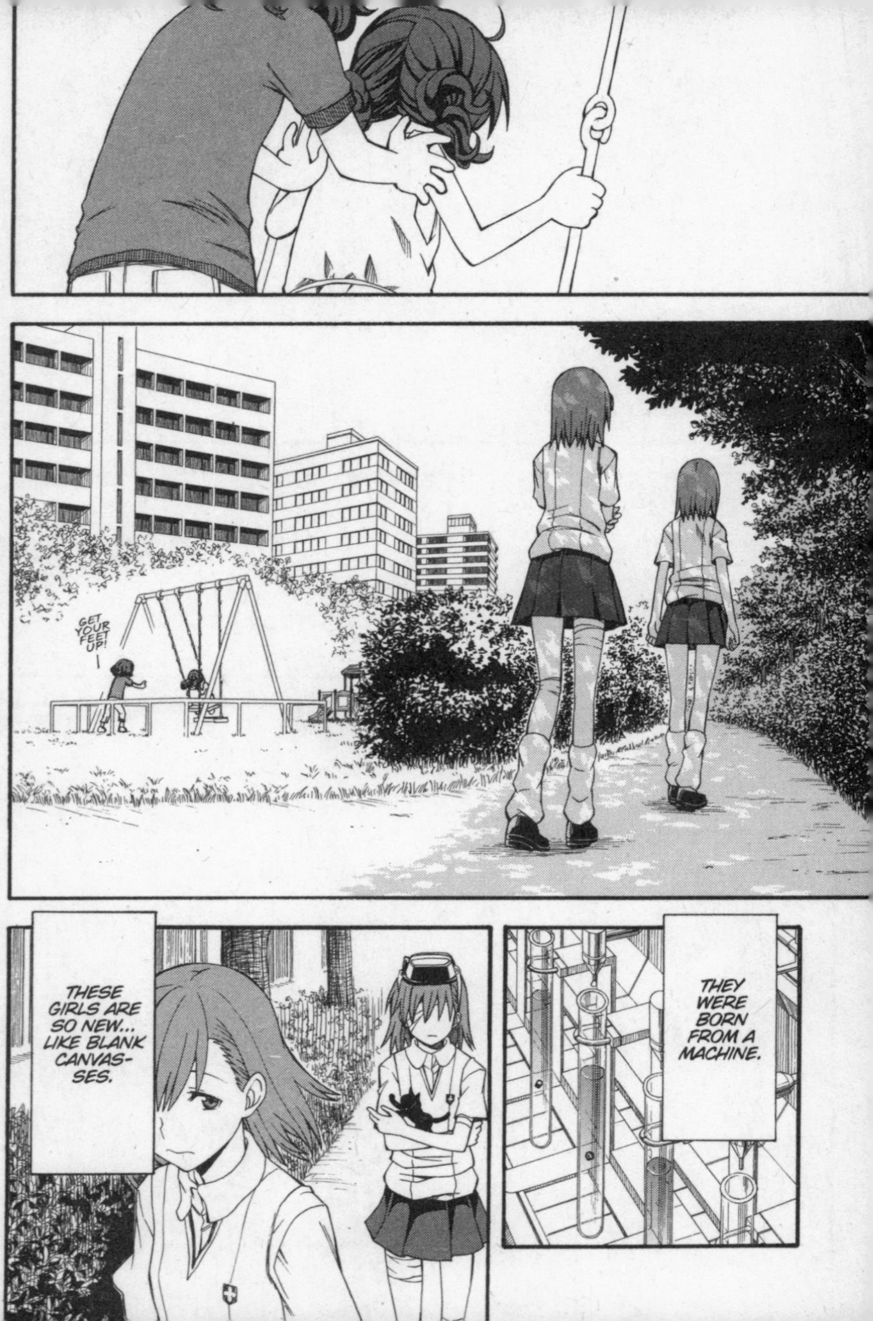
GET YOUR FEET UP!
THEY WERE BORN FROM A MACHINE.
THESE GIRLS ARE SO NEW... LIKE BLANK CANVAS-SES.

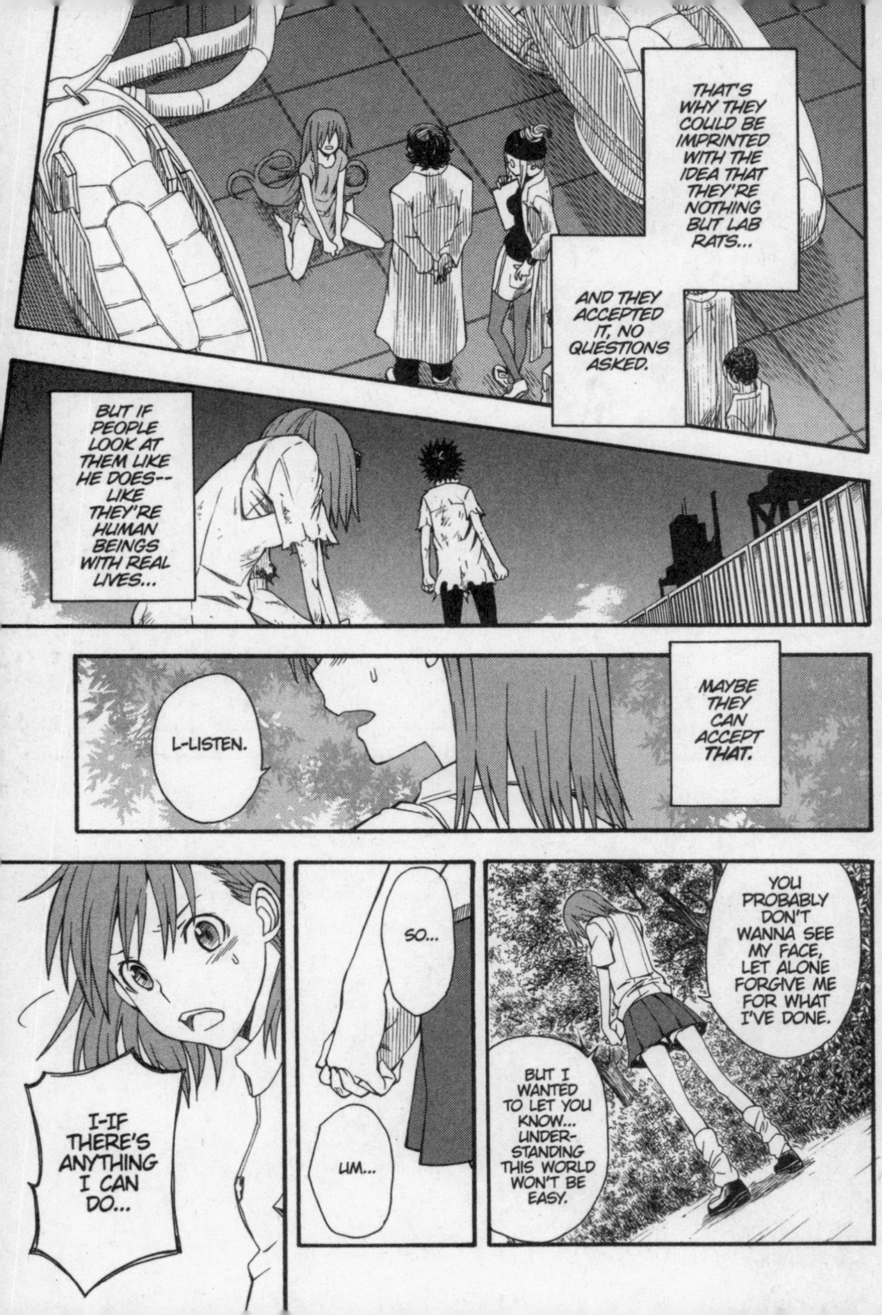
THAT'S WHY THEY COULD BE IMPRINTED WITH THE IDEA THAT THEY'RE NOTHING BUT LAB RATS...
AND THEY ACCEPTED IT, NO QUESTIONS ASKED.
BUT IF PEOPLE LOOK AT THEM LIKE HE DOES-- LIKE THEY'RE HUMAN BEINGS WITH REAL LIVES...
MAYBE THEY CAN ACCEPT THAT.
L-LISTEN.
YOU PROBABLY DON'T WANNA SEE MY FACE, LET ALONE FORGIVE ME FOR WHAT I'VE DONE.
BUT I WANTED TO LET YOU KNOW... UNDER-STANDING THIS WORLD WON'T BE EASY.
SO...
UM...
I-IF THERE'S ANYTHING I CAN DO...

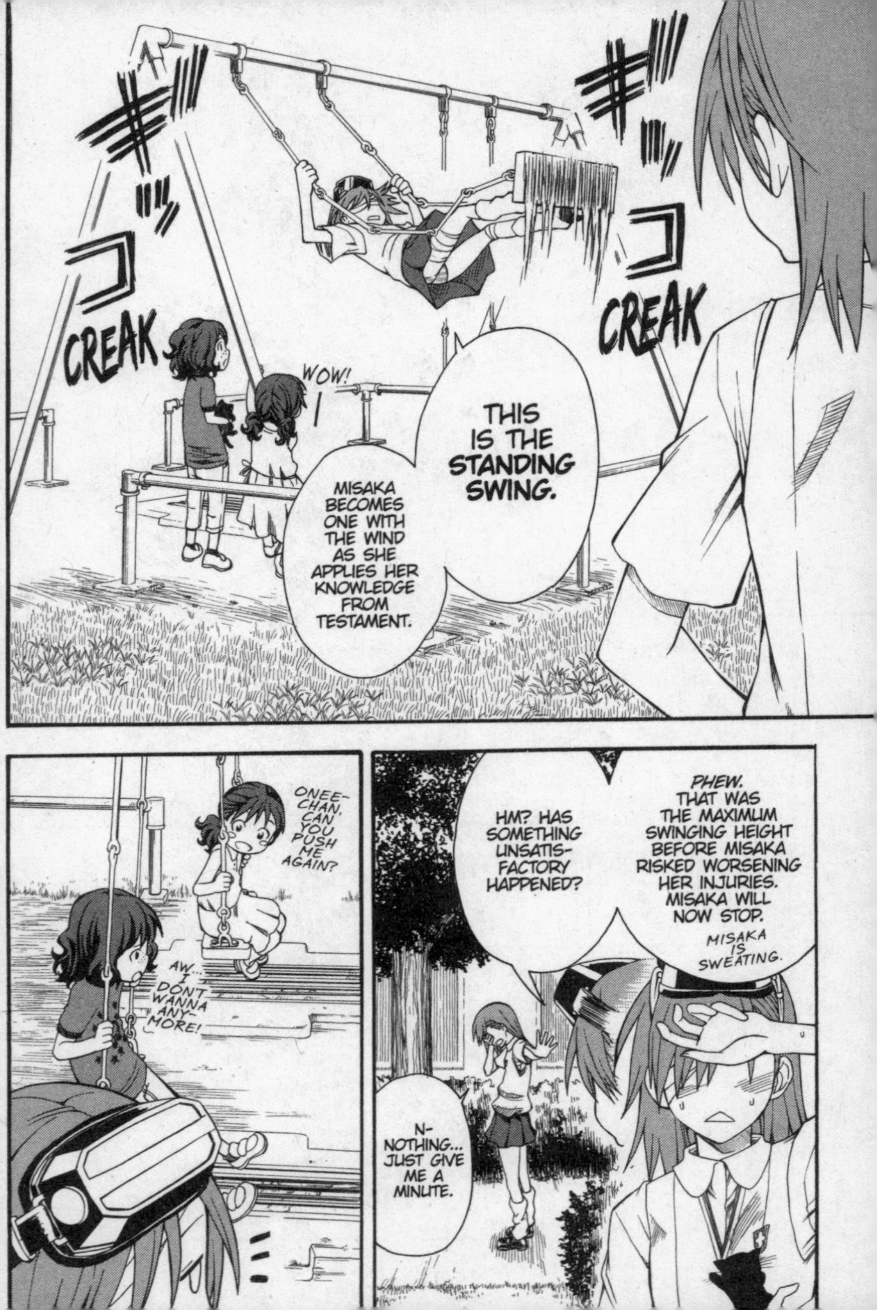
CREAK
THIS IS THE STANDING SWING.
MISAKA BECOMES ONE WITH THE WIND AS SHE APPLIES HER KNOWLEDGE FROM TESTAMENT.
WOW!
CREAK
PHEW. THAT WAS THE MAXIMUM SWINGING HEIGHT BEFORE MISAKA RISKED WORSENING HER INJURIES. MISAKA WILL NOW STOP.
MISAKA IS SWEATING.
HM? HAS SOMETHING UNSATIS-FACTORY HAPPENED?
N-NOTHING... JUST GIVE ME A MINUTE.
ONEE-CHAN, CAN YOU PUSH ME AGAIN?
AW... I DON'T WANNA ANY-MORE!

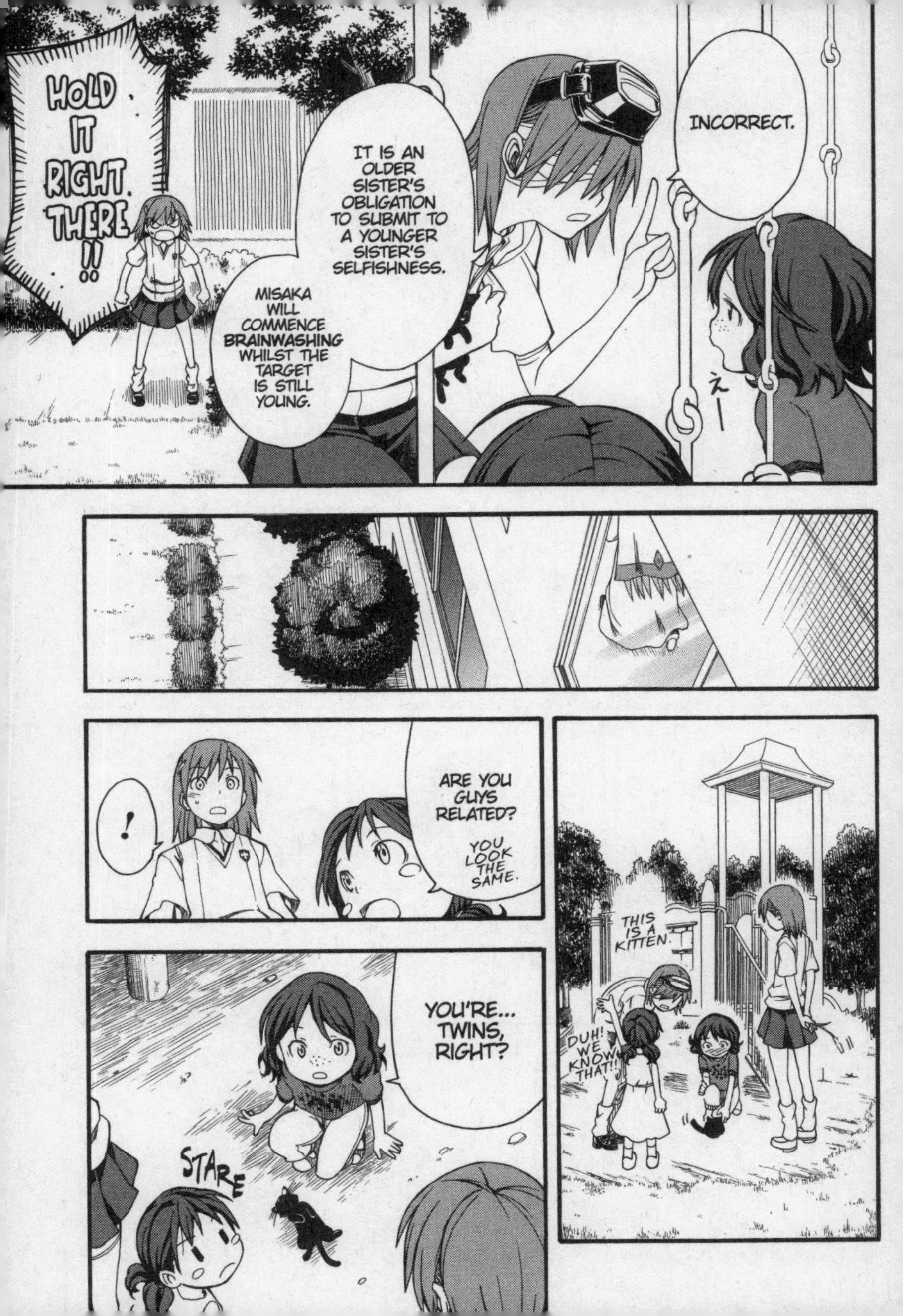
INCORRECT.
えー
IT IS AN OLDER SISTER'S OBLIGATION TO SUBMIT TO A YOUNGER SISTER'S SELFISHNESS.
MISAKA WILL COMMENCE BRAINWASHING WHILST THE TARGET IS STILL YOUNG.
HOLD IT RIGHT THERE!!
THIS IS A KITTEN.
DUH! WE KNOW THAT!!
ARE YOU GUYS RELATED?
YOU LOOK THE SAME.
!
YOU'RE... TWINS, RIGHT?
STARE

WHICH ONE OF YOU IS THE BIG SISTER...

AND WHICH ONE'S THE LITTLE ONE?

HUH?

RURI WANTS TO GUESS!

WAIT, WAIT!

THAT IS--

UH...

I THOUGHT SHE WANTED TO GUESS.

OH.

UM...

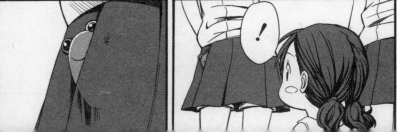

!

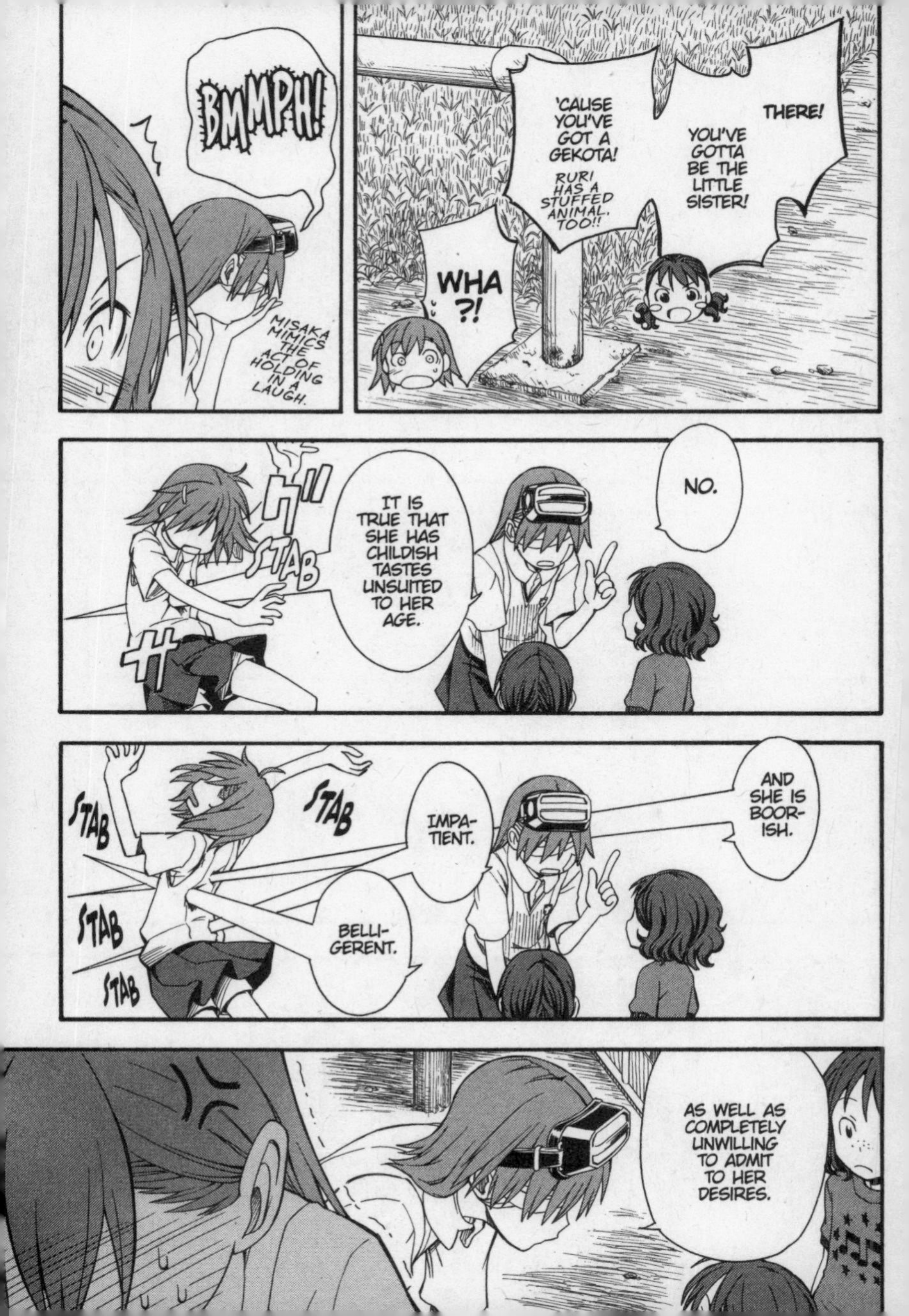
THERE!
YOU'VE GOTTA BE THE LITTLE SISTER!
'CAUSE YOU'VE GOT A GEKOTA!
RURI HAS A STUFFED ANIMAL, TOO!!
WHA?!
BMMPH!
MISAKA MIMICS THE ACT OF HOLDING IN A LAUGH.
NO.
IT IS TRUE THAT SHE HAS CHILDISH TASTES UNSUITED TO HER AGE.
STAB
AND SHE IS BOORISH.
IMPATIENT.
STAB
STAB
BELLIGERENT.
STAB
STAB
AS WELL AS COMPLETELY UNWILLING TO ADMIT TO HER DESIRES.

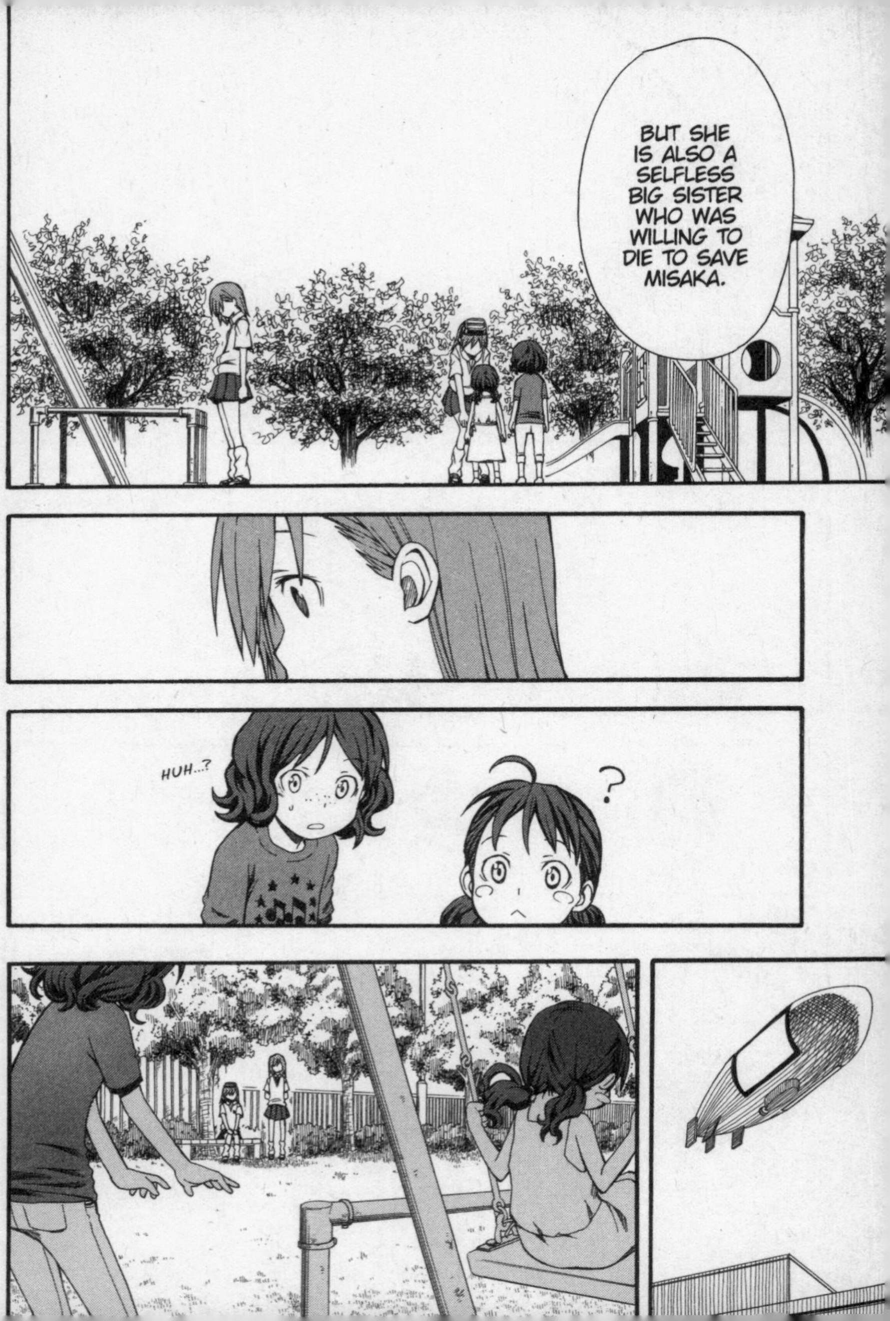
BUT SHE IS ALSO A SELFLESS BIG SISTER WHO WAS WILLING TO DIE TO SAVE MISAKA.
?
HUH...?

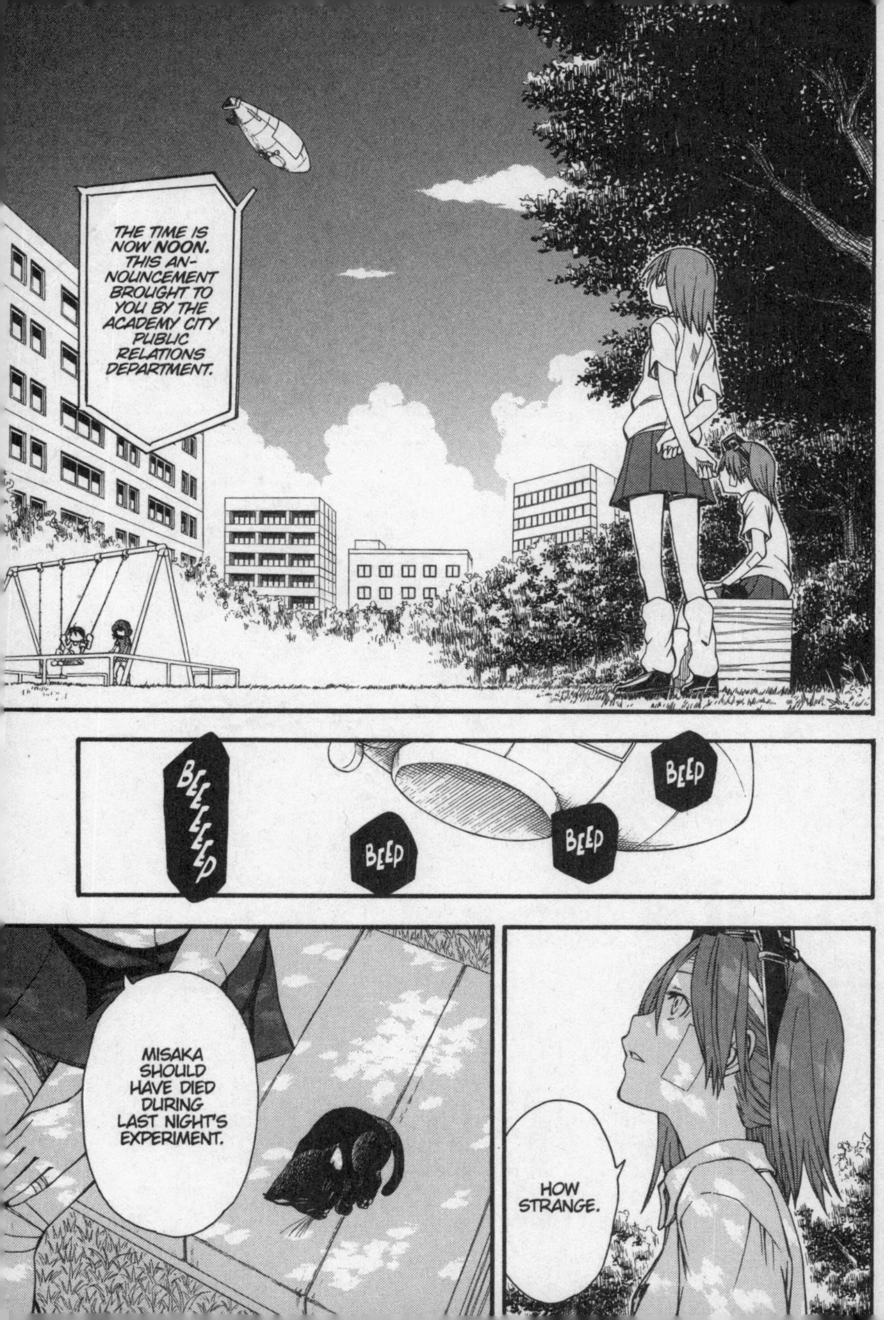
THE TIME IS NOW NOON. THIS ANNOUNCEMENT BROUGHT TO YOU BY THE ACADEMY CITY PUBLIC RELATIONS DEPARTMENT.
BEEP
BEEP
BEEP
BEEEEEEP
HOW STRANGE.
MISAKA SHOULD HAVE DIED DURING LAST NIGHT'S EXPERIMENT.

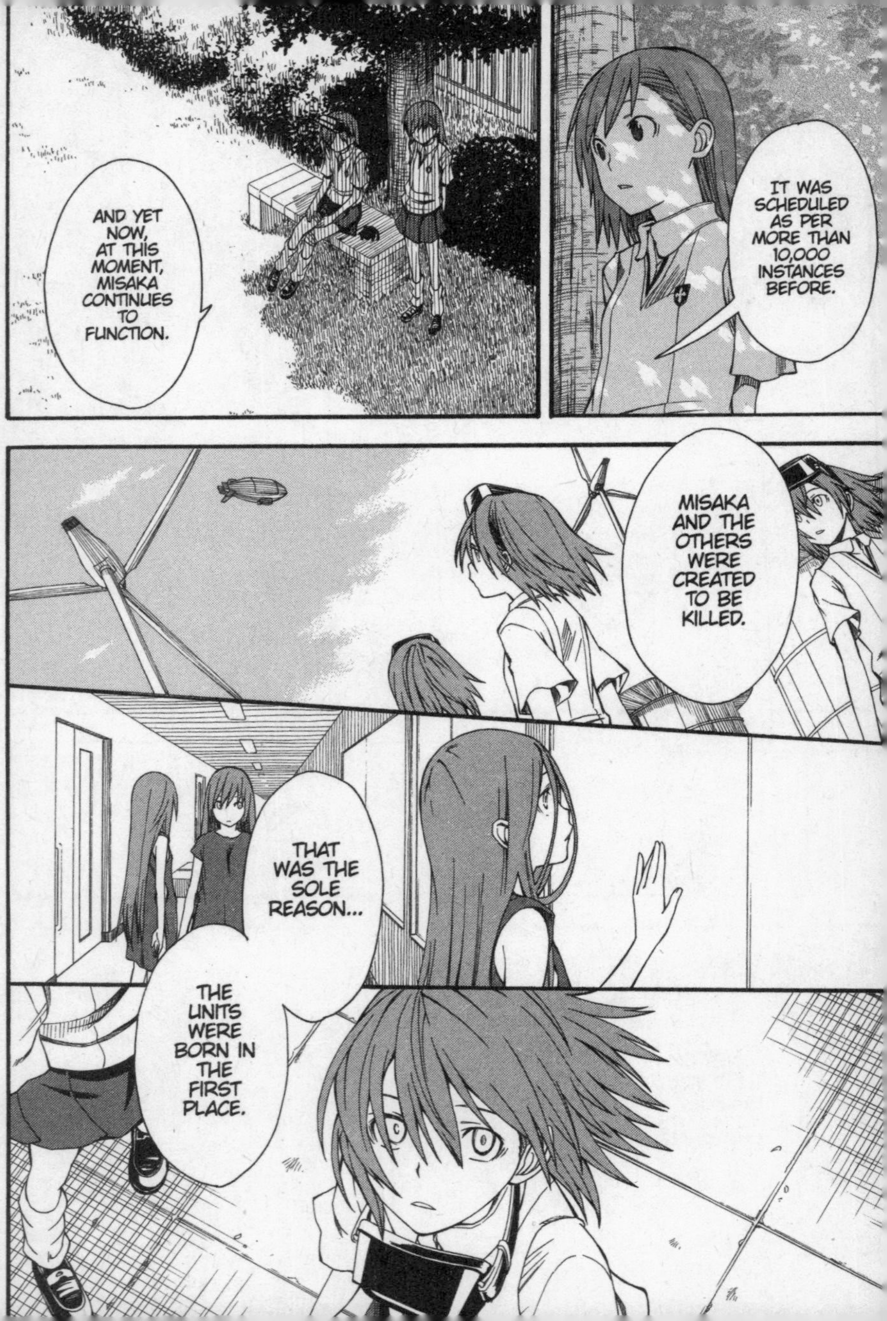
IT WAS SCHEDULED AS PER MORE THAN 10,000 INSTANCES BEFORE.
AND YET NOW, AT THIS MOMENT, MISAKA CONTINUES TO FUNCTION.
MISAKA AND THE OTHERS WERE CREATED TO BE KILLED.
THAT WAS THE SOLE REASON...
THE UNITS WERE BORN IN THE FIRST PLACE.

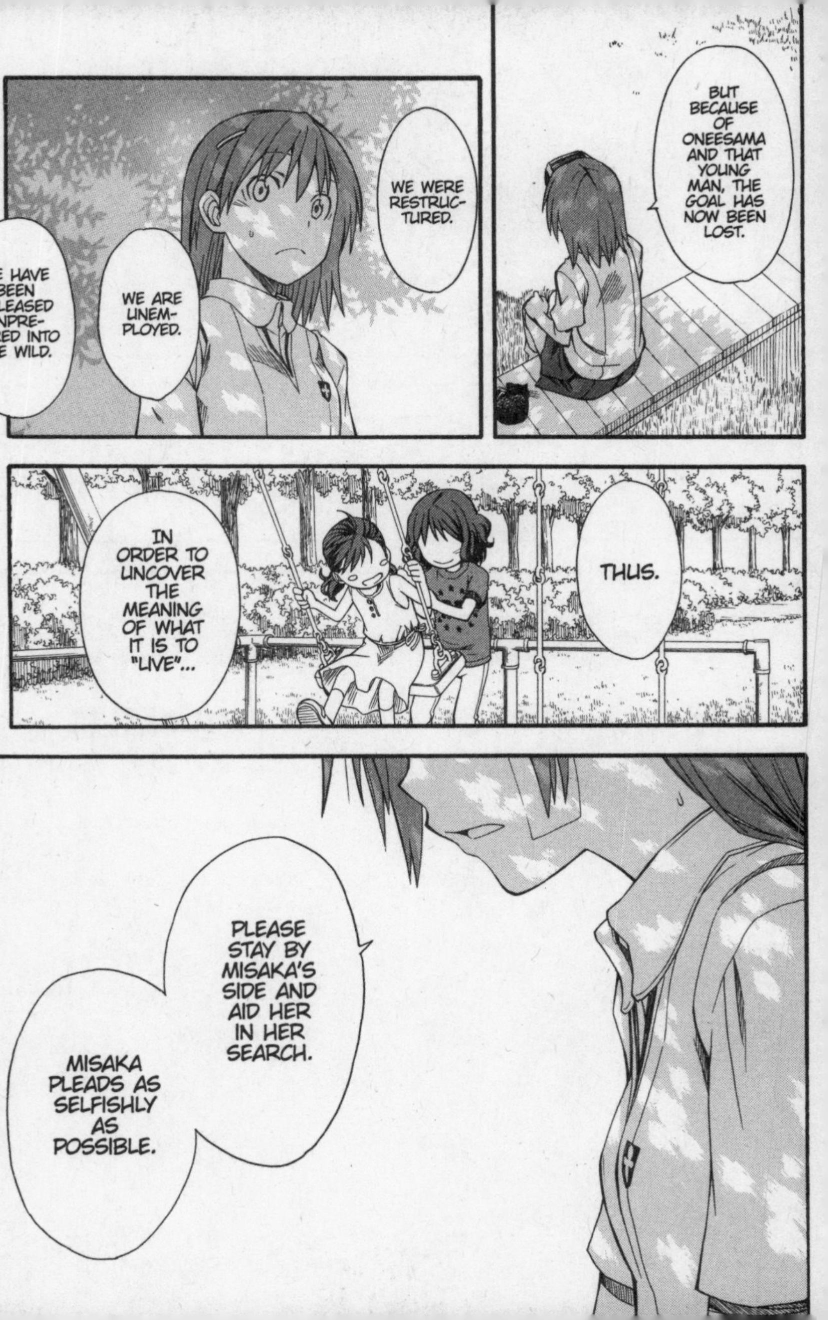
BUT BECAUSE OF ONEESAMA AND THAT YOUNG MAN, THE GOAL HAS NOW BEEN LOST.
WE WERE RESTRUC-TURED.
WE ARE UNEM-PLOYED.
WE HAVE BEEN RELEASED UNPRE-PARED INTO THE WILD.
THUS.
IN ORDER TO UNCOVER THE MEANING OF WHAT IT IS TO "LIVE"...
PLEASE STAY BY MISAKA'S SIDE AND AID HER IN HER SEARCH.
MISAKA PLEADS AS SELFISHLY AS POSSIBLE.

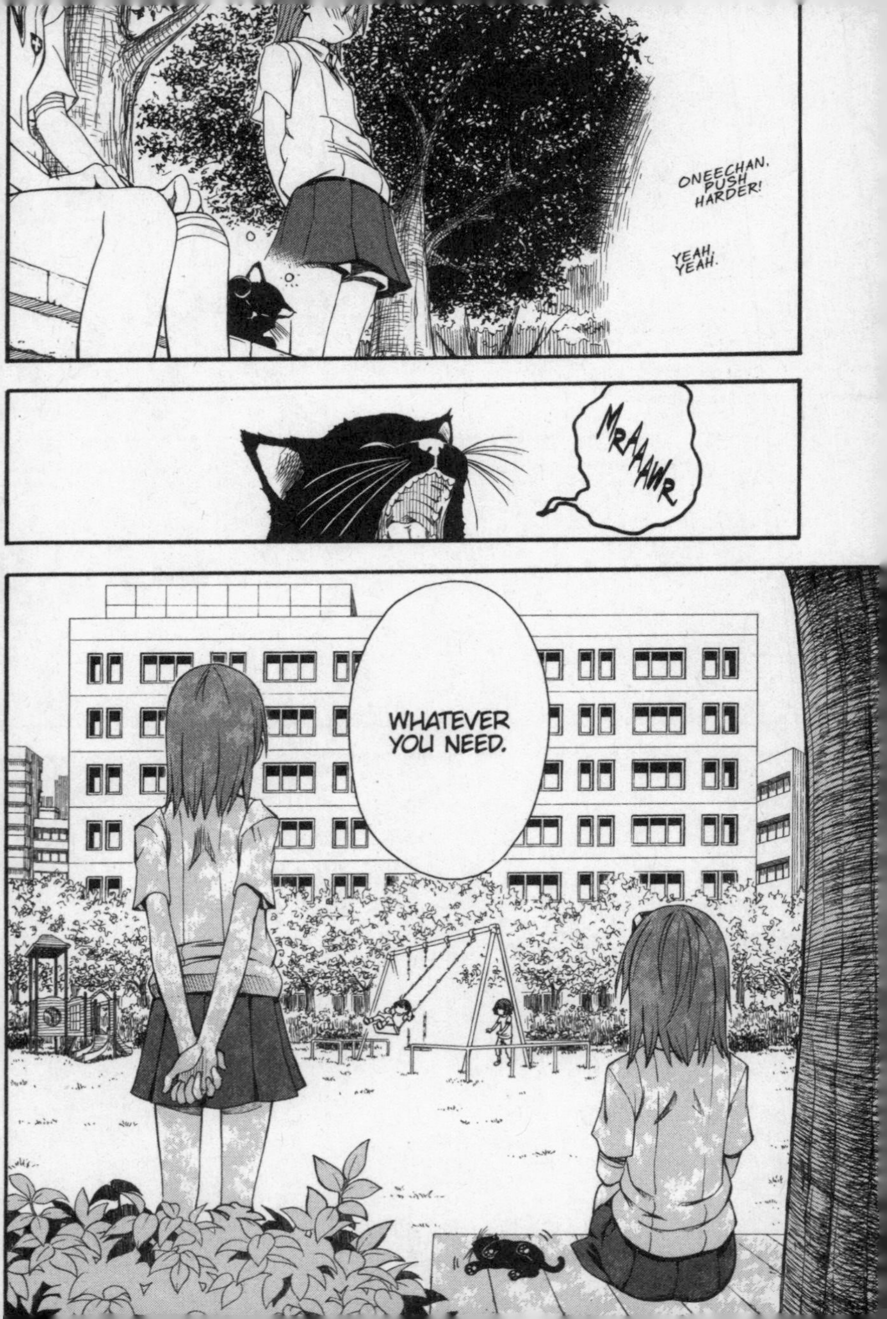
ONEECHAN, PUSH HARDER!
YEAH, YEAH.
MRAAAWR
WHATEVER YOU NEED.

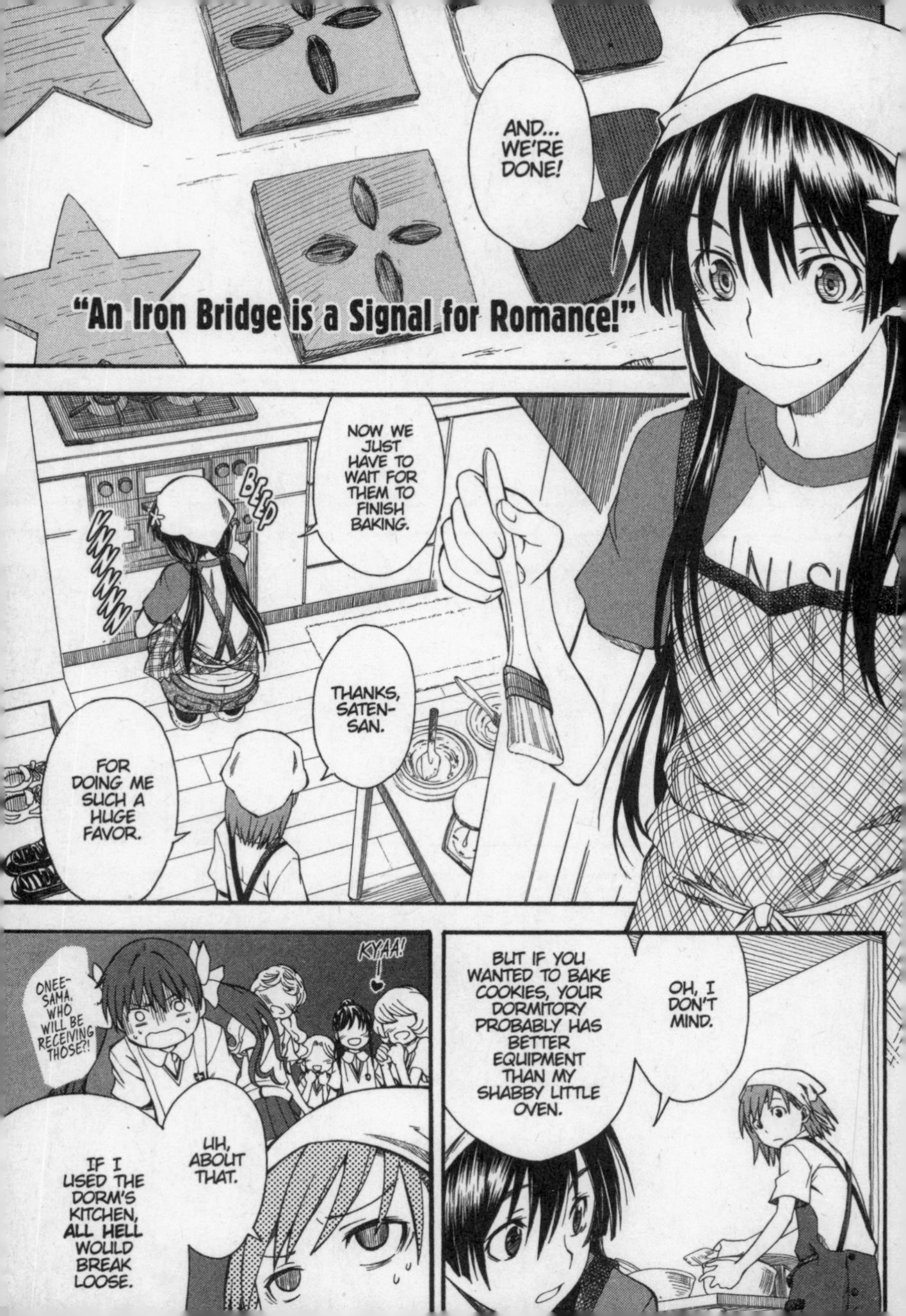
AND... WE'RE DONE!
"An Iron Bridge is a Signal for Romance!"
NOW WE JUST HAVE TO WAIT FOR THEM TO FINISH BAKING.
BEEP
VNNNNNN
THANKS, SATEN-SAN.
FOR DOING ME SUCH A HUGE FAVOR.
OH, I DON'T MIND.
BUT IF YOU WANTED TO BAKE COOKIES, YOUR DORMITORY PROBABLY HAS BETTER EQUIPMENT THAN MY SHABBY LITTLE OVEN.
UH, ABOUT THAT.
IF I USED THE DORM'S KITCHEN, ALL HELL WOULD BREAK LOOSE.
KYAA!
ONEE-SAMA, WHO WILL BE RECEIVING THOSE?!

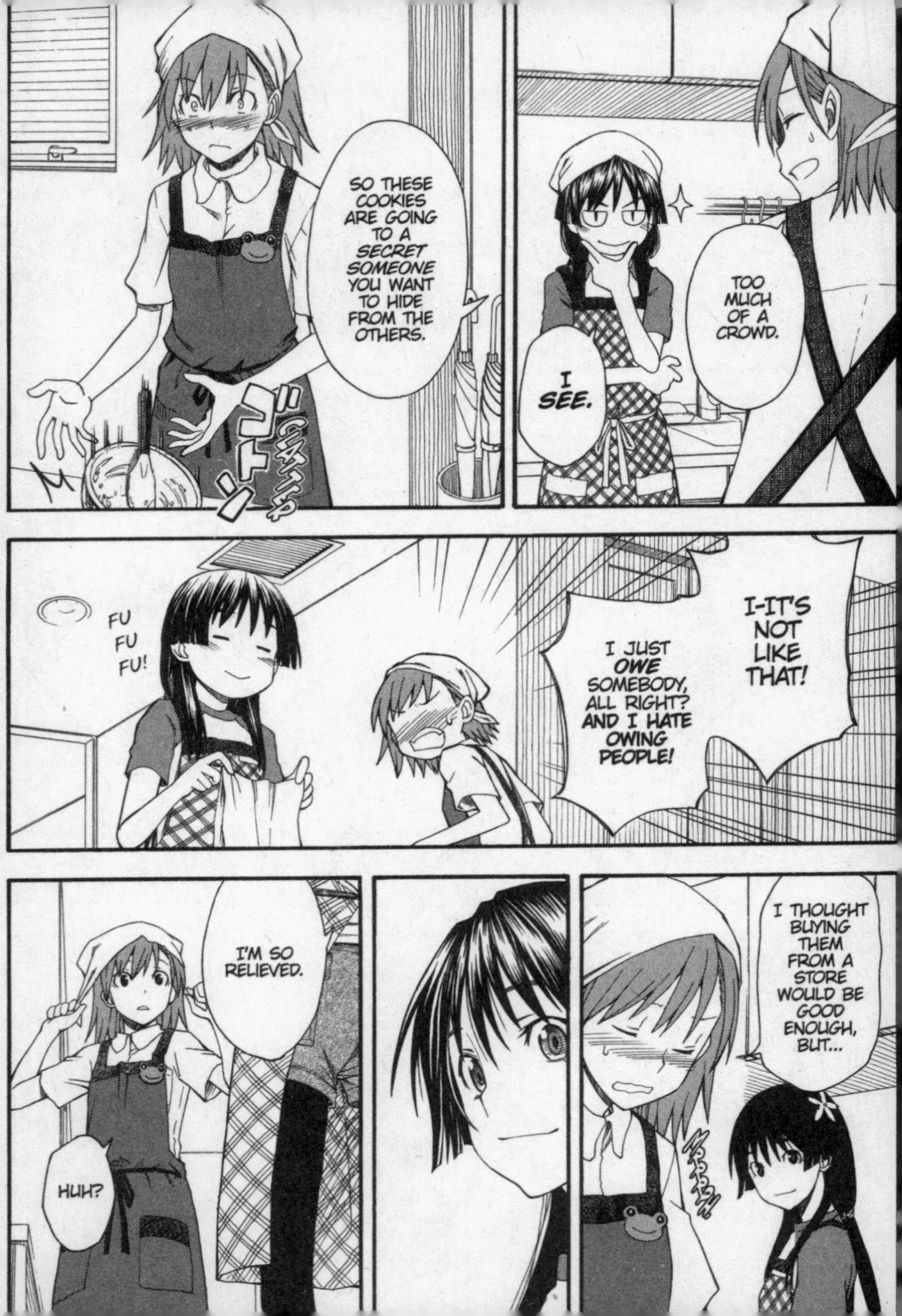
TOO MUCH OF A CROWD.
I SEE.
SO THESE COOKIES ARE GOING TO A SECRET SOMEONE YOU WANT TO HIDE FROM THE OTHERS.
CLATTER
I-IT'S NOT LIKE THAT!
I JUST OWE SOMEBODY, ALL RIGHT? AND I HATE OWING PEOPLE!
FU FU FU!
I THOUGHT BUYING THEM FROM A STORE WOULD BE GOOD ENOUGH, BUT...
I'M SO RELIEVED.
HUH?

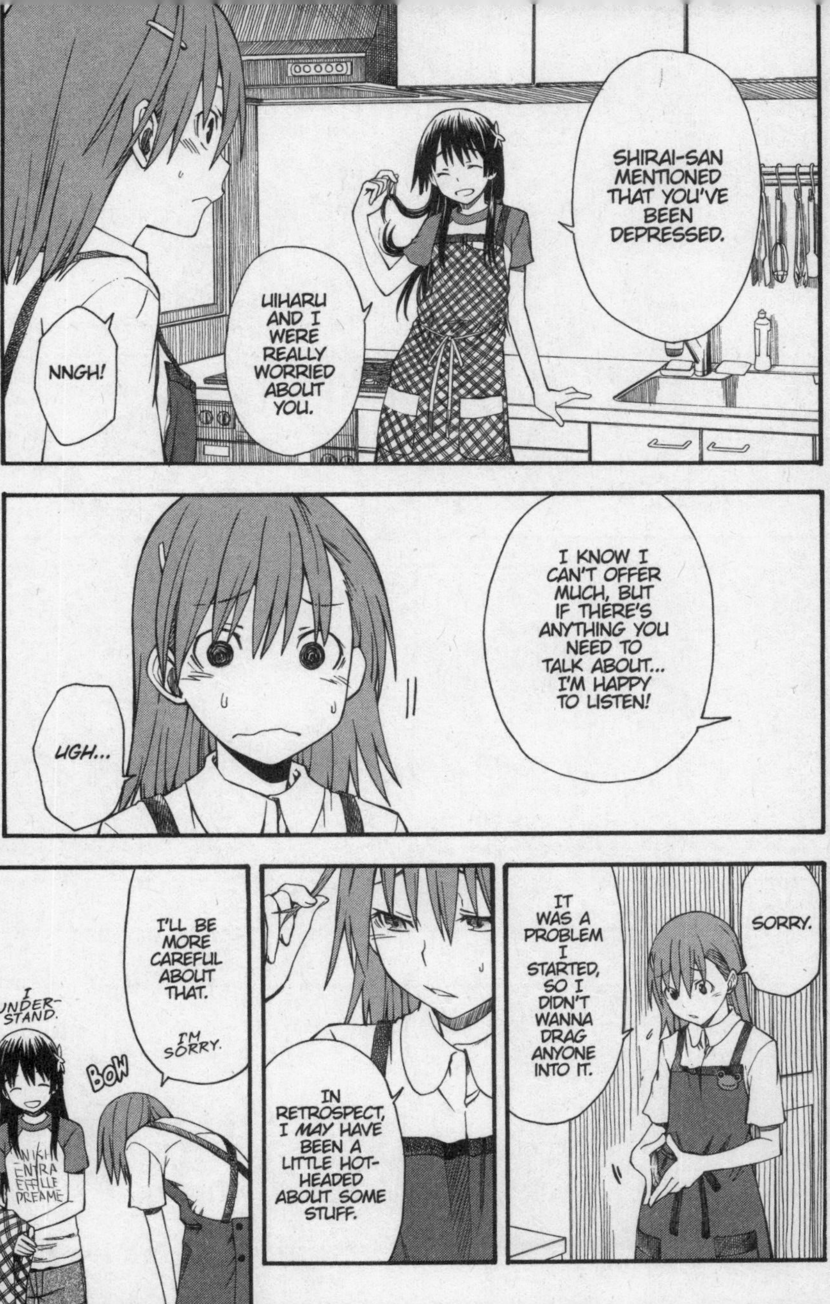
SHIRAI-SAN MENTIONED THAT YOU'VE BEEN DEPRESSED.
UIHARU AND I WERE REALLY WORRIED ABOUT YOU.
NNGH!
I KNOW I CAN'T OFFER MUCH, BUT IF THERE'S ANYTHING YOU NEED TO TALK ABOUT... I'M HAPPY TO LISTEN!
UGH...
SORRY.
IT WAS A PROBLEM I STARTED, SO I DIDN'T WANNA DRAG ANYONE INTO IT.
IN RETROSPECT, I *MAY* HAVE BEEN A LITTLE HOT-HEADED ABOUT SOME STUFF.
I'LL BE MORE CAREFUL ABOUT THAT.
I'M SORRY.
BOW
I UNDER-STAND.

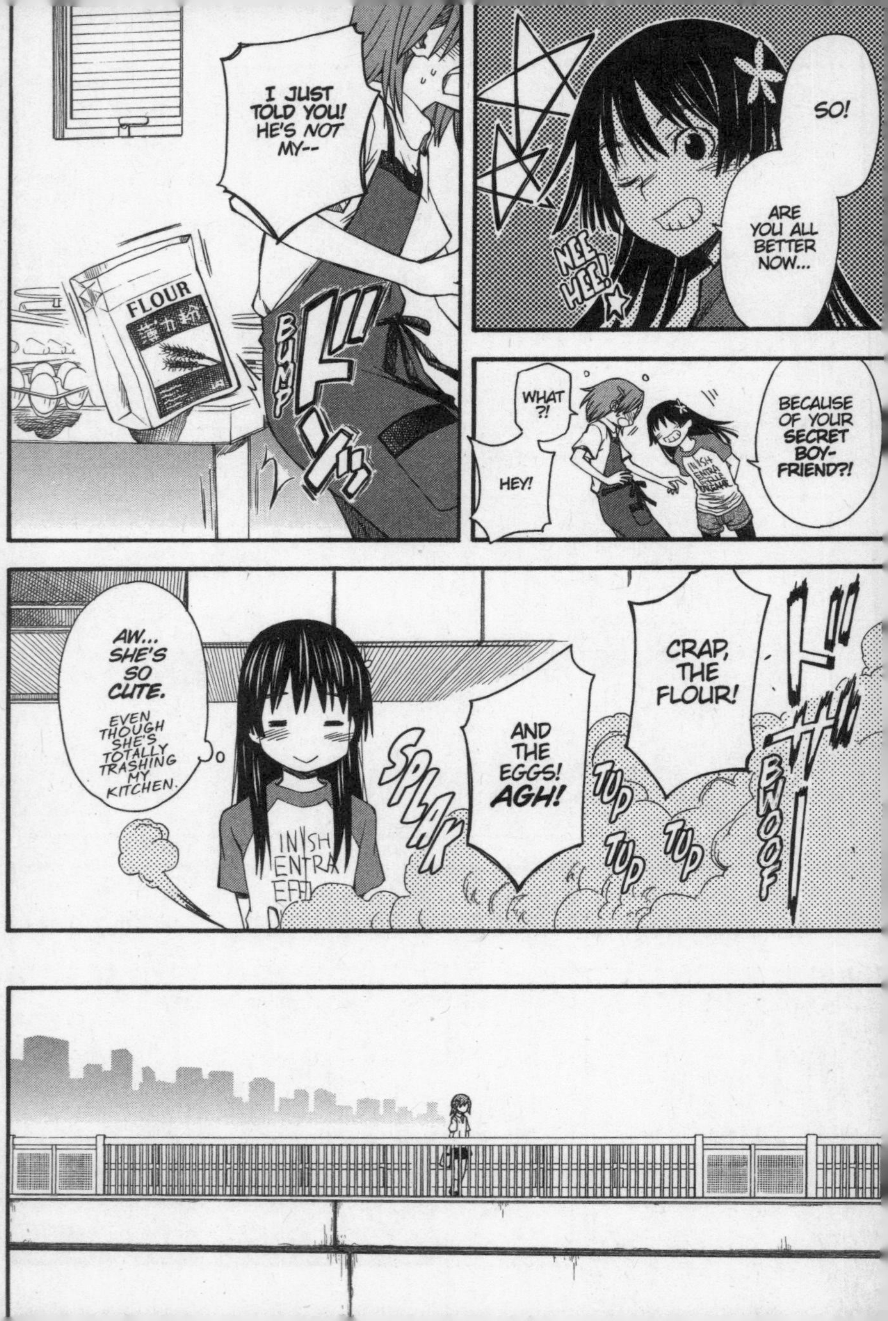
SO!
ARE YOU ALL BETTER NOW...
NEE HEE!
BECAUSE OF YOUR SECRET BOY-FRIEND?!
WHAT?!
HEY!
I JUST TOLD YOU! HE'S NOT MY--
FLOUR
BUMP
BWOOF
CRAP, THE FLOUR!
TUP TUP TUP
AND THE EGGS! AGH!
SPLAK
AW... SHE'S SO CUTE.
EVEN THOUGH SHE'S TOTALLY TRASHING MY KITCHEN.

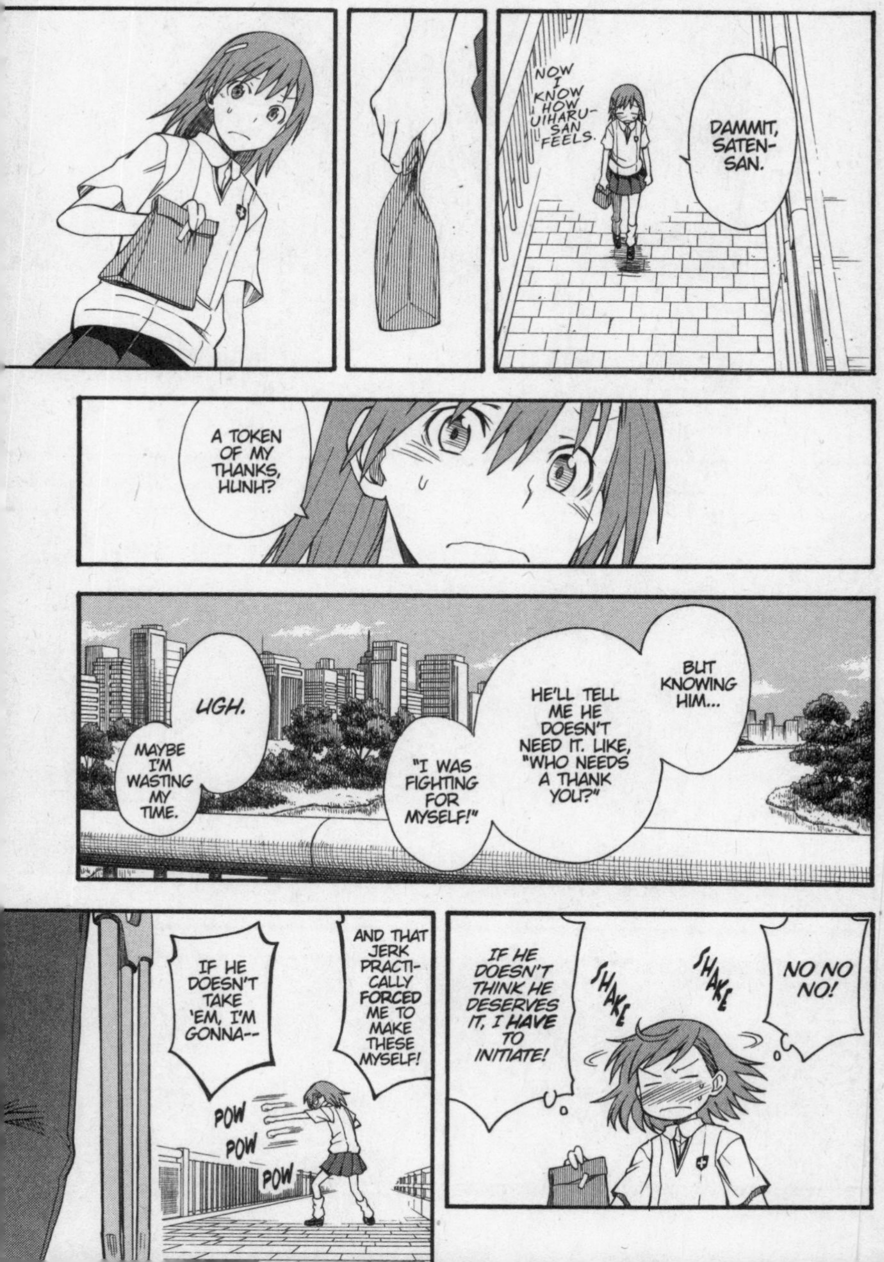
DAMMIT, SATEN-SAN.
NOW I KNOW HOW UIHARU-SAN FEELS.
A TOKEN OF MY THANKS, HUNH?
BUT KNOWING HIM...
HE'LL TELL ME HE DOESN'T NEED IT. LIKE, "WHO NEEDS A THANK YOU?"
"I WAS FIGHTING FOR MYSELF!"
UGH.
MAYBE I'M WASTING MY TIME.
NO NO NO!
SHAKE
SHAKE
IF HE DOESN'T THINK HE DESERVES IT, I HAVE TO INITIATE!
AND THAT JERK PRACTI-CALLY FORCED ME TO MAKE THESE MYSELF!
IF HE DOESN'T TAKE 'EM, I'M GONNA--
POW
POW
POW

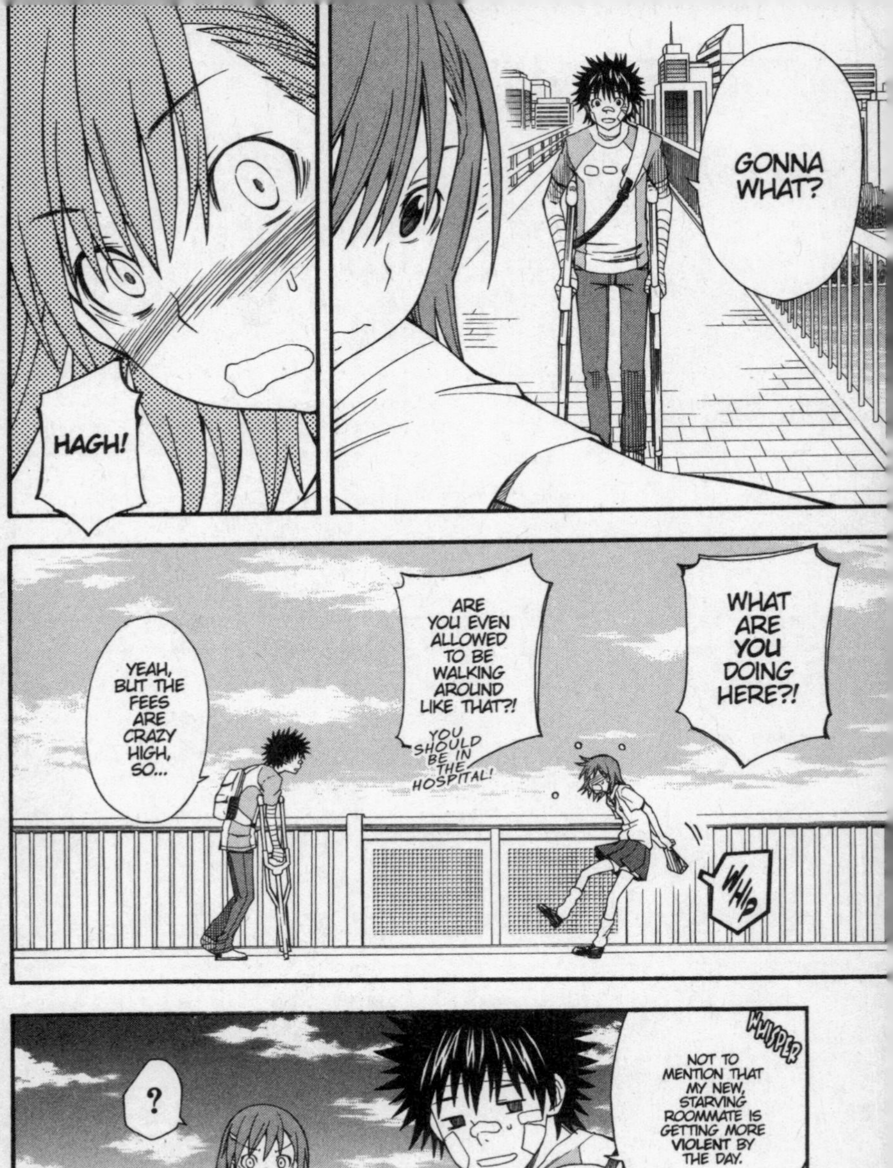
GONNA WHAT?
HAGH!
WHAT ARE YOU DOING HERE?!
WHIP
ARE YOU EVEN ALLOWED TO BE WALKING AROUND LIKE THAT?!
YOU SHOULD BE IN THE HOSPITAL!
YEAH, BUT THE FEES ARE CRAZY HIGH, SO...
WHISPER
NOT TO MENTION THAT MY NEW, STARVING ROOMMATE IS GETTING MORE VIOLENT BY THE DAY.
?

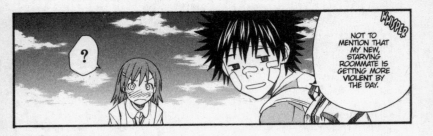

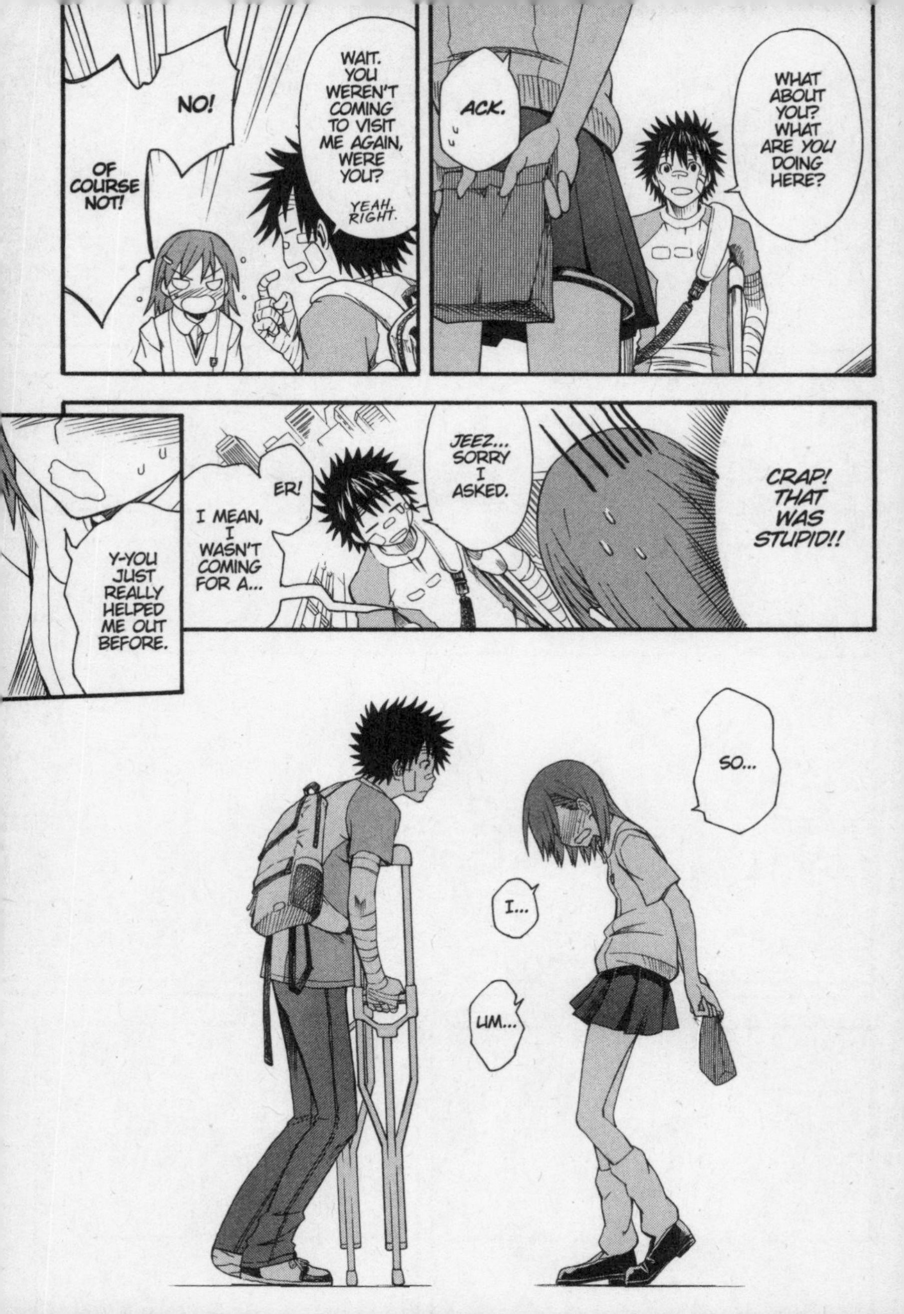
WHAT ABOUT YOU? WHAT ARE YOU DOING HERE?
ACK.
WAIT. YOU WEREN'T COMING TO VISIT ME AGAIN, WERE YOU?
YEAH, RIGHT.
NO!
OF COURSE NOT!
CRAP! THAT WAS STUPID!!
JEEZ... SORRY I ASKED.
ER!
I MEAN, I WASN'T COMING FOR A...
Y-YOU JUST REALLY HELPED ME OUT BEFORE.
SO...
I...
UM...

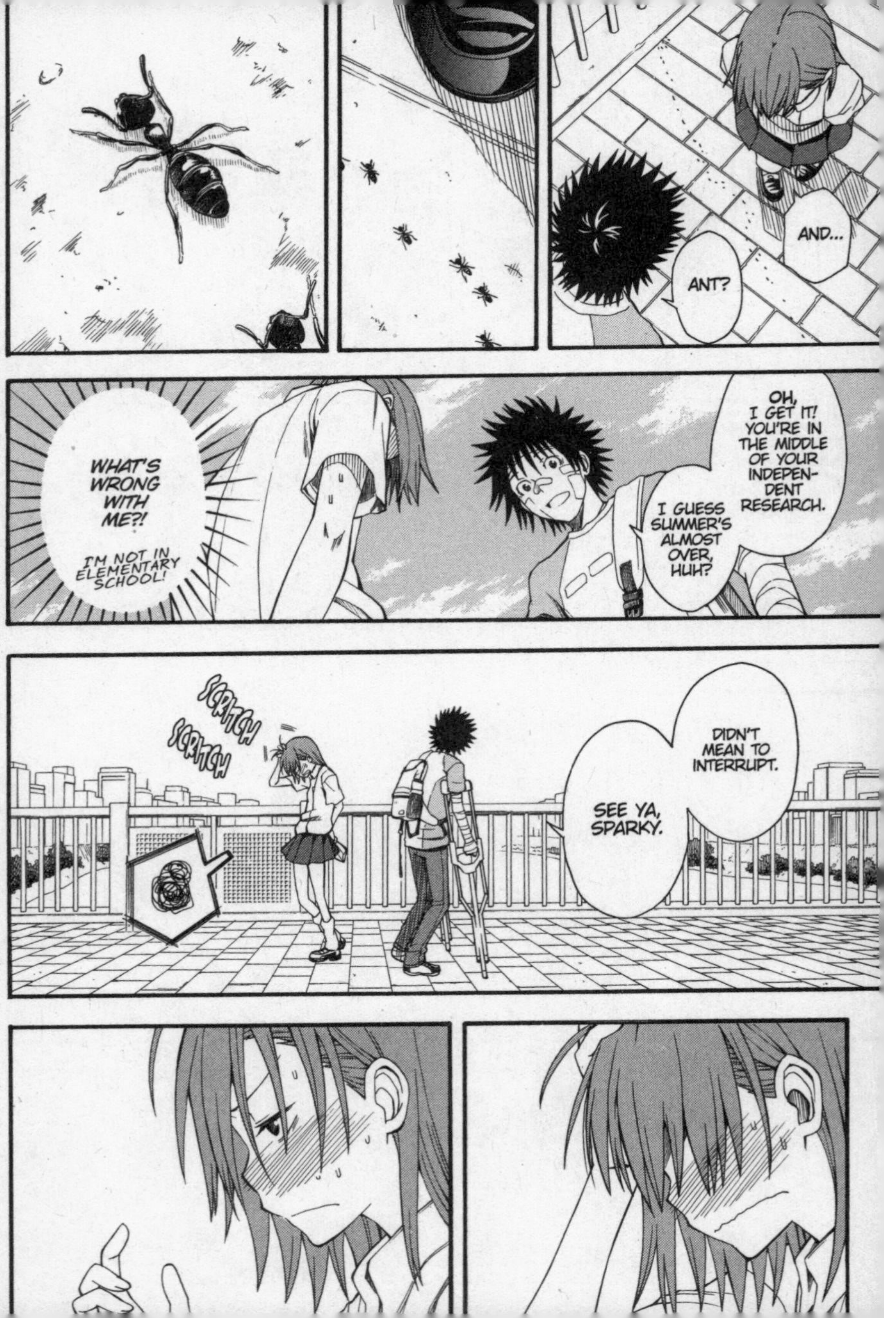
AND...
ANT?
OH, I GET IT! YOU'RE IN THE MIDDLE OF YOUR INDEPENDENT RESEARCH.
I GUESS SUMMER'S ALMOST OVER, HUH?
WHAT'S WRONG WITH ME?!
I'M NOT IN ELEMENTARY SCHOOL!
DIDN'T MEAN TO INTERRUPT.
SEE YA, SPARKY.
SCRATCH
SCRATCH

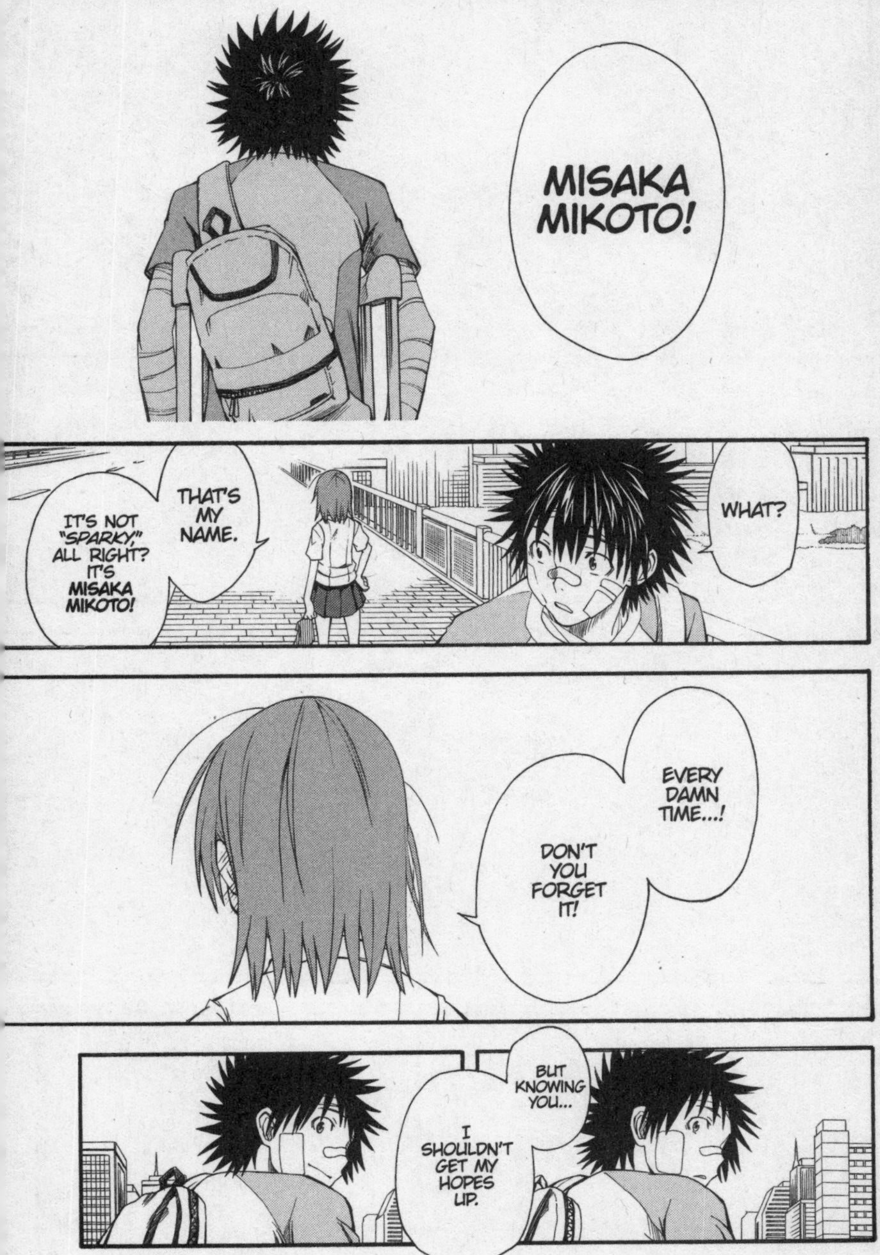
MISAKA MIKOTO!
WHAT?
THAT'S MY NAME.
IT'S NOT "SPARKY," ALL RIGHT? IT'S MISAKA MIKOTO!
EVERY DAMN TIME...!
DON'T YOU FORGET IT!
BUT KNOWING YOU...
I SHOULDN'T GET MY HOPES UP.

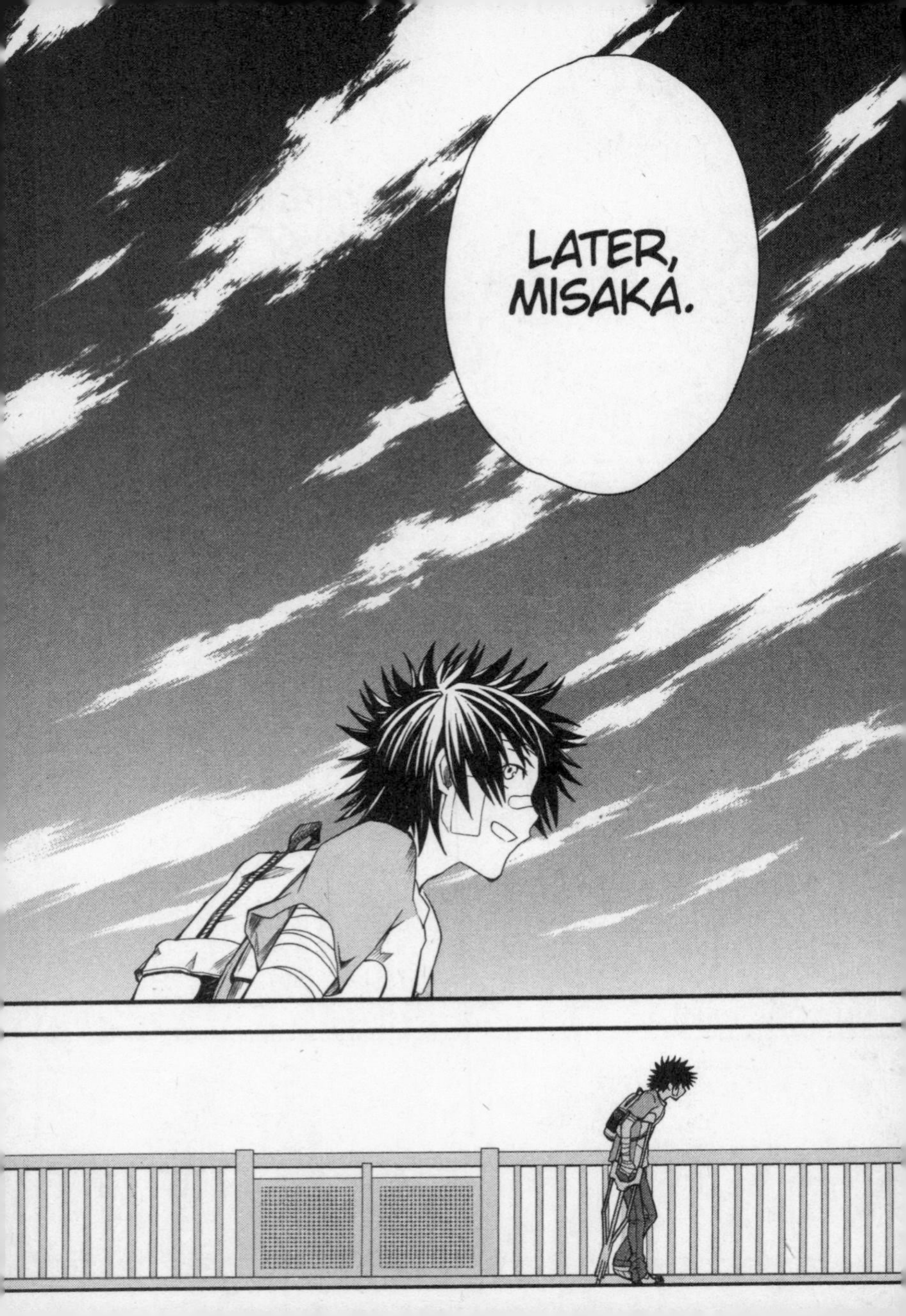
LATER, MISAKA.

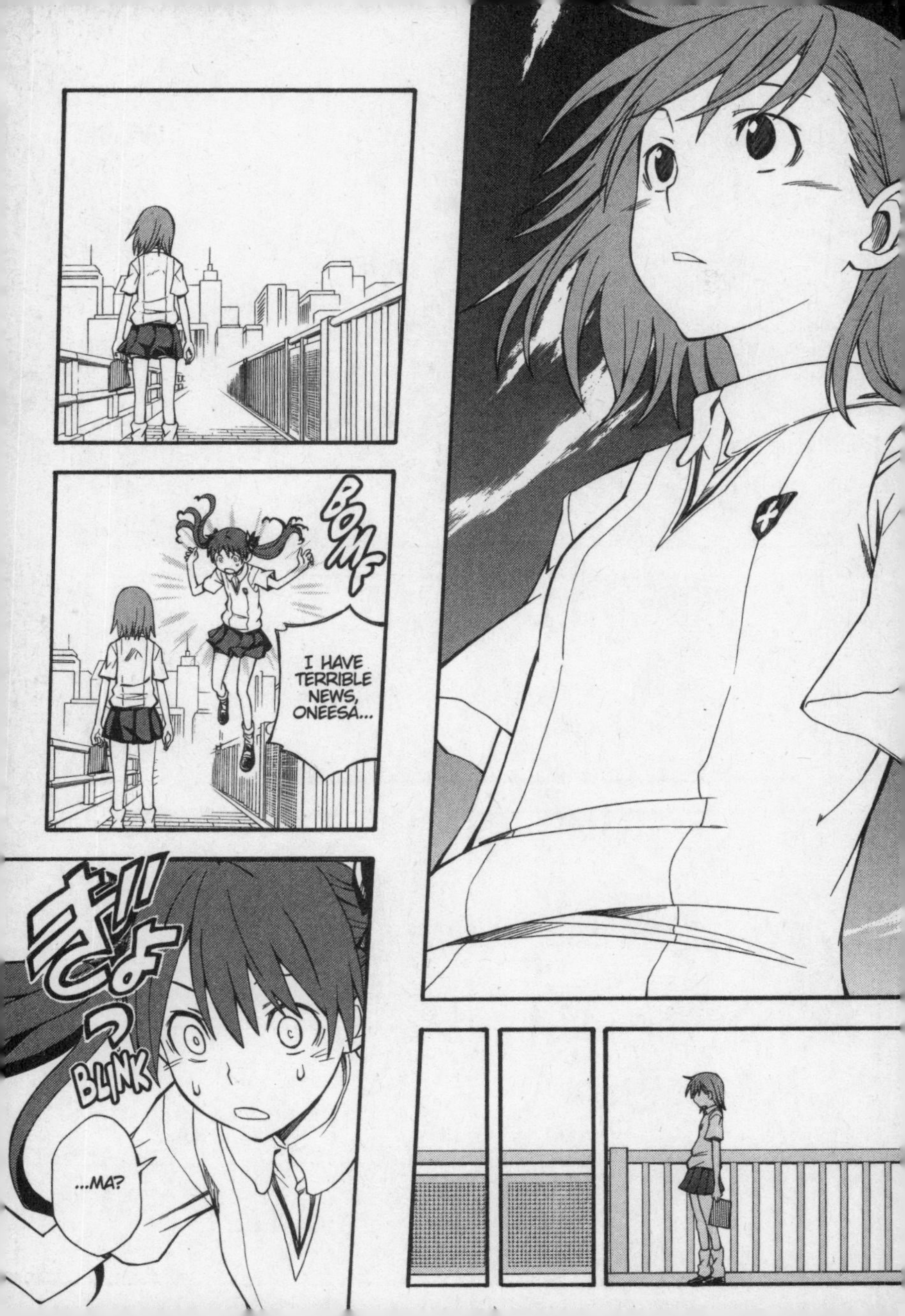
BOMF
I HAVE TERRIBLE NEWS, ONEESA...
ぎょっ
BLINK
...MA?

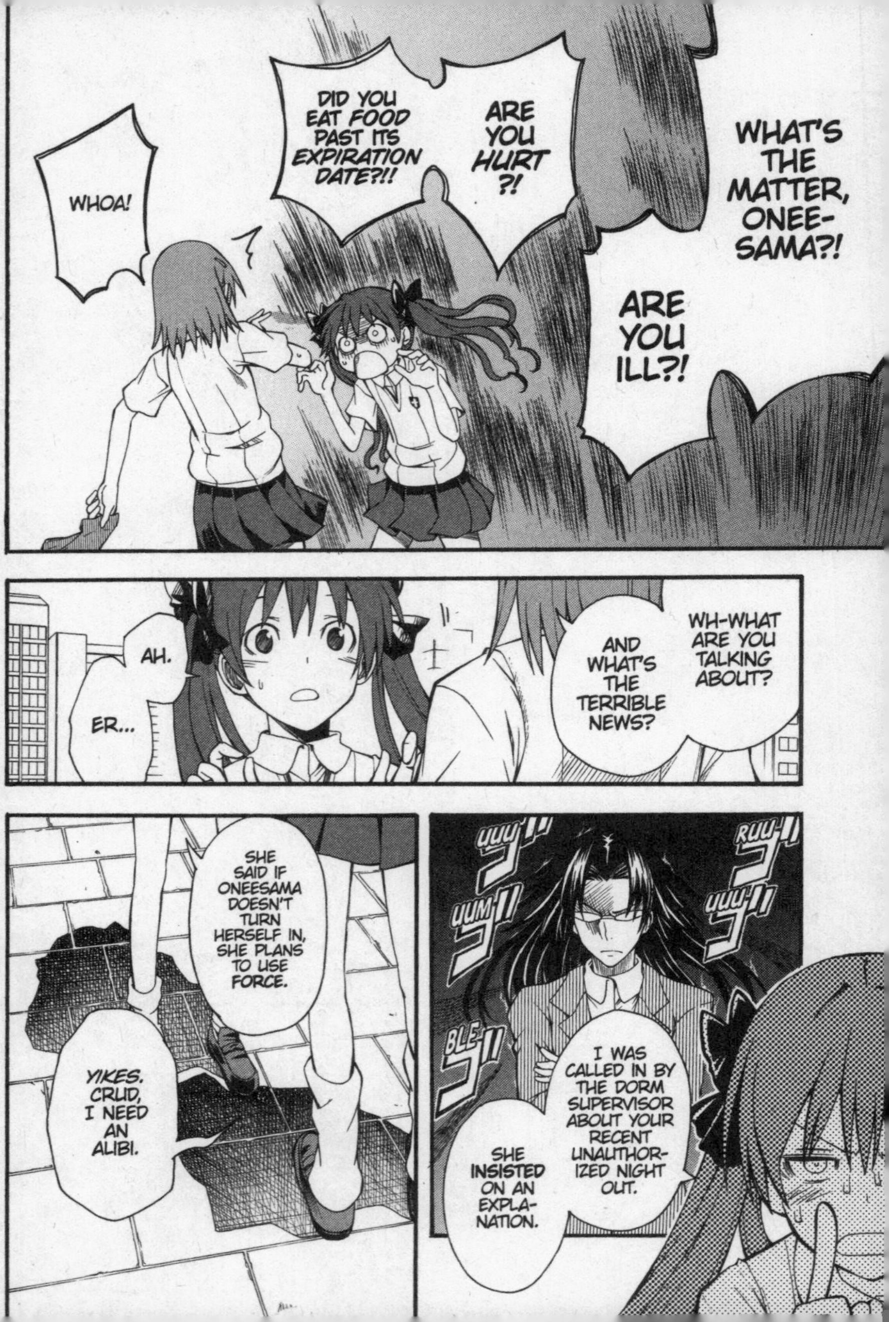
WHAT'S THE MATTER, ONEE-SAMA?!
ARE YOU ILL?!
ARE YOU HURT?!
DID YOU EAT FOOD PAST ITS EXPIRATION DATE?!!
WHOA!
WH-WHAT ARE YOU TALKING ABOUT?
AND WHAT'S THE TERRIBLE NEWS?
AH.
ER...
RUU-
UUU-
UUM-
UUU-
BLE-
I WAS CALLED IN BY THE DORM SUPERVISOR ABOUT YOUR RECENT UNAUTHOR-IZED NIGHT OUT.
SHE INSISTED ON AN EXPLA-NATION.
SHE SAID IF ONEESAMA DOESN'T TURN HERSELF IN, SHE PLANS TO USE FORCE.
YIKES. CRUD, I NEED AN ALIBI.

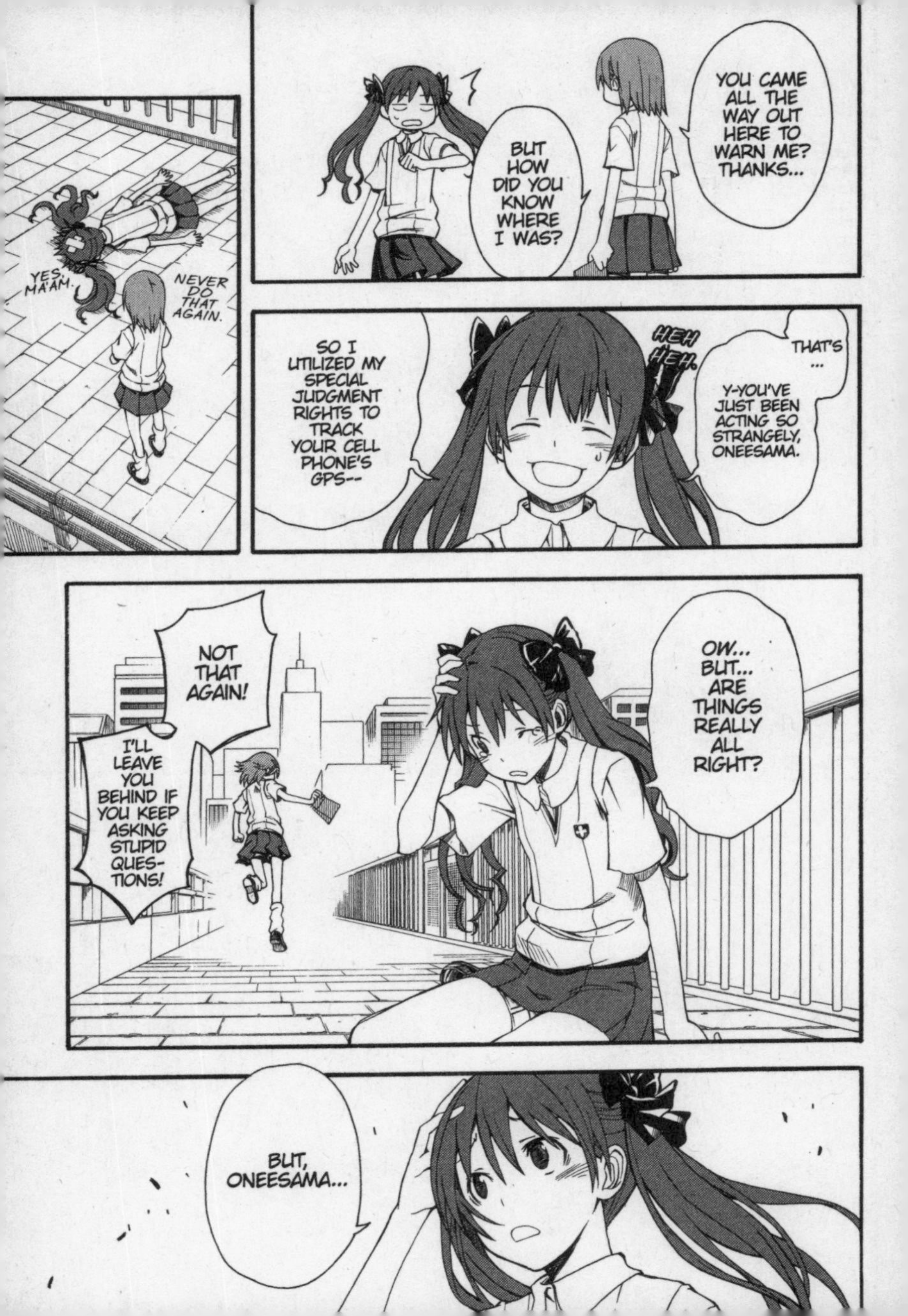
YOU CAME ALL THE WAY OUT HERE TO WARN ME? THANKS...
BUT HOW DID YOU KNOW WHERE I WAS?
THAT'S ...
Y-YOU'VE JUST BEEN ACTING SO STRANGELY, ONEESAMA.
HEH HEH.
SO I UTILIZED MY SPECIAL JUDGMENT RIGHTS TO TRACK YOUR CELL PHONE'S GPS--
NEVER DO THAT AGAIN.
YES, MA'AM.
OW... BUT... ARE THINGS REALLY ALL RIGHT?
NOT THAT AGAIN!
I'LL LEAVE YOU BEHIND IF YOU KEEP ASKING STUPID QUES-TIONS!
BUT, ONEESAMA...

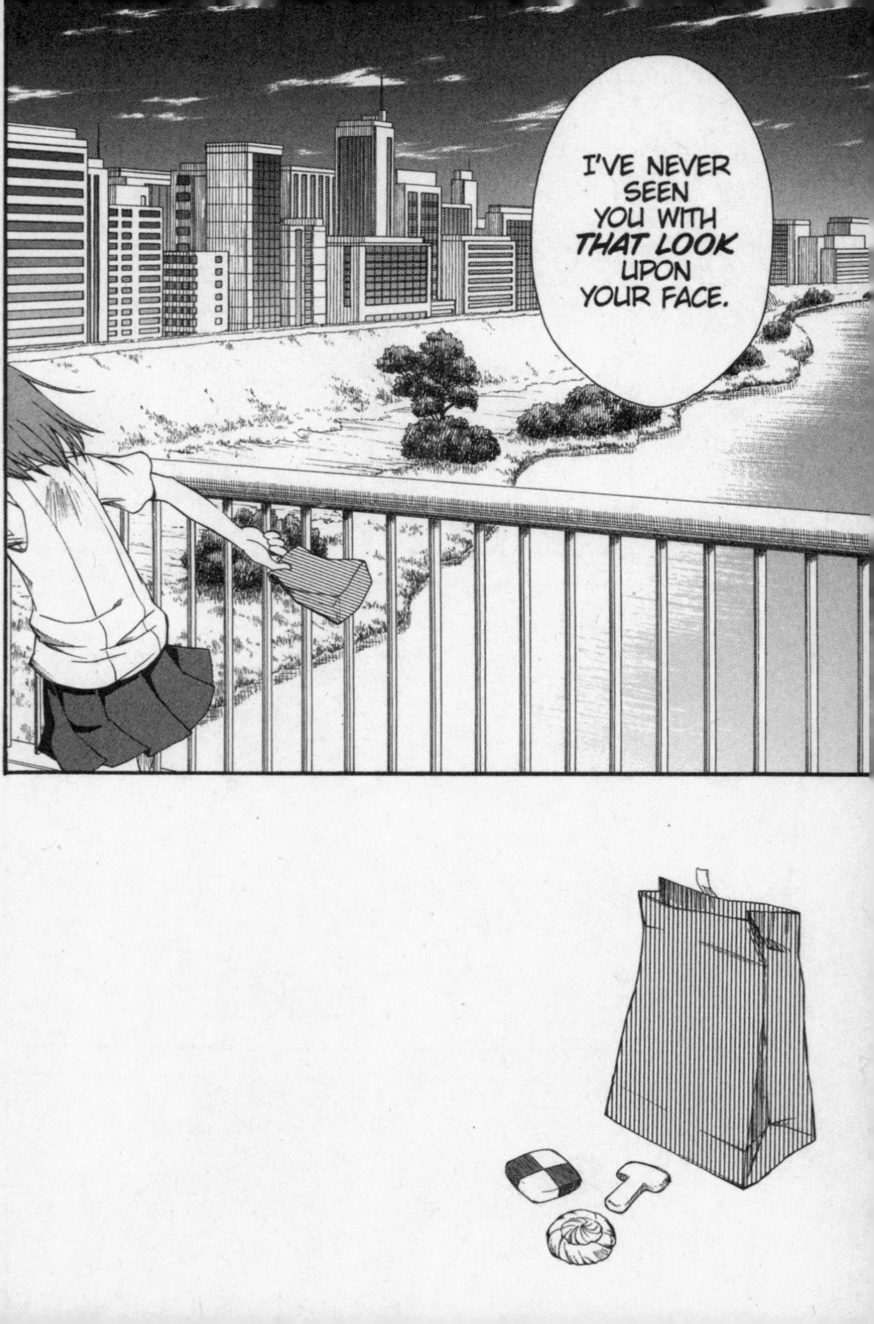
I'VE NEVER SEEN YOU WITH *THAT LOOK* UPON YOUR FACE.

A Certain SCIENTIFIC Railgun

A Certain Misaka's No Work

BUT BECAUSE OF ONEESAMA AND THAT YOUNG MAN, THE GOAL HAS NOW BEEN LOST.
WE WERE RESTRUC-TURED.
WE ARE UNEM-PLOYED.
WE HAVE BEEN RELEASED UNPREPARED INTO THE WILD.
BUT MISAKA DOES NOT MIND.
MISAKA HAS COME TO THINK...
THAT WORKING IS FOR SUCKERS!
Thumbs Up!!
HOLY CRAP IS HER PERSONALITY WEIRD AS HELL!

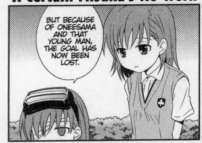

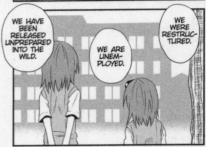

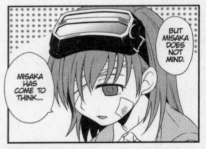

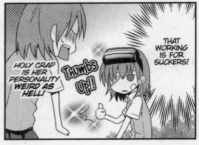

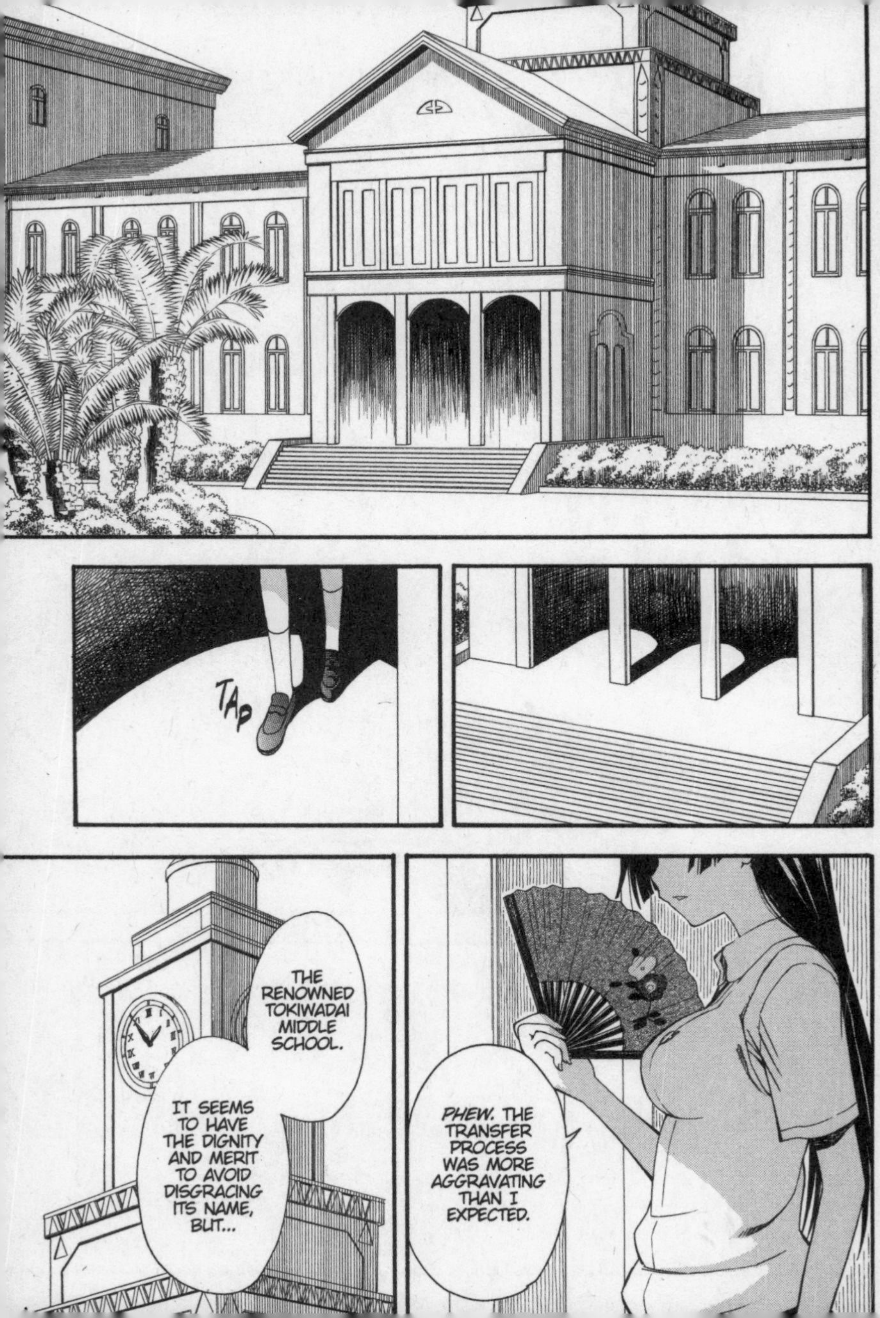
TAP
PHEW. THE TRANSFER PROCESS WAS MORE AGGRAVATING THAN I EXPECTED.
THE RENOWNED TOKIWADAI MIDDLE SCHOOL.
IT SEEMS TO HAVE THE DIGNITY AND MERIT TO AVOID DISGRACING ITS NAME, BUT...

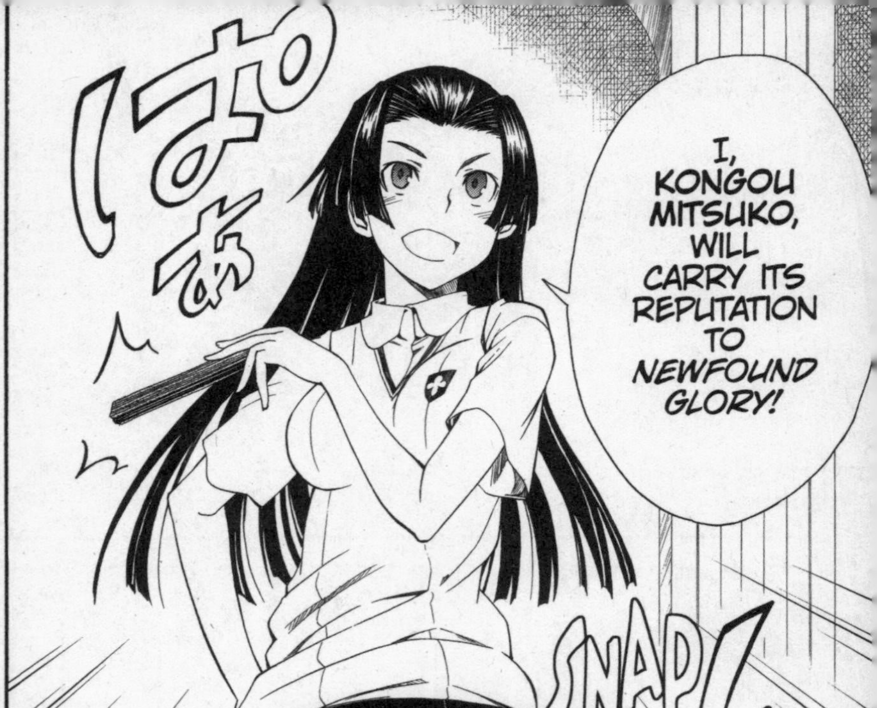
I, KONGOU MITSUKO, WILL CARRY ITS REPUTATION TO NEWFOUND GLORY!
SNAP
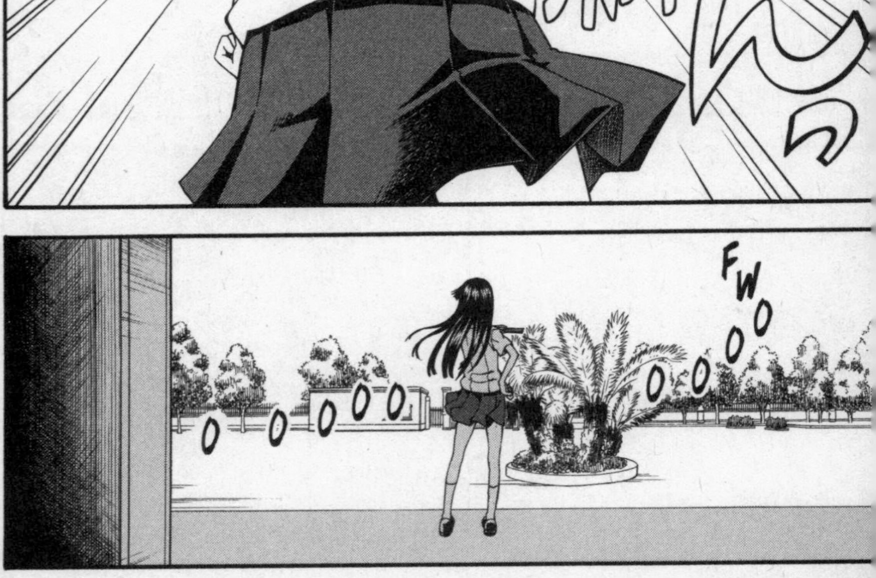
FWOOOO

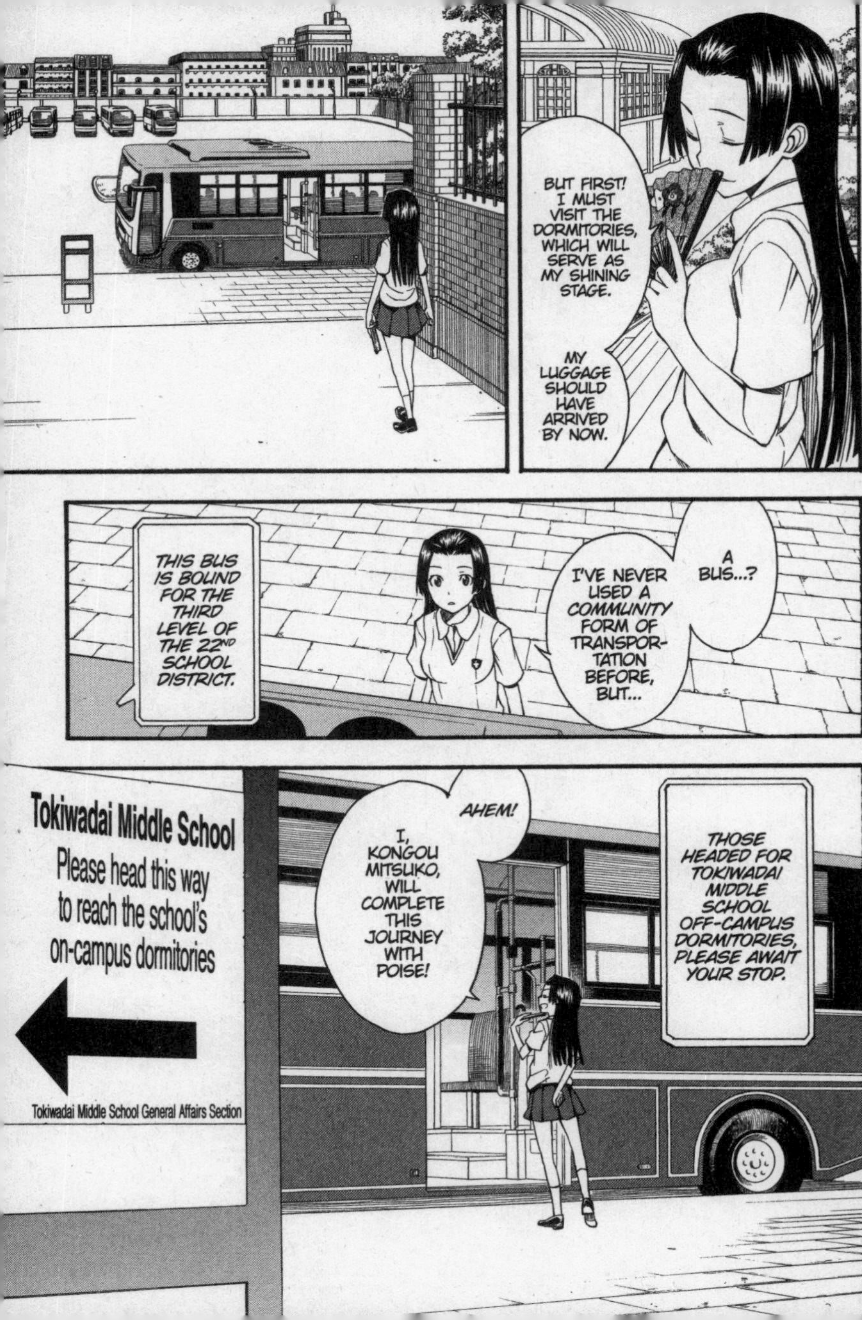
BUT FIRST! I MUST VISIT THE DORMITORIES, WHICH WILL SERVE AS MY SHINING STAGE.
MY LUGGAGE SHOULD HAVE ARRIVED BY NOW.
A BUS...?
I'VE NEVER USED A COMMUNITY FORM OF TRANSPOR-TATION BEFORE, BUT...
THIS BUS IS BOUND FOR THE THIRD LEVEL OF THE 22ND SCHOOL DISTRICT.
THOSE HEADED FOR TOKIWADAI MIDDLE SCHOOL OFF-CAMPUS DORMITORIES, PLEASE AWAIT YOUR STOP.
AHEM!
I, KONGOU MITSUKO, WILL COMPLETE THIS JOURNEY WITH POISE!
Tokiwadai Middle School
Please head this way to reach the school's on-campus dormitories
Tokiwadai Middle School General Affairs Section

CHAPTER 40: FACTION (1)

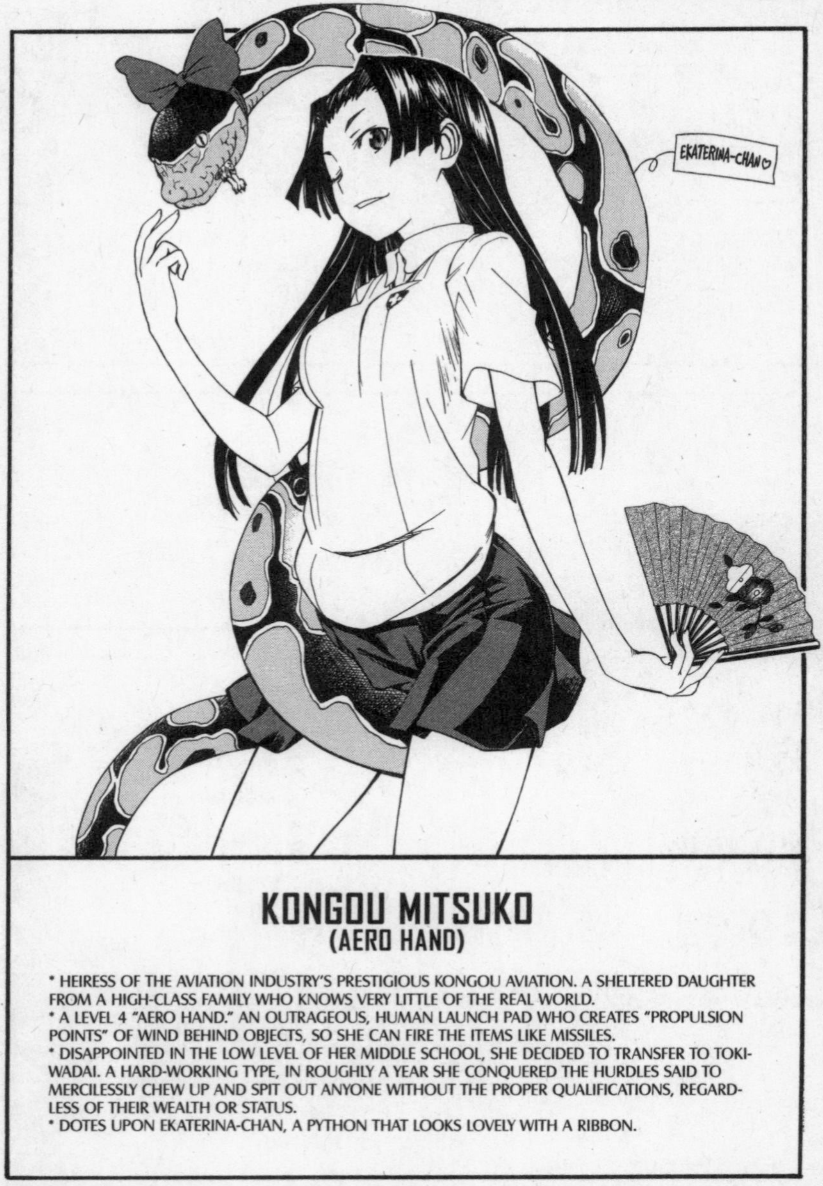
EKATERINA-CHAN♡

KONGOU MITSUKO
(AERO HAND)

* HEIRESS OF THE AVIATION INDUSTRY'S PRESTIGIOUS KONGOU AVIATION. A SHELTERED DAUGHTER FROM A HIGH-CLASS FAMILY WHO KNOWS VERY LITTLE OF THE REAL WORLD.
* A LEVEL 4 "AERO HAND." AN OUTRAGEOUS, HUMAN LAUNCH PAD WHO CREATES "PROPULSION POINTS" OF WIND BEHIND OBJECTS, SO SHE CAN FIRE THE ITEMS LIKE MISSILES.
* DISAPPOINTED IN THE LOW LEVEL OF HER MIDDLE SCHOOL, SHE DECIDED TO TRANSFER TO TOKIWADAI. A HARD-WORKING TYPE, IN ROUGHLY A YEAR SHE CONQUERED THE HURDLES SAID TO MERCILESSLY CHEW UP AND SPIT OUT ANYONE WITHOUT THE PROPER QUALIFICATIONS, REGARDLESS OF THEIR WEALTH OR STATUS.
* DOTES UPON EKATERINA-CHAN, A PYTHON THAT LOOKS LOVELY WITH A RIBBON.

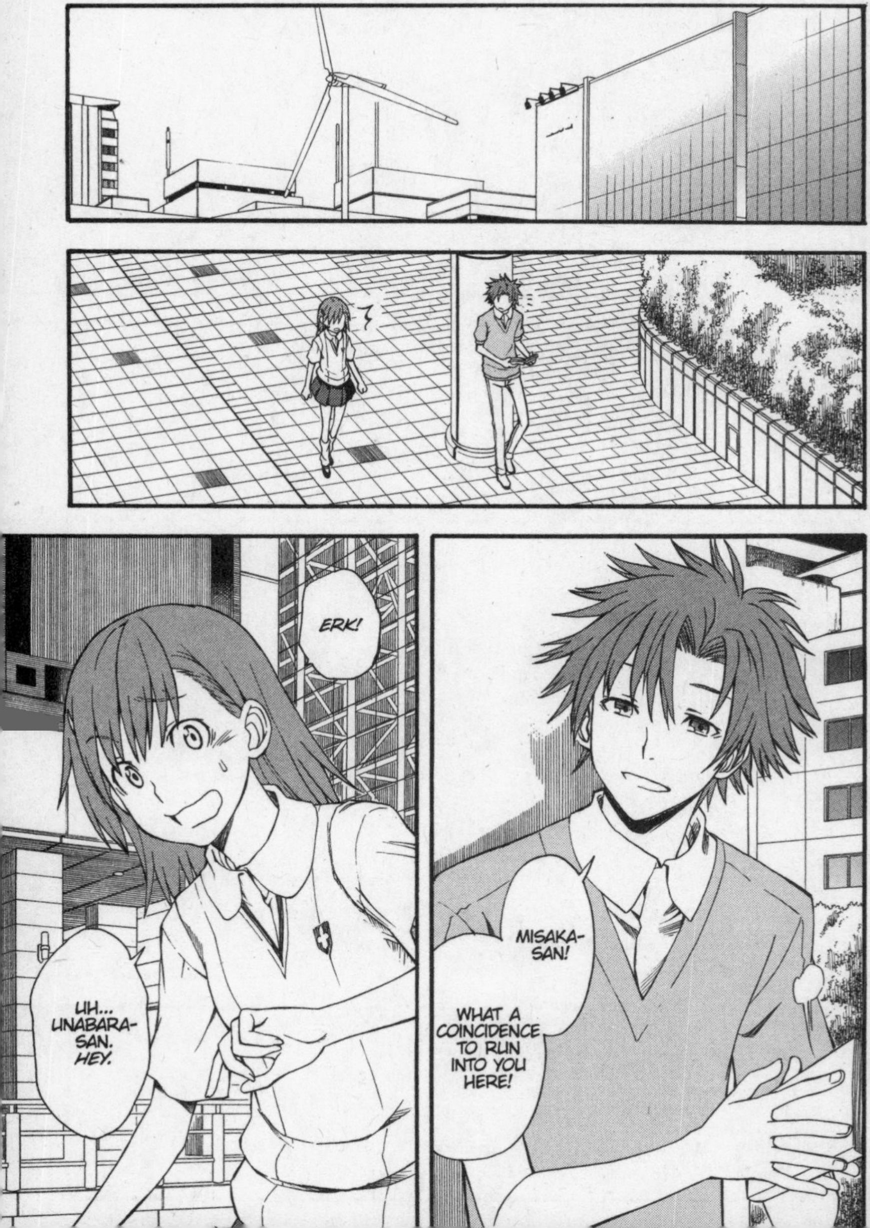
MISAKA-SAN!
WHAT A COINCIDENCE TO RUN INTO YOU HERE!
ERK!
UH... UNABARA-SAN. HEY.

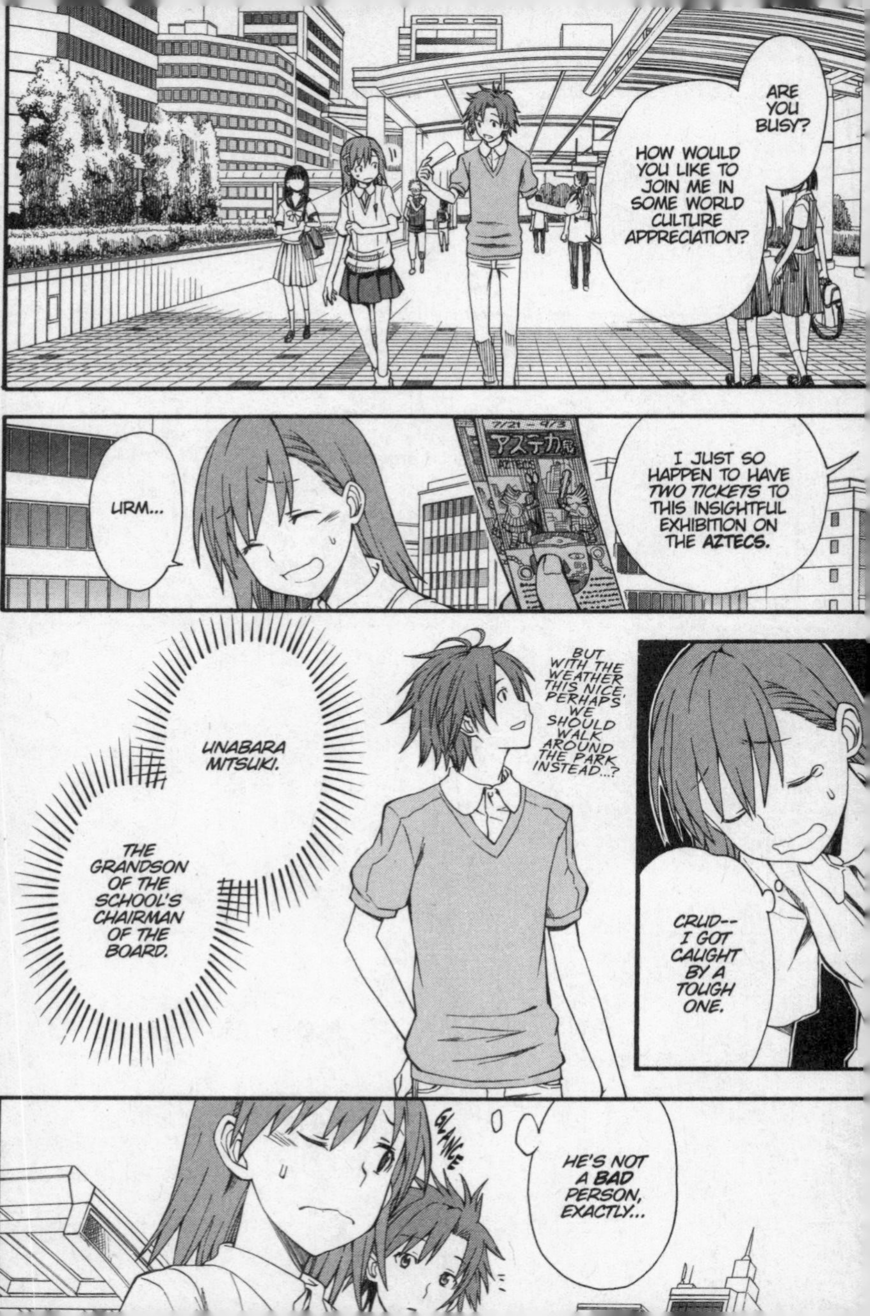
ARE YOU BUSY?
HOW WOULD YOU LIKE TO JOIN ME IN SOME WORLD CULTURE APPRECIATION?
I JUST SO HAPPEN TO HAVE *TWO TICKETS* TO THIS INSIGHTFUL EXHIBITION ON THE **AZTECS.**
7/21 - 9/3
AZTECS
URM...
CRUD-- I GOT CAUGHT BY A TOUGH ONE.
BUT WITH THE WEATHER THIS NICE, PERHAPS WE SHOULD WALK AROUND THE PARK INSTEAD...?
UNABARA MITSUKI.
THE GRANDSON OF THE SCHOOL'S CHAIRMAN OF THE BOARD.
GLANCE
HE'S NOT A *BAD* PERSON, EXACTLY...

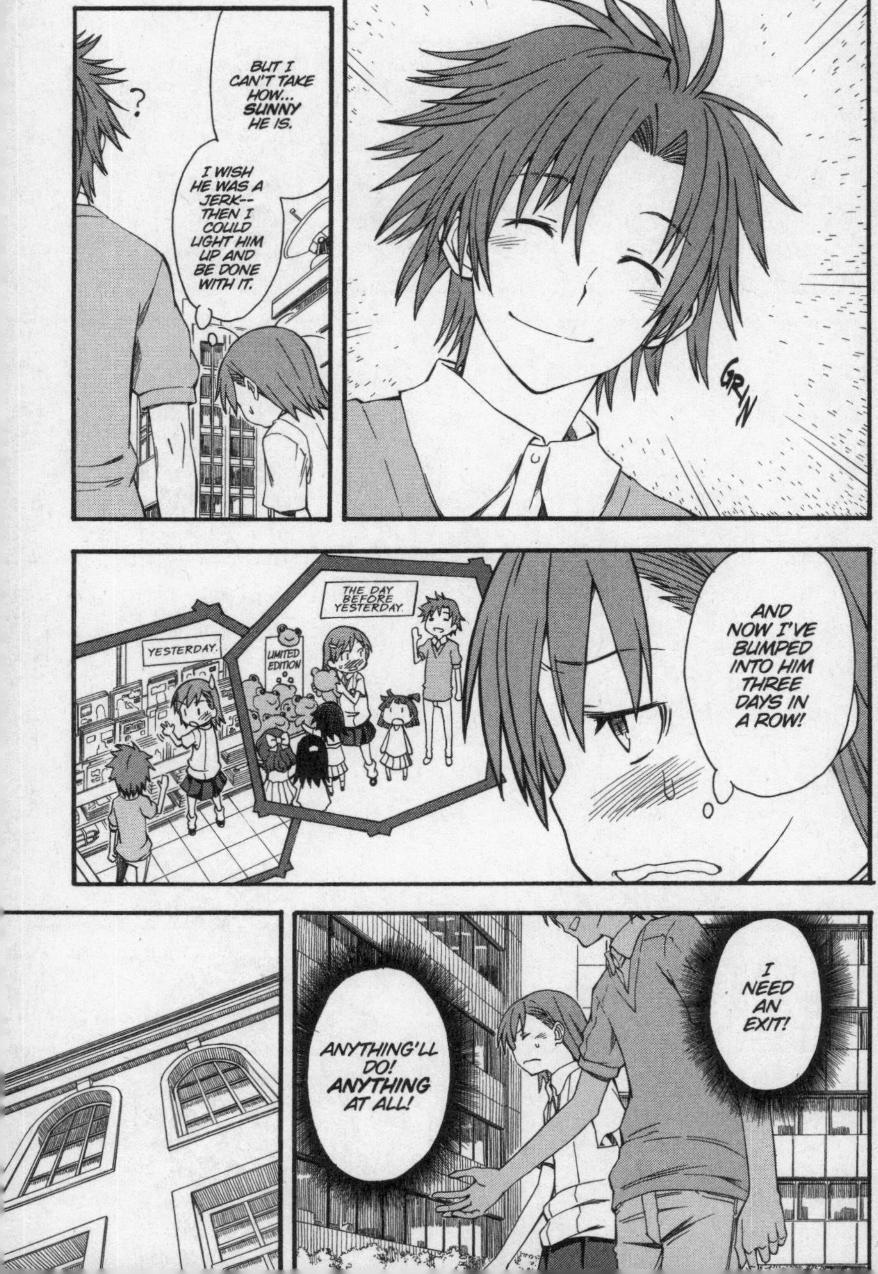
GRIN
BUT I CAN'T TAKE HOW... SUNNY HE IS.
?
I WISH HE WAS A JERK-- THEN I COULD LIGHT HIM UP AND BE DONE WITH IT.
AND NOW I'VE BUMPED INTO HIM THREE DAYS IN A ROW!
THE DAY BEFORE YESTERDAY.
LIMITED EDITION
YESTERDAY.
I NEED AN EXIT!
ANYTHING'LL DO! ANYTHING AT ALL!

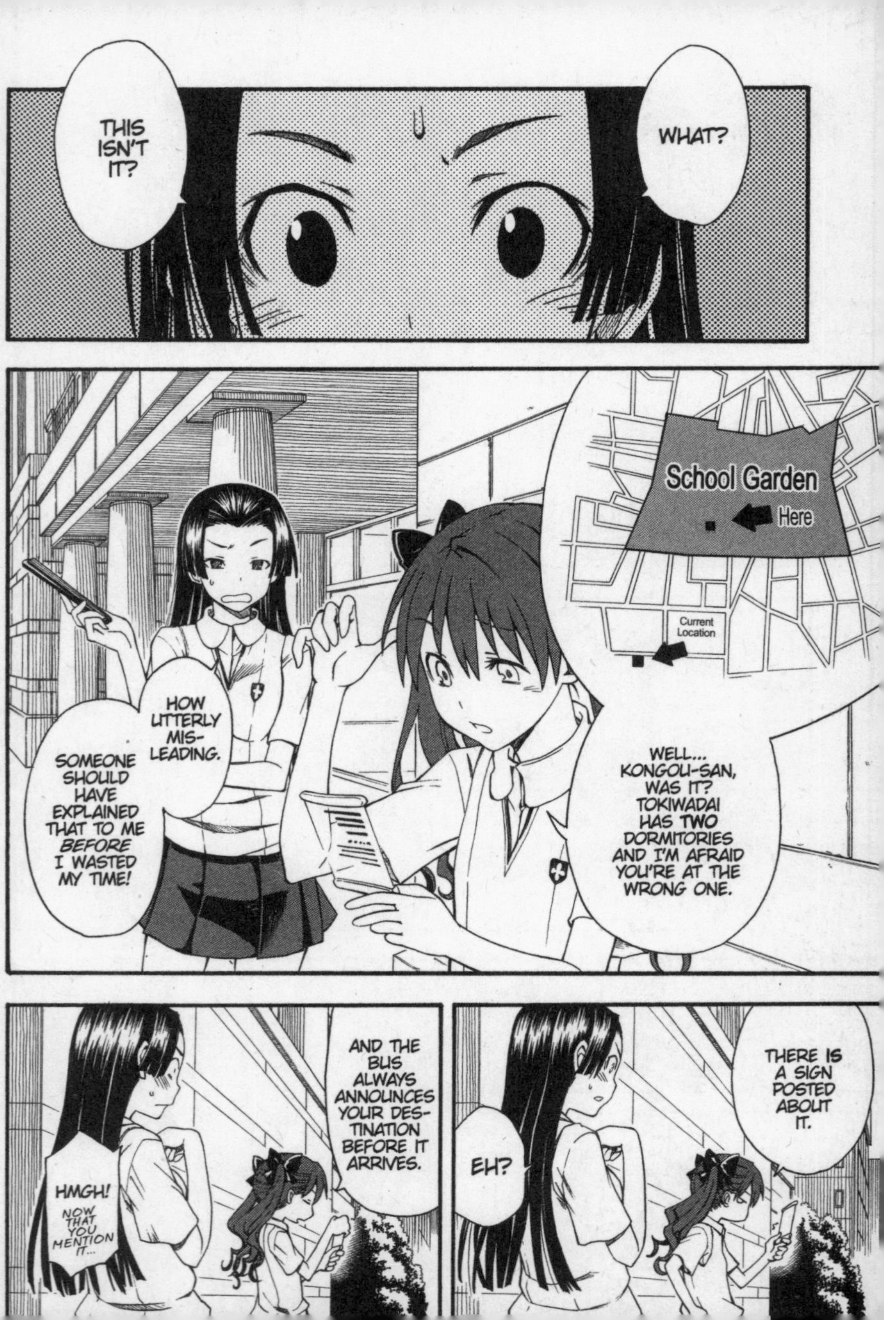
WHAT?
THIS ISN'T IT?
School Garden
Here
Current Location
WELL... KONGOU-SAN, WAS IT? TOKIWADAI HAS TWO DORMITORIES AND I'M AFRAID YOU'RE AT THE WRONG ONE.
HOW UTTERLY MIS-LEADING.
SOMEONE SHOULD HAVE EXPLAINED THAT TO ME BEFORE I WASTED MY TIME!
THERE IS A SIGN POSTED ABOUT IT.
EH?
AND THE BUS ALWAYS ANNOUNCES YOUR DES-TINATION BEFORE IT ARRIVES.
HMGH!
NOW THAT YOU MENTION IT...

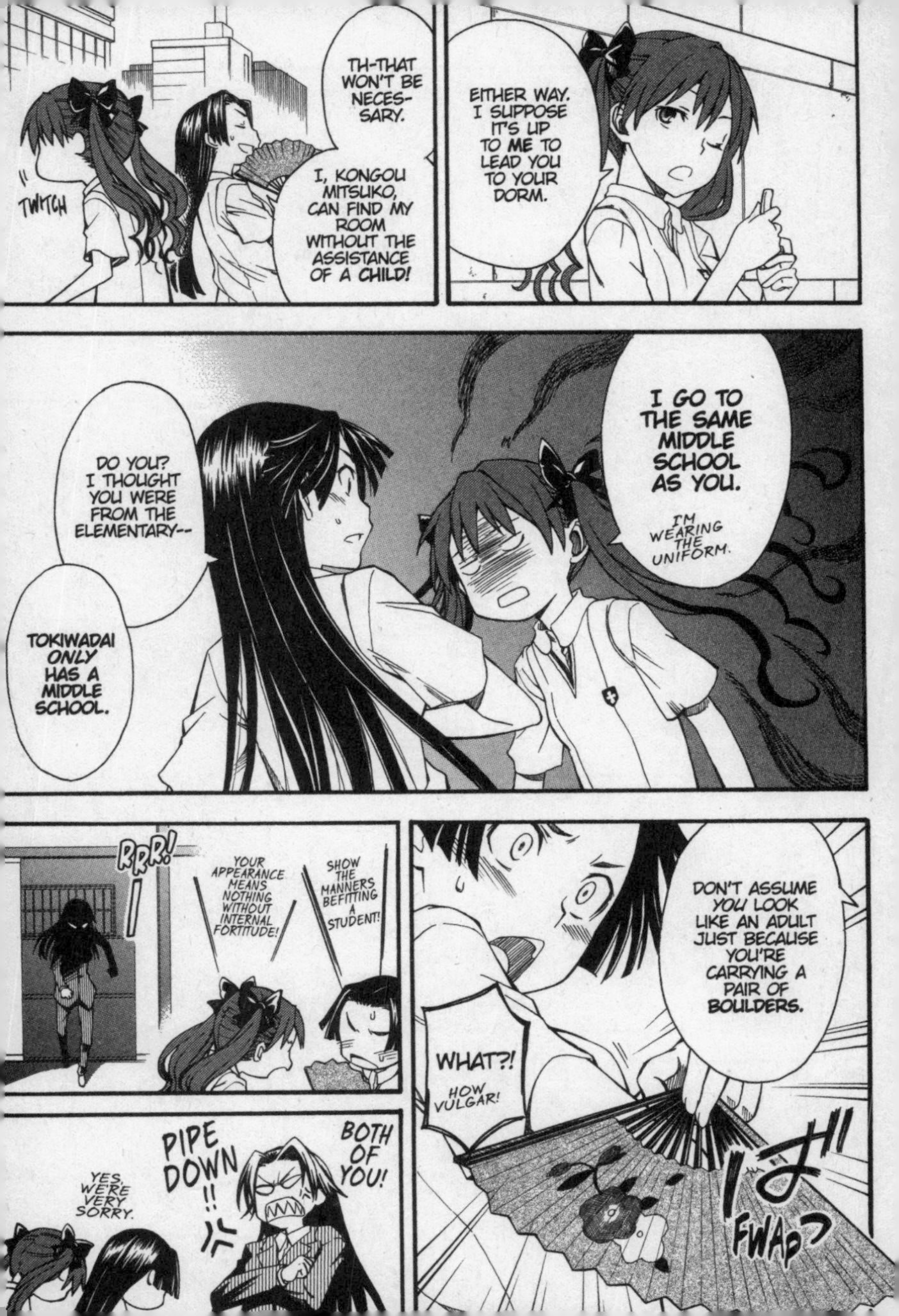
EITHER WAY. I SUPPOSE IT'S UP TO ME TO LEAD YOU TO YOUR DORM.
TH-THAT WON'T BE NECES-SARY.
I, KONGOU MITSUKO, CAN FIND MY ROOM WITHOUT THE ASSISTANCE OF A CHILD!
TWITCH
I GO TO THE SAME MIDDLE SCHOOL AS YOU.
I'M WEARING THE UNIFORM.
DO YOU? I THOUGHT YOU WERE FROM THE ELEMENTARY--
TOKIWADAI ONLY HAS A MIDDLE SCHOOL.
DON'T ASSUME YOU LOOK LIKE AN ADULT JUST BECAUSE YOU'RE CARRYING A PAIR OF BOULDERS.
WHAT?!
HOW VULGAR!
FWAP
RRR!
SHOW THE MANNERS BEFITTING A STUDENT!
YOUR APPEARANCE MEANS NOTHING WITHOUT INTERNAL FORTITUDE!
BOTH OF YOU!
PIPE DOWN!!
YES, WE'RE VERY SORRY.

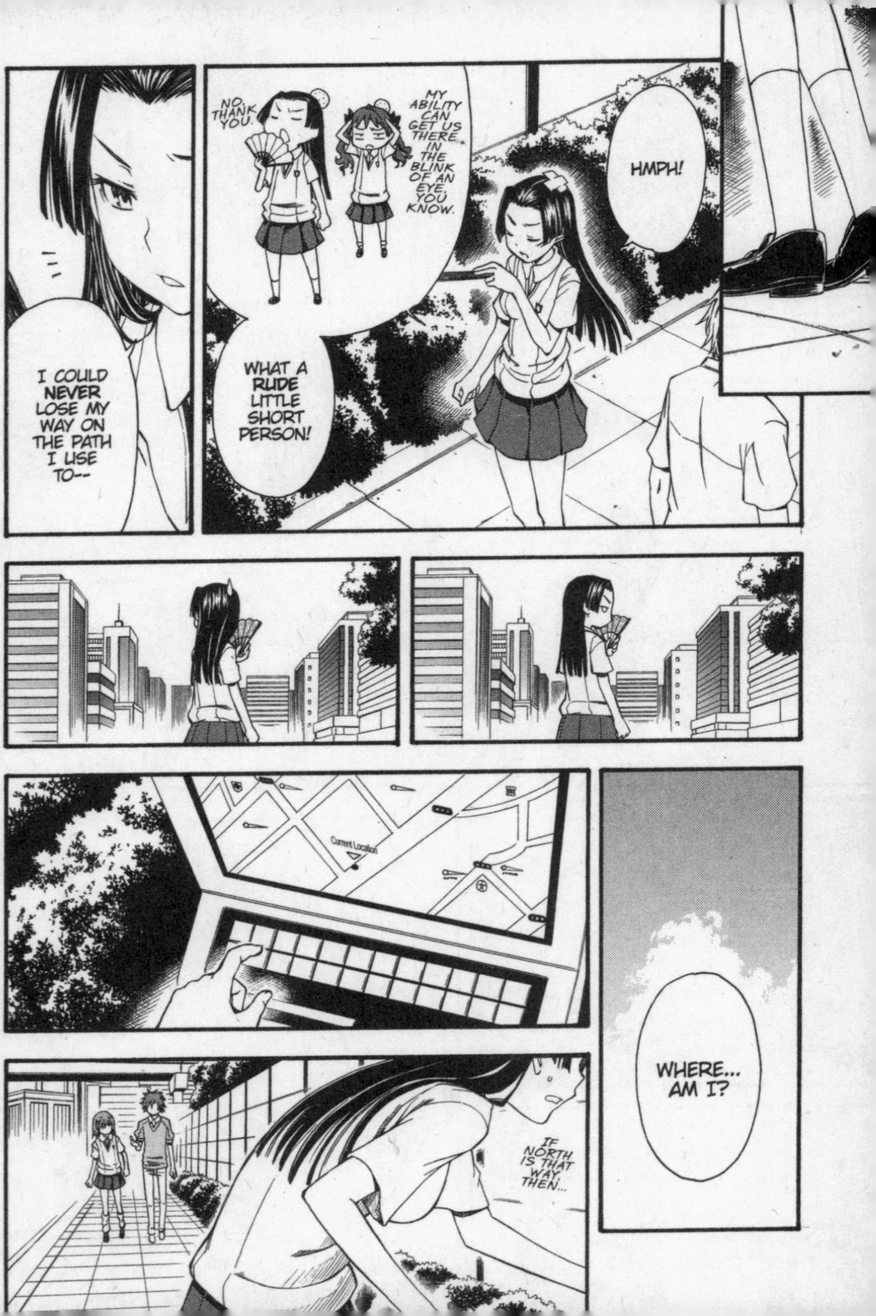
HMPH!
MY ABILITY CAN GET US THERE IN THE BLINK OF AN EYE, YOU KNOW.
NO, THANK YOU.
WHAT A RUDE LITTLE SHORT PERSON!
I COULD NEVER LOSE MY WAY ON THE PATH I USE TO--
WHERE... AM I?
Current Location
IF NORTH IS THAT WAY, THEN...

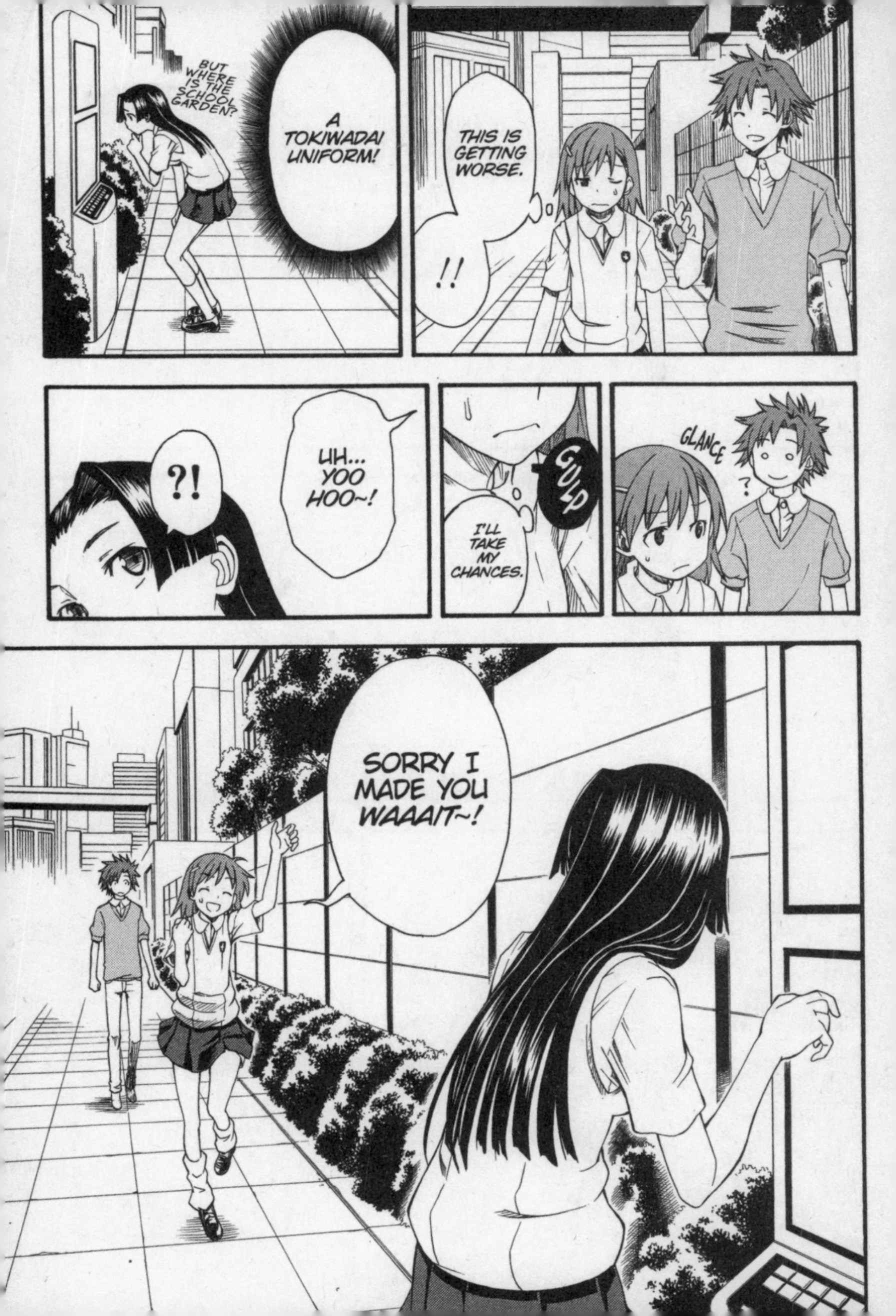
THIS IS GETTING WORSE.
!!
A TOKIWADAI UNIFORM!
BUT WHERE IS THE SCHOOL GARDEN?
GLANCE
?
GULP
I'LL TAKE MY CHANCES.
UH... YOO HOO~!
?!
SORRY I MADE YOU WAAAIT~!

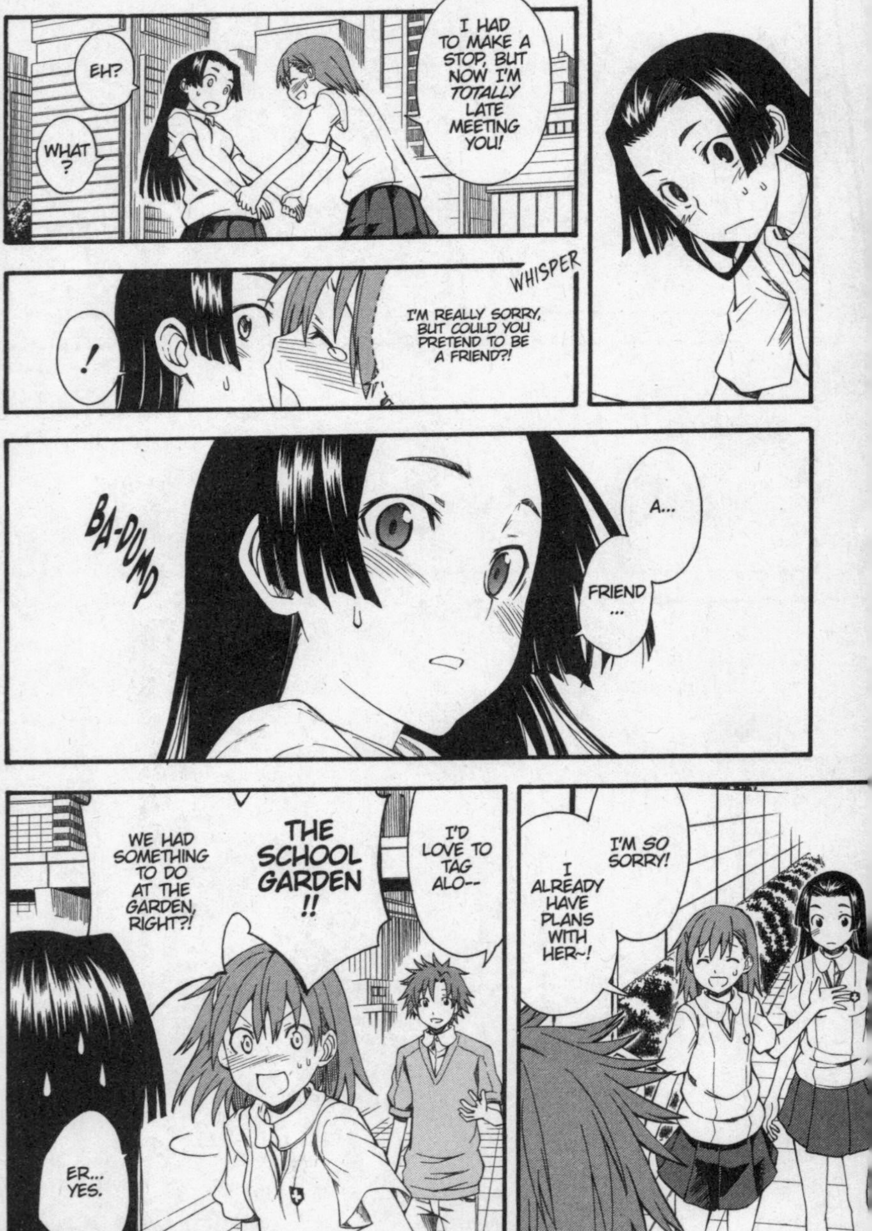
I HAD TO MAKE A STOP, BUT NOW I'M *TOTALLY* LATE MEETING YOU!
EH?
WHAT?
WHISPER
I'M REALLY SORRY, BUT COULD YOU PRETEND TO BE A FRIEND?!
!
A...
FRIEND...
BA-DUMP
I'M SO SORRY!
I ALREADY HAVE PLANS WITH HER~!
I'D LOVE TO TAG ALO--
THE SCHOOL GARDEN!!
WE HAD SOMETHING TO DO AT THE GARDEN, RIGHT?!
ER... YES.

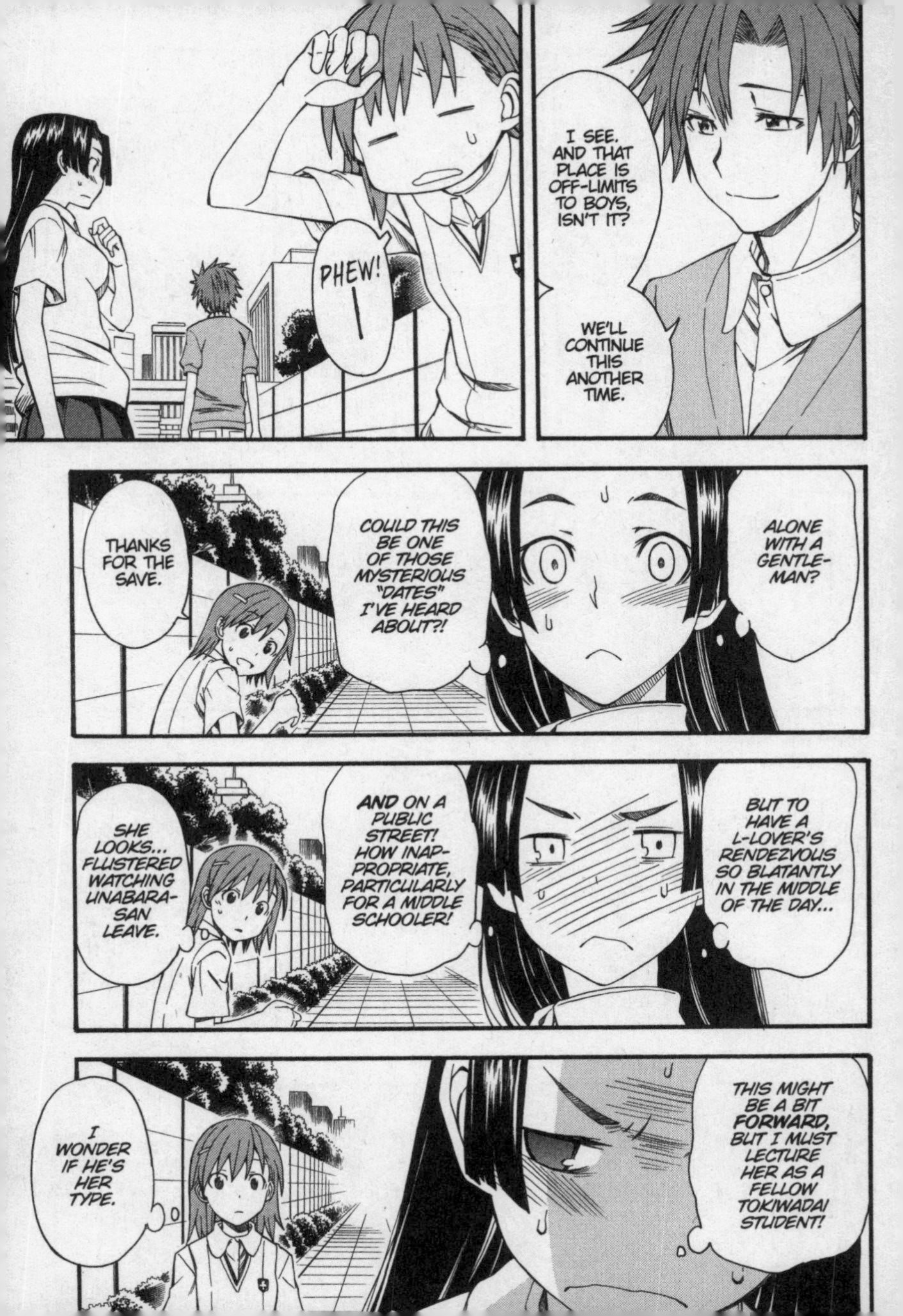
I SEE. AND THAT PLACE IS OFF-LIMITS TO BOYS, ISN'T IT?
WE'LL CONTINUE THIS ANOTHER TIME.
PHEW!
ALONE WITH A GENTLE-MAN?
COULD THIS BE ONE OF THOSE MYSTERIOUS "DATES" I'VE HEARD ABOUT?!
THANKS FOR THE SAVE.
BUT TO HAVE A L-LOVER'S RENDEZVOUS SO BLATANTLY IN THE MIDDLE OF THE DAY...
AND ON A PUBLIC STREET! HOW INAPPROPRIATE, PARTICULARLY FOR A MIDDLE SCHOOLER!
SHE LOOKS... FLUSTERED WATCHING UNABARA-SAN LEAVE.
THIS MIGHT BE A BIT FORWARD, BUT I MUST LECTURE HER AS A FELLOW TOKIWADAI STUDENT!
I WONDER IF HE'S HER TYPE.

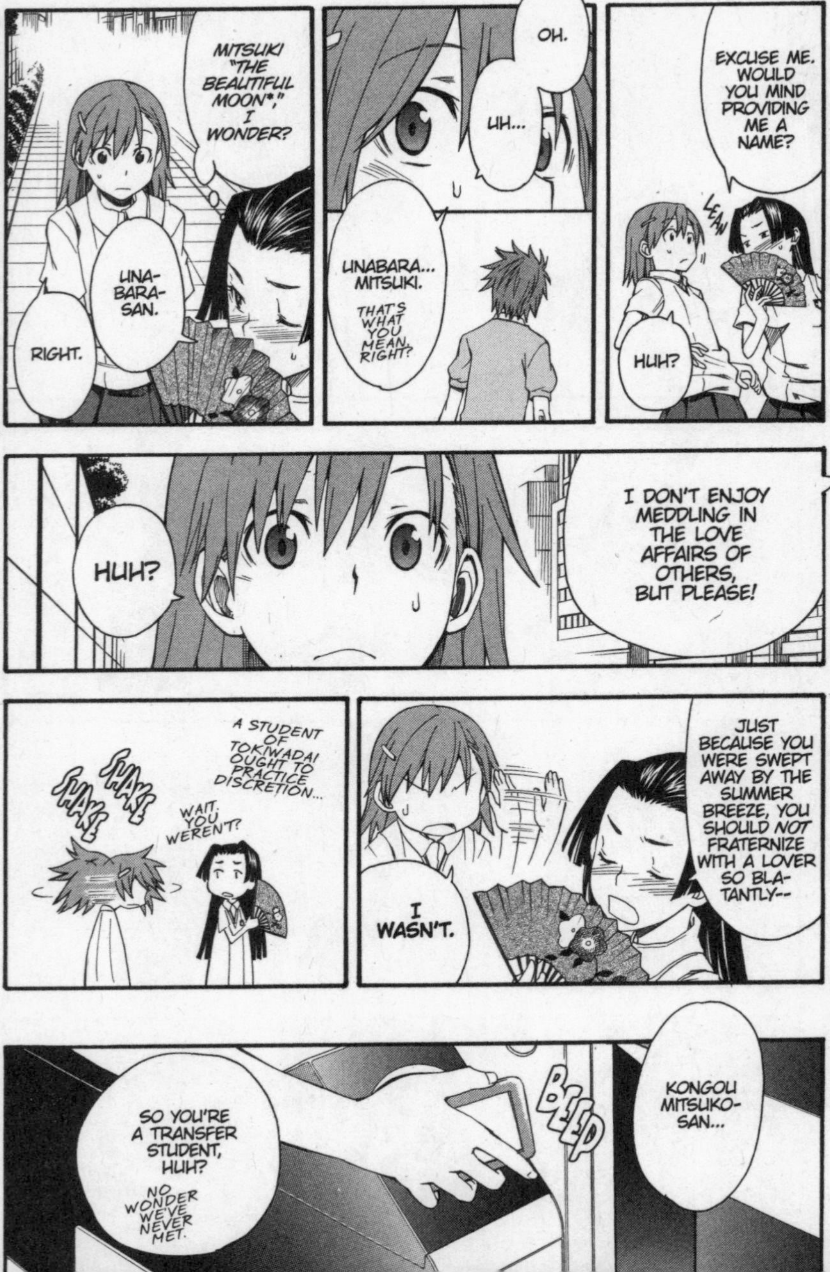
EXCUSE ME. WOULD YOU MIND PROVIDING ME A NAME?
LEAN
HUH?
OH.
UH...
UNABARA... MITSUKI.
THAT'S WHAT YOU MEAN, RIGHT?
MITSUKI "THE BEAUTIFUL MOON*," I WONDER?
UNA-BARA-SAN.
RIGHT.
I DON'T ENJOY MEDDLING IN THE LOVE AFFAIRS OF OTHERS, BUT PLEASE!
HUH?
JUST BECAUSE YOU WERE SWEPT AWAY BY THE SUMMER BREEZE, YOU SHOULD NOT FRATERNIZE WITH A LOVER SO BLA-TANTLY--
I WASN'T.
A STUDENT OF TOKIWADAI OUGHT TO PRACTICE DISCRETION...
WAIT. YOU WEREN'T?
SHAKE
SHAKE
KONGOU MITSUKO-SAN...
BEEP
SO YOU'RE A TRANSFER STUDENT, HUH?
NO WONDER WE'VE NEVER MET.

*The actual kanji for "Mitsuki" mentioned here has the kanji for "light" and "honor" (光貴), whereas Mitsuko suggested more feminine kanji for the same name (美月).

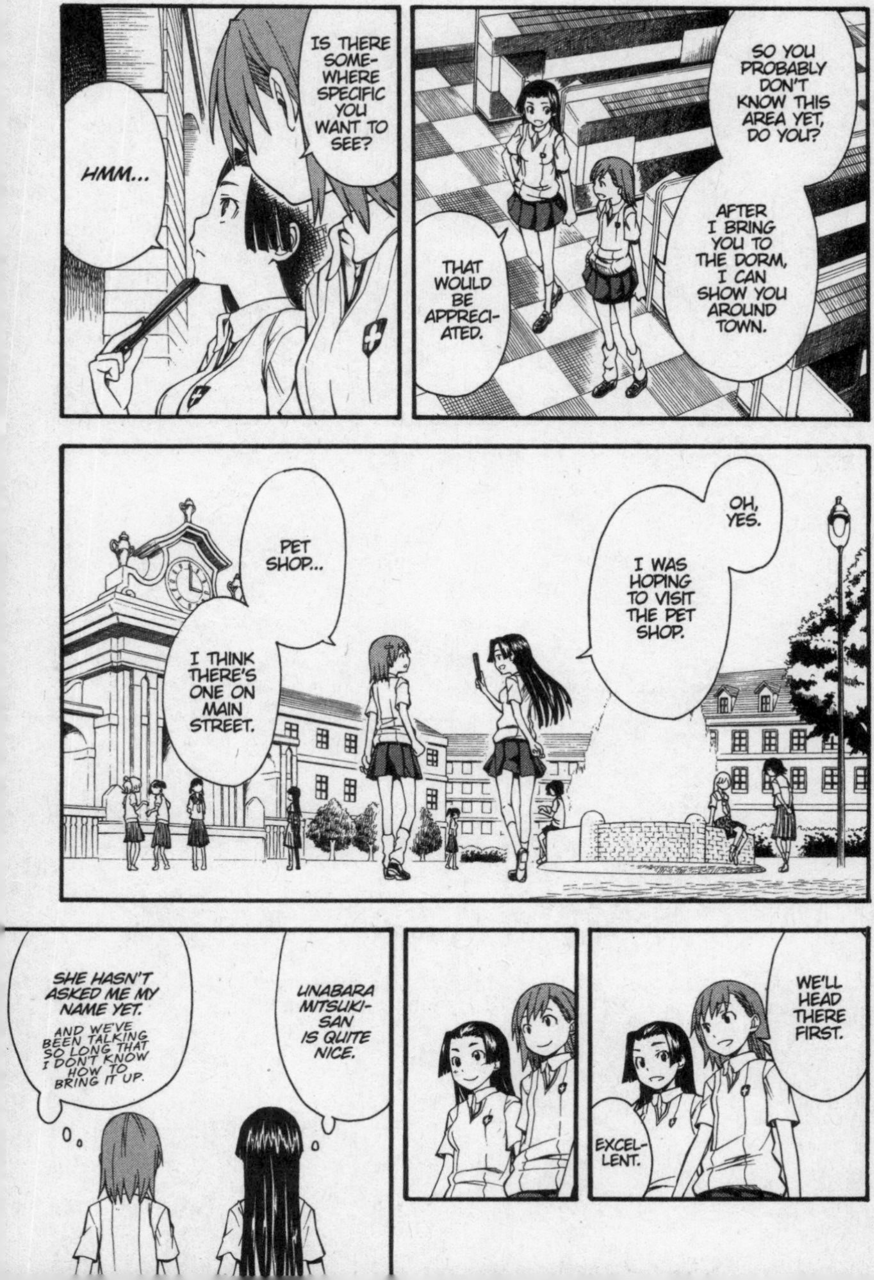
SO YOU PROBABLY DON'T KNOW THIS AREA YET, DO YOU?
AFTER I BRING YOU TO THE DORM, I CAN SHOW YOU AROUND TOWN.
THAT WOULD BE APPRECIATED.
IS THERE SOMEWHERE SPECIFIC YOU WANT TO SEE?
HMM...
OH, YES.
I WAS HOPING TO VISIT THE PET SHOP.
PET SHOP...
I THINK THERE'S ONE ON MAIN STREET.
WE'LL HEAD THERE FIRST.
EXCELLENT.
UNABARA MITSUKI-SAN IS QUITE NICE.
SHE HASN'T ASKED ME MY NAME YET.
AND WE'VE BEEN TALKING SO LONG THAT I DON'T KNOW HOW TO BRING IT UP.

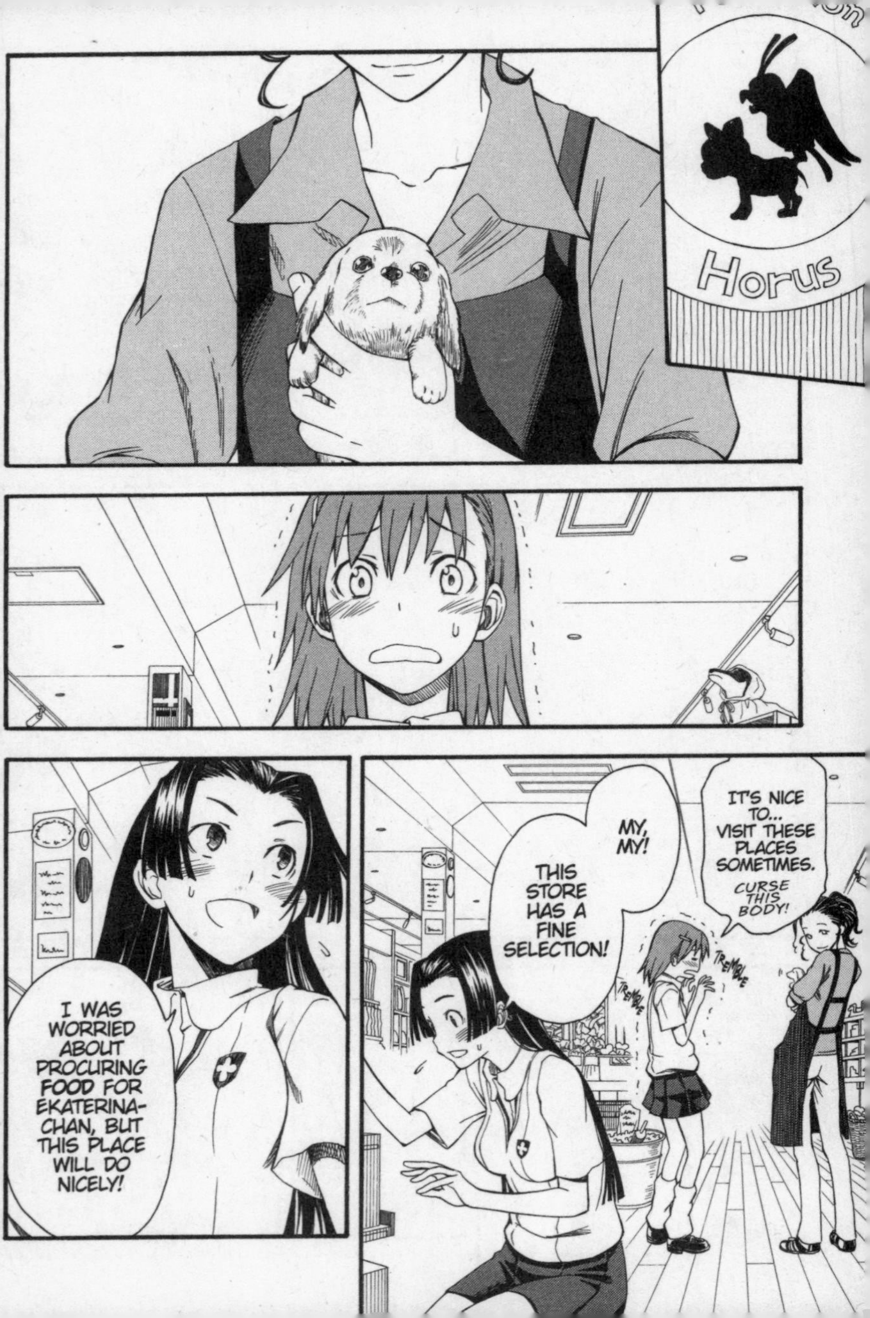
Horus
IT'S NICE TO... VISIT THESE PLACES SOMETIMES.
CURSE THIS BODY!
TREMBLE
TREMBLE
MY, MY!
THIS STORE HAS A FINE SELECTION!
I WAS WORRIED ABOUT PROCURING FOOD FOR EKATERINA-CHAN, BUT THIS PLACE WILL DO NICELY!

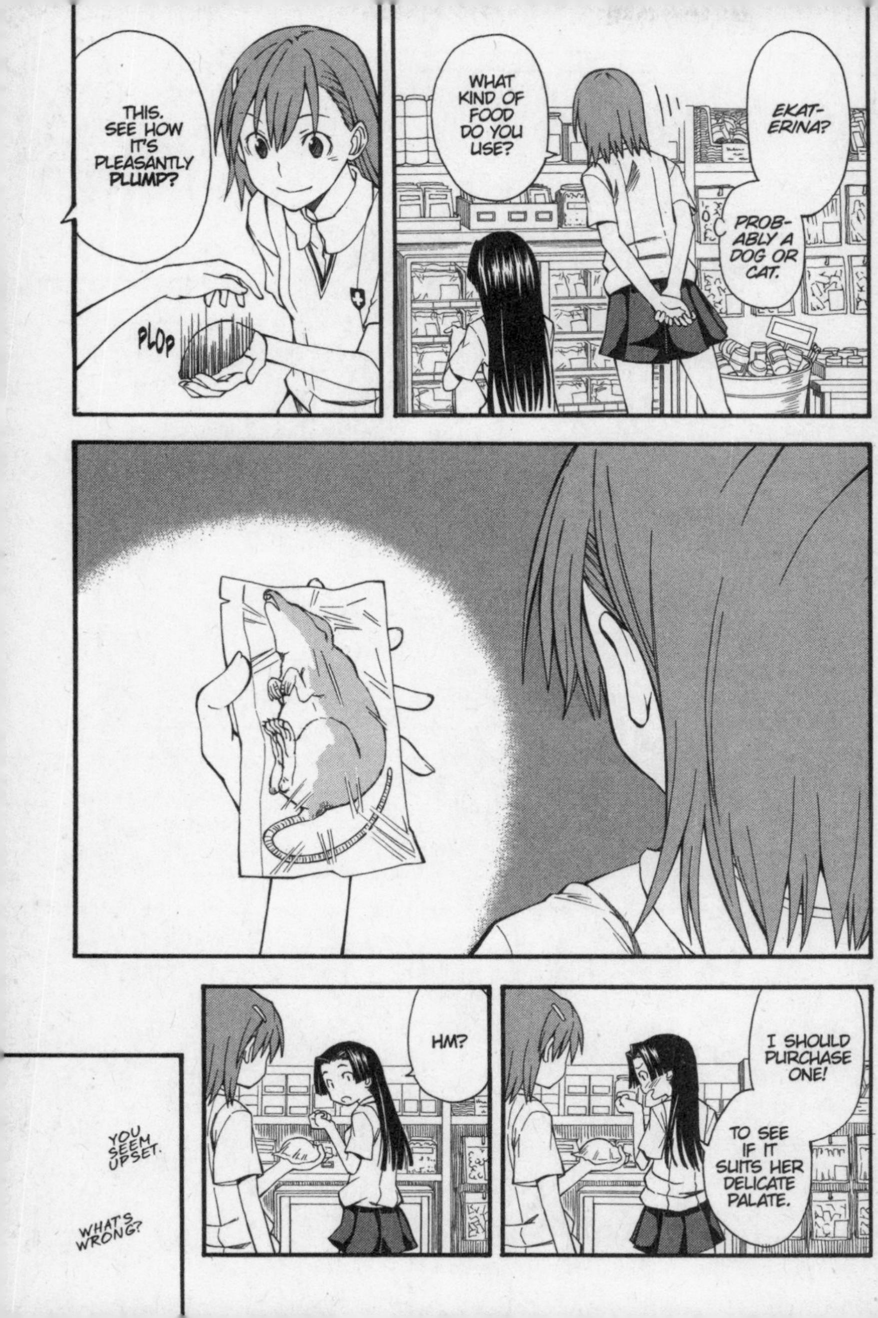

EKAT-ERINA?
PROB-ABLY A DOG OR CAT.
WHAT KIND OF FOOD DO YOU USE?
THIS. SEE HOW IT'S PLEASANTLY PLUMP?
PLOP
I SHOULD PURCHASE ONE!
TO SEE IF IT SUITS HER DELICATE PALATE.
HM?
YOU SEEM UPSET.
WHAT'S WRONG?

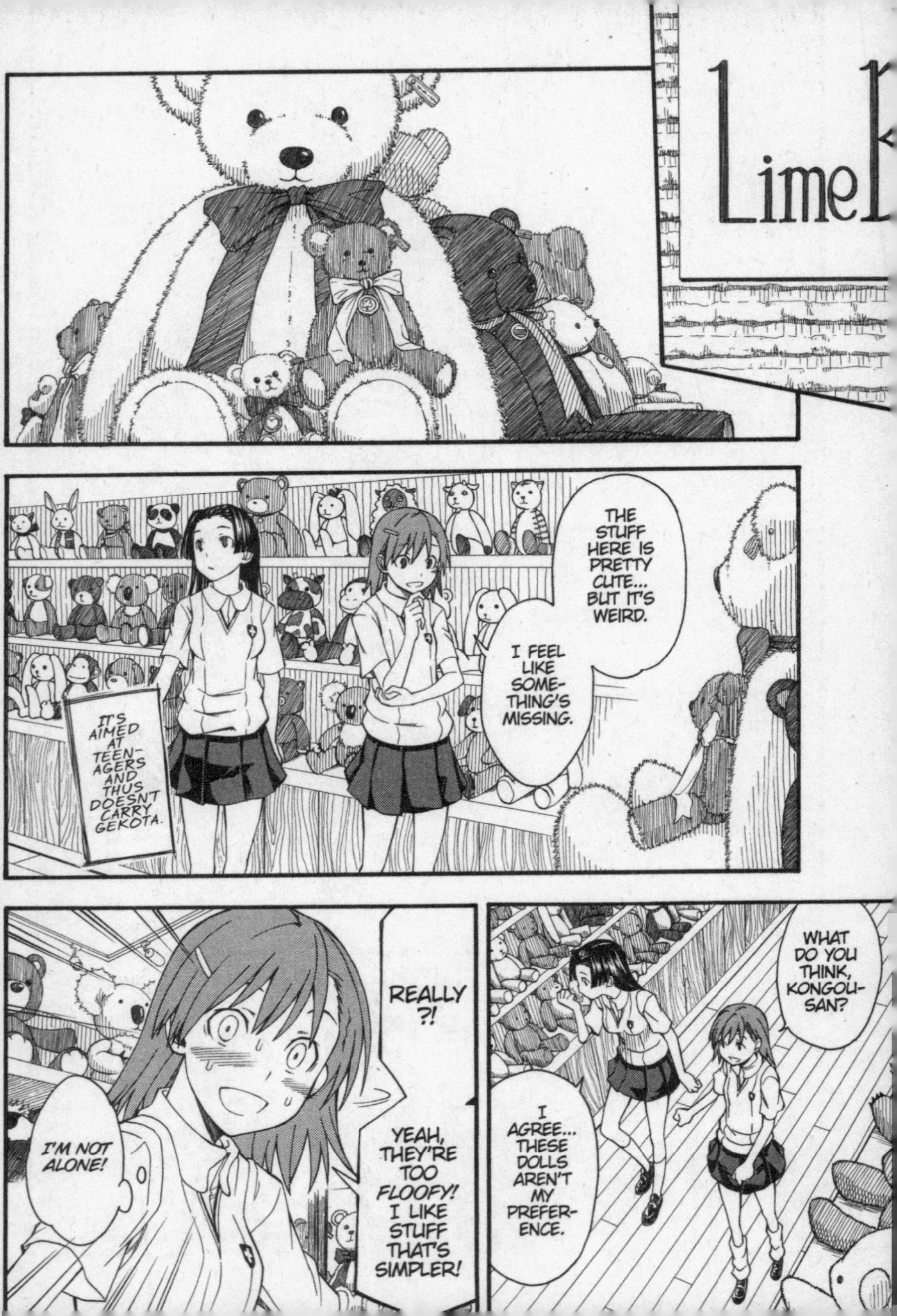
Lime
THE STUFF HERE IS PRETTY CUTE... BUT IT'S WEIRD.
I FEEL LIKE SOME-THING'S MISSING.
IT'S AIMED AT TEEN-AGERS AND THUS DOESN'T CARRY GEKOTA.
WHAT DO YOU THINK, KONGOU-SAN?
I AGREE... THESE DOLLS AREN'T MY PREFER-ENCE.
REALLY?!
YEAH, THEY'RE TOO FLOOFY! I LIKE STUFF THAT'S SIMPLER!
I'M NOT ALONE!

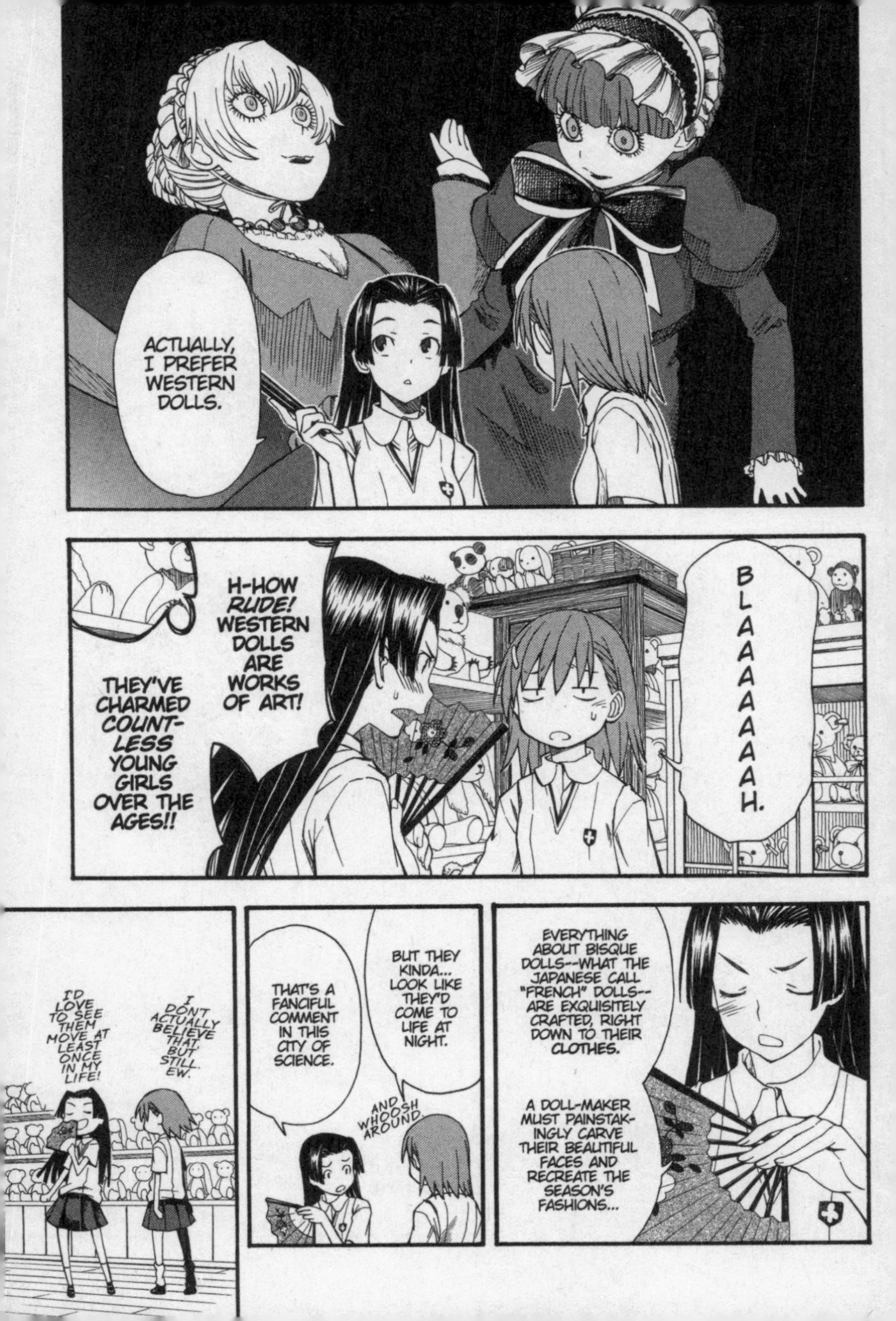
ACTUALLY, I PREFER WESTERN DOLLS.
BLAAAAAAAAH.
H-HOW *RUDE!* WESTERN DOLLS ARE WORKS OF ART!
THEY'VE CHARMED COUNT-LESS YOUNG GIRLS OVER THE AGES!!
EVERYTHING ABOUT BISQUE DOLLS--WHAT THE JAPANESE CALL "FRENCH" DOLLS--ARE EXQUISITELY CRAFTED, RIGHT DOWN TO THEIR CLOTHES.
A DOLL-MAKER MUST PAINSTAK-INGLY CARVE THEIR BEAUTIFUL FACES AND RECREATE THE SEASON'S FASHIONS...
BUT THEY KINDA... LOOK LIKE THEY'D COME TO LIFE AT NIGHT.
AND WHOOSH AROUND.
THAT'S A FANCIFUL COMMENT IN THIS CITY OF SCIENCE.
I DON'T ACTUALLY BELIEVE THAT, BUT STILL. EW.
I'D LOVE TO SEE THEM MOVE AT LEAST ONCE IN MY LIFE!

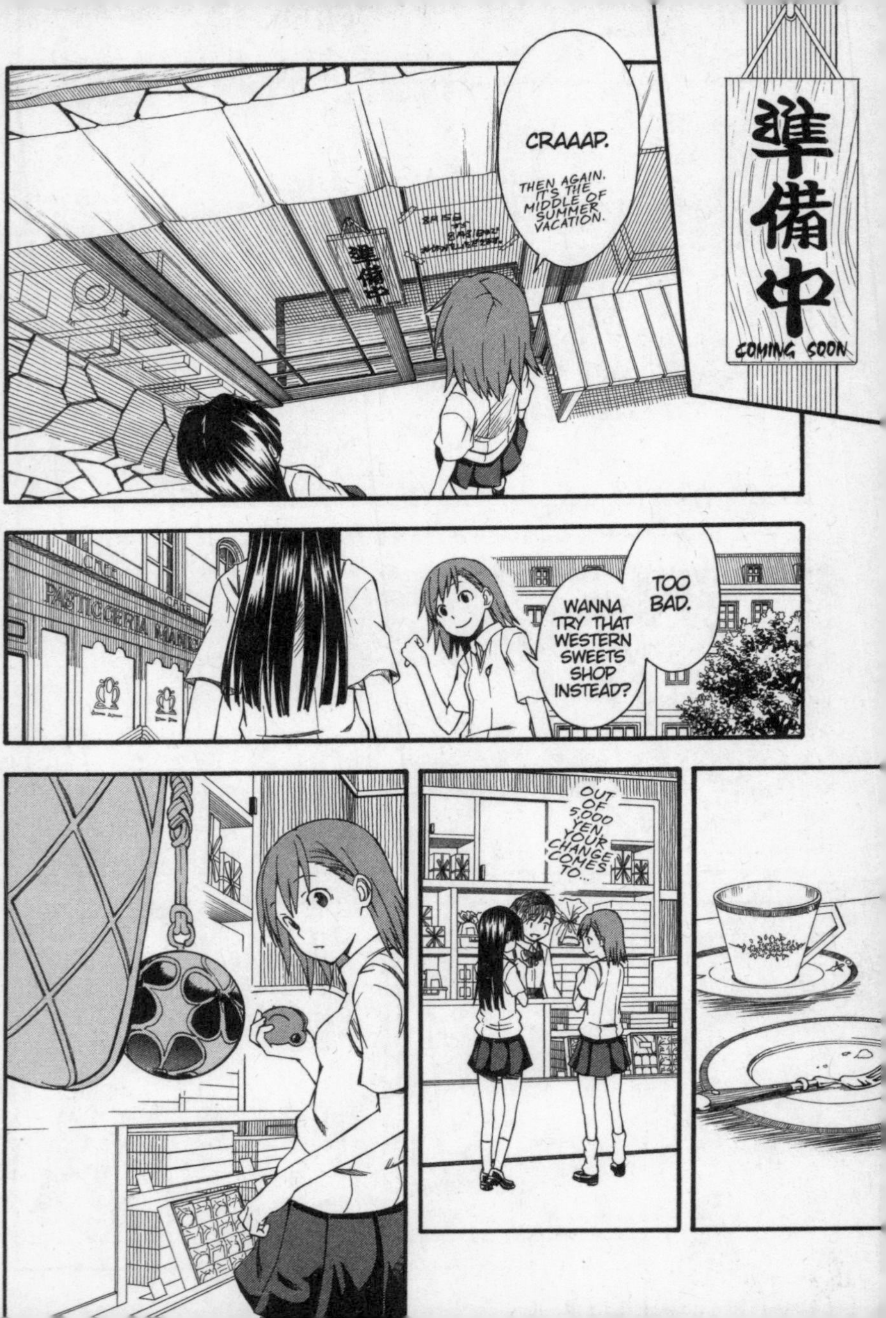
準備中
COMING SOON
CRAAAP.
THEN AGAIN, IT'S THE MIDDLE OF SUMMER VACATION.
TOO BAD.
WANNA TRY THAT WESTERN SWEETS SHOP INSTEAD?
OUT OF 5,000 YEN, YOUR CHANGE COMES TO...

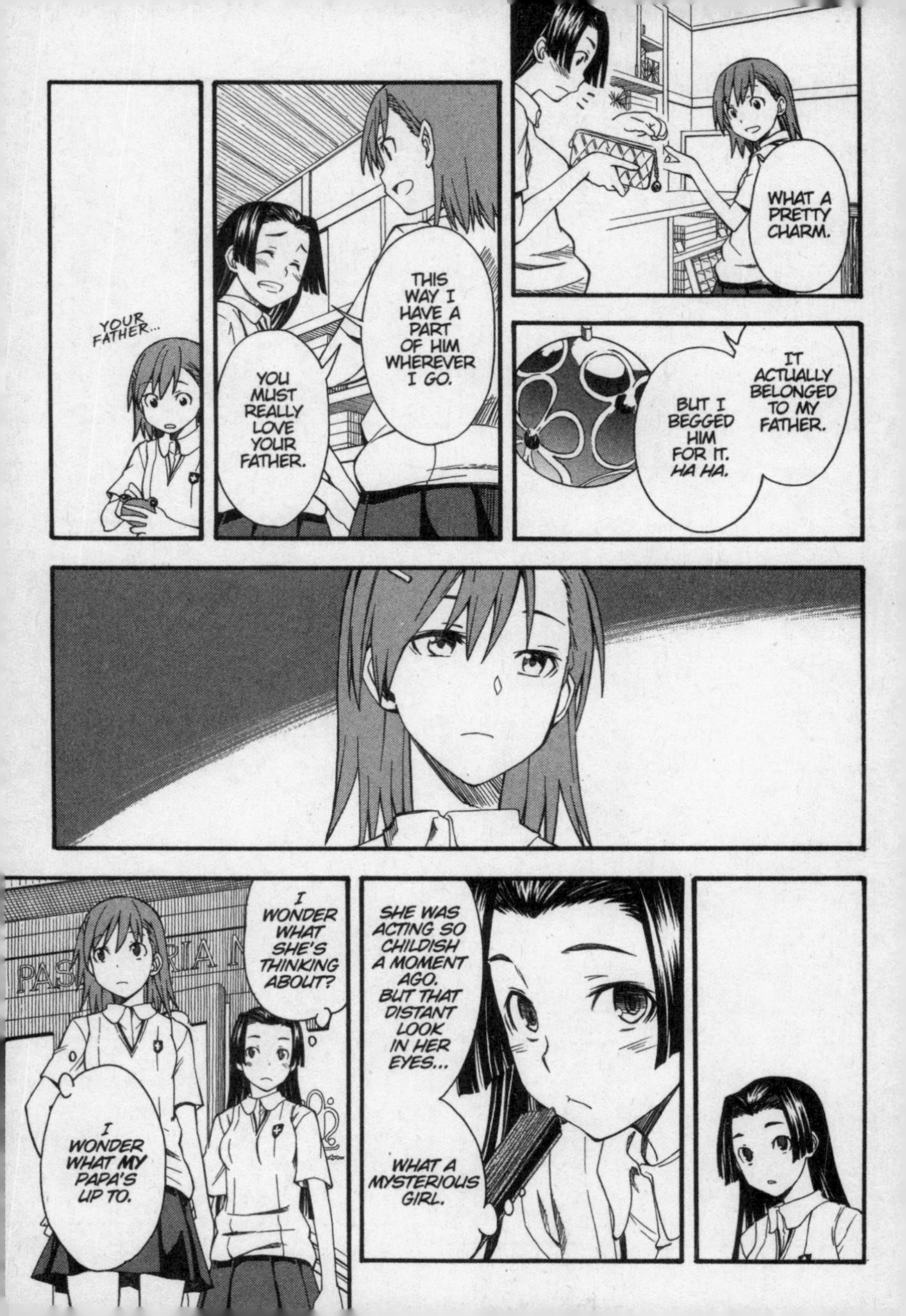
WHAT A PRETTY CHARM.
IT ACTUALLY BELONGED TO MY FATHER.
BUT I BEGGED HIM FOR IT. HA HA.
THIS WAY I HAVE A PART OF HIM WHEREVER I GO.
YOU MUST REALLY LOVE YOUR FATHER.
YOUR FATHER...
SHE WAS ACTING SO CHILDISH A MOMENT AGO. BUT THAT DISTANT LOOK IN HER EYES...
WHAT A MYSTERIOUS GIRL.
I WONDER WHAT SHE'S THINKING ABOUT?
I WONDER WHAT MY PAPA'S UP TO.

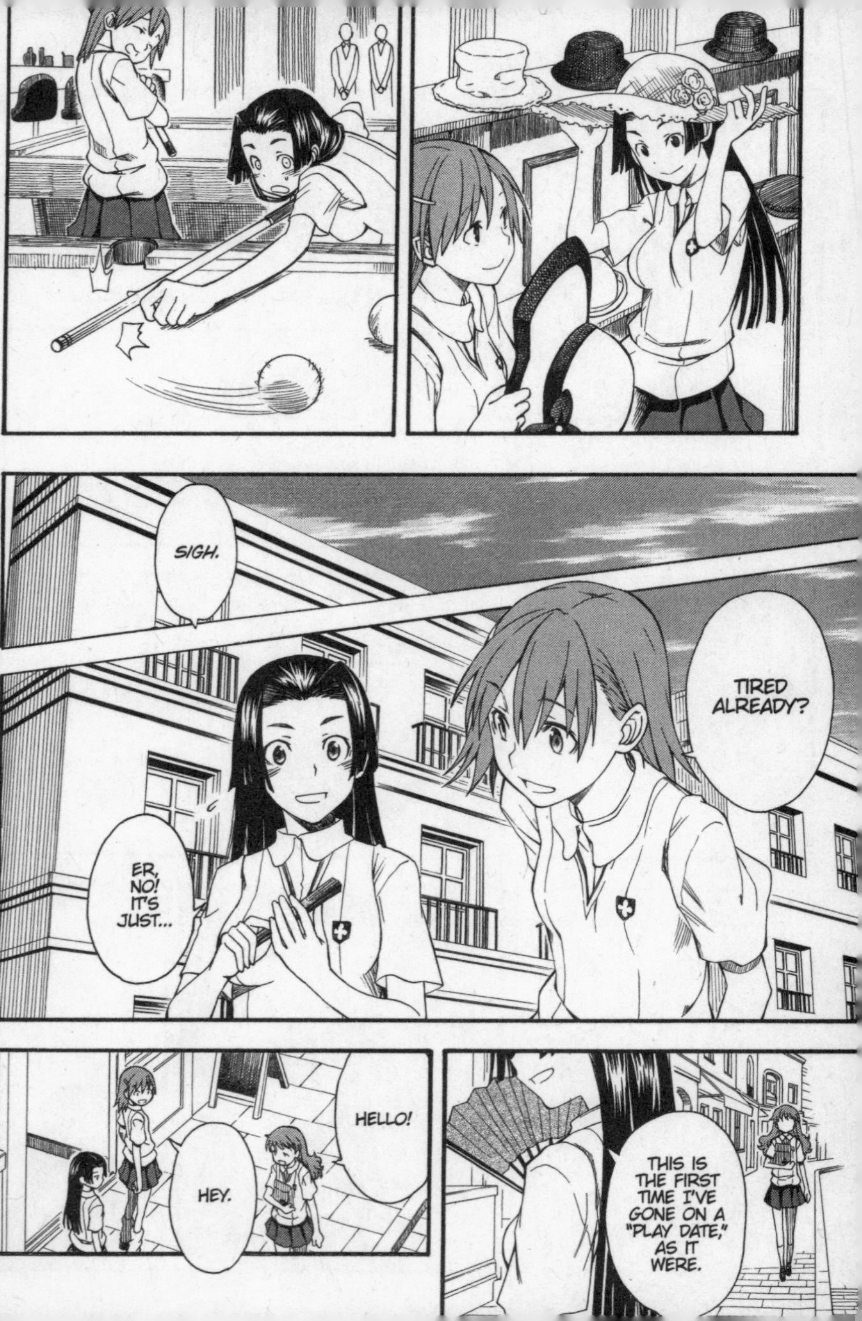
SIGH.
TIRED ALREADY?
ER, NO! IT'S JUST...
THIS IS THE FIRST TIME I'VE GONE ON A "PLAY DATE," AS IT WERE.
HELLO!
HEY.

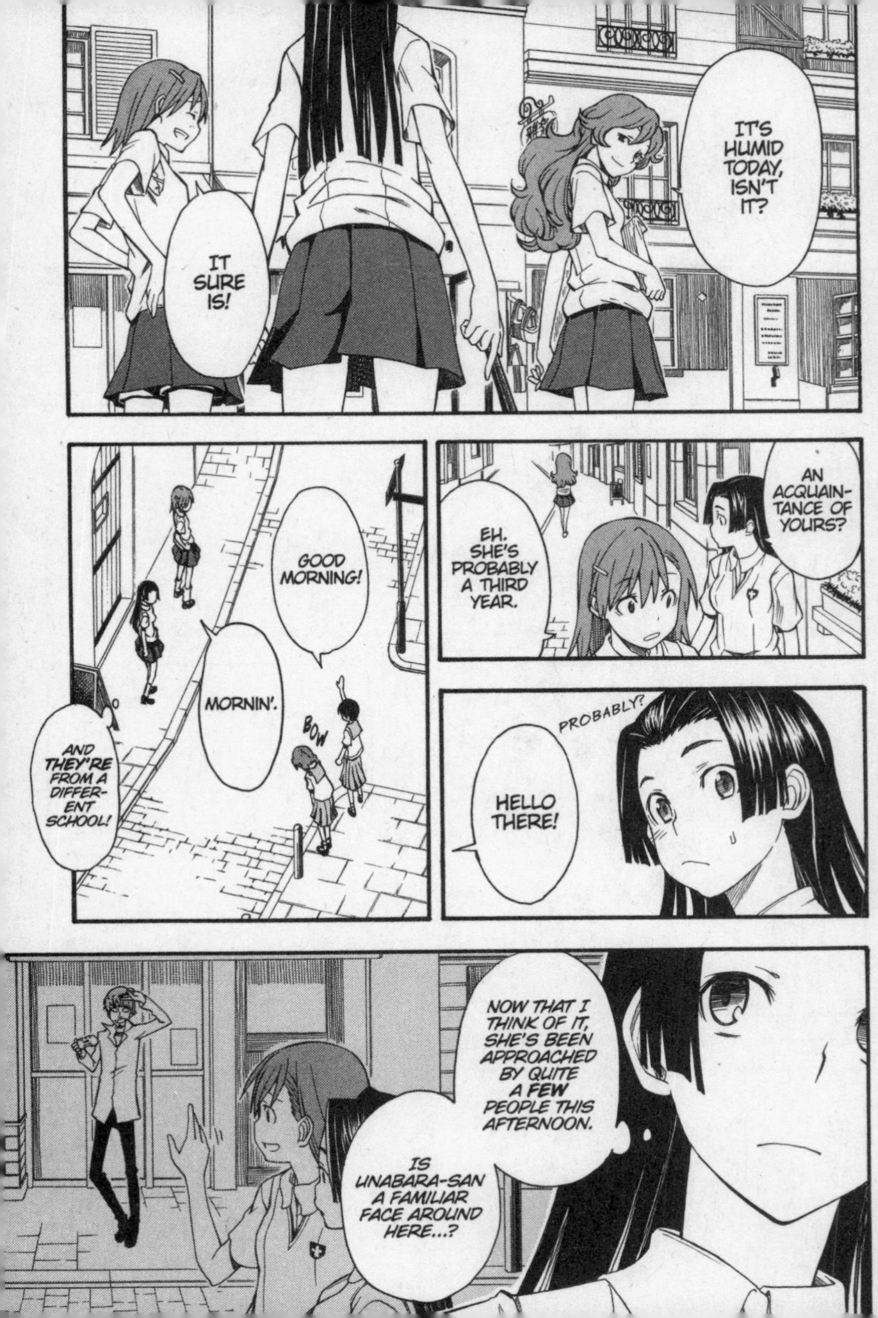
IT'S HUMID TODAY, ISN'T IT?
IT SURE IS!
AN ACQUAINTANCE OF YOURS?
EH. SHE'S PROBABLY A THIRD YEAR.
PROBABLY?
HELLO THERE!
GOOD MORNING!
MORNIN'.
BOW
AND THEY'RE FROM A DIFFERENT SCHOOL!
NOW THAT I THINK OF IT, SHE'S BEEN APPROACHED BY QUITE A FEW PEOPLE THIS AFTERNOON.
IS UNABARA-SAN A FAMILIAR FACE AROUND HERE...?

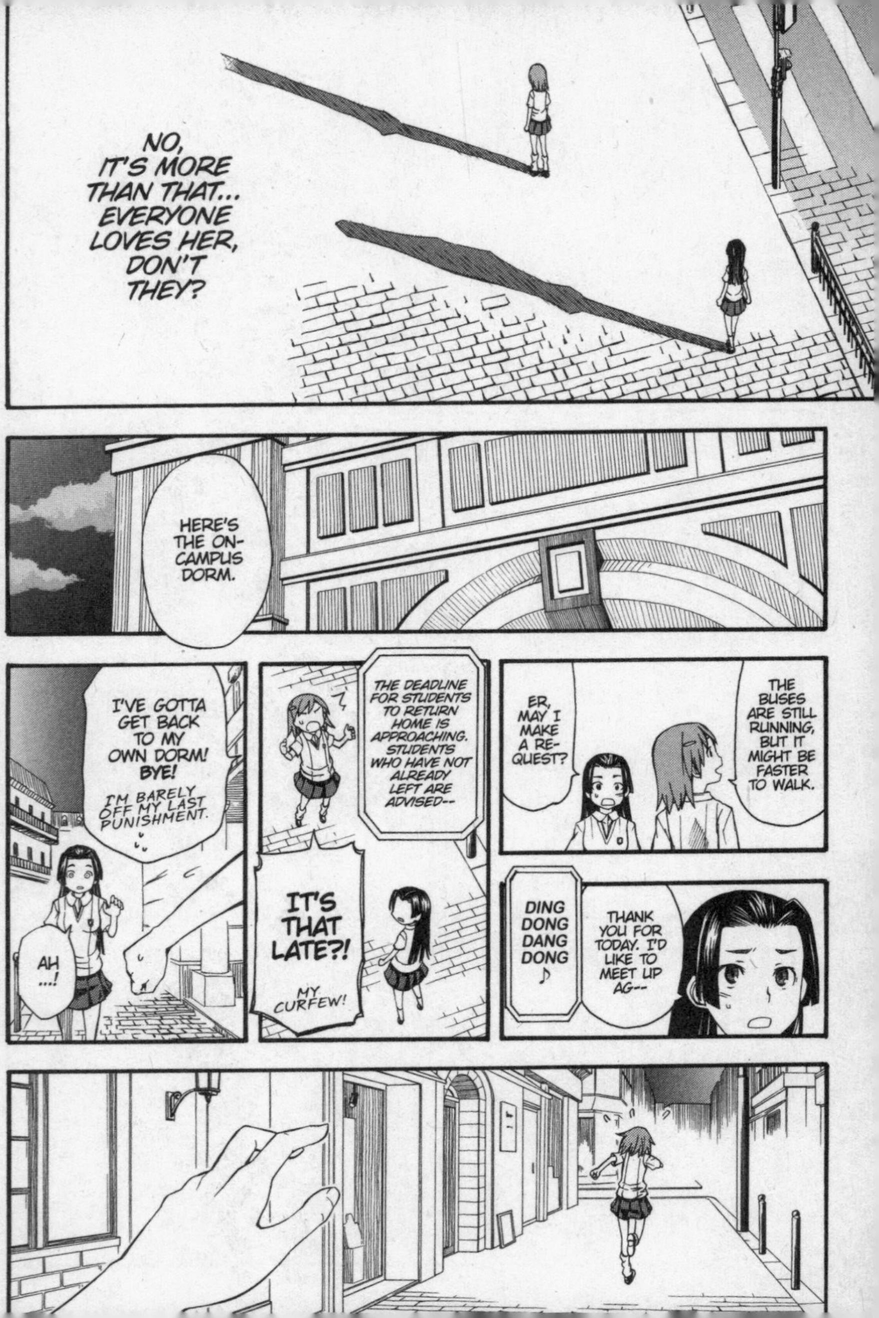
NO, IT'S MORE THAN THAT... EVERYONE LOVES HER, DON'T THEY?
HERE'S THE ON-CAMPUS DORM.
THE BUSES ARE STILL RUNNING, BUT IT MIGHT BE FASTER TO WALK.
ER, MAY I MAKE A REQUEST?
THANK YOU FOR TODAY. I'D LIKE TO MEET UP AG--
DING DONG DANG DONG ♪
THE DEADLINE FOR STUDENTS TO RETURN HOME IS APPROACHING. STUDENTS WHO HAVE NOT ALREADY LEFT ARE ADVISED--
IT'S THAT LATE?!
MY CURFEW!
I'VE GOTTA GET BACK TO MY OWN DORM! BYE!
I'M BARELY OFF MY LAST PUNISHMENT.
AH ...!

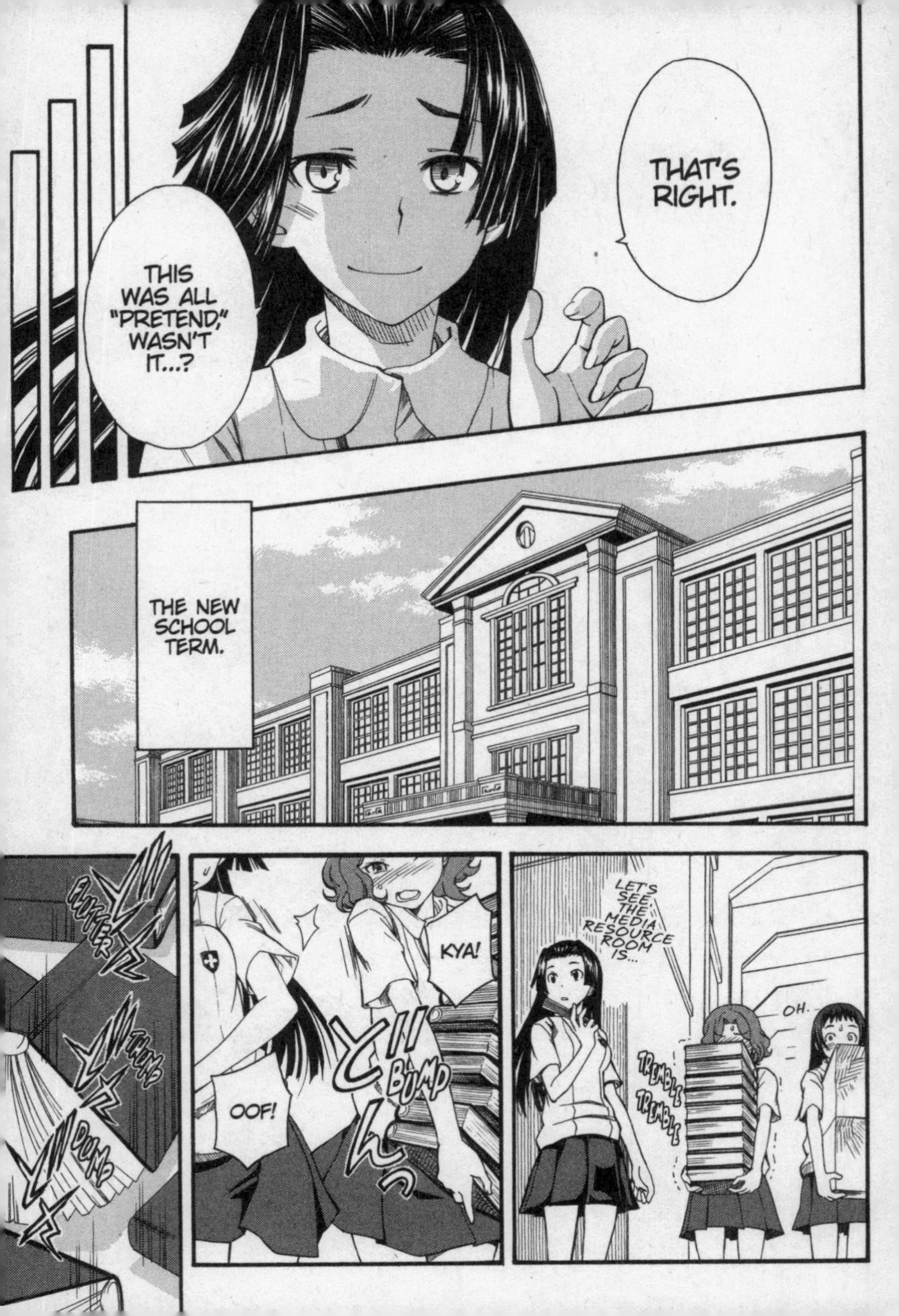
THAT'S RIGHT.
THIS WAS ALL "PRETEND," WASN'T IT...?
THE NEW SCHOOL TERM.
LET'S SEE THE MEDIA RESOURCE ROOM IS...
OH.
TREMBLE TREMBLE
KYA!
BUMP
OOF!
FLICKER
THUMP
DUMP

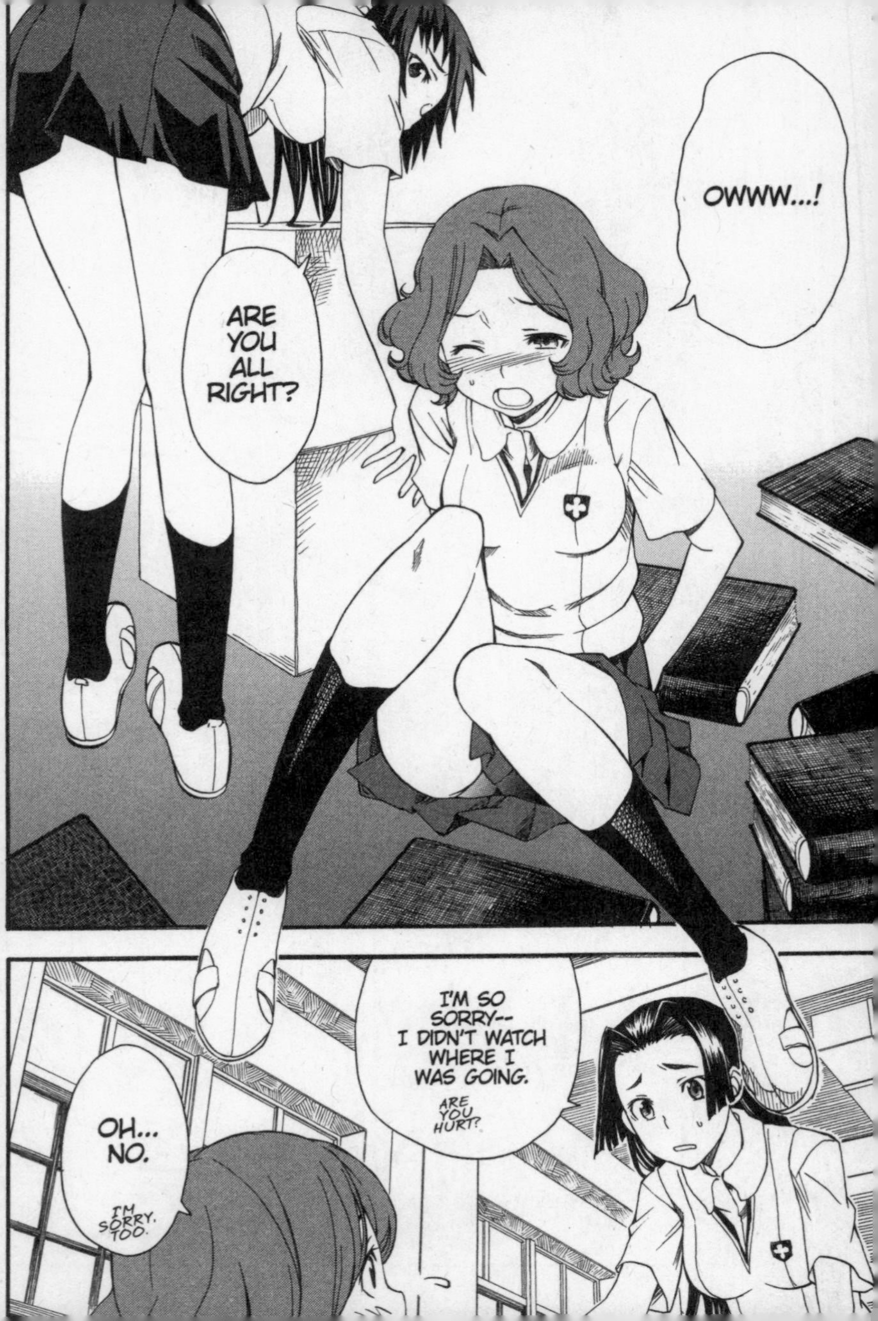
OWWW...!
ARE YOU ALL RIGHT?
I'M SO SORRY-- I DIDN'T WATCH WHERE I WAS GOING.
ARE YOU HURT?
OH... NO.
I'M SORRY, TOO.

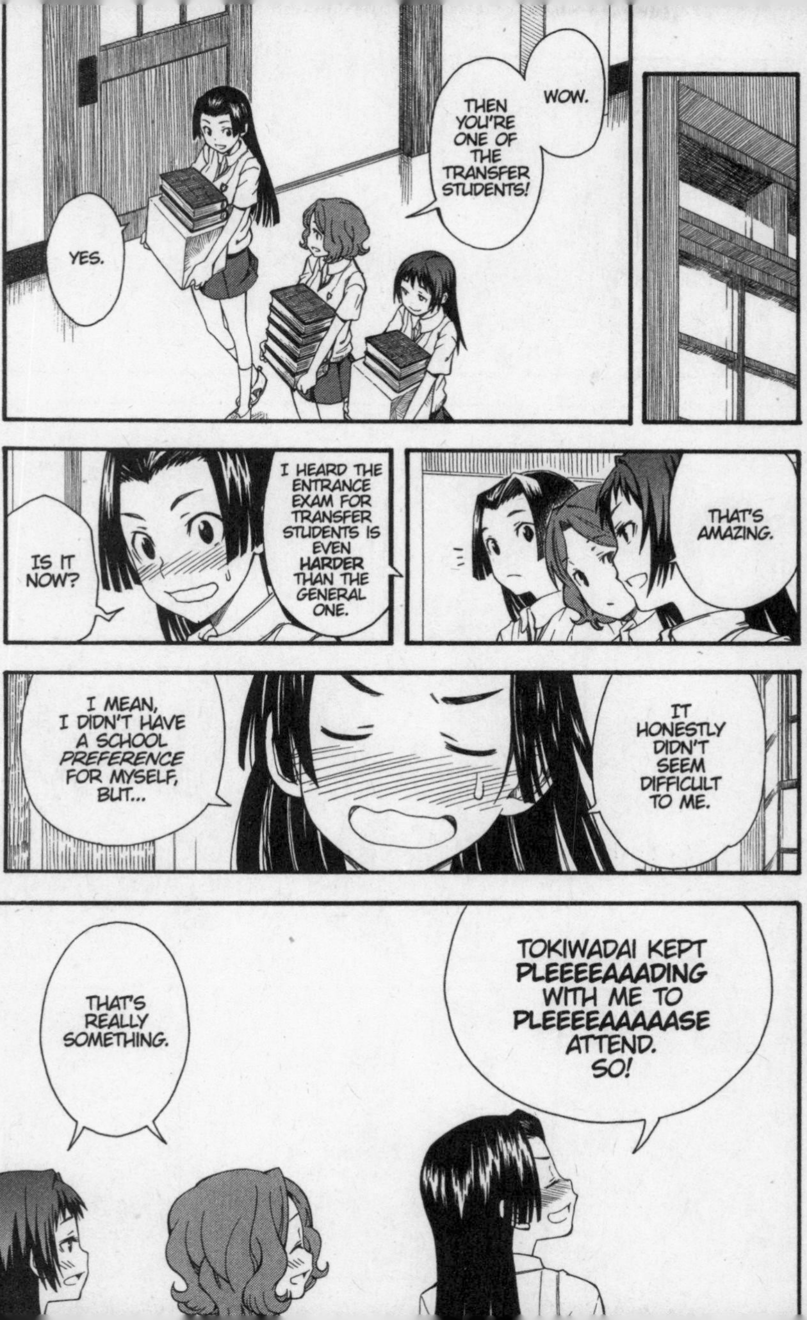
WOW.
THEN YOU'RE ONE OF THE TRANSFER STUDENTS!
YES.
THAT'S AMAZING.
I HEARD THE ENTRANCE EXAM FOR TRANSFER STUDENTS IS EVEN HARDER THAN THE GENERAL ONE.
IS IT NOW?
IT HONESTLY DIDN'T SEEM DIFFICULT TO ME.
I MEAN, I DIDN'T HAVE A SCHOOL *PREFERENCE* FOR MYSELF, BUT...
TOKIWADAI KEPT PLEEEEAAADING WITH ME TO PLEEEEAAAAASE ATTEND. SO!
THAT'S REALLY SOMETHING.

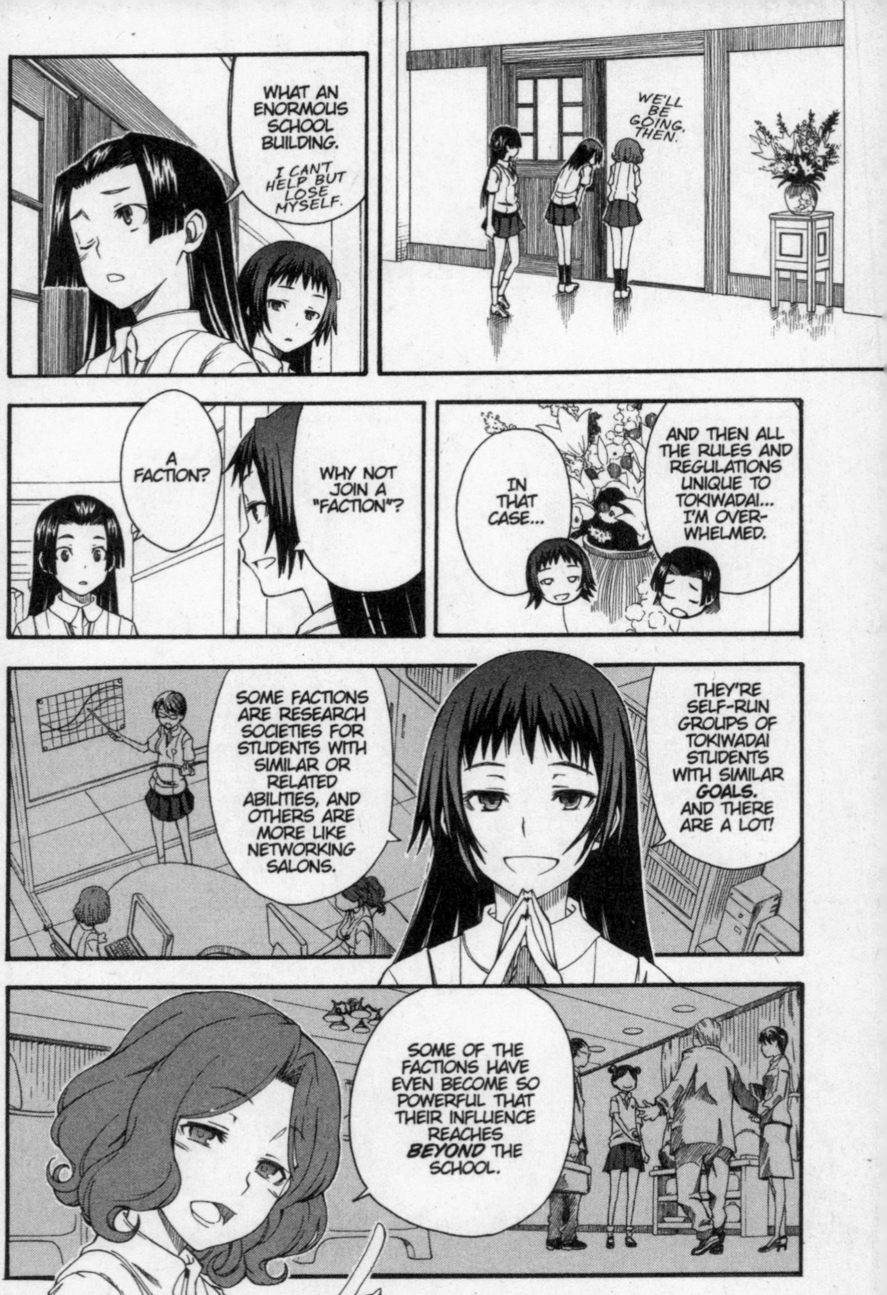
WE'LL BE GOING, THEN.
WHAT AN ENORMOUS SCHOOL BUILDING.
I CAN'T HELP BUT LOSE MYSELF.
AND THEN ALL THE RULES AND REGULATIONS UNIQUE TO TOKIWADAI... I'M OVER-WHELMED.
IN THAT CASE...
WHY NOT JOIN A "FACTION"?
A FACTION?
THEY'RE SELF-RUN GROUPS OF TOKIWADAI STUDENTS WITH SIMILAR **GOALS.** AND THERE ARE A LOT!
SOME FACTIONS ARE RESEARCH SOCIETIES FOR STUDENTS WITH SIMILAR OR RELATED ABILITIES, AND OTHERS ARE MORE LIKE NETWORKING SALONS.
SOME OF THE FACTIONS HAVE EVEN BECOME SO POWERFUL THAT THEIR INFLUENCE REACHES ***BEYOND*** THE SCHOOL.

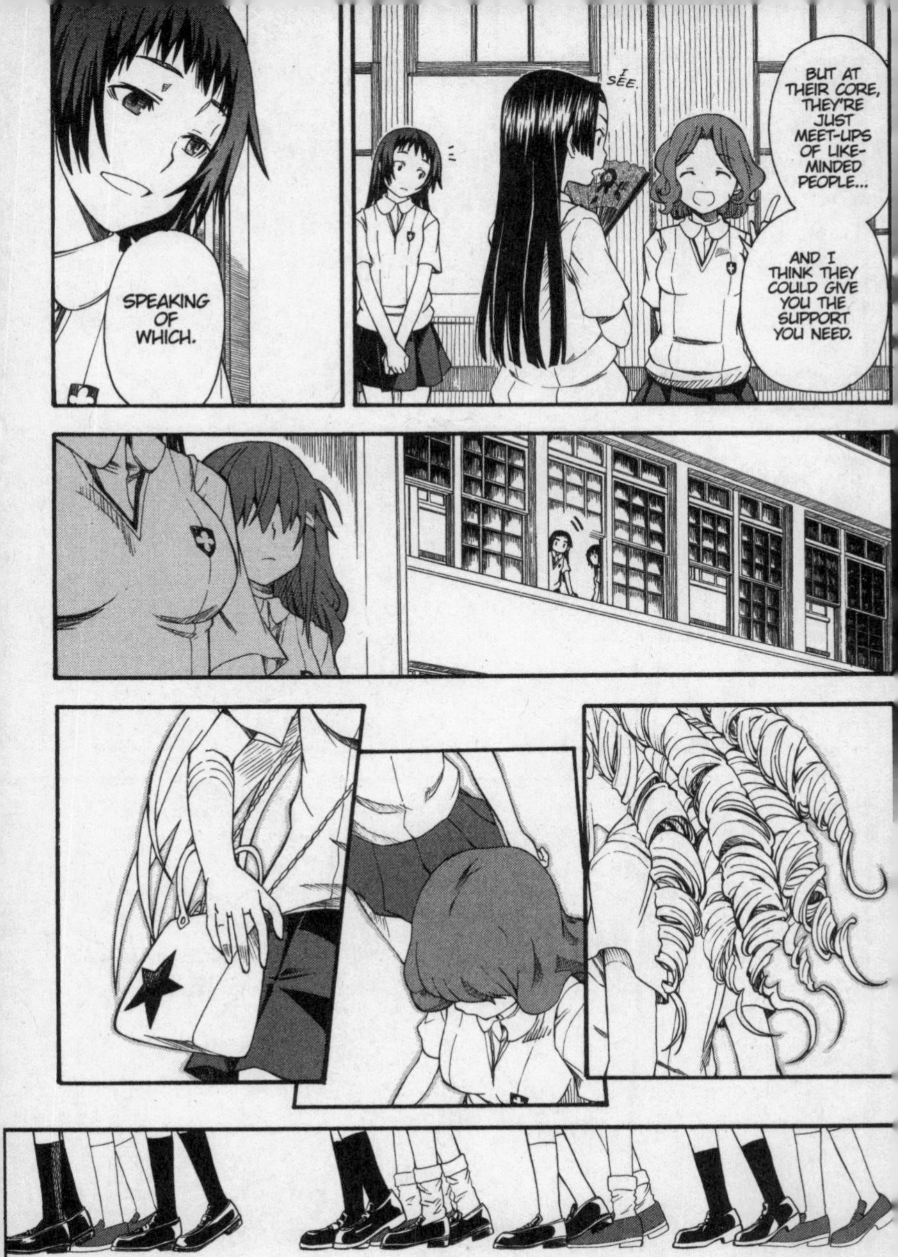
BUT AT THEIR CORE, THEY'RE JUST MEET-UPS OF LIKE-MINDED PEOPLE...
AND I THINK THEY COULD GIVE YOU THE SUPPORT YOU NEED.
I SEE.
SPEAKING OF WHICH.

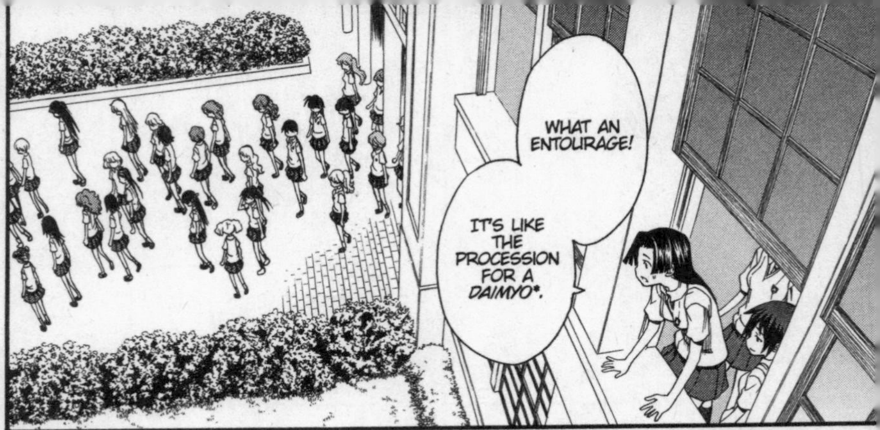
WHAT AN ENTOURAGE!
IT'S LIKE THE PROCESSION FOR A *DAIMYO**.

*Powerful feudal lords in ancient Japan.

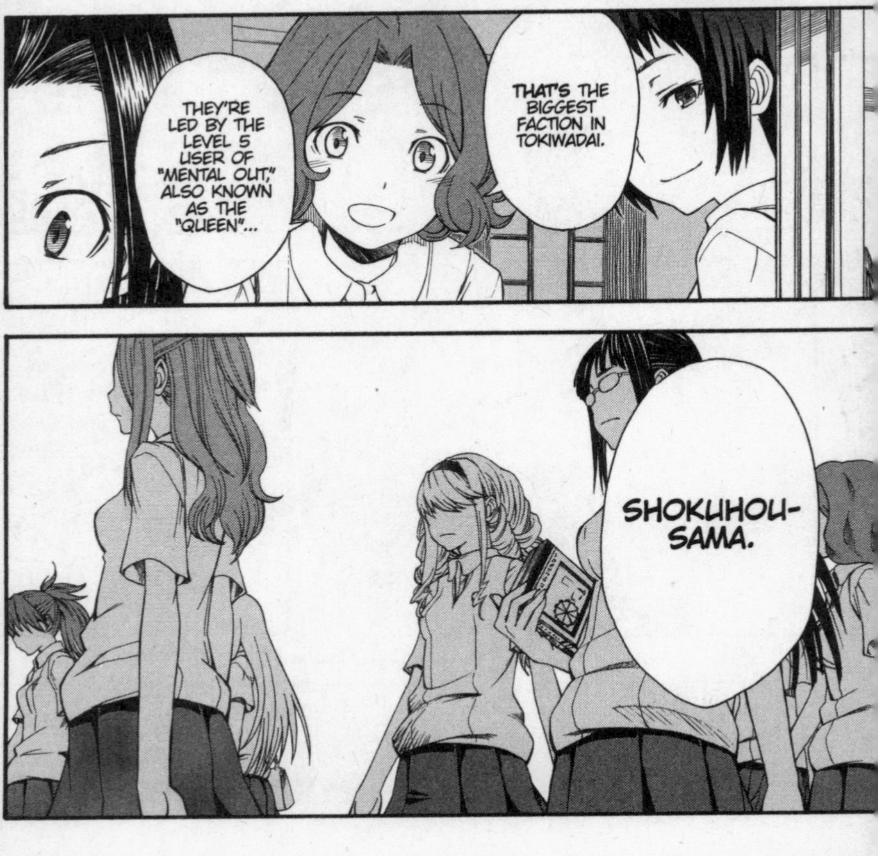
THAT'S THE BIGGEST FACTION IN TOKIWADAI.
THEY'RE LED BY THE LEVEL 5 USER OF "MENTAL OUT," ALSO KNOWN AS THE "QUEEN"...
SHOKUHOU-SAMA.

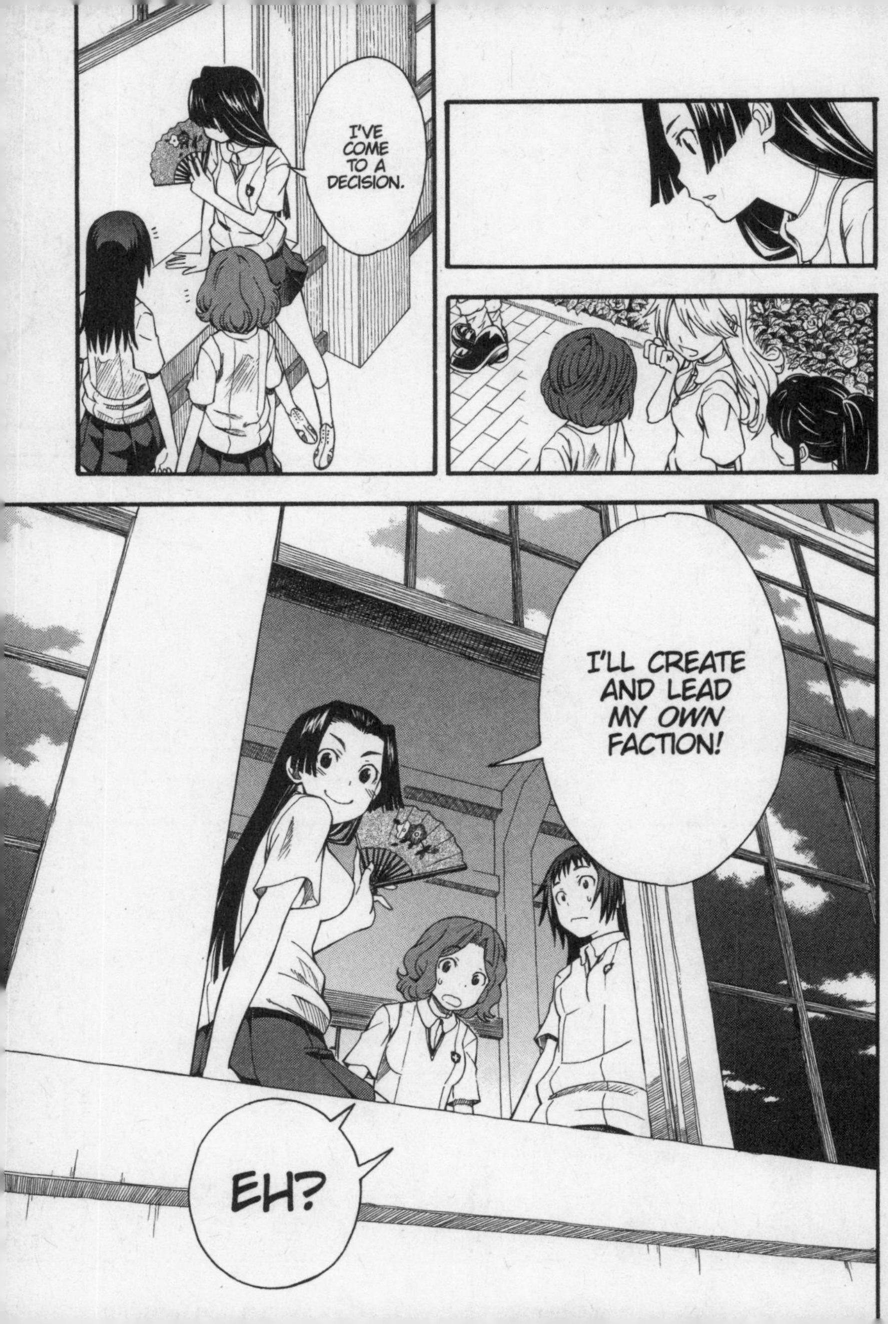
I'VE COME TO A DECISION.
I'LL CREATE AND LEAD MY *OWN* FACTION!
EH?

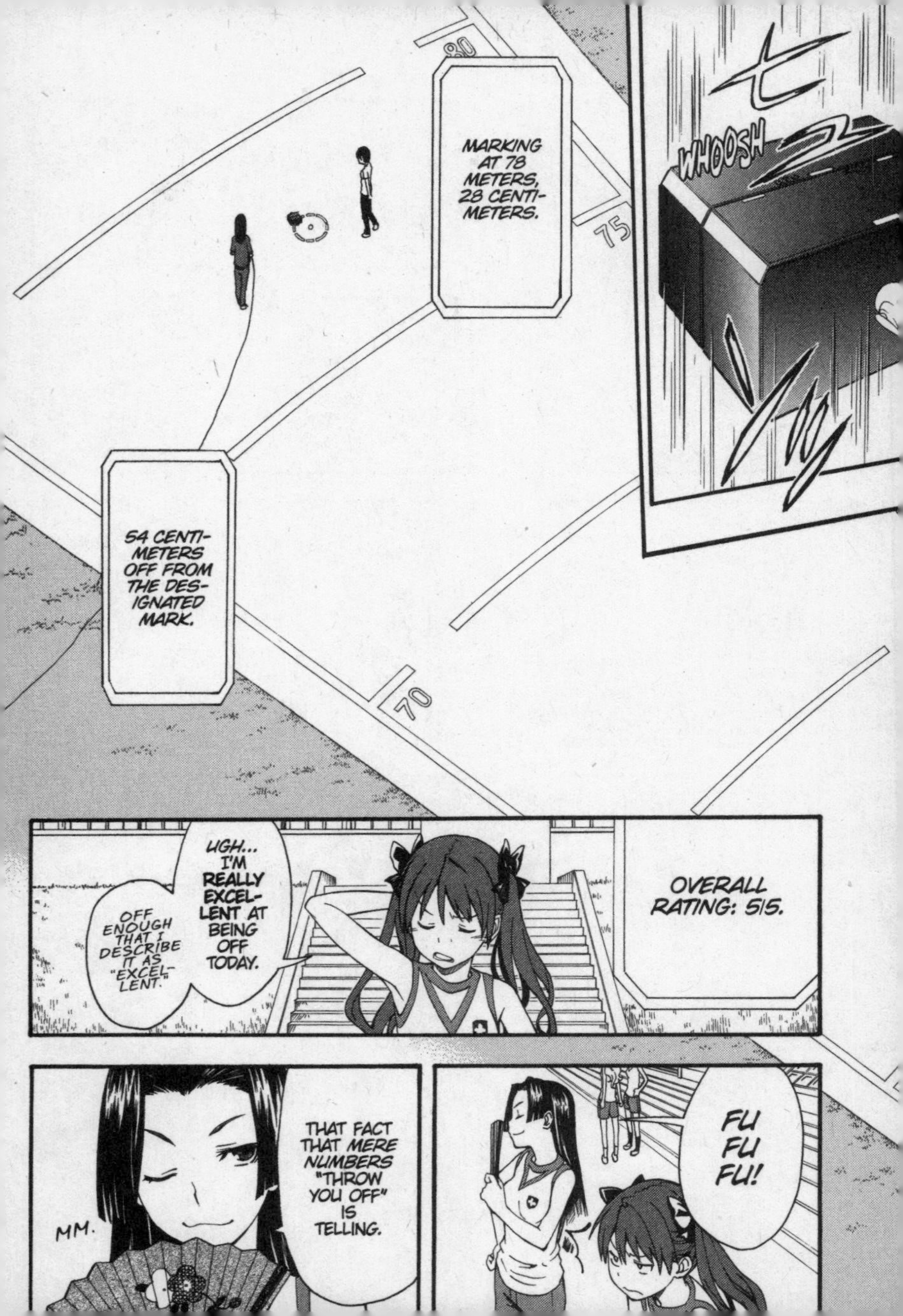
WHOOSH
MARKING AT 78 METERS, 28 CENTIMETERS.
54 CENTIMETERS OFF FROM THE DESIGNATED MARK.
70
75
80
OVERALL RATING: 515.
UGH... I'M REALLY EXCELLENT AT BEING OFF TODAY.
OFF ENOUGH THAT I DESCRIBE IT AS "EXCELLENT."
FU FU FU!
THAT FACT THAT MERE NUMBERS "THROW YOU OFF" IS TELLING.
MM.

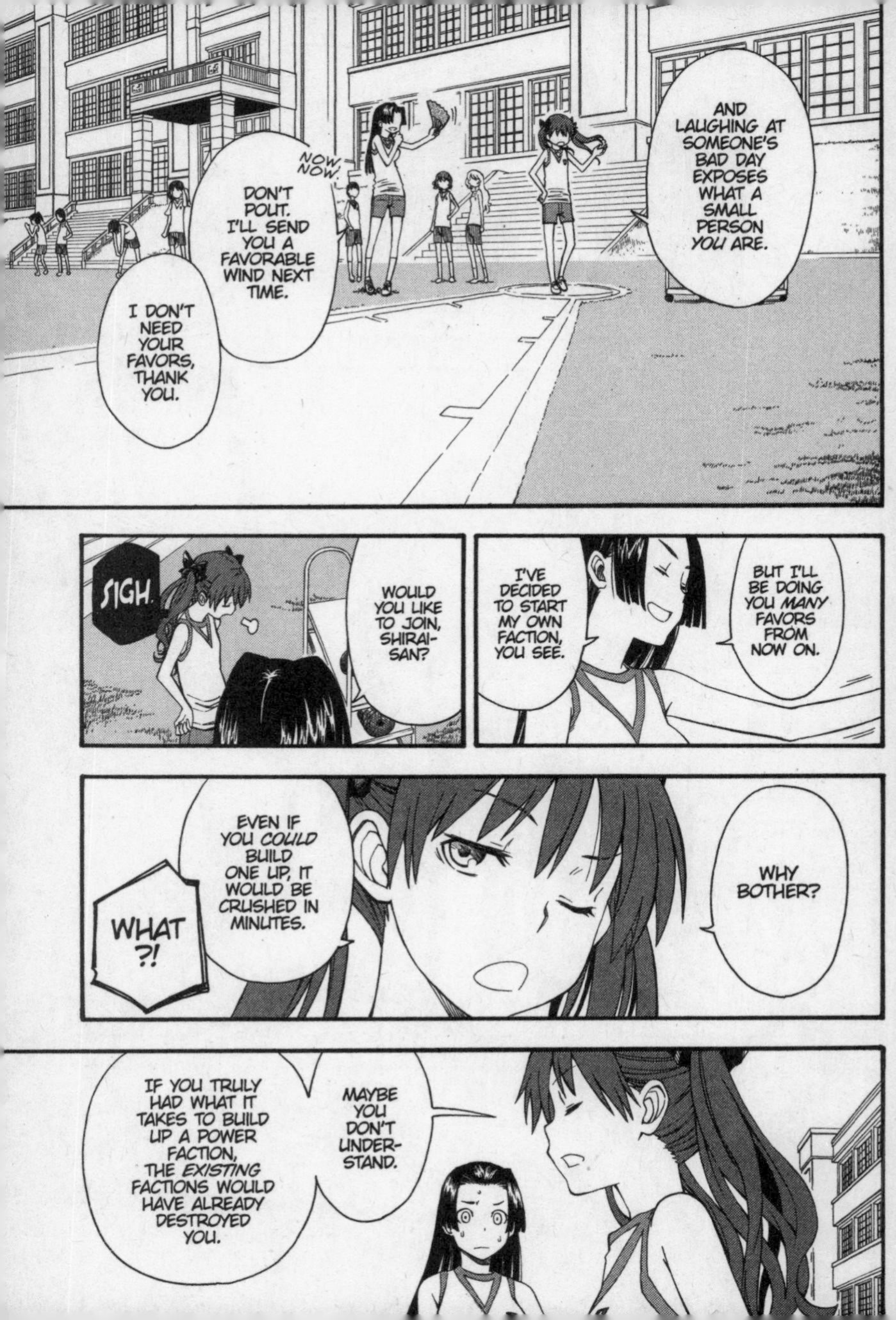
AND LAUGHING AT SOMEONE'S BAD DAY EXPOSES WHAT A SMALL PERSON *YOU* ARE.
NOW, NOW.
DON'T POUT. I'LL SEND YOU A FAVORABLE WIND NEXT TIME.
I DON'T NEED YOUR FAVORS, THANK YOU.
BUT I'LL BE DOING YOU *MANY* FAVORS FROM NOW ON.
I'VE DECIDED TO START MY OWN FACTION, YOU SEE.
WOULD YOU LIKE TO JOIN, SHIRAI-SAN?
SIGH.
WHY BOTHER?
EVEN IF YOU *COULD* BUILD ONE UP, IT WOULD BE CRUSHED IN MINUTES.
WHAT ?!
MAYBE YOU DON'T UNDER-STAND.
IF YOU TRULY HAD WHAT IT TAKES TO BUILD UP A POWER FACTION, THE *EXISTING* FACTIONS WOULD HAVE ALREADY DESTROYED YOU.

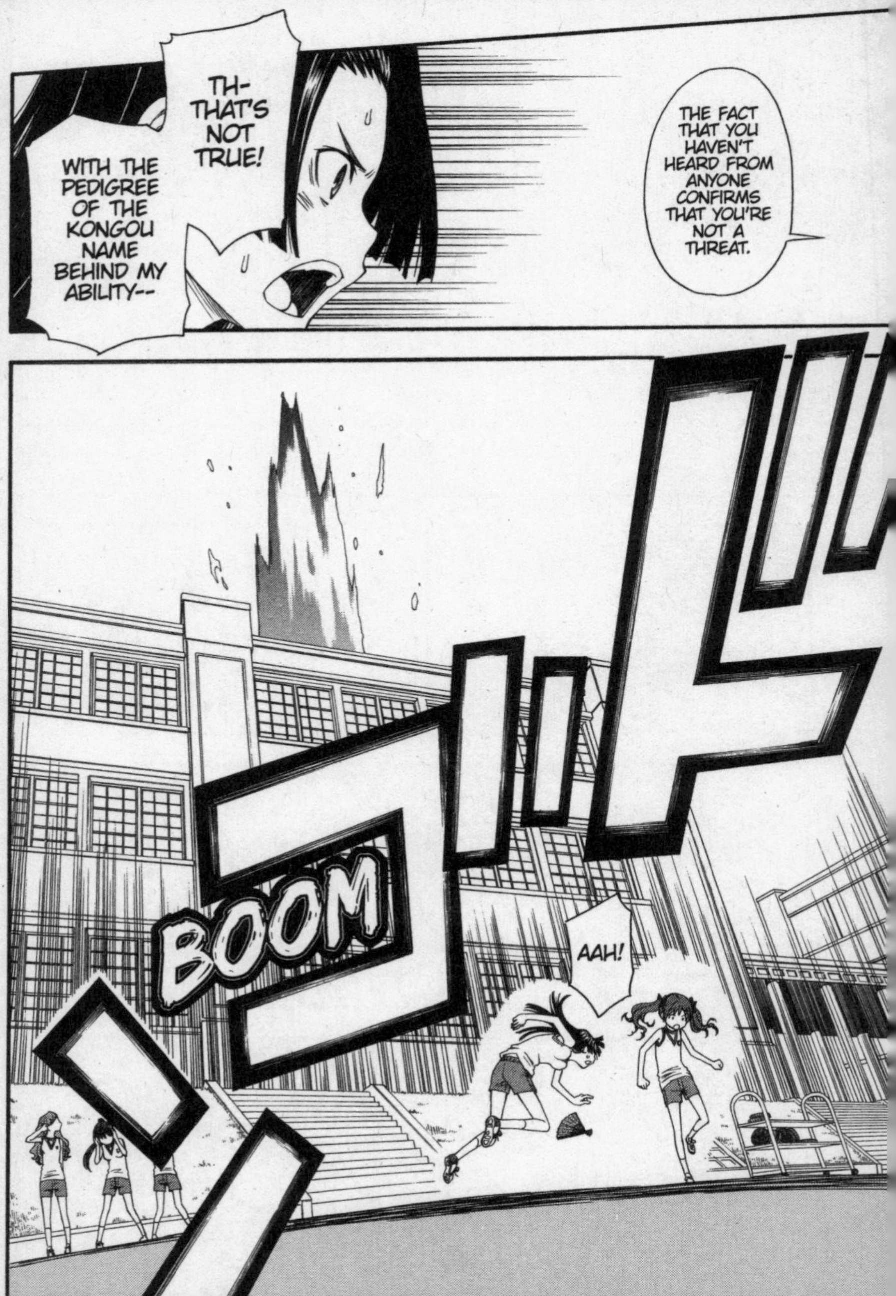
THE FACT THAT YOU HAVEN'T HEARD FROM ANYONE CONFIRMS THAT YOU'RE NOT A THREAT.
TH- THAT'S NOT TRUE!
WITH THE PEDIGREE OF THE KONGOU NAME BEHIND MY ABILITY--
BOOM
AAH!

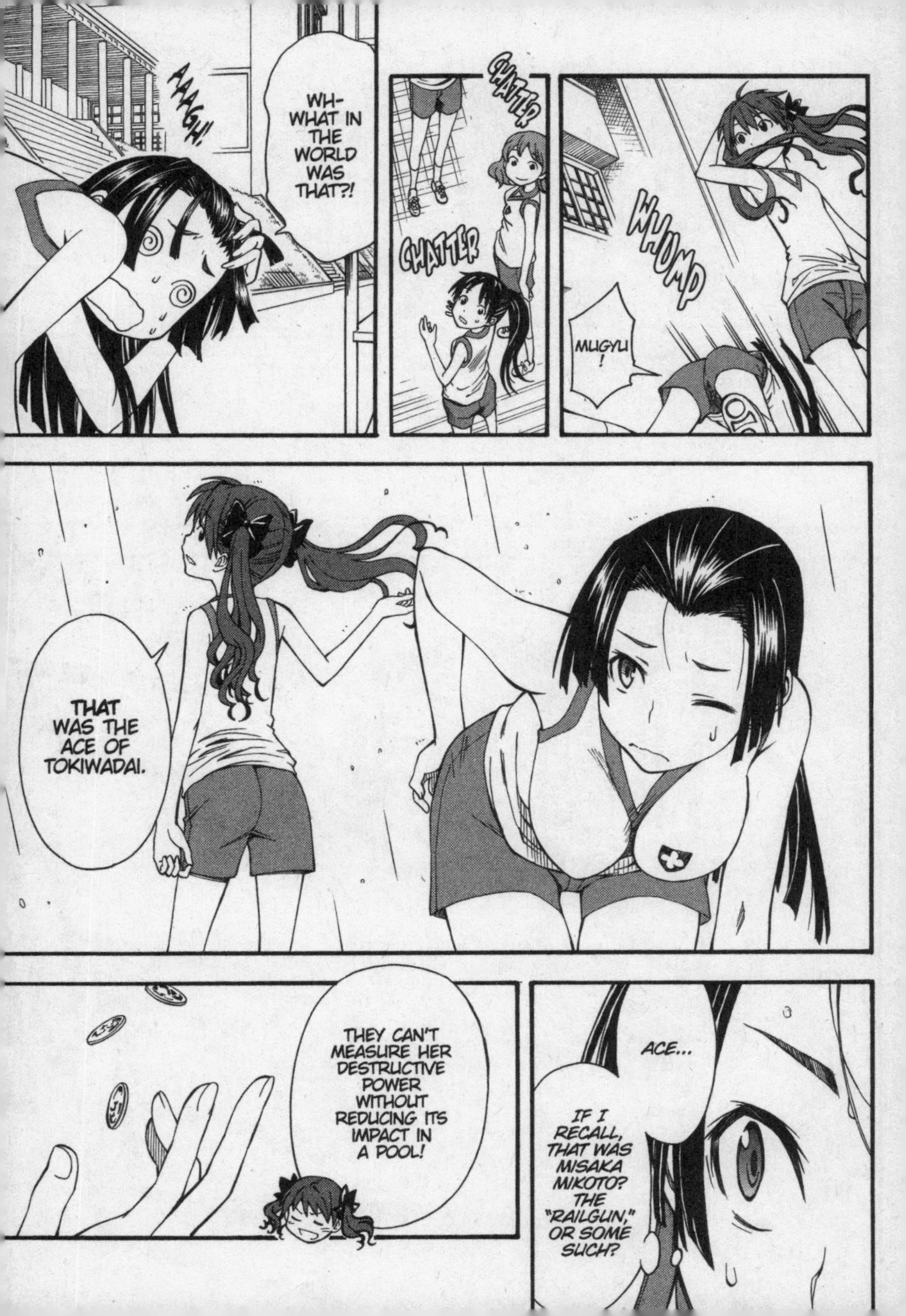
WHUMP
MUGYU!
CHATTER
CHATTER
AAAGH!
WH- WHAT IN THE WORLD WAS THAT?!
THAT WAS THE ACE OF TOKIWADAI.
ACE...
IF I RECALL, THAT WAS MISAKA MIKOTO? THE "RAILGUN," OR SOME SUCH?
THEY CAN'T MEASURE HER DESTRUCTIVE POWER WITHOUT REDUCING ITS IMPACT IN A POOL!

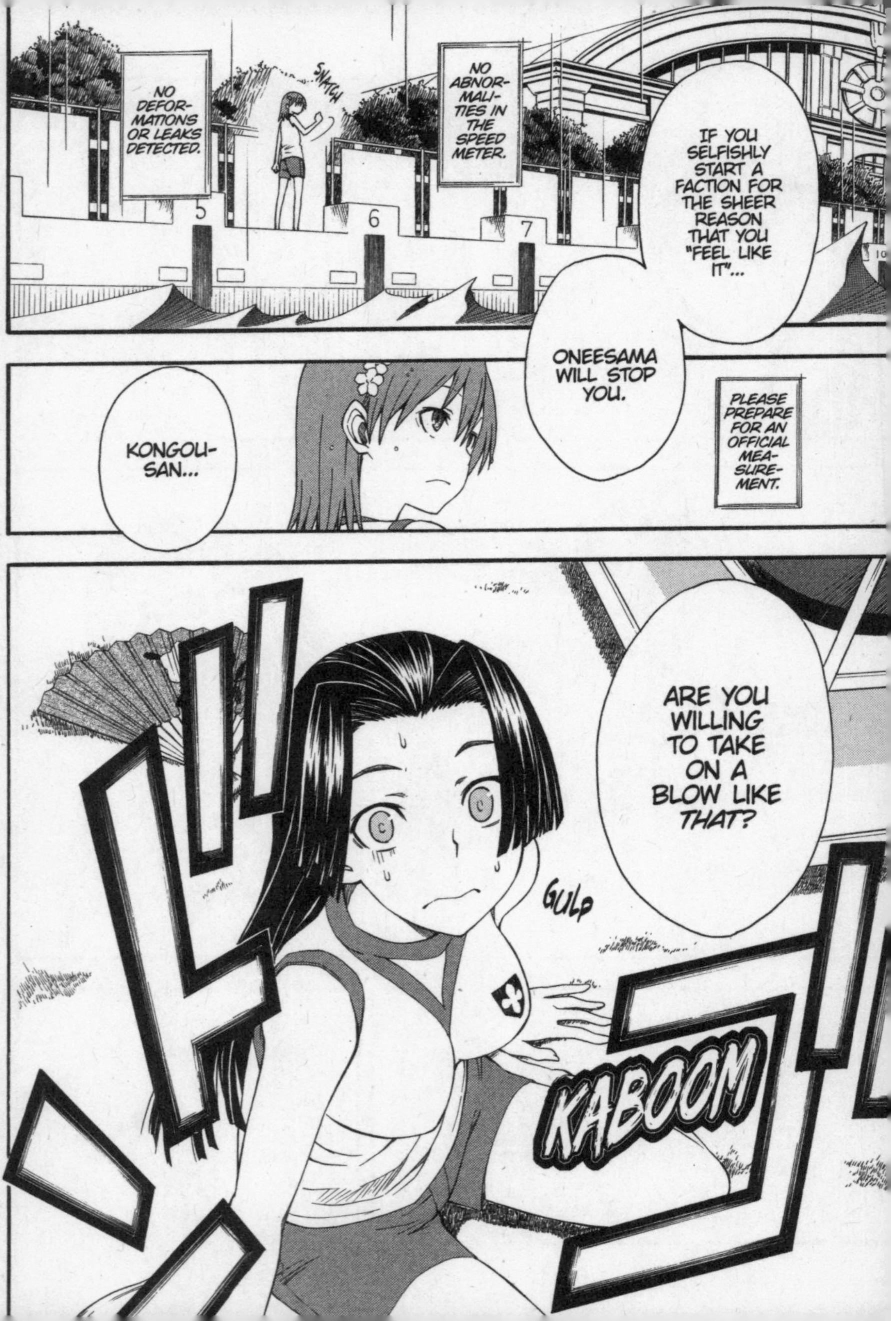
IF YOU SELFISHLY START A FACTION FOR THE SHEER REASON THAT YOU "FEEL LIKE IT"...
ONEESAMA WILL STOP YOU.
NO ABNORMALITIES IN THE SPEED METER.
SNATCH
NO DEFORMATIONS OR LEAKS DETECTED.
5
6
7
PLEASE PREPARE FOR AN OFFICIAL MEASUREMENT.
KONGOU-SAN...
ARE YOU WILLING TO TAKE ON A BLOW LIKE *THAT*?
GULP
KABOOM

A Certain SCIENTIFIC Railgun

A Certain Uiharu's Blossom

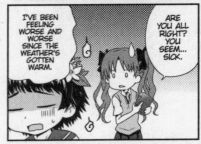

ARE YOU ALL RIGHT? YOU SEEM... SICK.
I'VE BEEN FEELING WORSE AND WORSE SINCE THE WEATHER'S GOTTEN WARM.
THAT'S NORMAL AT THE CHANGE OF SEASONS.
I'LL FINISH UP HERE SO YOU CAN GO HOME AND REST--
ABUNDANT...
......
IT'S... FEEDING OFF HER?
GULP

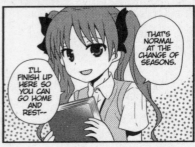

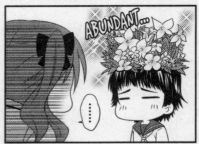

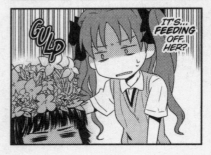

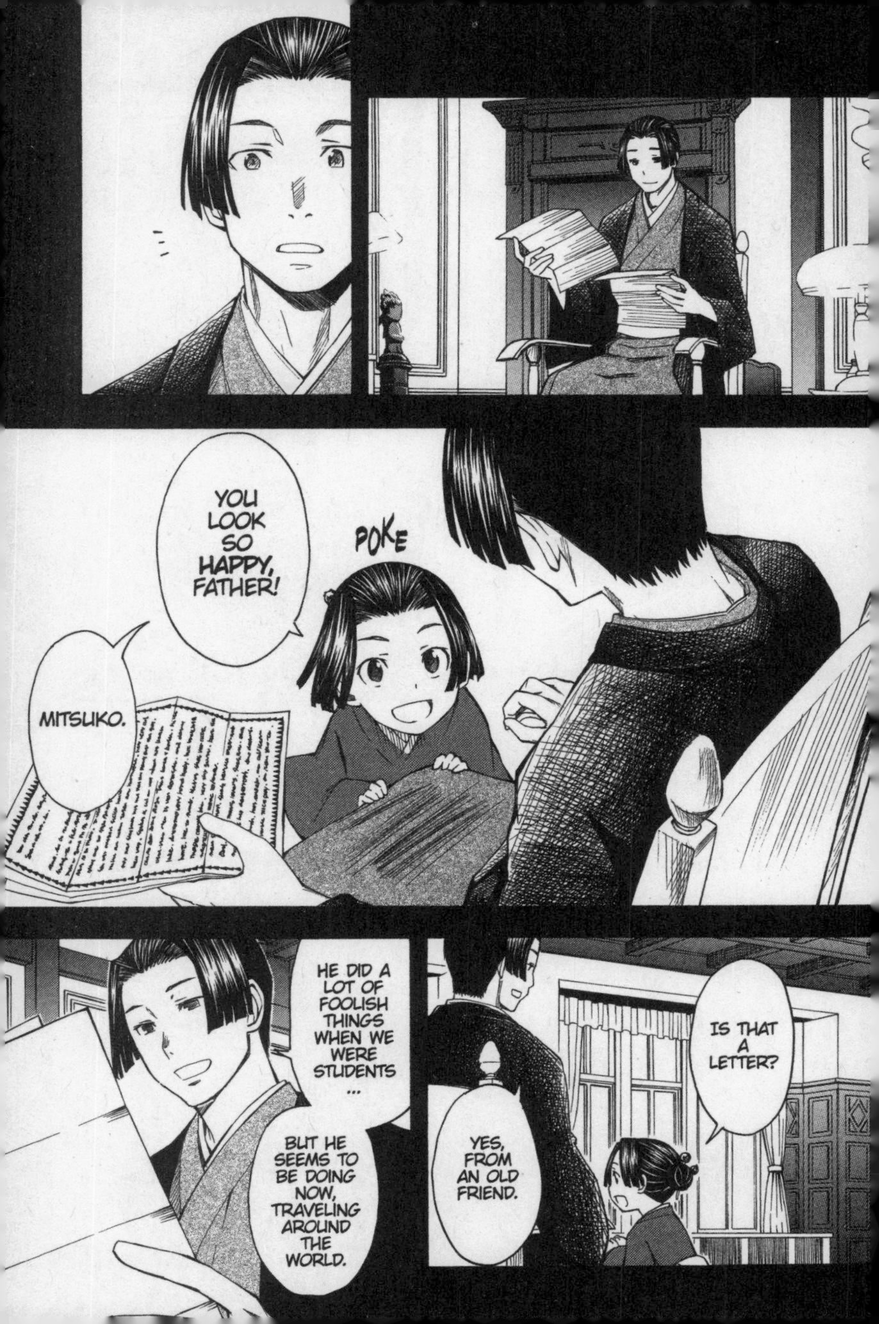
POKE
YOU LOOK SO HAPPY, FATHER!
MITSUKO.
IS THAT A LETTER?
YES, FROM AN OLD FRIEND.
HE DID A LOT OF FOOLISH THINGS WHEN WE WERE STUDENTS ...
BUT HE SEEMS TO BE DOING NOW, TRAVELING AROUND THE WORLD.

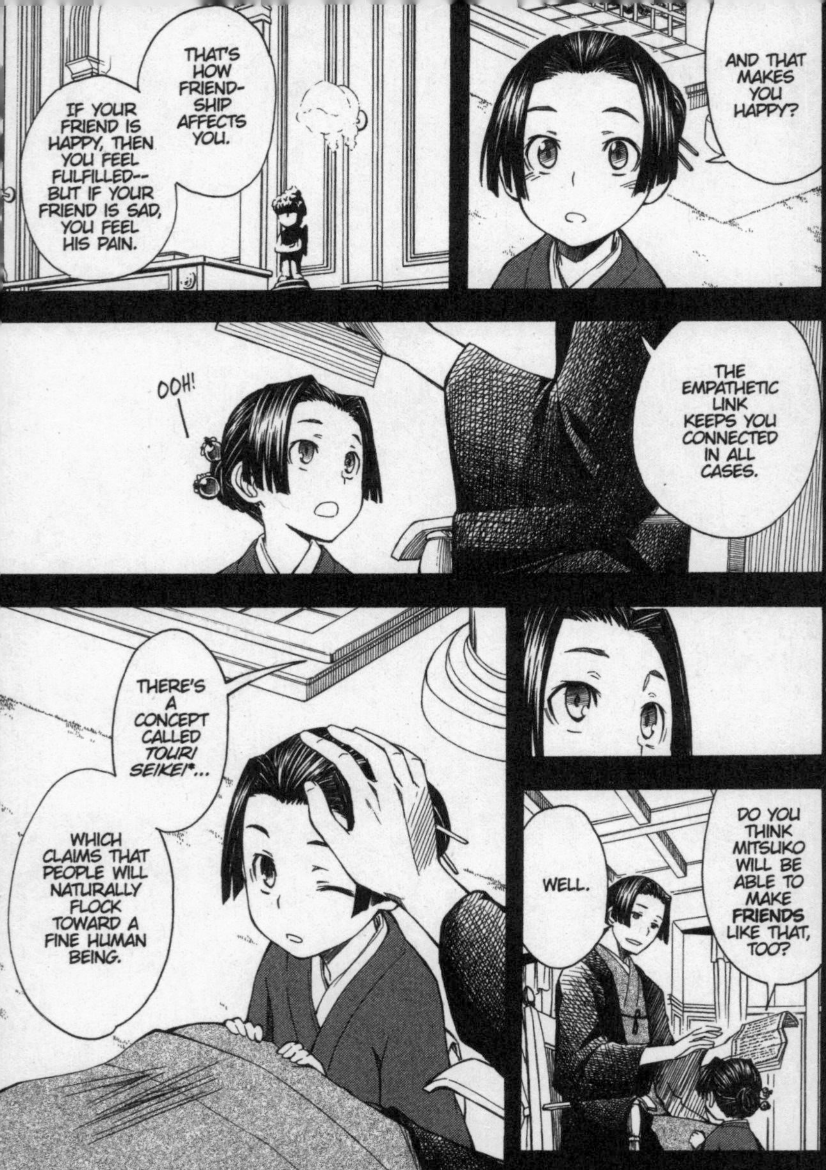
AND THAT MAKES YOU HAPPY?
THAT'S HOW FRIEND-SHIP AFFECTS YOU.
IF YOUR FRIEND IS HAPPY, THEN YOU FEEL FULFILLED-- BUT IF YOUR FRIEND IS SAD, YOU FEEL HIS PAIN.
THE EMPATHETIC LINK KEEPS YOU CONNECTED IN ALL CASES.
OOH!
DO YOU THINK MITSUKO WILL BE ABLE TO MAKE FRIENDS LIKE THAT, TOO?
WELL.
THERE'S A CONCEPT CALLED *TOURI SEIKEI**...
WHICH CLAIMS THAT PEOPLE WILL NATURALLY FLOCK TOWARD A FINE HUMAN BEING.

IF YOU IMPROVE YOURSELF AND MAINTAIN A CONSIDERATE HEART...

THEN THOSE GOOD ENOUGH TO BE YOUR FRIENDS WILL FIND THEIR WAY TO YOU.

WOW!

OF COURSE I AM!

WOOOW.

KONGOU-SAN'S IN FIRST PLACE AGAIN.

OOH! THEY POSTED THE TEST RESULTS!

INDIVIDUAL RE

1st	Kongou Mitsuko	498 points
2nd	Yokosuka Saaya	494 points

I WILL THEREFORE ALLOW YOU TO BECOME MY FRIENDS!

UH... THANKS?

BUT YOU CAME IN THIRD, NACCHAN!

YOU'RE SO SMART!

AW... NO, I'M NOT.

HUH?

YOU'RE ALL EXCELLENT STUDENTS!

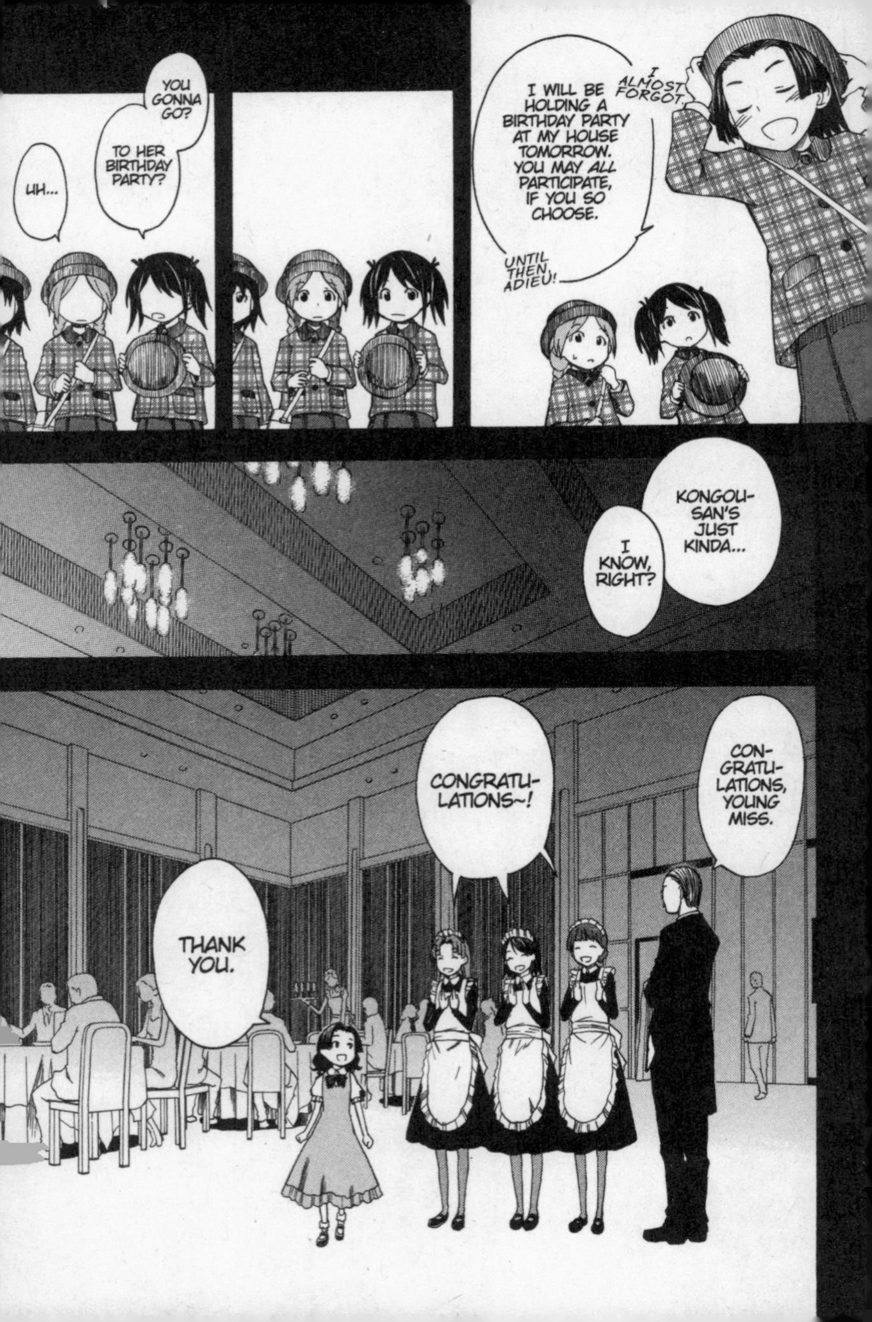
I ALMOST FORGOT.
I WILL BE HOLDING A BIRTHDAY PARTY AT MY HOUSE TOMORROW. YOU MAY ALL PARTICIPATE, IF YOU SO CHOOSE.
UNTIL THEN, ADIEU!
YOU GONNA GO?
TO HER BIRTHDAY PARTY?
UH...
KONGOU-SAN'S JUST KINDA...
I KNOW, RIGHT?
CON-GRATU-LATIONS, YOUNG MISS.
CONGRATU-LATIONS~!
THANK YOU.

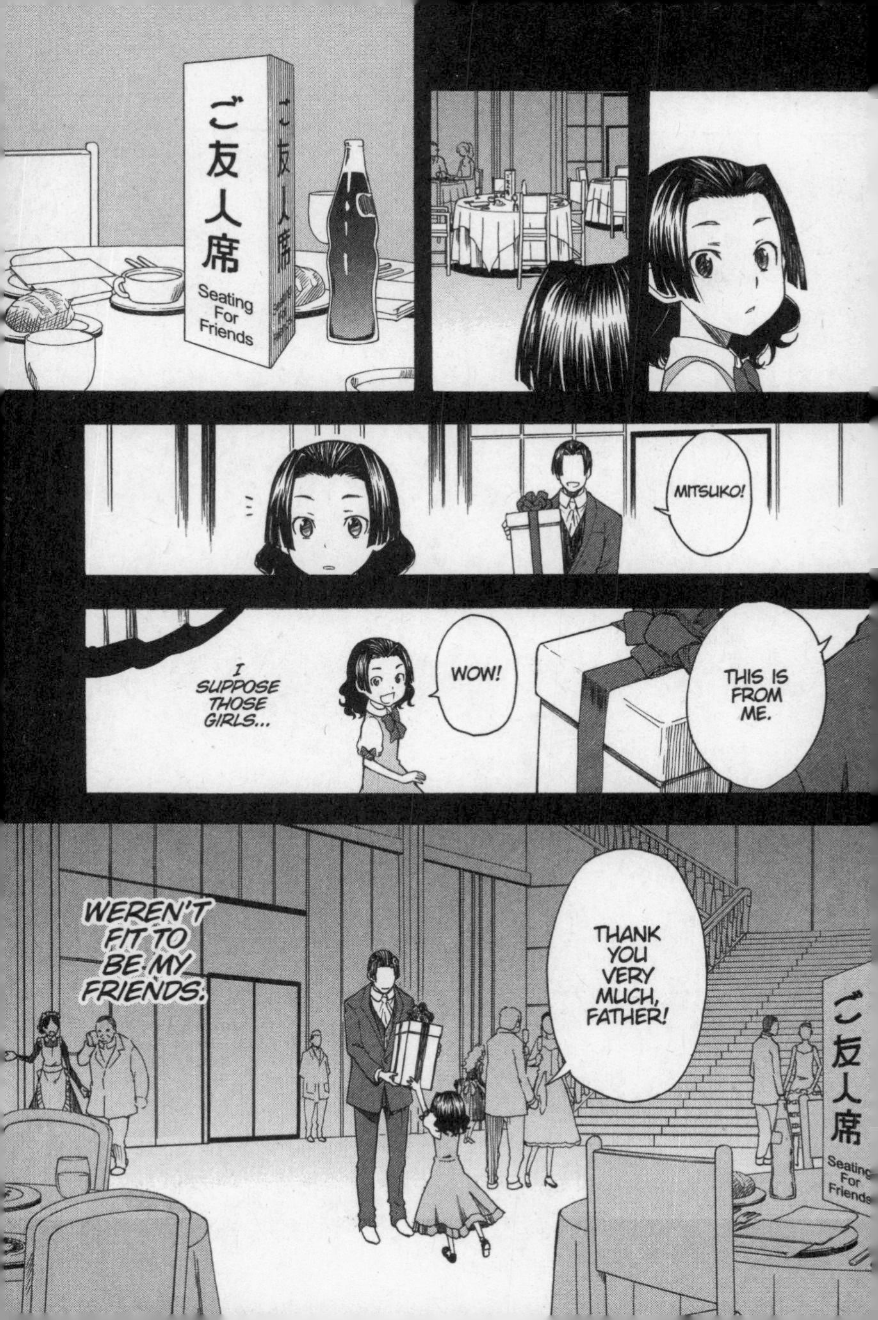
ご友人席
Seating For Friends
MITSUKO!
THIS IS FROM ME.
WOW!
I SUPPOSE THOSE GIRLS...
THANK YOU VERY MUCH, FATHER!
ご友人席
Seating For Friends
WEREN'T FIT TO BE MY FRIENDS.

CHAPTER 41: FACTION (2)

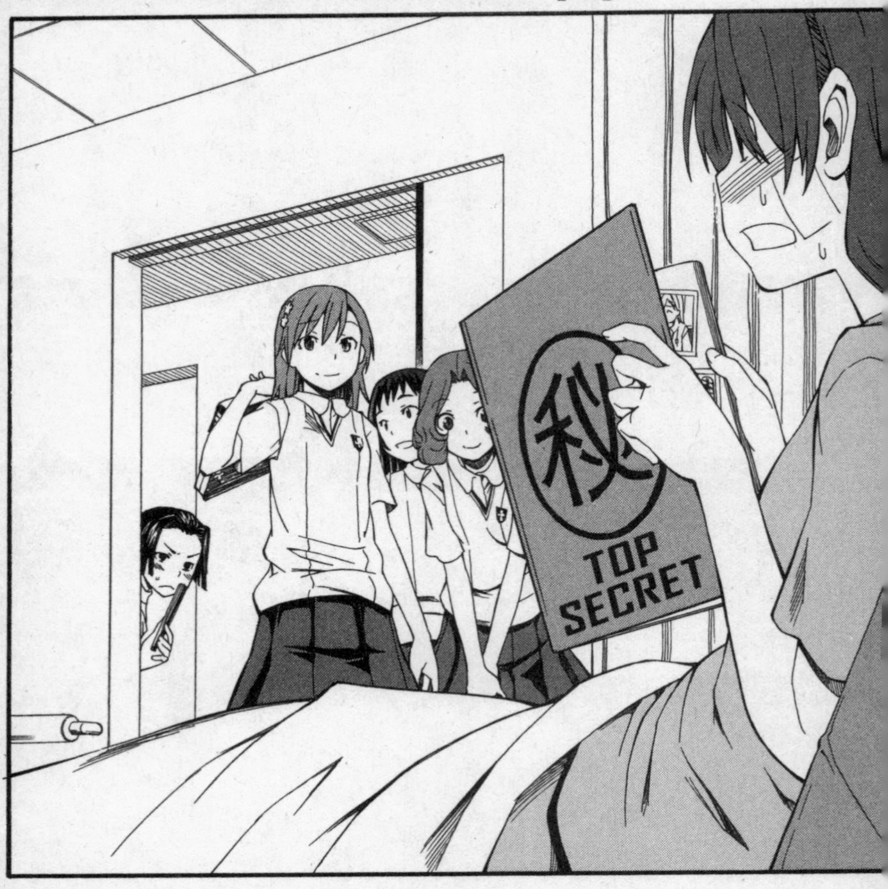
秘
TOP SECRET

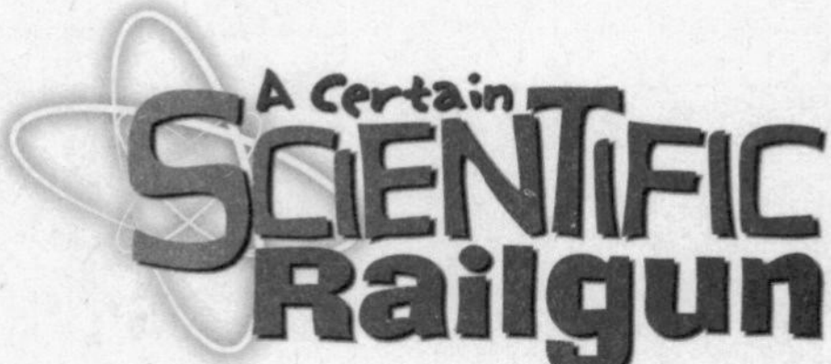
A Certain
SCIENTIFIC
Railgun

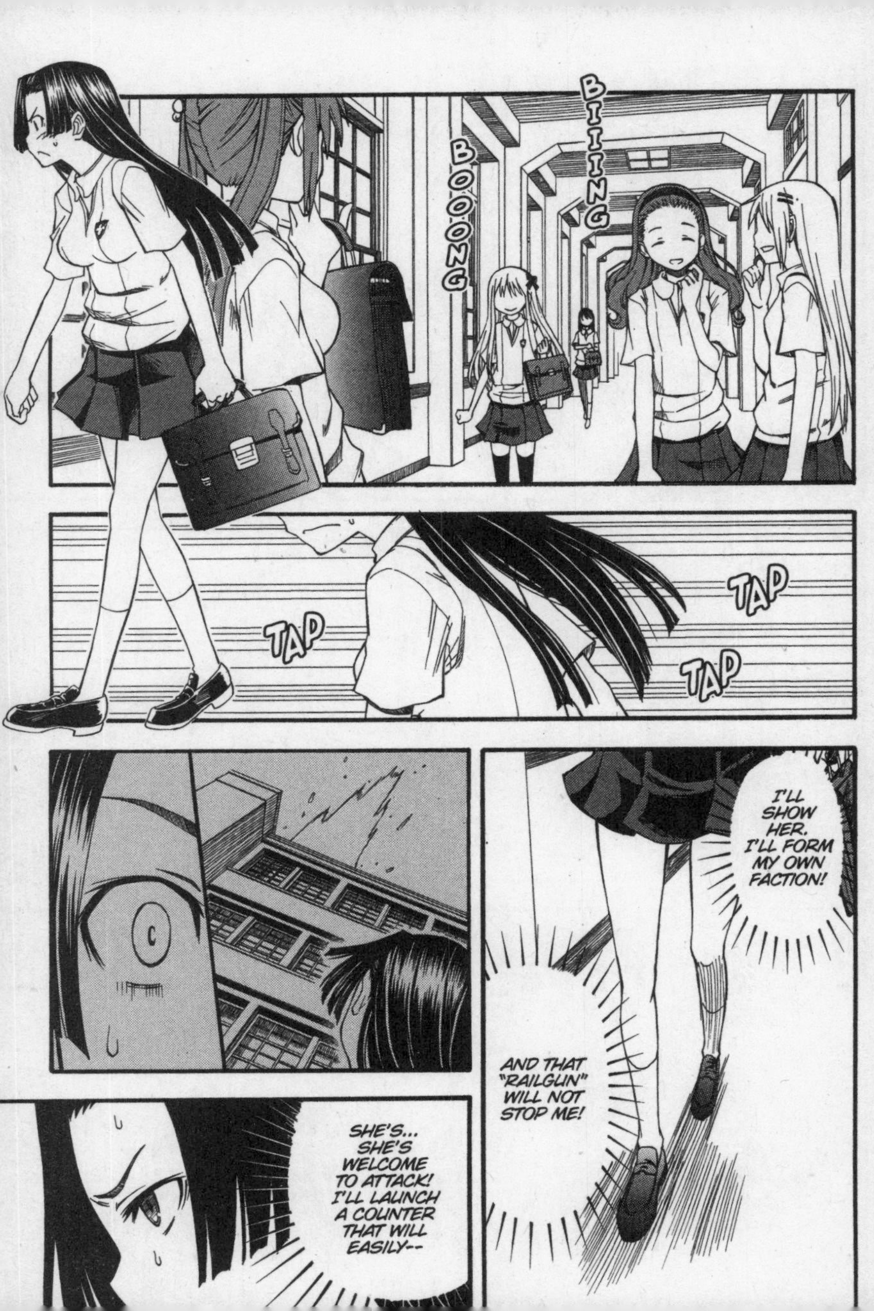
BIIING
BOOOONG
TAP
TAP
TAP
I'LL SHOW HER. I'LL FORM MY OWN FACTION!
AND THAT "RAILGUN" WILL NOT STOP ME!
SHE'S... SHE'S WELCOME TO ATTACK! I'LL LAUNCH A COUNTER THAT WILL EASILY--

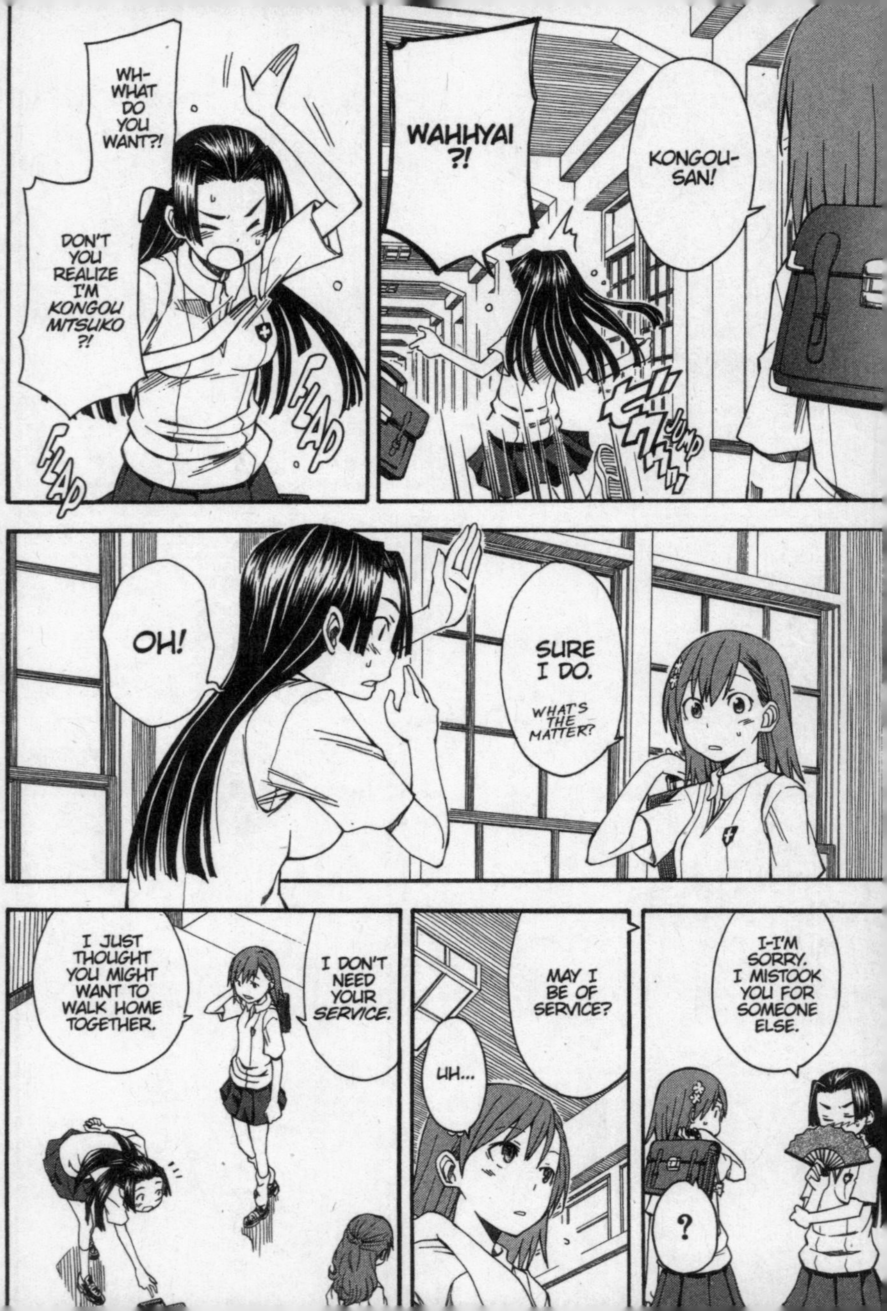
KONGOU-SAN!
WAHHYAI ?!
JUMP
WH-WHAT DO YOU WANT?!
DON'T YOU REALIZE I'M KONGOU MITSUKO ?!
FLAP
FLAP
SURE I DO.
WHAT'S THE MATTER?
OH!
I-I'M SORRY. I MISTOOK YOU FOR SOMEONE ELSE.
?
MAY I BE OF SERVICE?
UH...
I DON'T NEED YOUR SERVICE.
I JUST THOUGHT YOU MIGHT WANT TO WALK HOME TOGETHER.

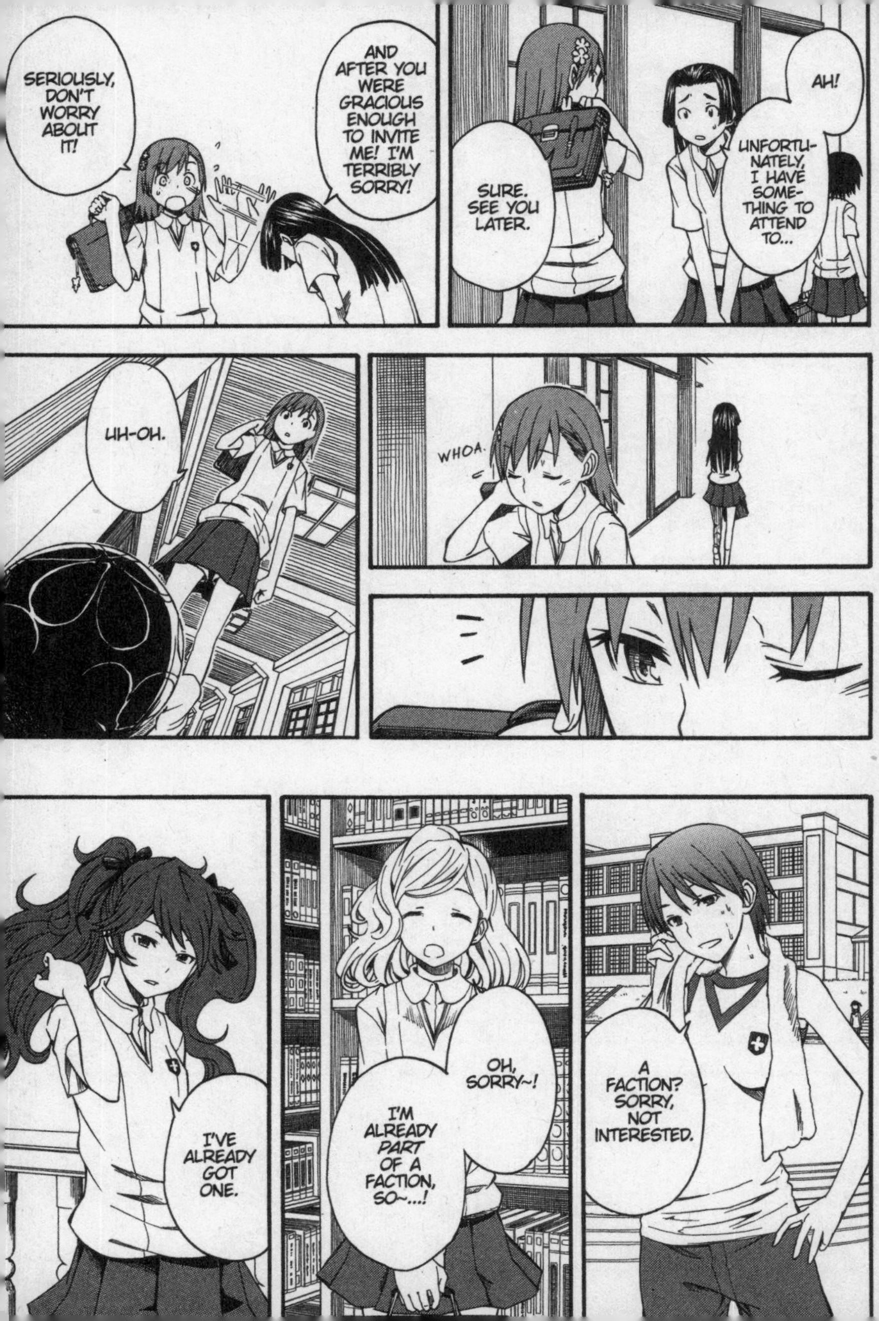
AH!
UNFORTUNATELY, I HAVE SOMETHING TO ATTEND TO...
SURE. SEE YOU LATER.
AND AFTER YOU WERE GRACIOUS ENOUGH TO INVITE ME! I'M TERRIBLY SORRY!
SERIOUSLY, DON'T WORRY ABOUT IT!
WHOA.
UH-OH.
A FACTION? SORRY, NOT INTERESTED.
OH, SORRY~!
I'M ALREADY PART OF A FACTION, SO~...!
I'VE ALREADY GOT ONE.

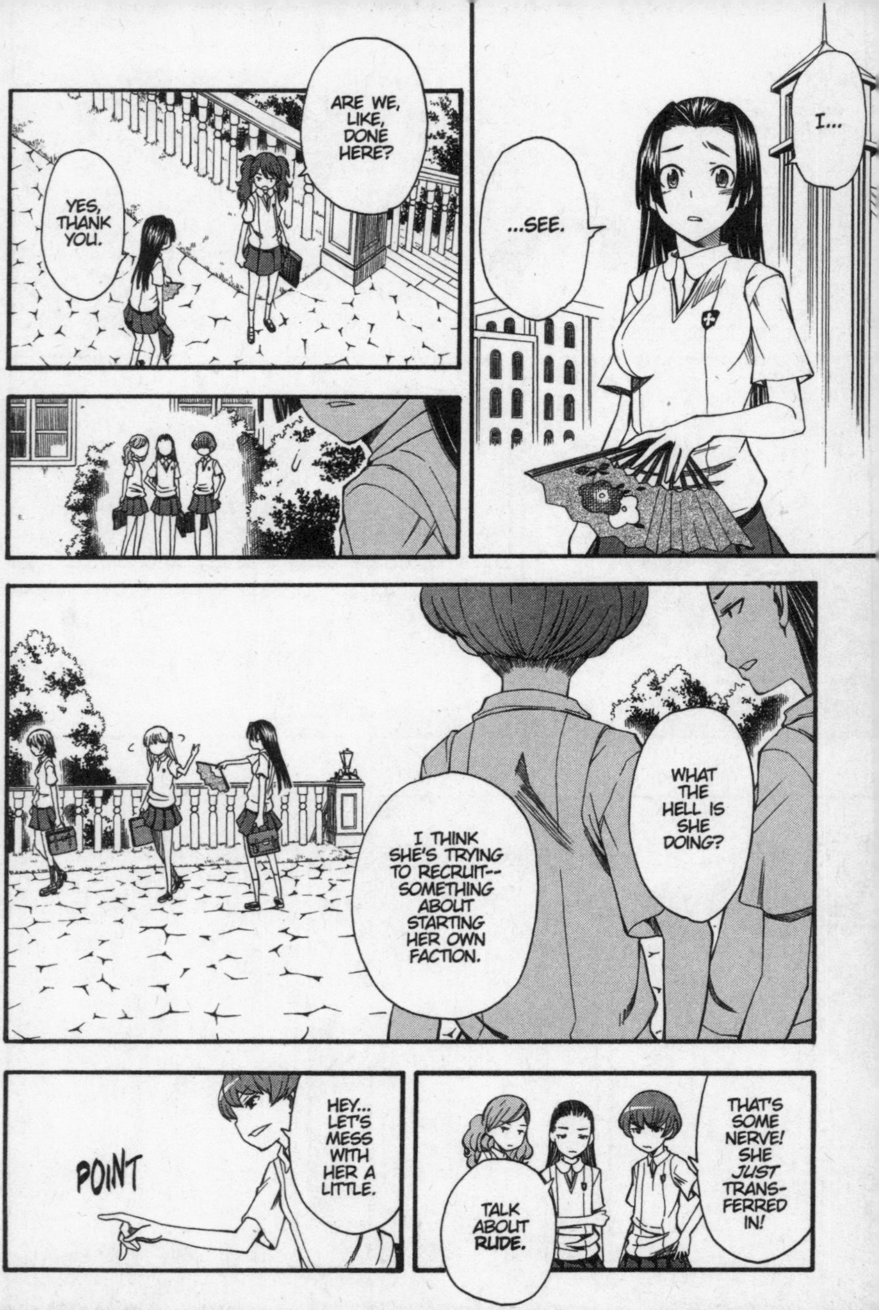
I...
...SEE.
ARE WE, LIKE, DONE HERE?
YES, THANK YOU.
WHAT THE HELL IS SHE DOING?
I THINK SHE'S TRYING TO RECRUIT-- SOMETHING ABOUT STARTING HER OWN FACTION.
THAT'S SOME NERVE! SHE JUST TRANS-FERRED IN!
TALK ABOUT RUDE.
HEY... LET'S MESS WITH HER A LITTLE.
POINT

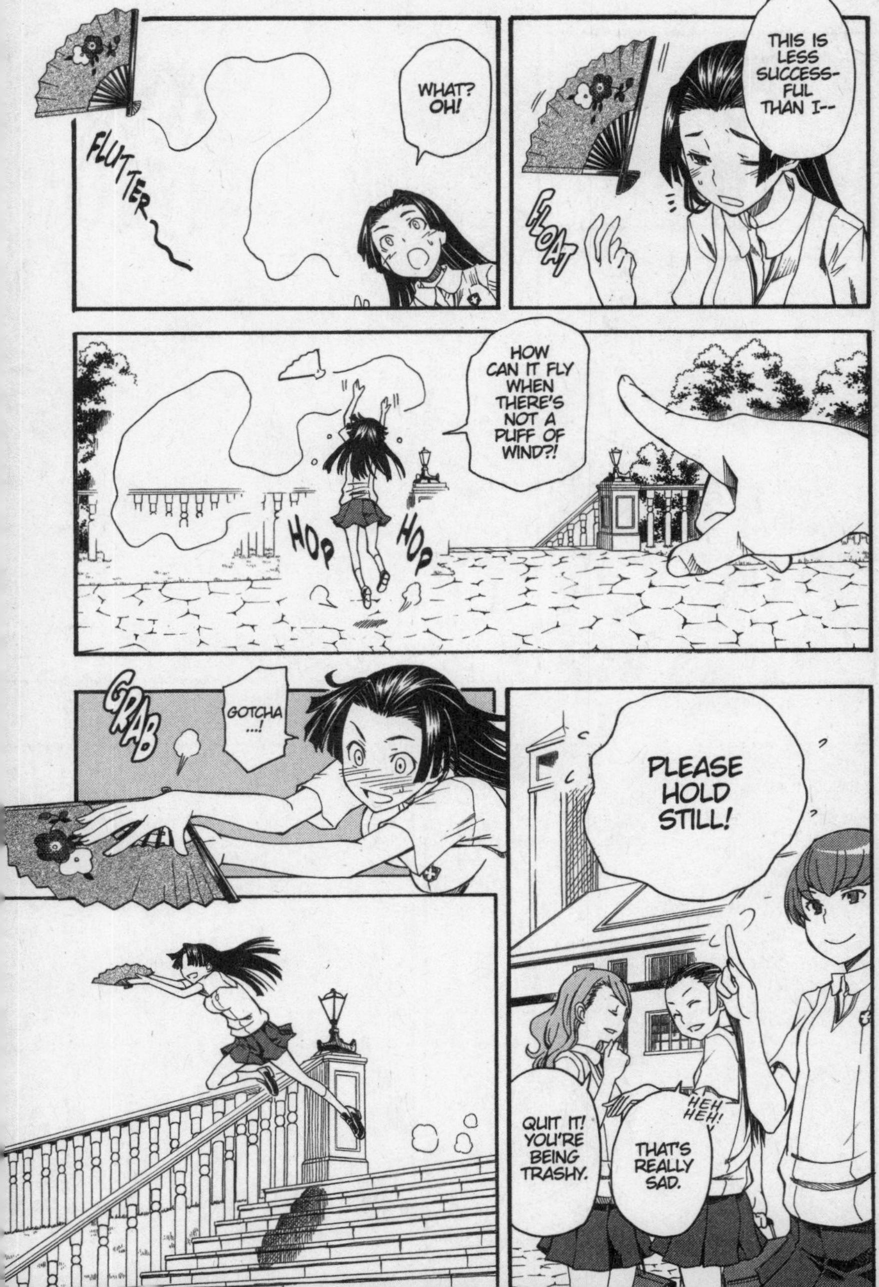
THIS IS LESS SUCCESS-FUL THAN I--
FLOAT
WHAT? OH!
FLUTTER~
HOW CAN IT FLY WHEN THERE'S NOT A PUFF OF WIND?!
HOP
HOP
PLEASE HOLD STILL!
HEH HEH!
THAT'S REALLY SAD.
QUIT IT! YOU'RE BEING TRASHY.
GRAB
GOTCHA...!

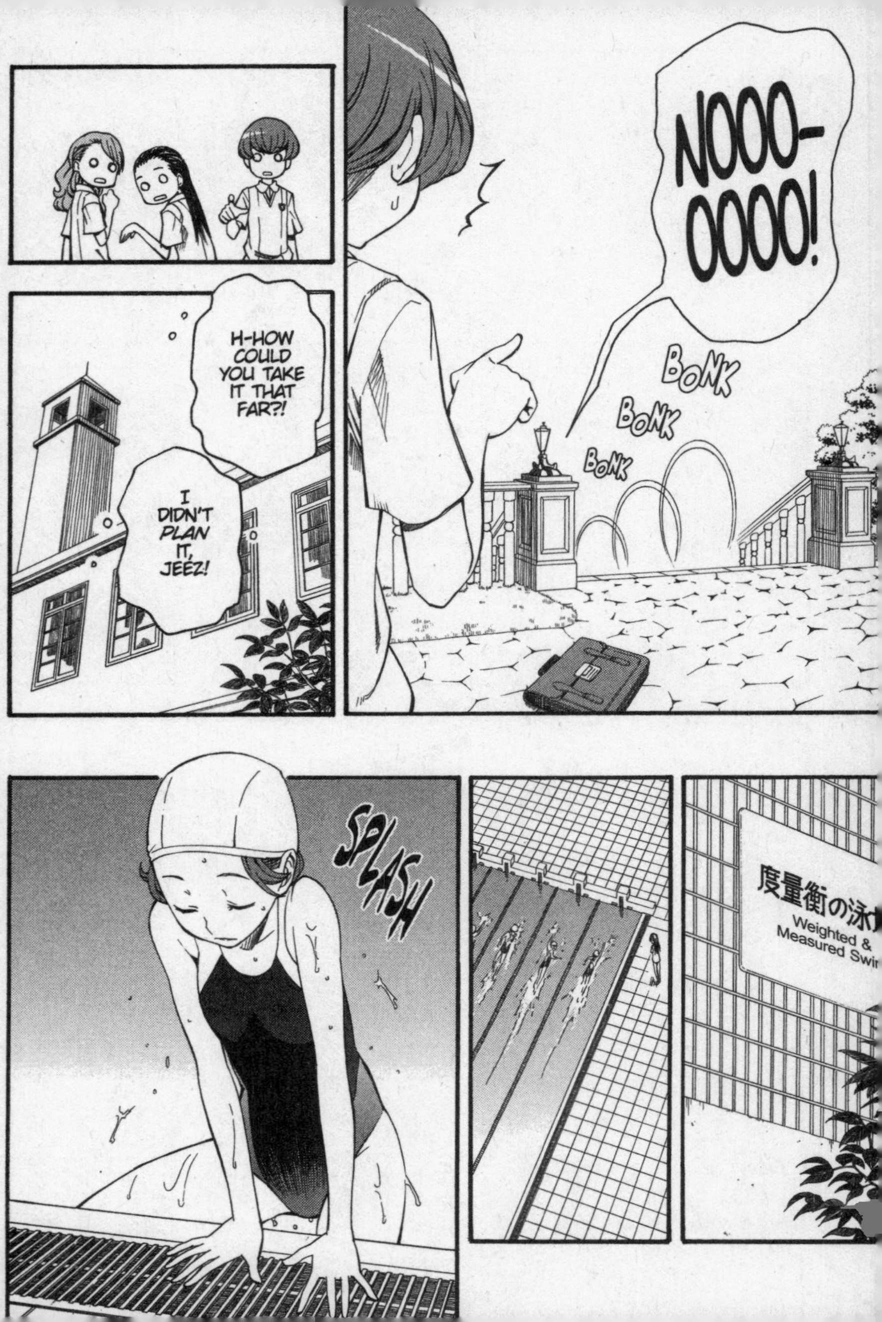
NOOO-OOOO!
BONK
BONK
BONK
H-HOW COULD YOU TAKE IT THAT FAR?!
I DIDN'T *PLAN* IT, JEEZ!
度量衡の泳
Weighted &
Measured
SPLASH

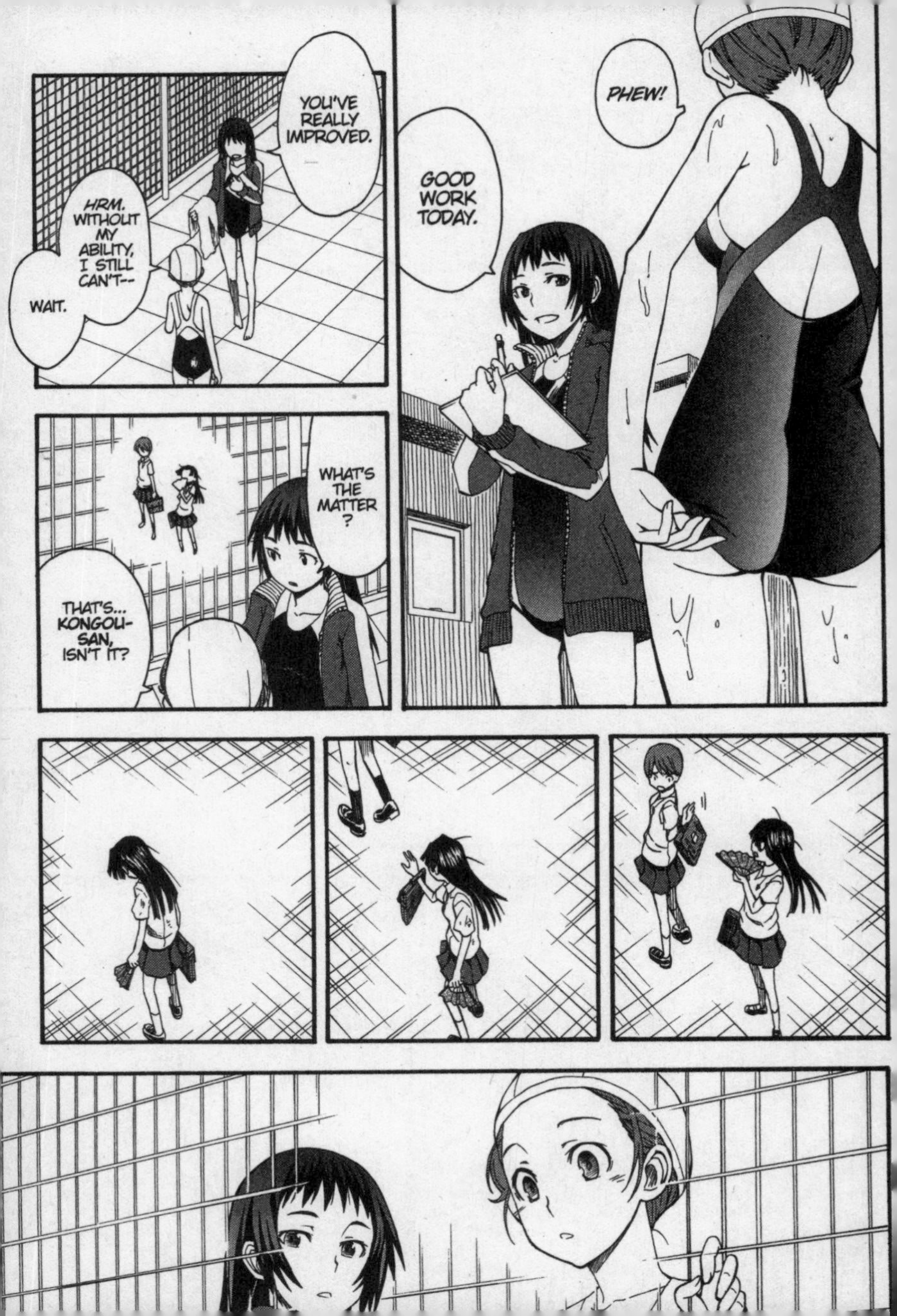
PHEW!
GOOD WORK TODAY.
YOU'VE REALLY IMPROVED.
HRM. WITHOUT MY ABILITY, I STILL CAN'T--
WAIT.
WHAT'S THE MATTER?
THAT'S... KONGOU-SAN, ISN'T IT?

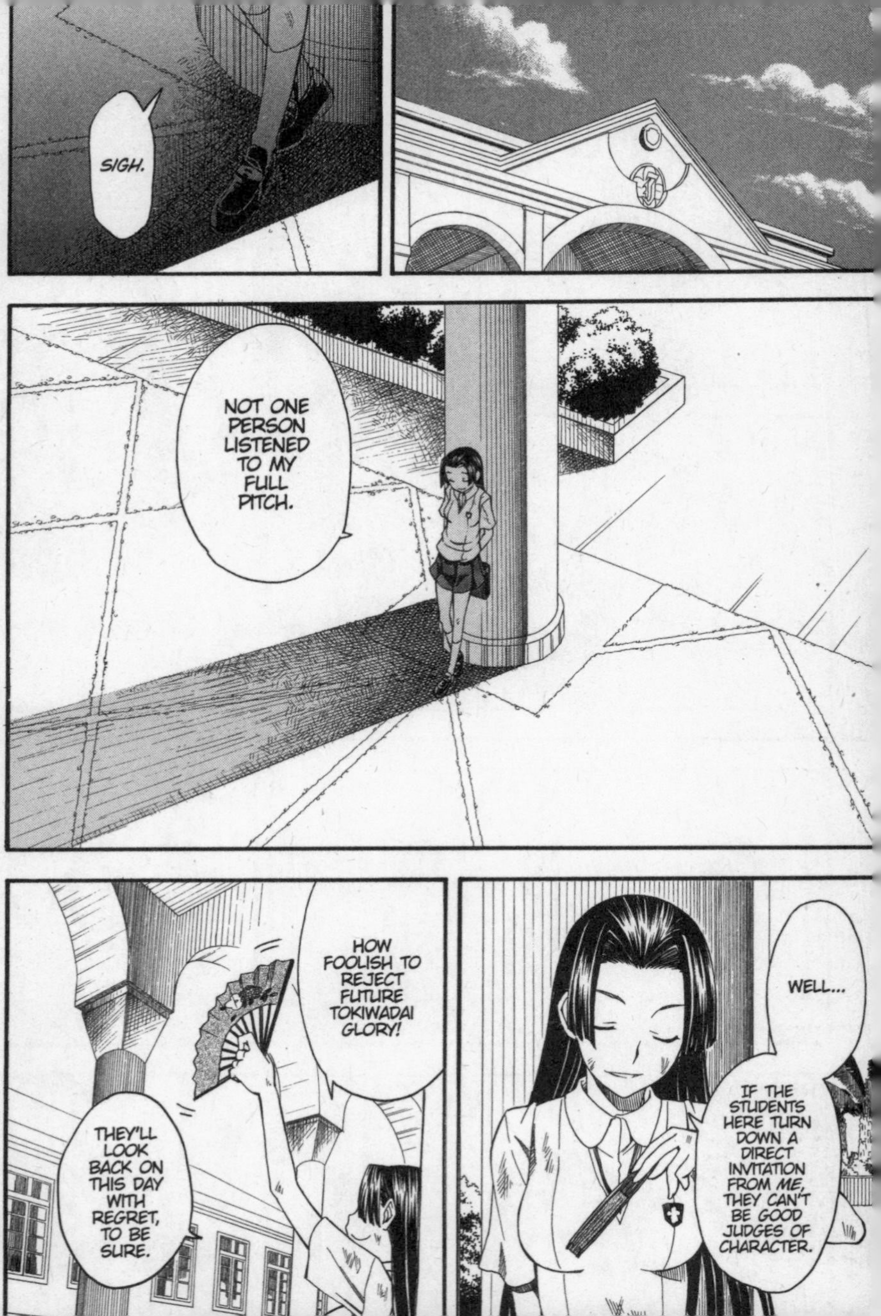
SIGH.
NOT ONE PERSON LISTENED TO MY FULL PITCH.
WELL...
IF THE STUDENTS HERE TURN DOWN A DIRECT INVITATION FROM *ME*, THEY CAN'T BE GOOD JUDGES OF CHARACTER.
HOW FOOLISH TO REJECT FUTURE TOKIWADAI GLORY!
THEY'LL LOOK BACK ON THIS DAY WITH REGRET, TO BE SURE.

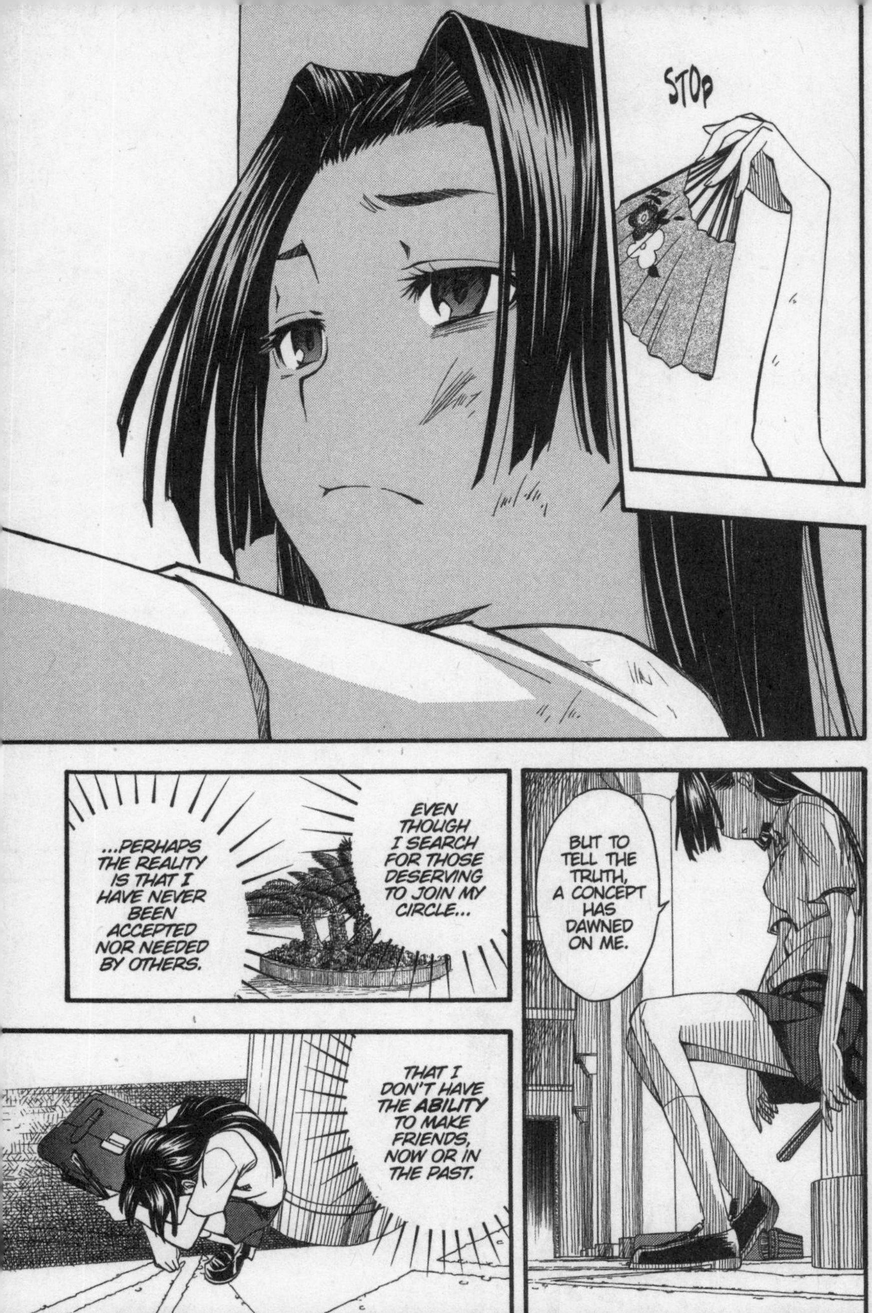
STOP
BUT TO TELL THE TRUTH, A CONCEPT HAS DAWNED ON ME.
EVEN THOUGH I SEARCH FOR THOSE DESERVING TO JOIN MY CIRCLE...
...PERHAPS THE REALITY IS THAT I HAVE NEVER BEEN ACCEPTED NOR NEEDED BY OTHERS.
THAT I DON'T HAVE THE ABILITY TO MAKE FRIENDS, NOW OR IN THE PAST.

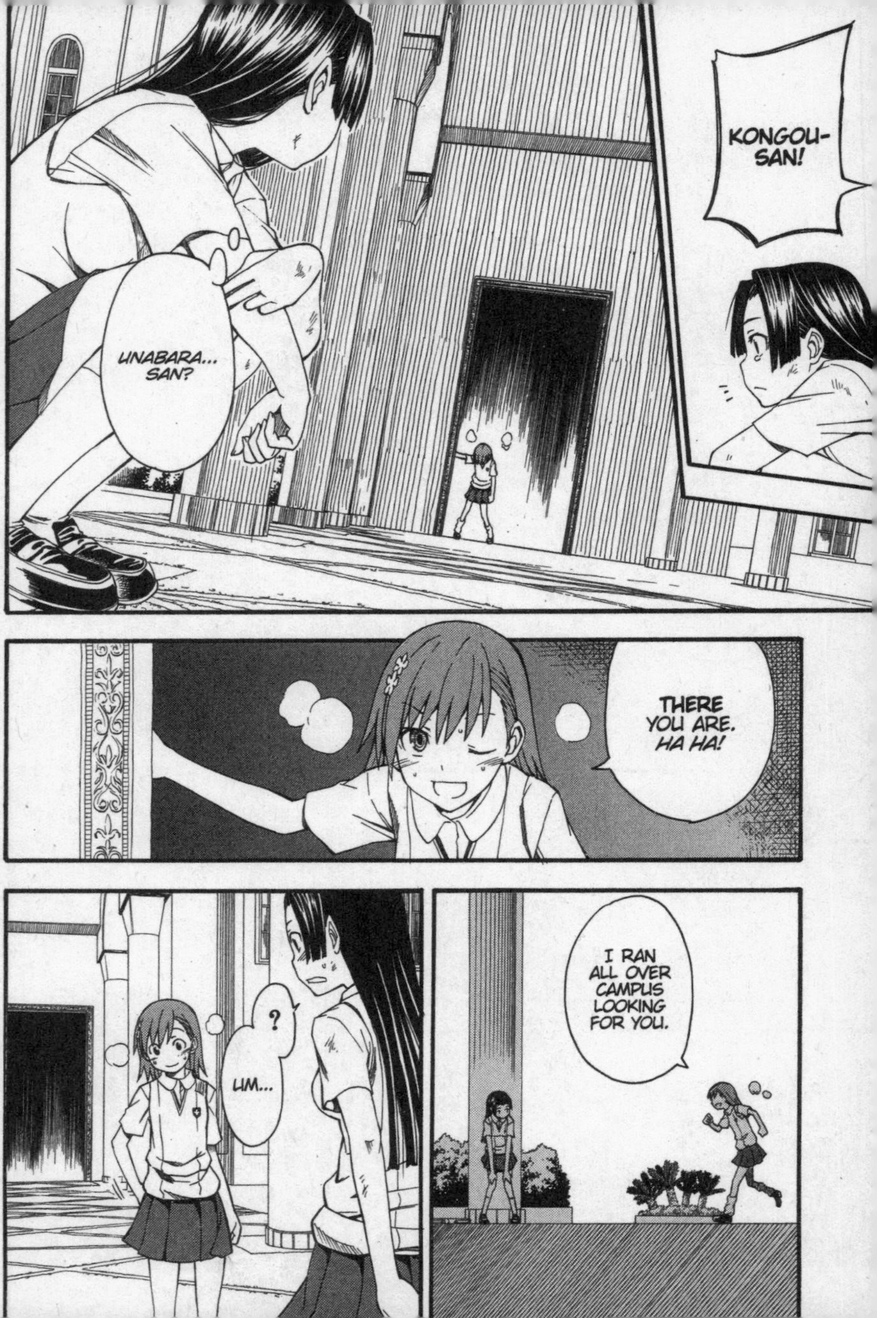
KONGOU-SAN!
UNABARA... SAN?
THERE YOU ARE. HA HA!
I RAN ALL OVER CAMPUS LOOKING FOR YOU.
?
UM...

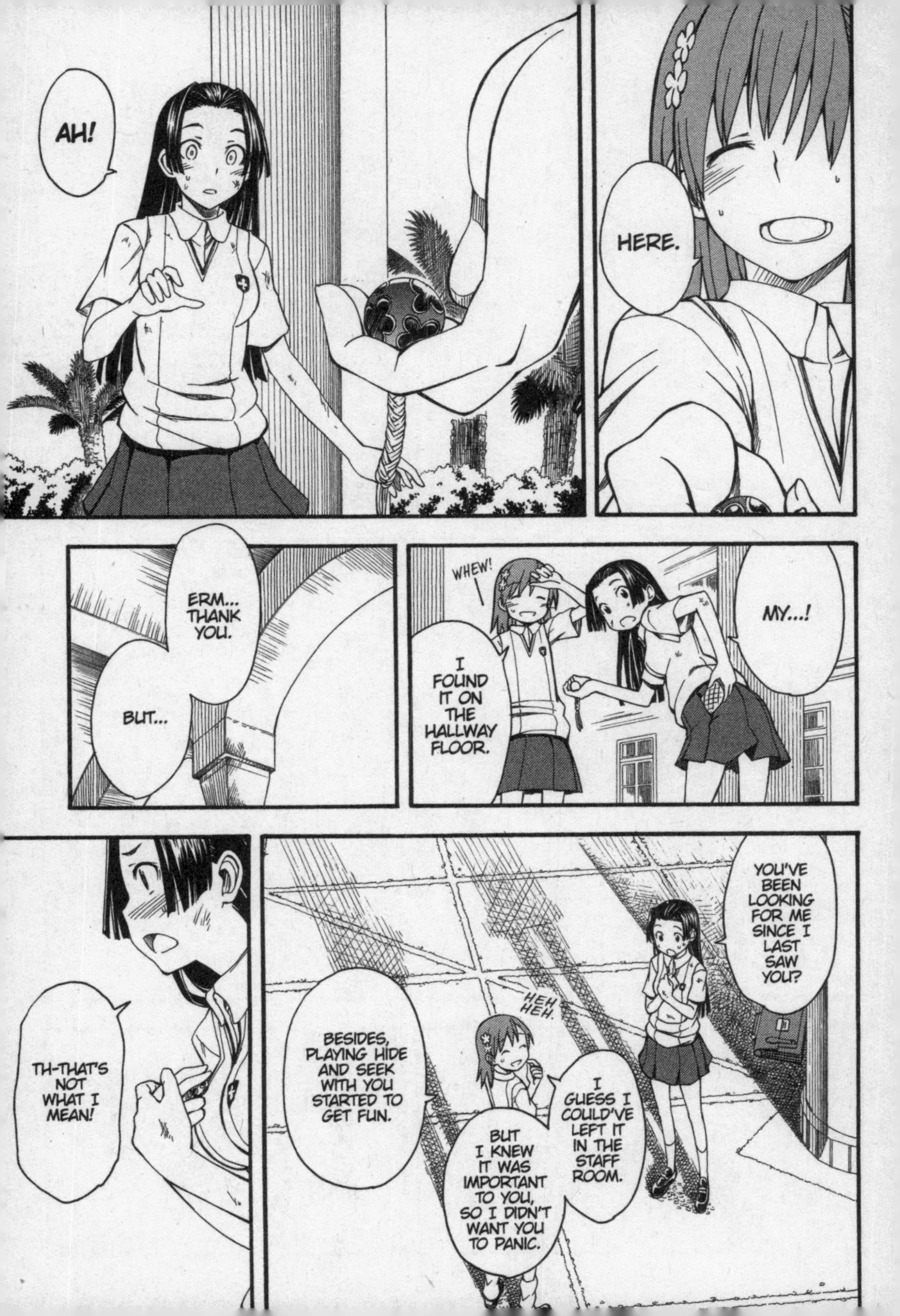
HERE.
AH!
MY...!
WHEW!
I FOUND IT ON THE HALLWAY FLOOR.
ERM... THANK YOU.
BUT...
YOU'VE BEEN LOOKING FOR ME SINCE I LAST SAW YOU?
HEH HEH.
I GUESS I COULD'VE LEFT IT IN THE STAFF ROOM.
BUT I KNEW IT WAS IMPORTANT TO YOU, SO I DIDN'T WANT YOU TO PANIC.
BESIDES, PLAYING HIDE AND SEEK WITH YOU STARTED TO GET FUN.
TH-THAT'S NOT WHAT I MEAN!

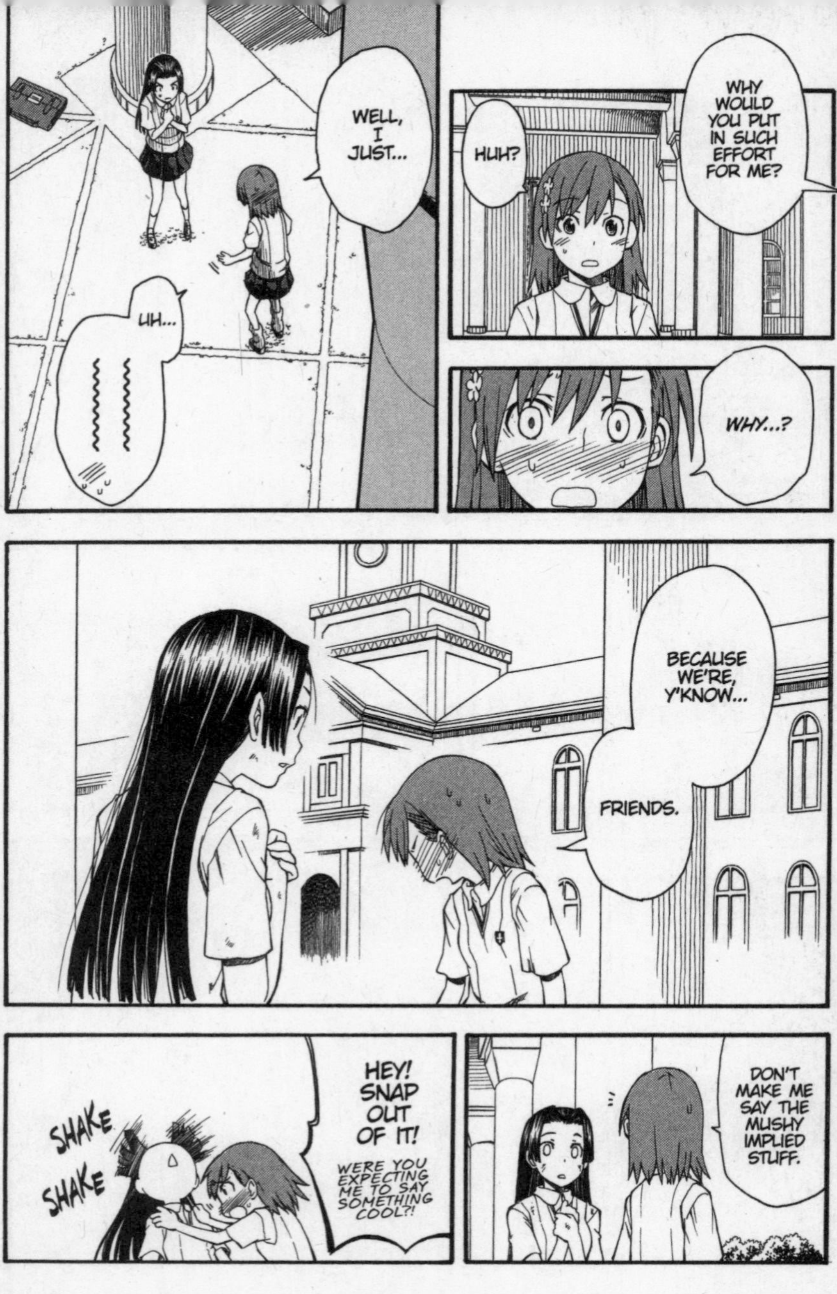
WHY WOULD YOU PUT IN SUCH EFFORT FOR ME?
HUH?
WHY...?
WELL, I JUST...
UH...
BECAUSE WE'RE, Y'KNOW...
FRIENDS.
DON'T MAKE ME SAY THE MUSHY IMPLIED STUFF.
HEY! SNAP OUT OF IT!
WERE YOU EXPECTING ME TO SAY SOMETHING COOL?!
SHAKE
SHAKE

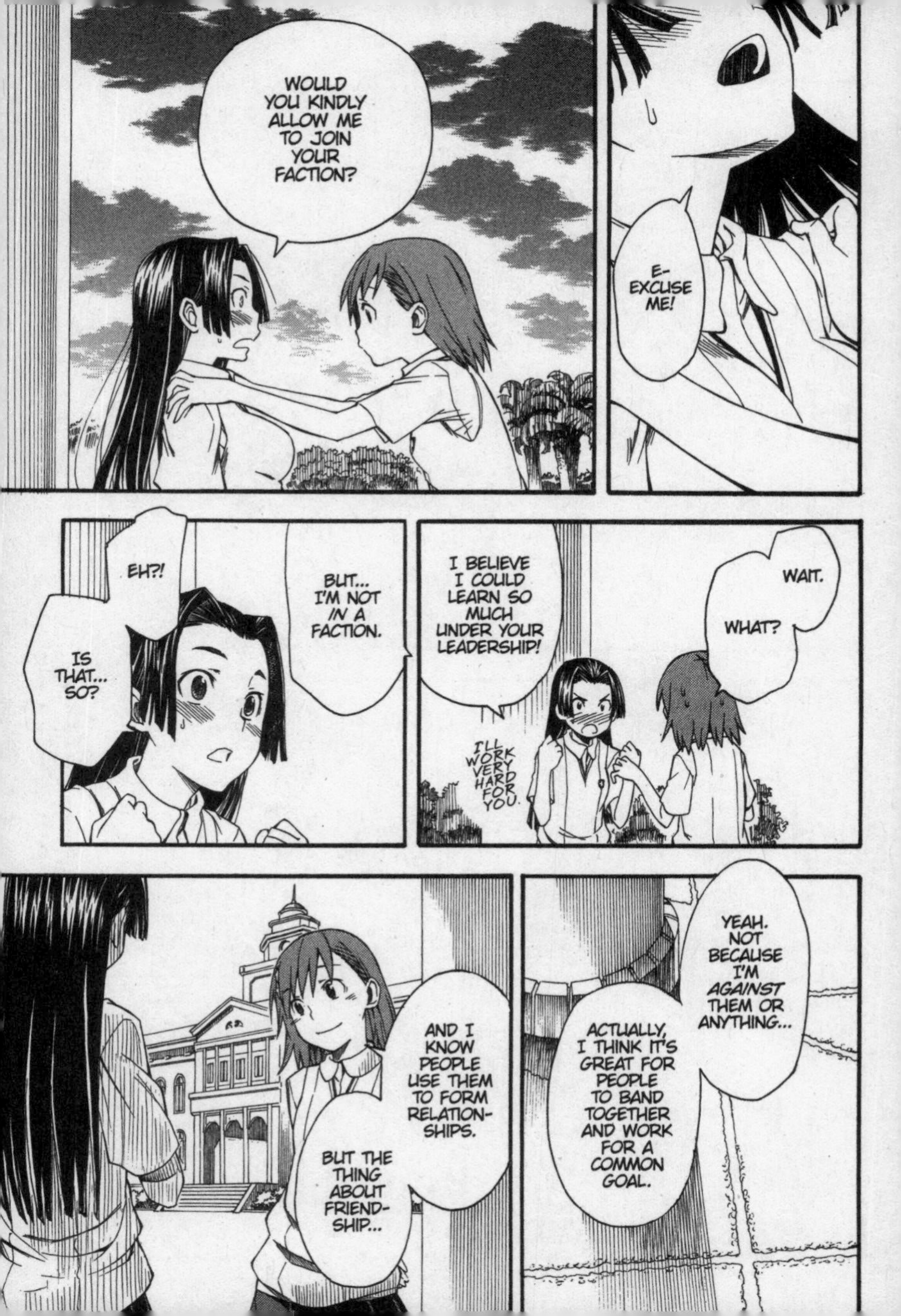
E- EXCUSE ME!
WOULD YOU KINDLY ALLOW ME TO JOIN YOUR FACTION?
WAIT.
WHAT?
I BELIEVE I COULD LEARN SO MUCH UNDER YOUR LEADERSHIP!
I'LL WORK VERY HARD FOR YOU.
BUT... I'M NOT *IN* A FACTION.
EH?!
IS THAT... SO?
YEAH. NOT BECAUSE I'M *AGAINST* THEM OR ANYTHING...
ACTUALLY, I THINK IT'S GREAT FOR PEOPLE TO BAND TOGETHER AND WORK FOR A COMMON GOAL.
AND I KNOW PEOPLE USE THEM TO FORM RELATIONSHIPS.
BUT THE THING ABOUT FRIENDSHIP...

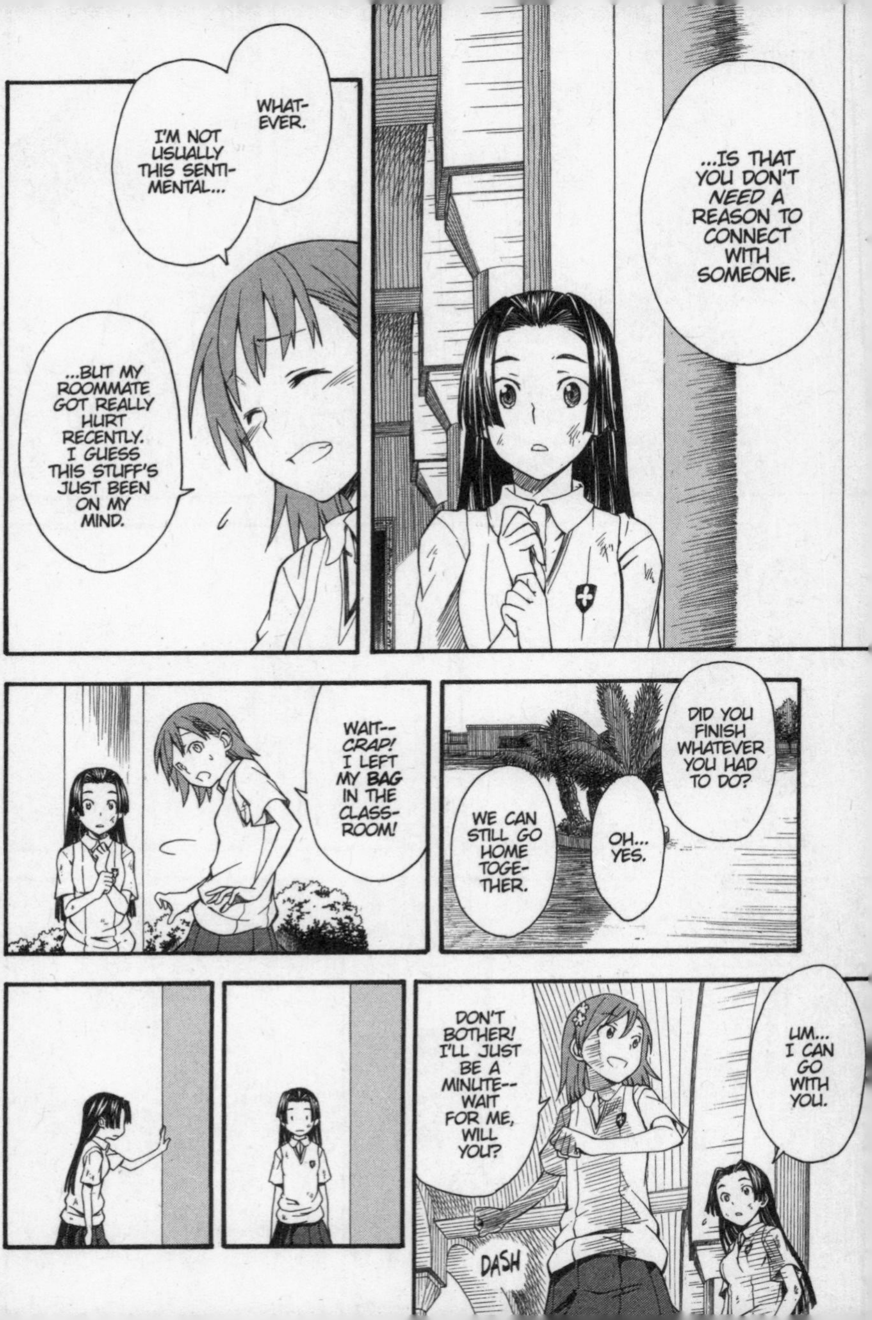
...IS THAT YOU DON'T NEED A REASON TO CONNECT WITH SOMEONE.
WHAT-EVER.
I'M NOT USUALLY THIS SENTI-MENTAL...
...BUT MY ROOMMATE GOT REALLY HURT RECENTLY. I GUESS THIS STUFF'S JUST BEEN ON MY MIND.
DID YOU FINISH WHATEVER YOU HAD TO DO?
OH... YES.
WE CAN STILL GO HOME TOGE-THER.
WAIT-- CRAP! I LEFT MY BAG IN THE CLASS-ROOM!
UM... I CAN GO WITH YOU.
DON'T BOTHER! I'LL JUST BE A MINUTE-- WAIT FOR ME, WILL YOU?
DASH

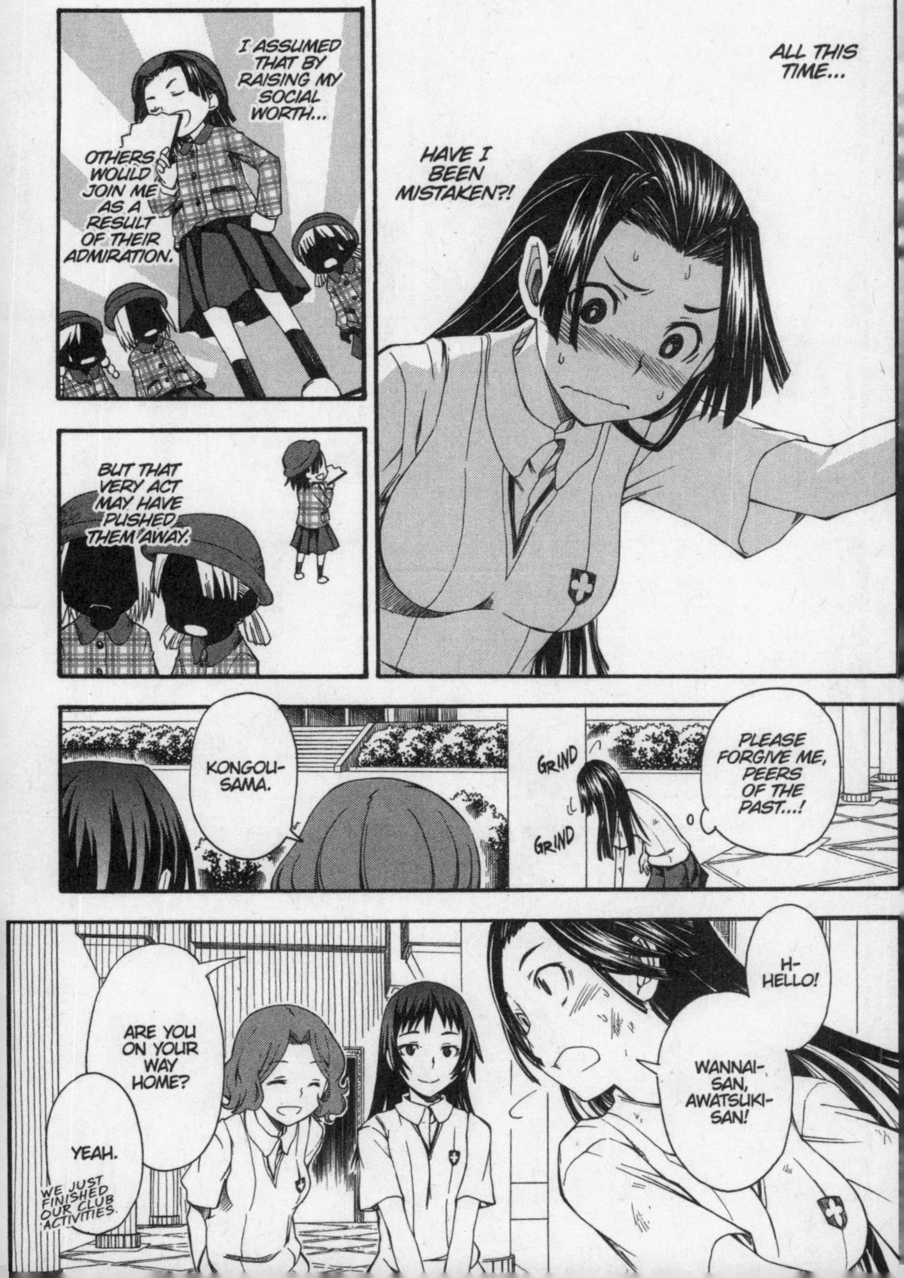
ALL THIS TIME...
HAVE I BEEN MISTAKEN?!
I ASSUMED THAT BY RAISING MY SOCIAL WORTH...
OTHERS WOULD JOIN ME AS A RESULT OF THEIR ADMIRATION.
BUT THAT VERY ACT MAY HAVE PUSHED THEM AWAY.
GRIND
GRIND
PLEASE FORGIVE ME, PEERS OF THE PAST...!
KONGOU-SAMA.
H-HELLO!
WANNAI-SAN, AWATSUKI-SAN!
ARE YOU ON YOUR WAY HOME?
YEAH.
WE JUST FINISHED OUR CLUB ACTIVITIES.

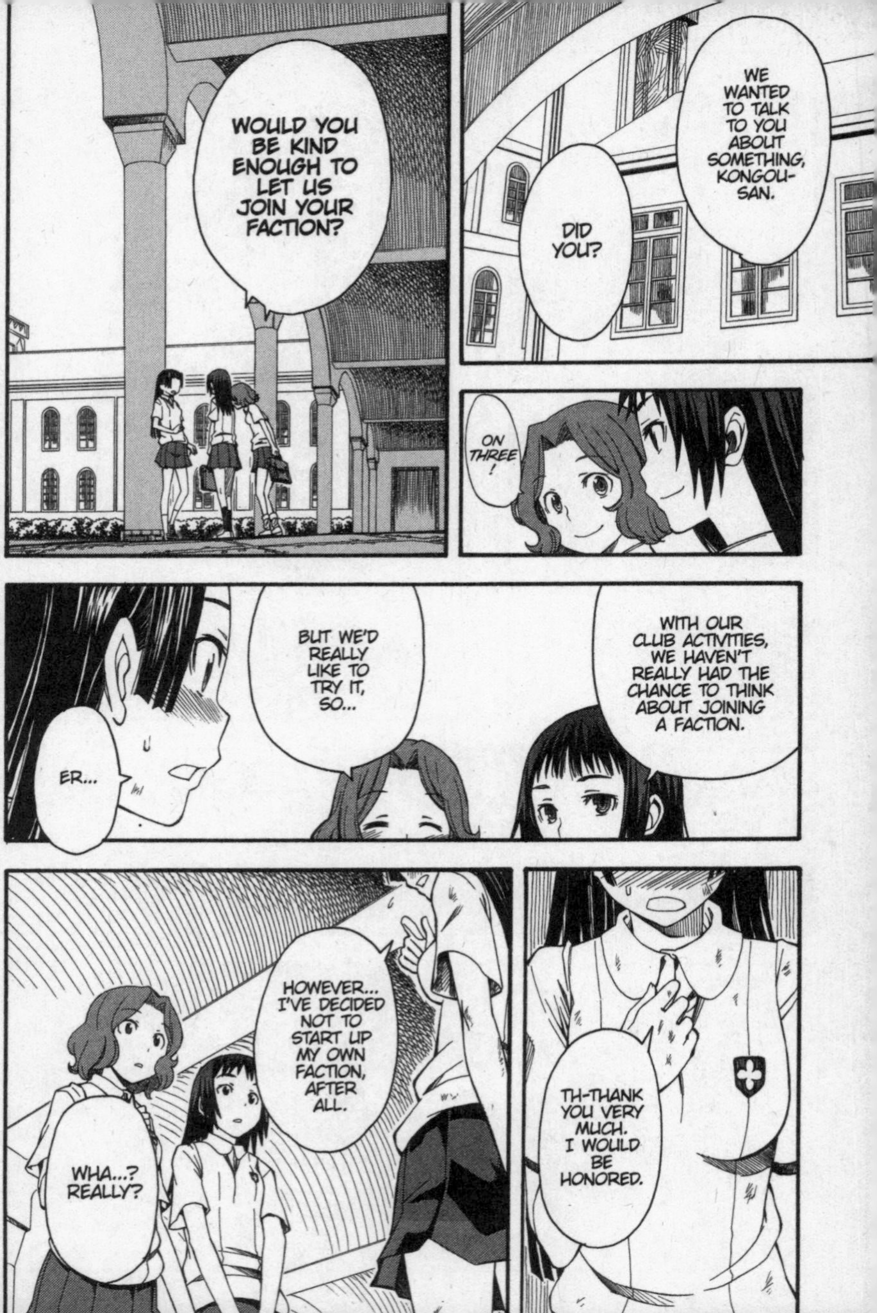
WE WANTED TO TALK TO YOU ABOUT SOMETHING, KONGOU-SAN.
DID YOU?
ON THREE!
WOULD YOU BE KIND ENOUGH TO LET US JOIN YOUR FACTION?
WITH OUR CLUB ACTIVITIES, WE HAVEN'T REALLY HAD THE CHANCE TO THINK ABOUT JOINING A FACTION.
BUT WE'D REALLY LIKE TO TRY IT, SO...
ER...
TH-THANK YOU VERY MUCH. I WOULD BE HONORED.
HOWEVER... I'VE DECIDED NOT TO START UP MY OWN FACTION, AFTER ALL.
WHA...? REALLY?

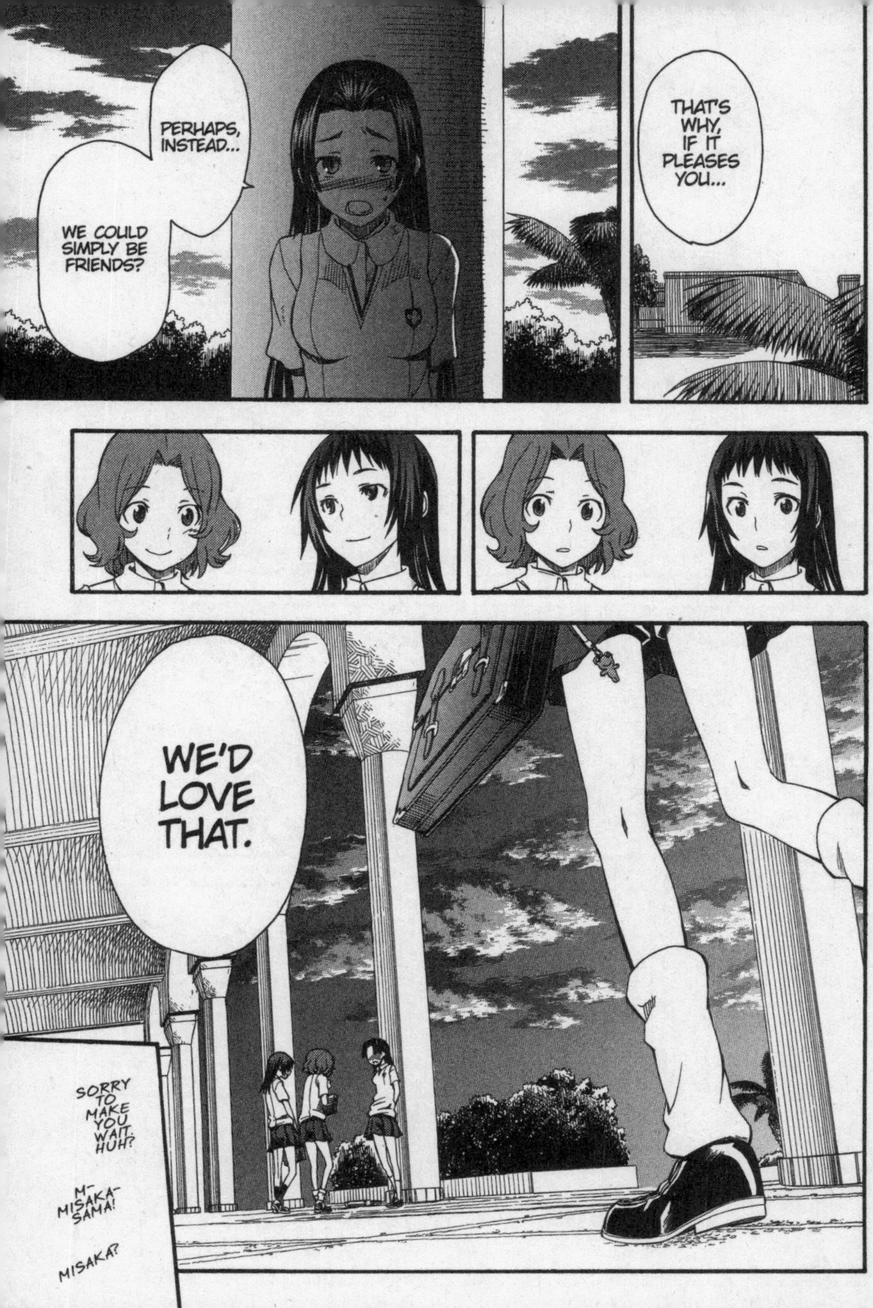
THAT'S WHY, IF IT PLEASES YOU...
PERHAPS, INSTEAD...
WE COULD SIMPLY BE FRIENDS?
WE'D LOVE THAT.
SORRY TO MAKE YOU WAIT. HUH?
M-MISAKA-SAMA!
MISAKA?

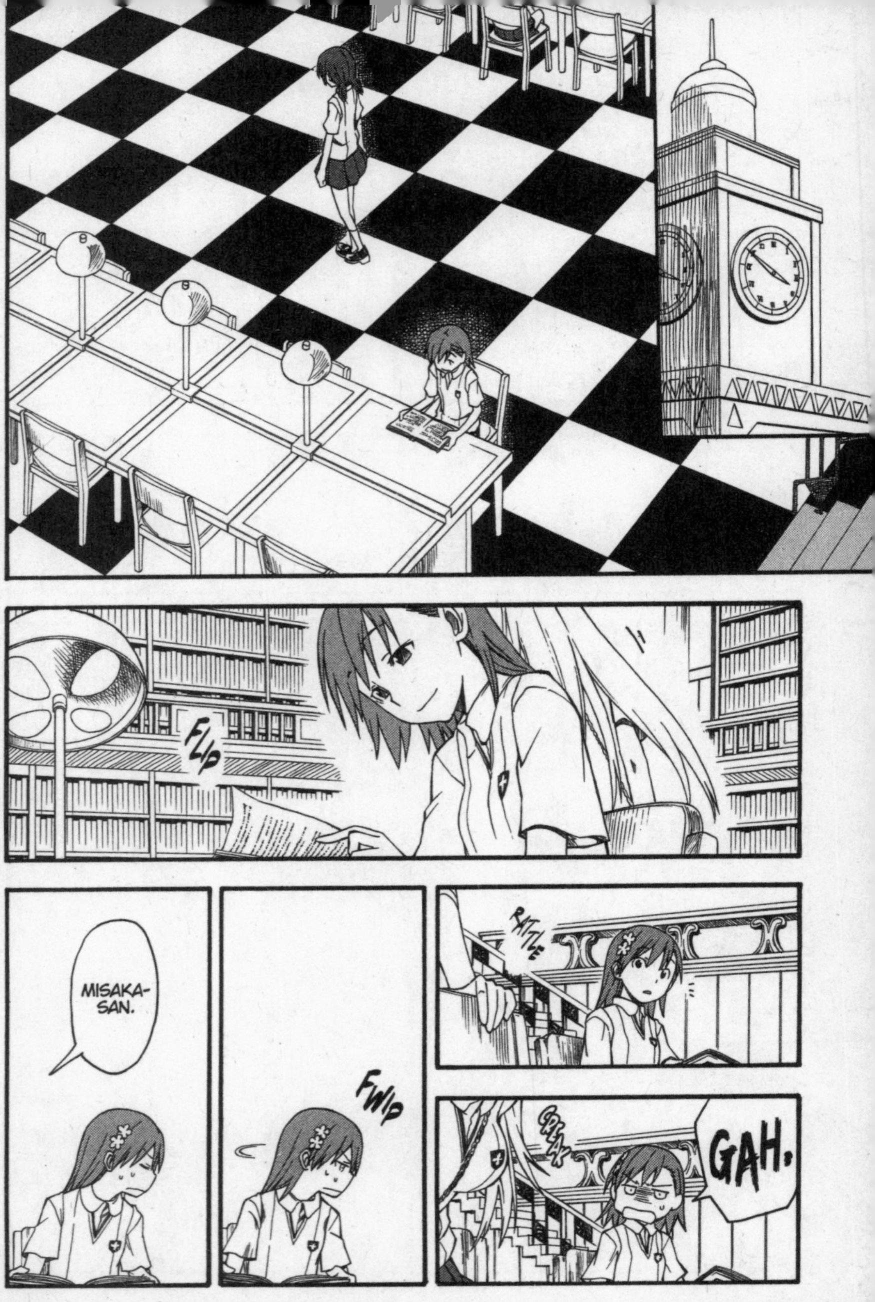
FLIP
RATTLE
CREAK
GAH.
FWIP
MISAKA-SAN.

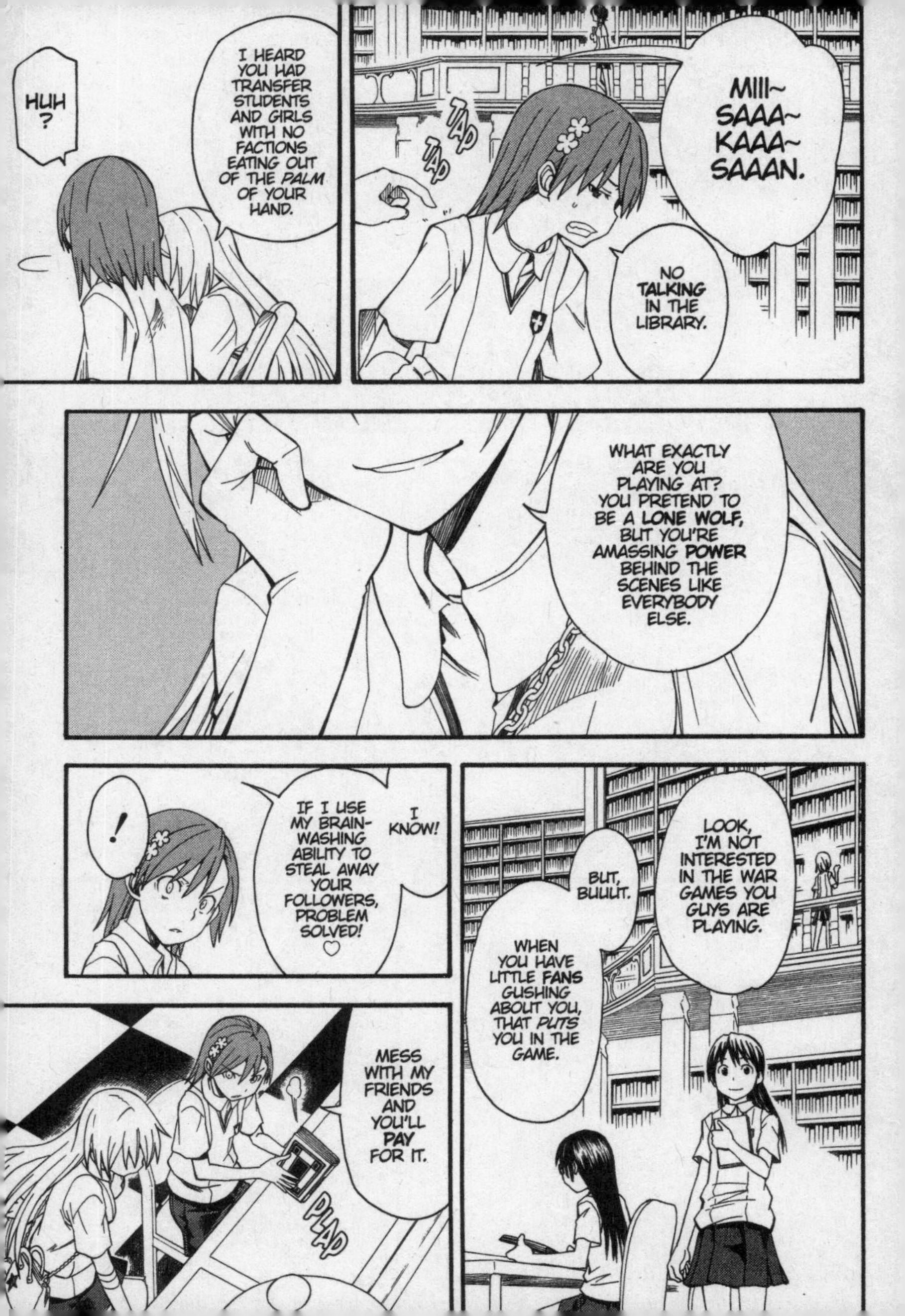
MIII~ SAAA~ KAAA~ SAAAN.
TAP TAP
NO TALKING IN THE LIBRARY.
I HEARD YOU HAD TRANSFER STUDENTS AND GIRLS WITH NO FACTIONS EATING OUT OF THE *PALM* OF YOUR HAND.
HUH?
WHAT EXACTLY ARE YOU PLAYING AT? YOU PRETEND TO BE A **LONE WOLF**, BUT YOU'RE AMASSING **POWER** BEHIND THE SCENES LIKE EVERYBODY ELSE.
LOOK, I'M NOT INTERESTED IN THE WAR GAMES YOU GUYS ARE PLAYING.
BUT, BUUUT.
WHEN YOU HAVE LITTLE **FANS** GUSHING ABOUT YOU, THAT *PUTS* YOU IN THE GAME.
I KNOW!
IF I USE MY BRAIN-WASHING ABILITY TO STEAL AWAY YOUR FOLLOWERS, PROBLEM SOLVED! ♡
!
MESS WITH MY FRIENDS AND YOU'LL **PAY** FOR IT.
PLAP

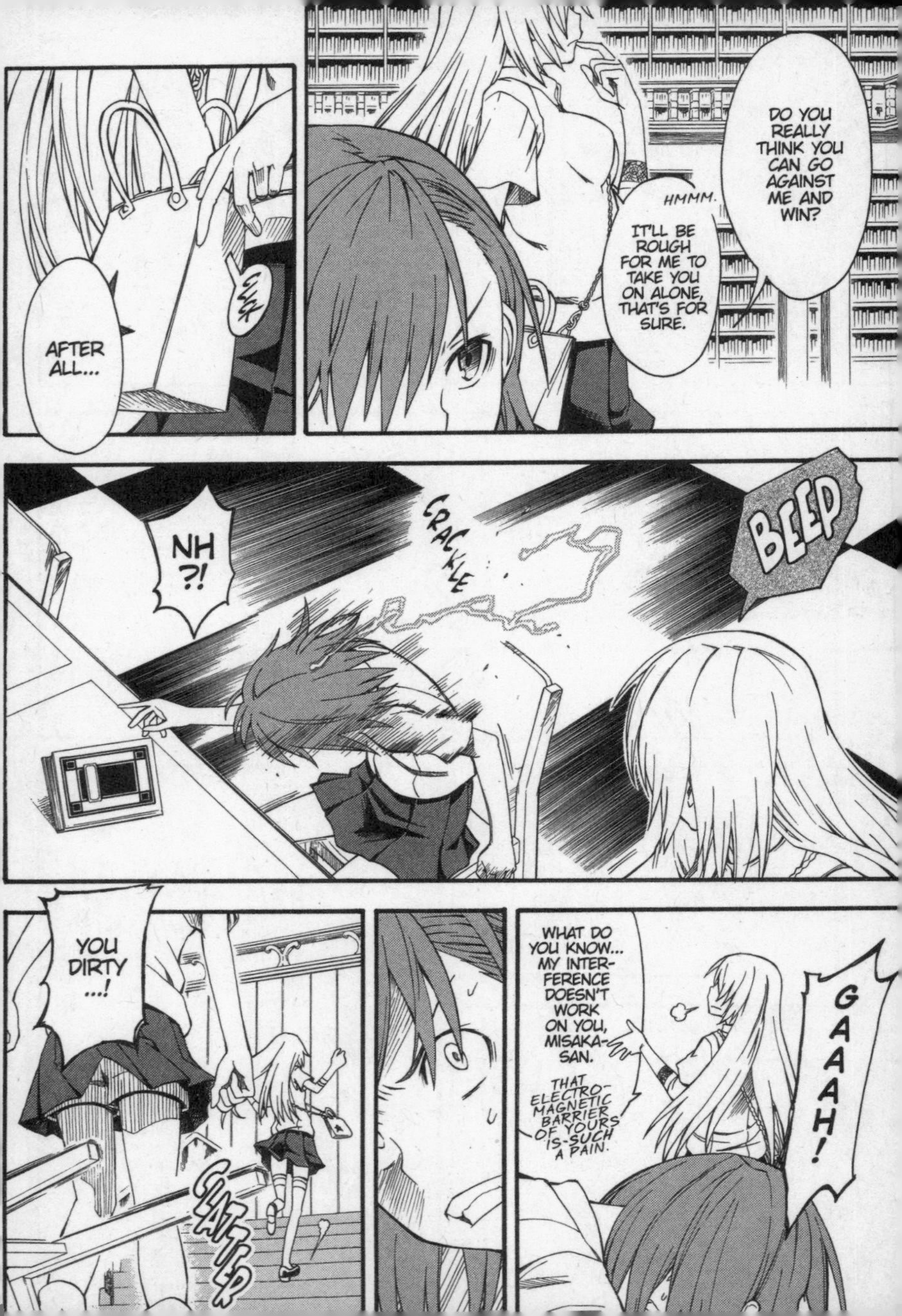
DO YOU REALLY THINK YOU CAN GO AGAINST ME AND WIN?
HMMM.
IT'LL BE ROUGH FOR ME TO TAKE YOU ON ALONE, THAT'S FOR SURE.
CLICK
AFTER ALL...
BEEP
CRACKLE
NH ?!
GAAAH!
WHAT DO YOU KNOW... MY INTERFERENCE DOESN'T WORK ON YOU, MISAKA-SAN.
THAT ELECTROMAGNETIC BARRIER OF YOURS IS SUCH A PAIN.
YOU DIRTY ...!
CLATTER

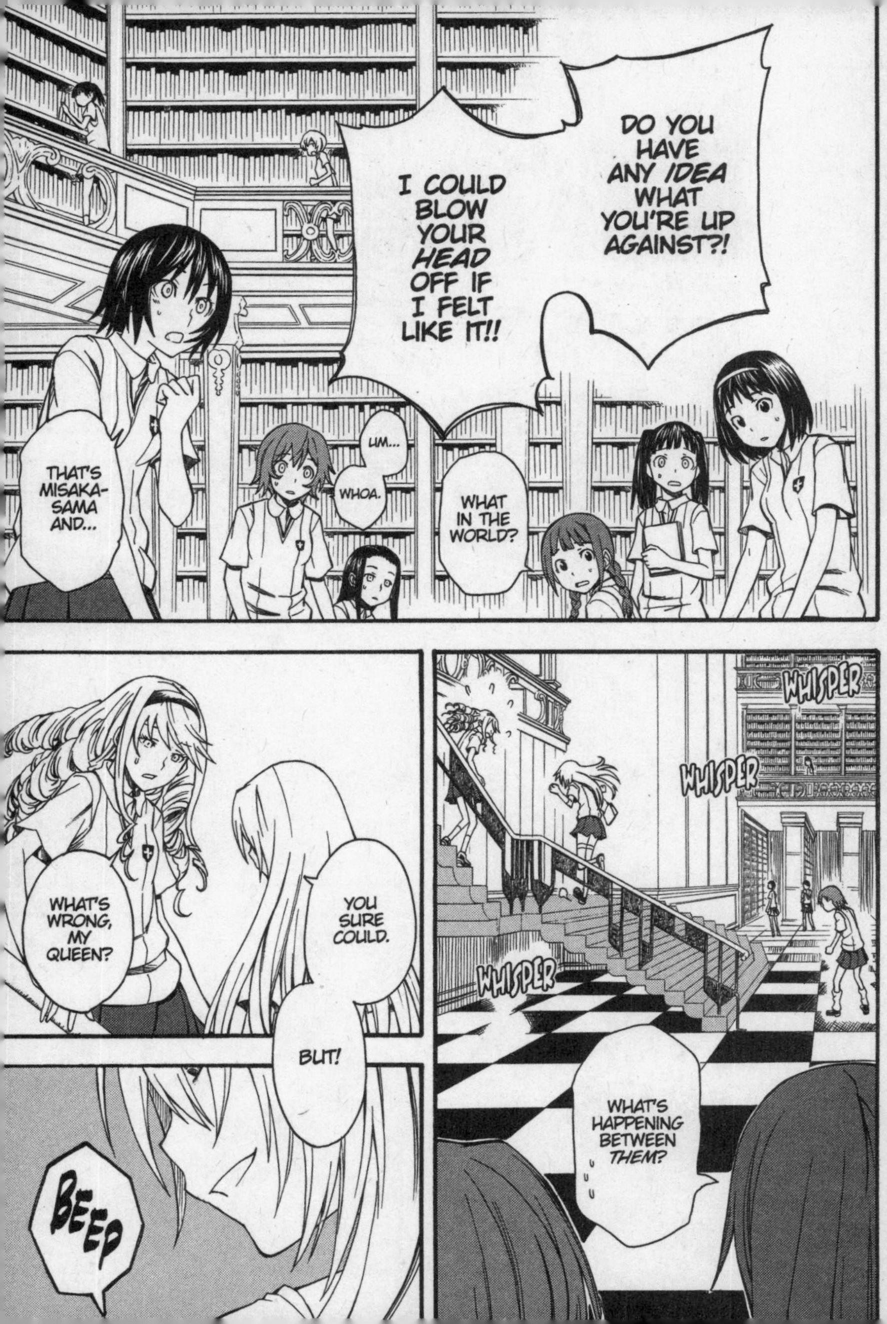
DO YOU HAVE ANY *IDEA* WHAT YOU'RE UP AGAINST?!
I COULD BLOW YOUR *HEAD* OFF IF I FELT LIKE IT!!
WHAT IN THE WORLD?
UM...
WHOA.
THAT'S MISAKA-SAMA AND...
WHISPER
WHISPER
WHISPER
YOU SURE COULD.
WHAT'S WRONG, MY QUEEN?
WHAT'S HAPPENING BETWEEN *THEM*?
BUT!
BEEP

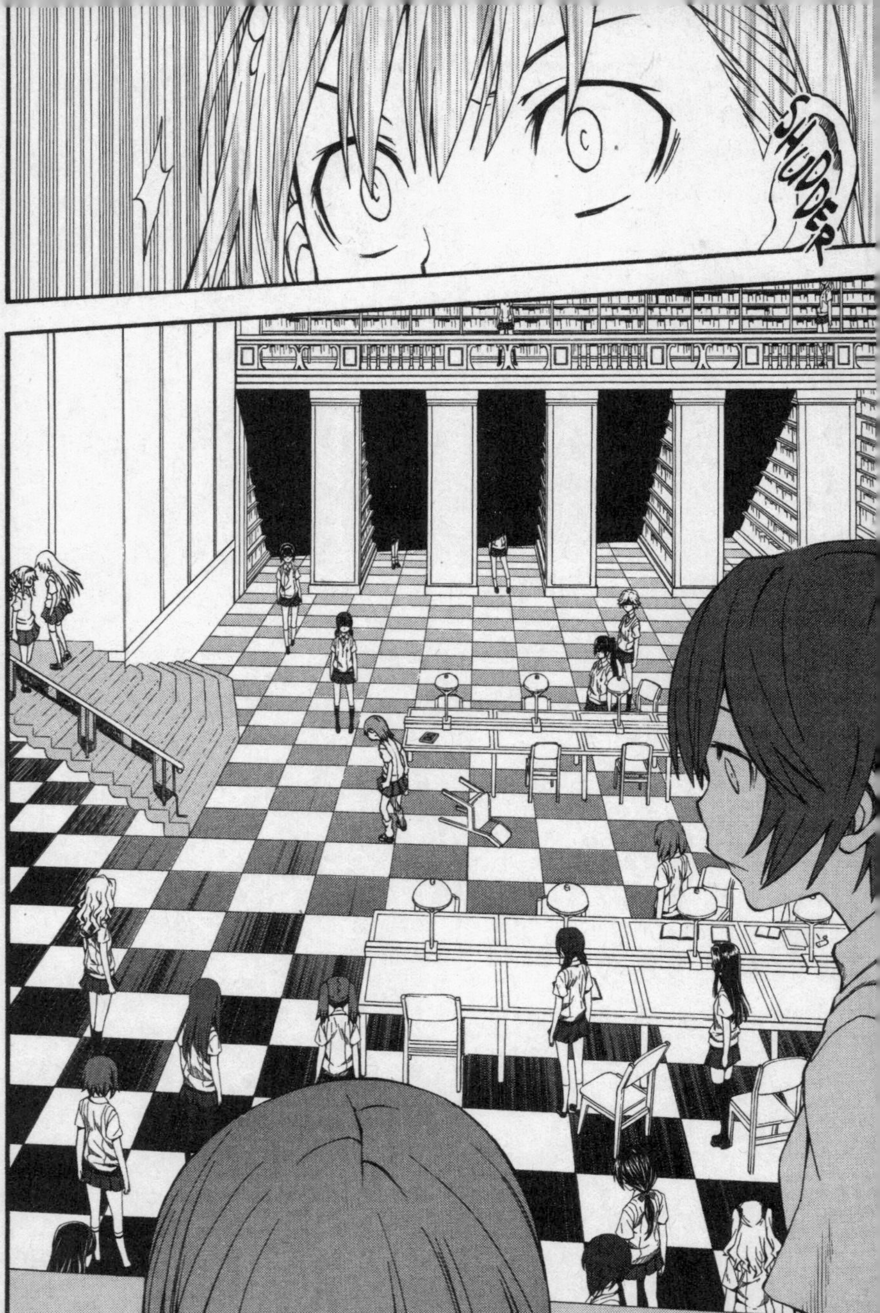
SHUDDER

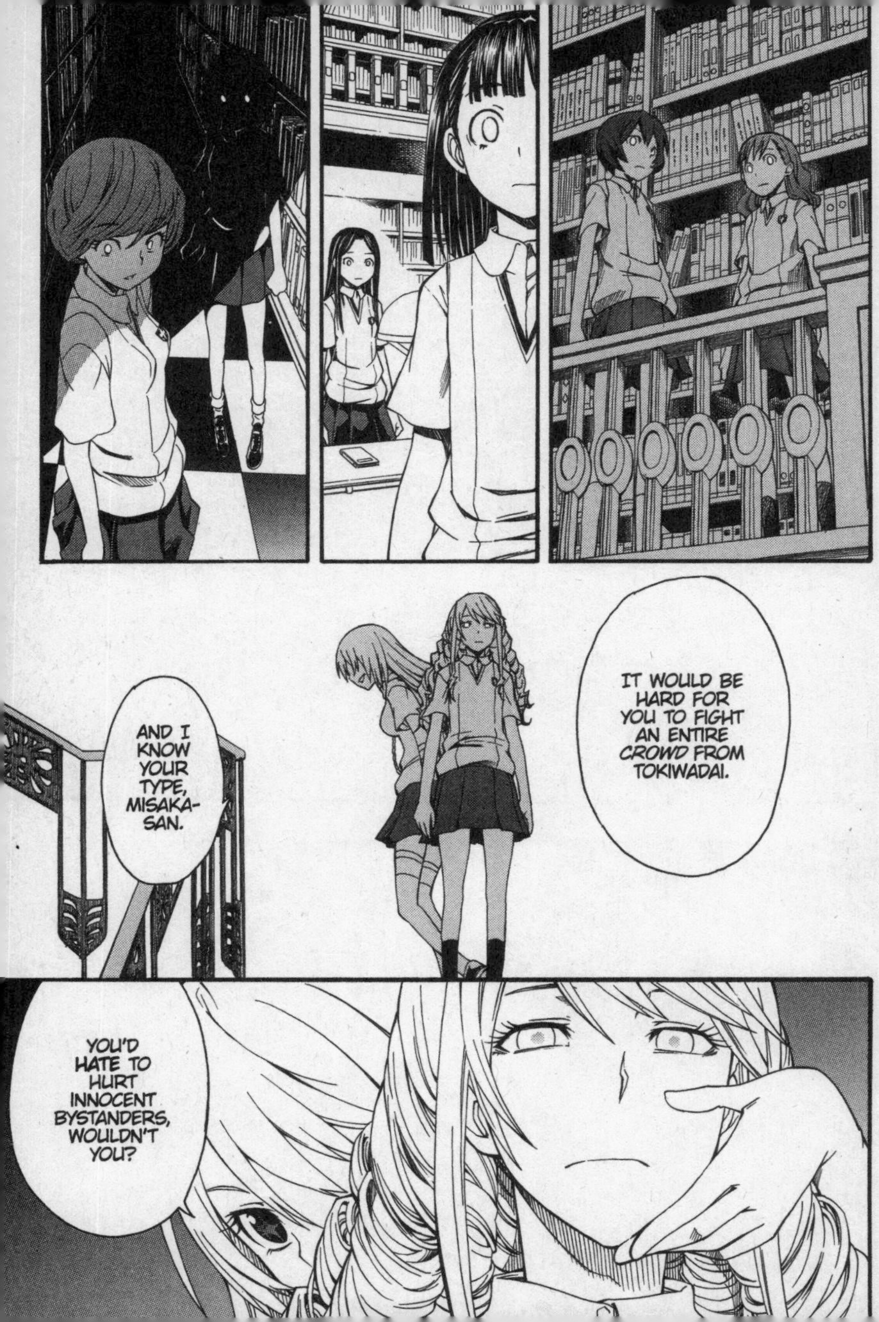
IT WOULD BE HARD FOR YOU TO FIGHT AN ENTIRE *CROWD* FROM TOKIWADAI.
AND I KNOW YOUR TYPE, MISAKA-SAN.
YOU'D HATE TO HURT INNOCENT BYSTANDERS, WOULDN'T YOU?

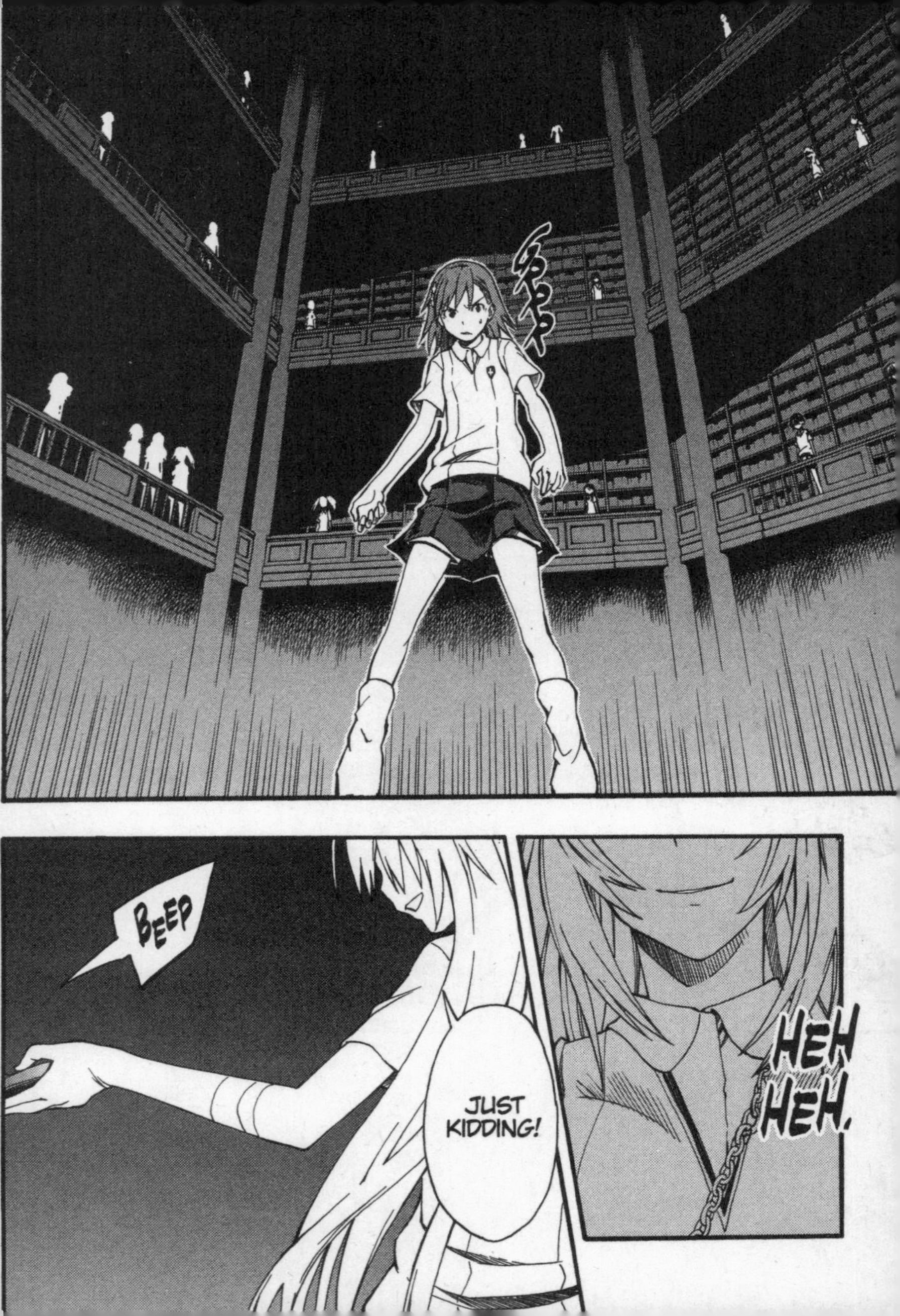
HEH HEH.
BEEP
JUST KIDDING!

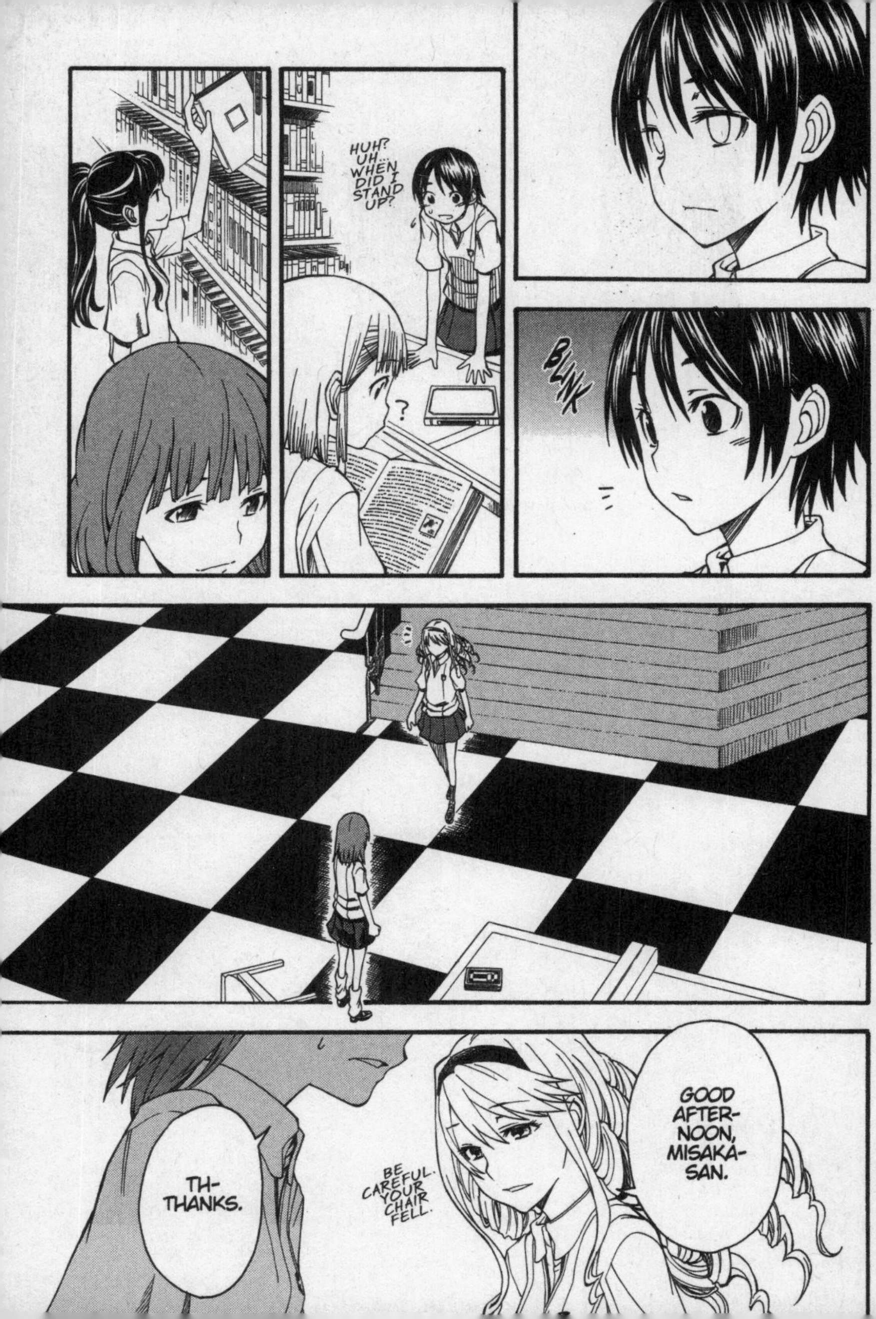
BLINK
HUH? UH... WHEN DID I STAND UP?
?
GOOD AFTERNOON, MISAKA-SAN.
BE CAREFUL. YOUR CHAIR FELL.
TH-THANKS.

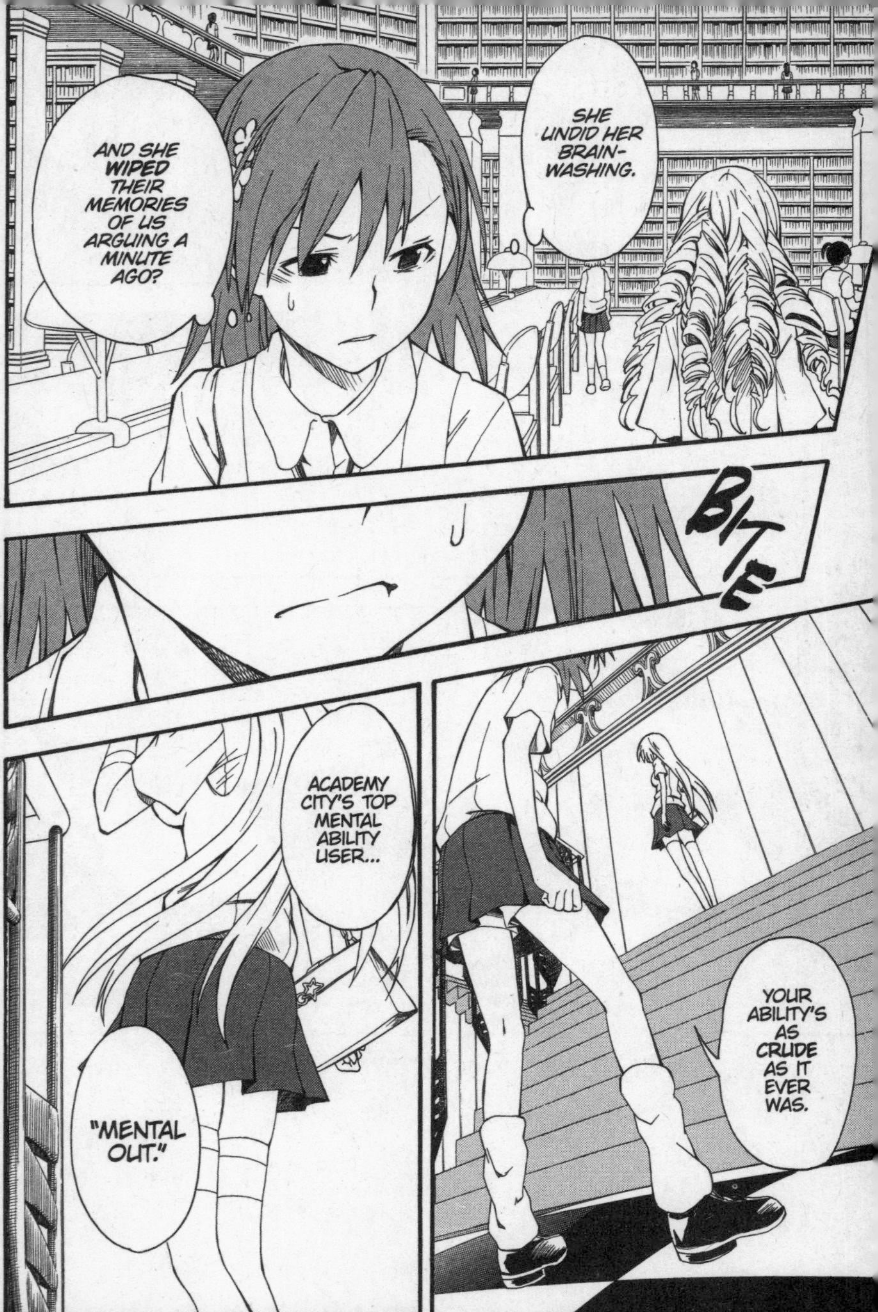
SHE UNDID HER BRAIN-WASHING.
AND SHE WIPED THEIR MEMORIES OF US ARGUING A MINUTE AGO?
BITE
YOUR ABILITY'S AS CRUDE AS IT EVER WAS.
ACADEMY CITY'S TOP MENTAL ABILITY USER...
"MENTAL OUT."

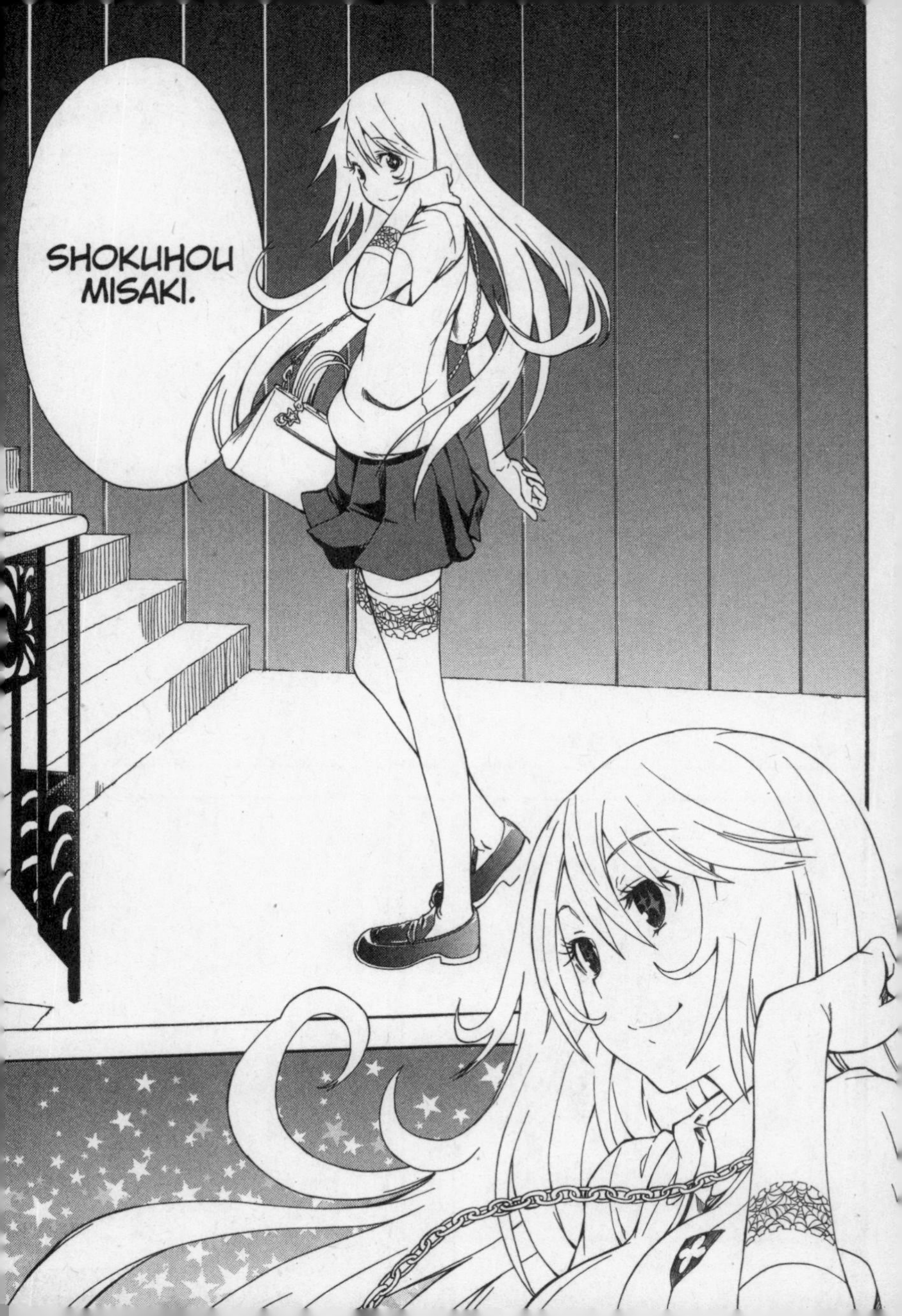
SHOKUHOU MISAKI.

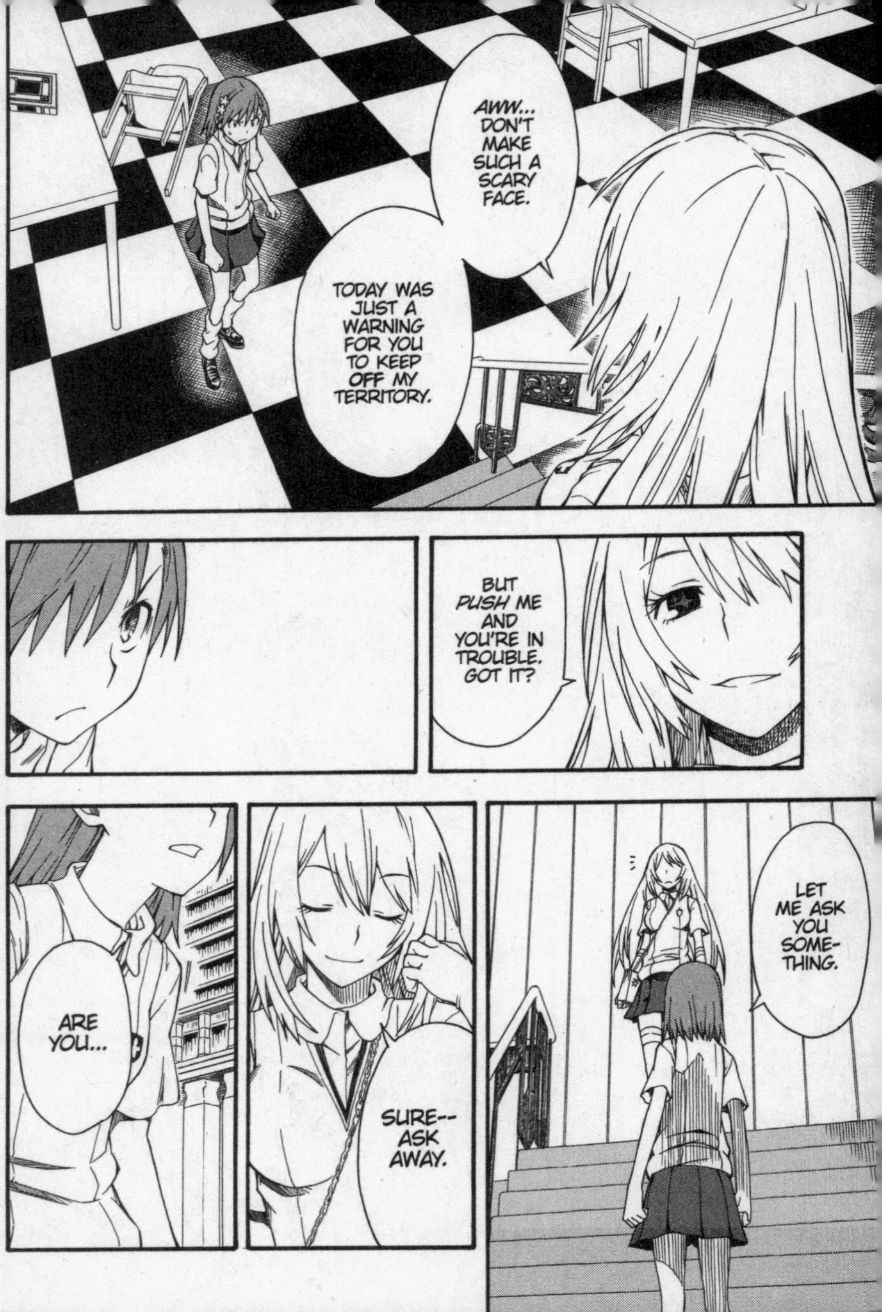
AWW... DON'T MAKE SUCH A SCARY FACE.
TODAY WAS JUST A WARNING FOR YOU TO KEEP OFF MY TERRITORY.
BUT *PUSH* ME AND YOU'RE IN TROUBLE. GOT IT?
LET ME ASK YOU SOME-THING.
SURE-- ASK AWAY.
ARE YOU...

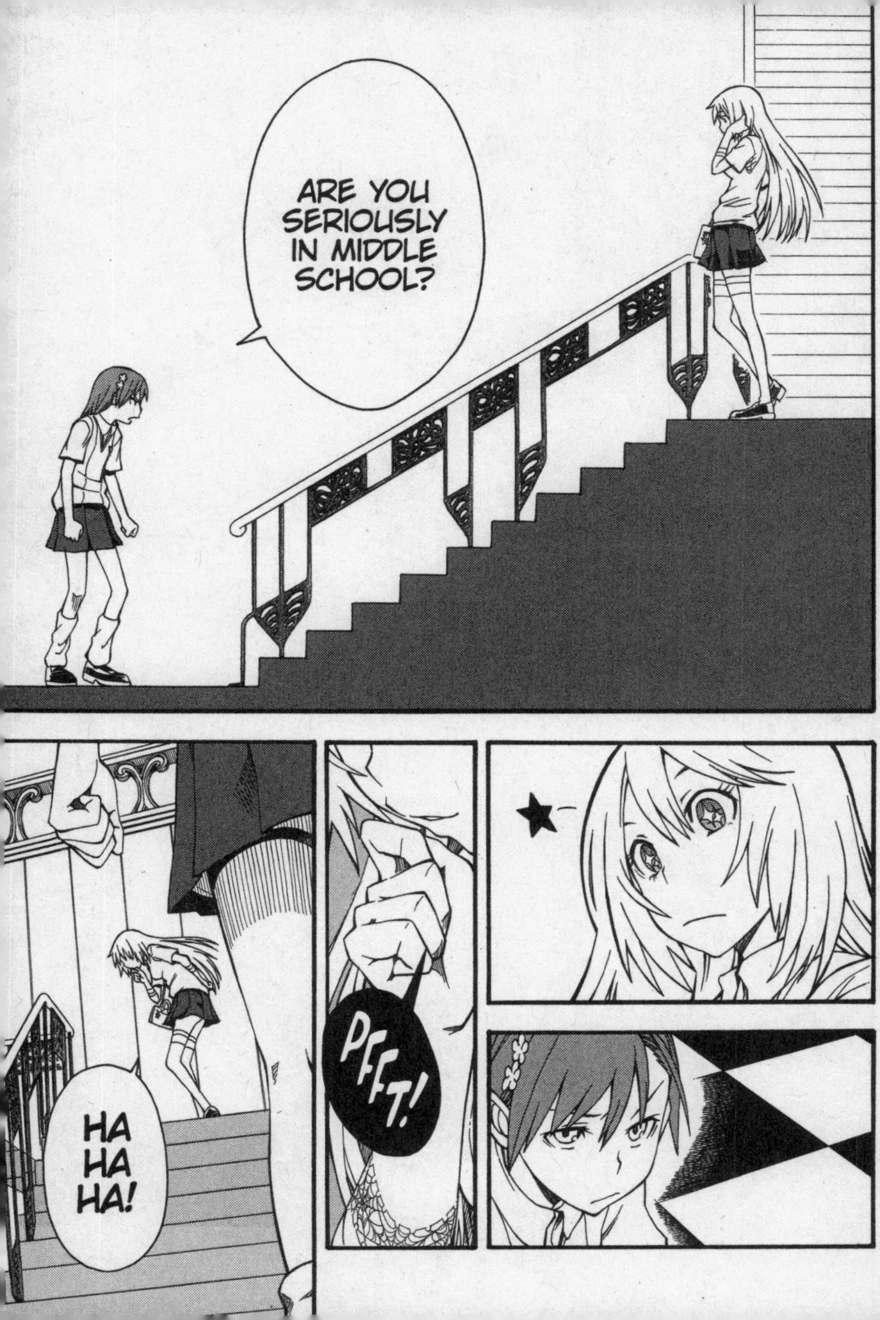
ARE YOU SERIOUSLY IN MIDDLE SCHOOL?
PFFT!
HA HA HA!

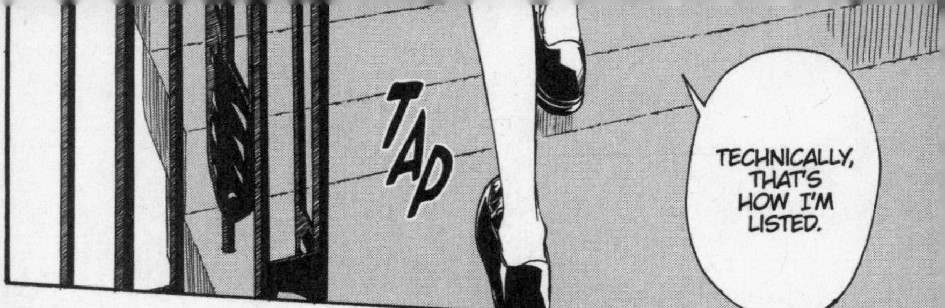
TECHNICALLY, THAT'S HOW I'M LISTED.
TAP
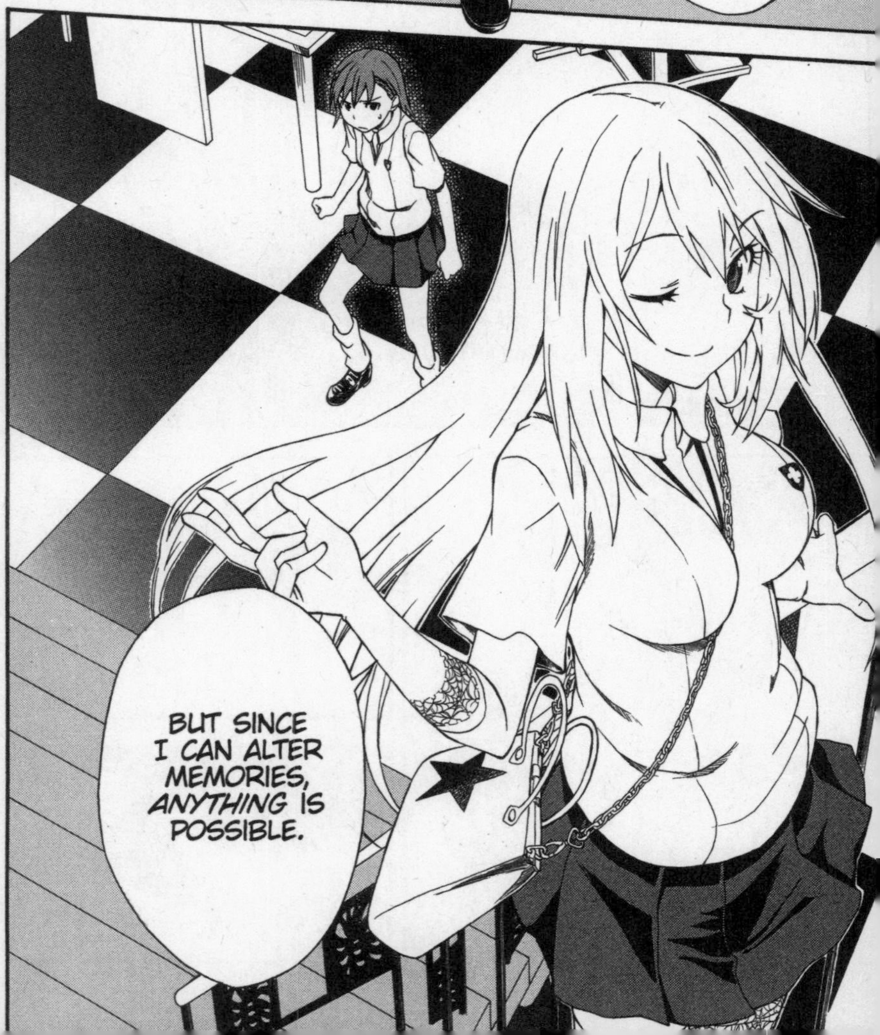
BUT SINCE I CAN ALTER MEMORIES, *ANYTHING* IS POSSIBLE.

A Certain SCIENTIFIC Railgun

A Certain Chest Measurement Ranking

LET ME ASK YOU SOMETHING.

SURE-- ASK AWAY.

BOIIING

ARE YOU SERIOUSLY IN MIDDLE SCHOOL?

DOOM

?

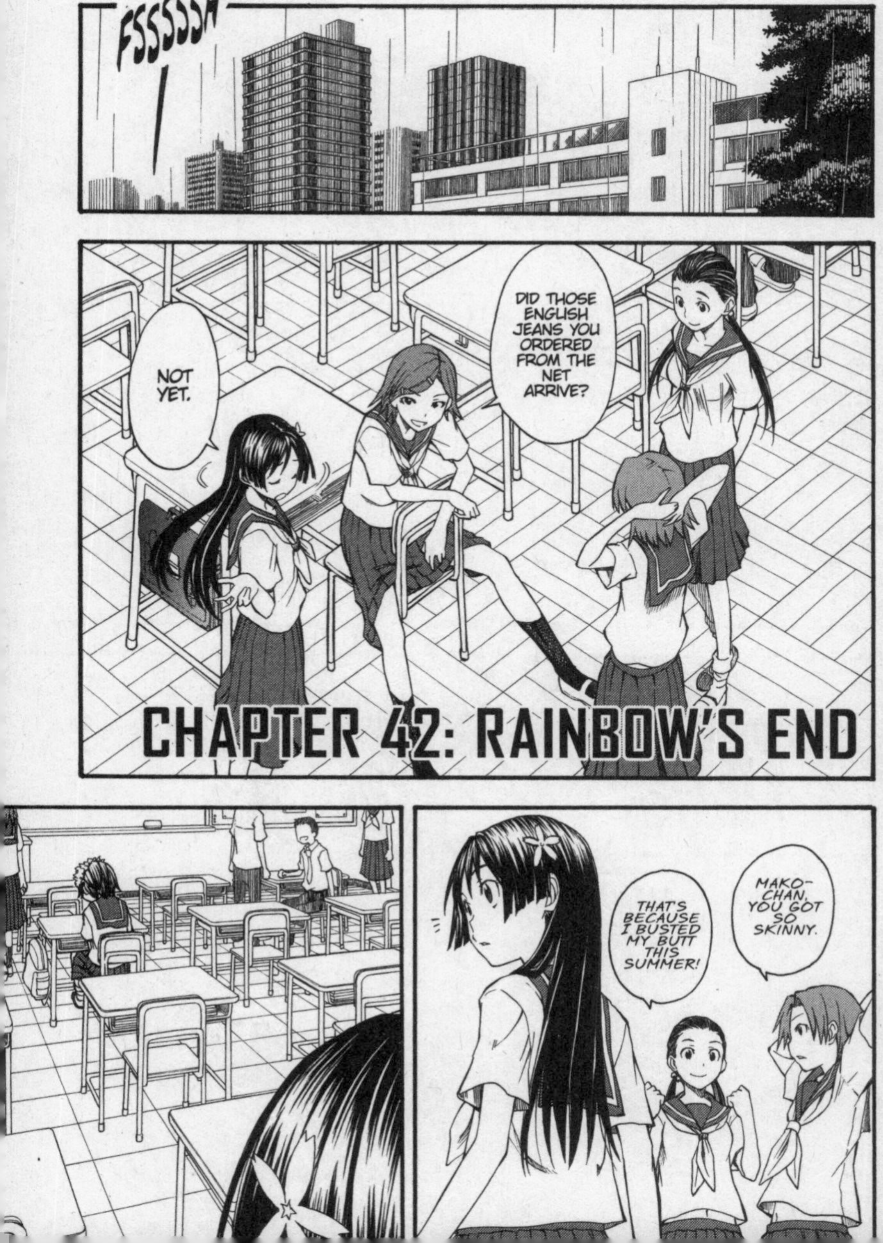
FSSSSSH
DID THOSE ENGLISH JEANS YOU ORDERED FROM THE NET ARRIVE?
NOT YET.
CHAPTER 42: RAINBOW'S END
MAKO-CHAN, YOU GOT SO SKINNY.
THAT'S BECAUSE I BUSTED MY BUTT THIS SUMMER!

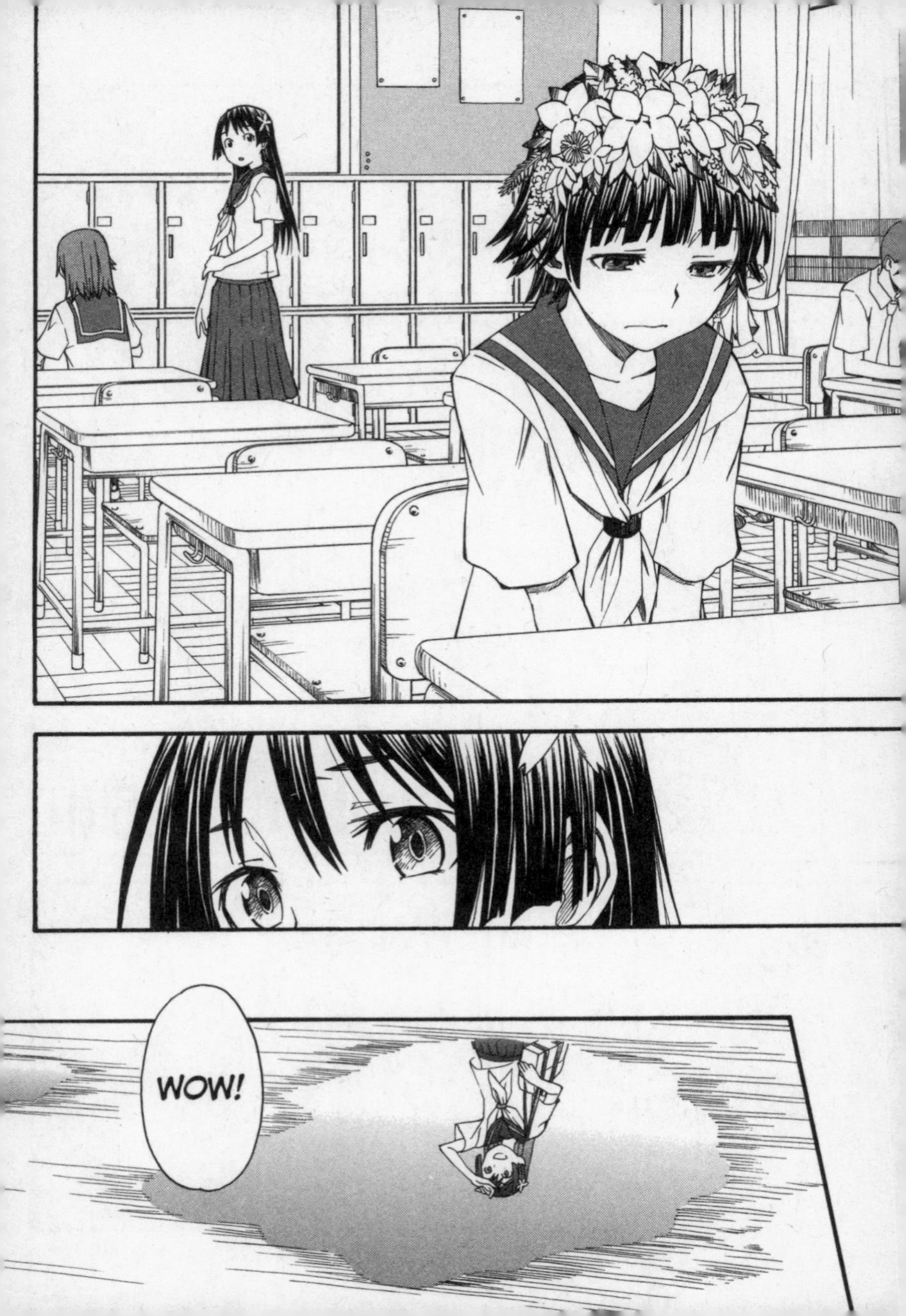
WOW!

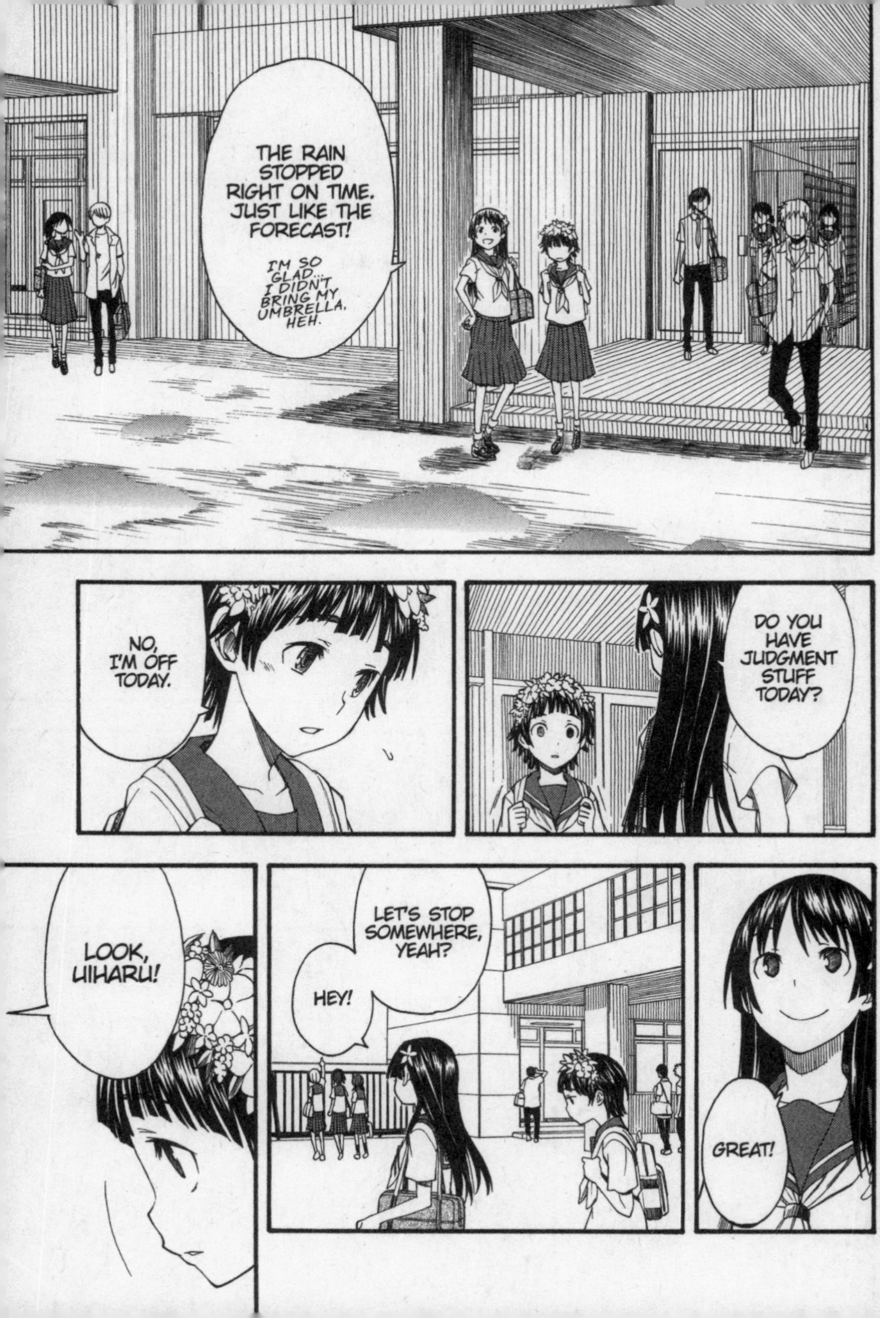
THE RAIN STOPPED RIGHT ON TIME. JUST LIKE THE FORECAST!
I'M SO GLAD... I DIDN'T BRING MY UMBRELLA, HEH.
DO YOU HAVE JUDGMENT STUFF TODAY?
NO, I'M OFF TODAY.
GREAT!
LET'S STOP SOMEWHERE, YEAH?
HEY!
LOOK, UIHARU!

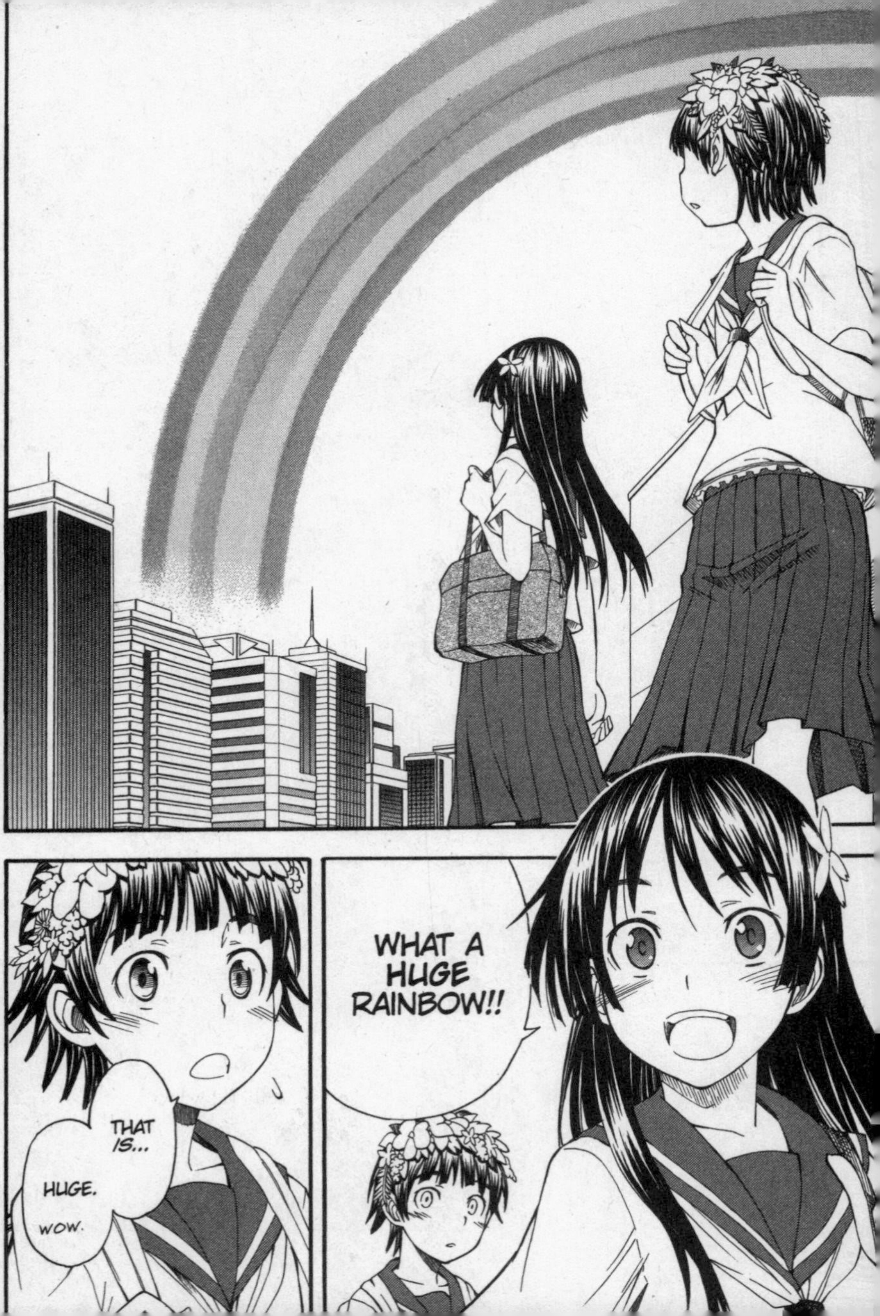
WHAT A HUGE RAINBOW!!
THAT IS... HUGE.
WOW.

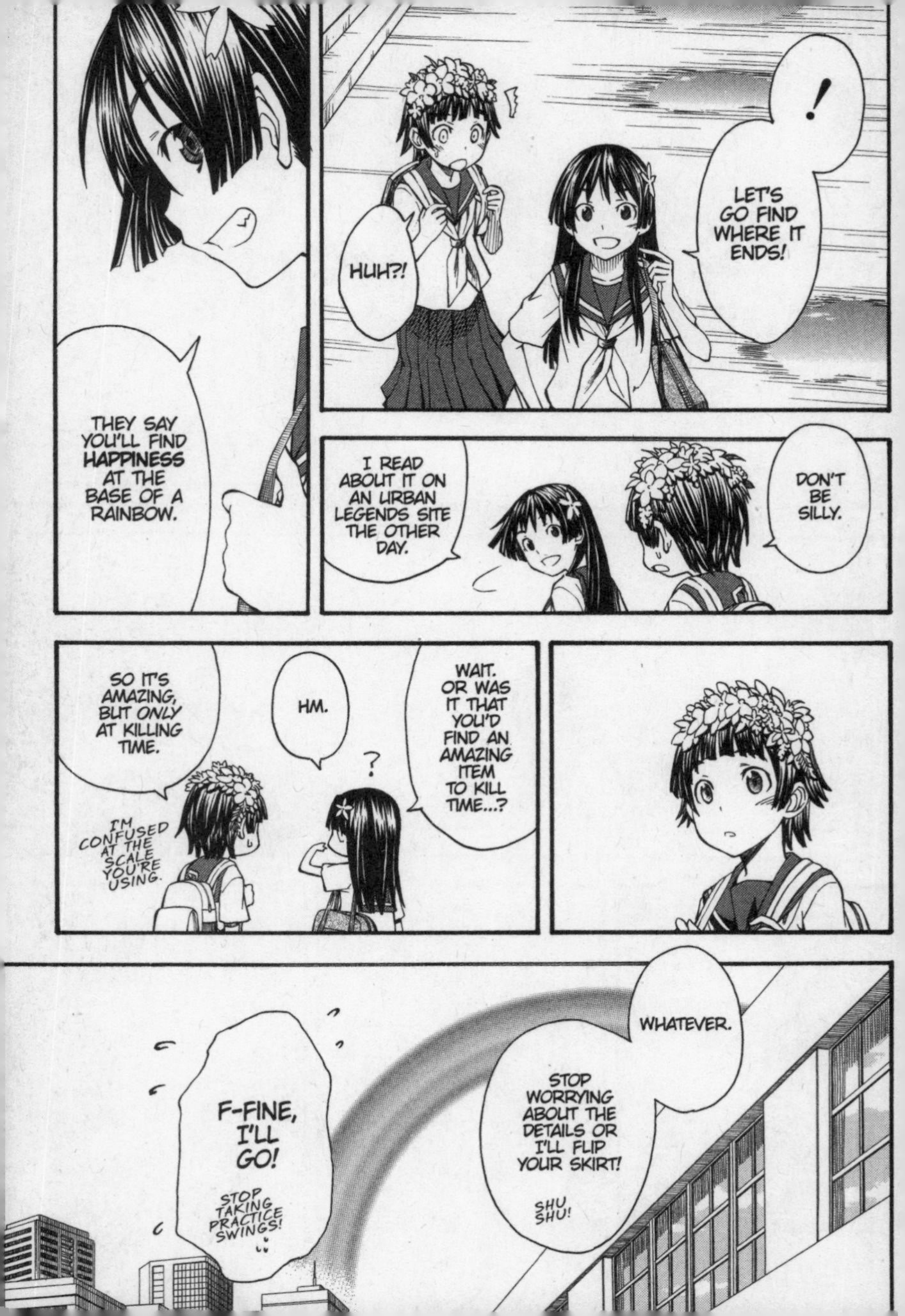
!
LET'S GO FIND WHERE IT ENDS!
HUH?!
DON'T BE SILLY.
I READ ABOUT IT ON AN URBAN LEGENDS SITE THE OTHER DAY.
THEY SAY YOU'LL FIND HAPPINESS AT THE BASE OF A RAINBOW.
WAIT. OR WAS IT THAT YOU'D FIND AN AMAZING ITEM TO KILL TIME...?
?
HM.
SO IT'S AMAZING, BUT ONLY AT KILLING TIME.
I'M CONFUSED AT THE SCALE YOU'RE USING.
WHATEVER.
STOP WORRYING ABOUT THE DETAILS OR I'LL FLIP YOUR SKIRT!
SHU SHU!
F-FINE, I'LL GO!
STOP TAKING PRACTICE SWINGS!

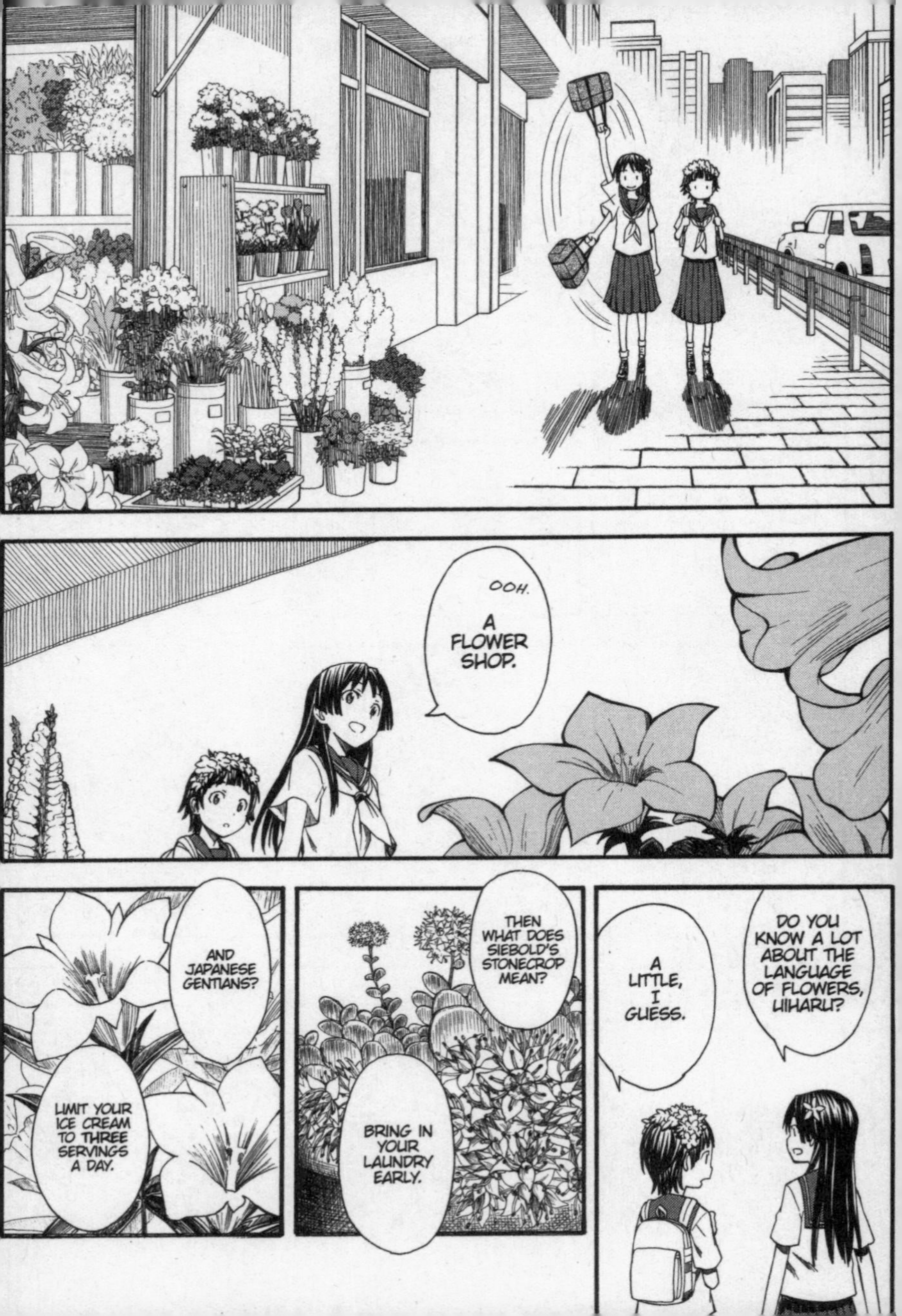
OOH.
A FLOWER SHOP.
DO YOU KNOW A LOT ABOUT THE LANGUAGE OF FLOWERS, UIHARU?
A LITTLE, I GUESS.
THEN WHAT DOES SIEBOLD'S STONECROP MEAN?
BRING IN YOUR LAUNDRY EARLY.
AND JAPANESE GENTIANS?
LIMIT YOUR ICE CREAM TO THREE SERVINGS A DAY.

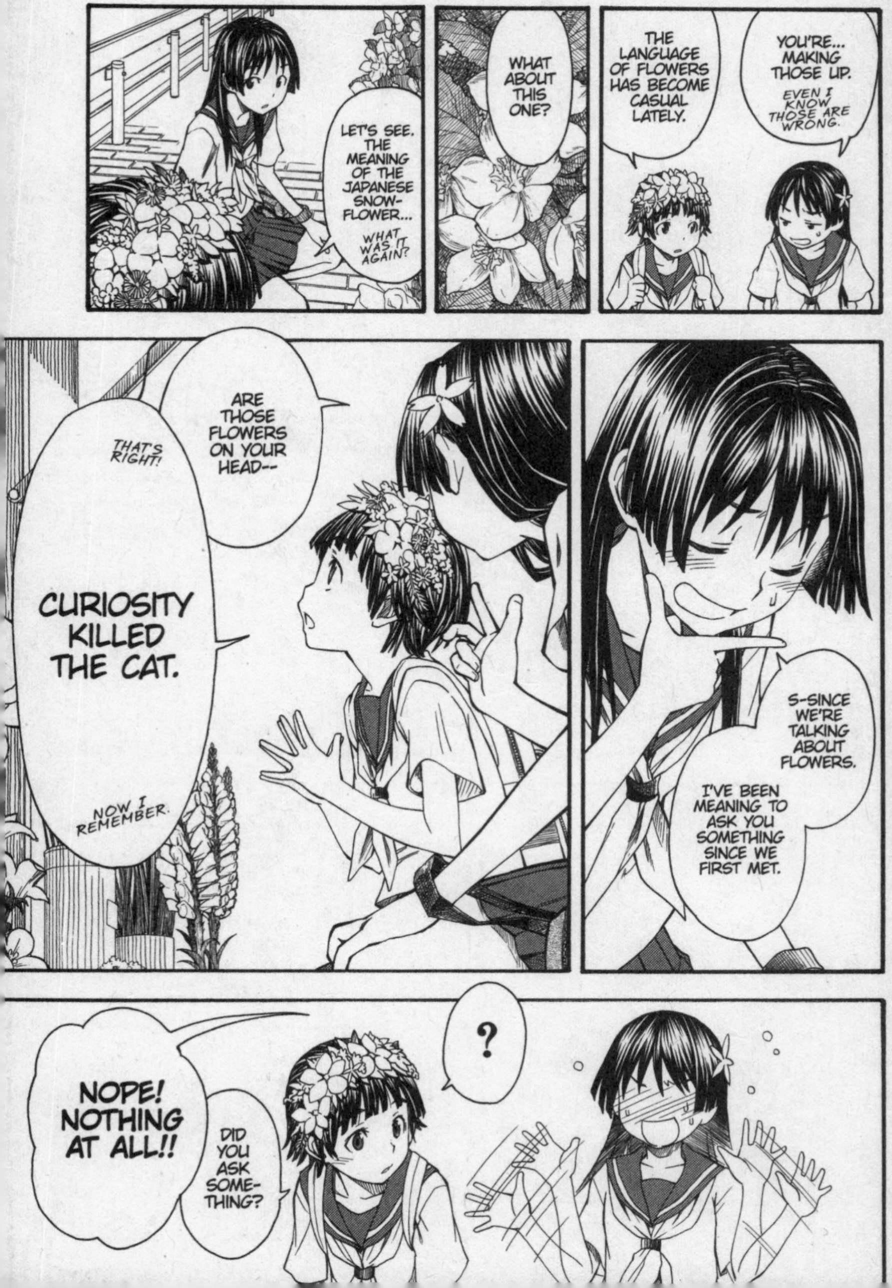
YOU'RE... MAKING THOSE UP.
EVEN I KNOW THOSE ARE WRONG.
THE LANGUAGE OF FLOWERS HAS BECOME CASUAL LATELY.
WHAT ABOUT THIS ONE?
LET'S SEE. THE MEANING OF THE JAPANESE SNOW-FLOWER...
WHAT WAS IT AGAIN?
S-SINCE WE'RE TALKING ABOUT FLOWERS.
I'VE BEEN MEANING TO ASK YOU SOMETHING SINCE WE FIRST MET.
ARE THOSE FLOWERS ON YOUR HEAD--
THAT'S RIGHT!
CURIOSITY KILLED THE CAT.
NOW I REMEMBER.
?
DID YOU ASK SOME-THING?
NOPE! NOTHING AT ALL!!

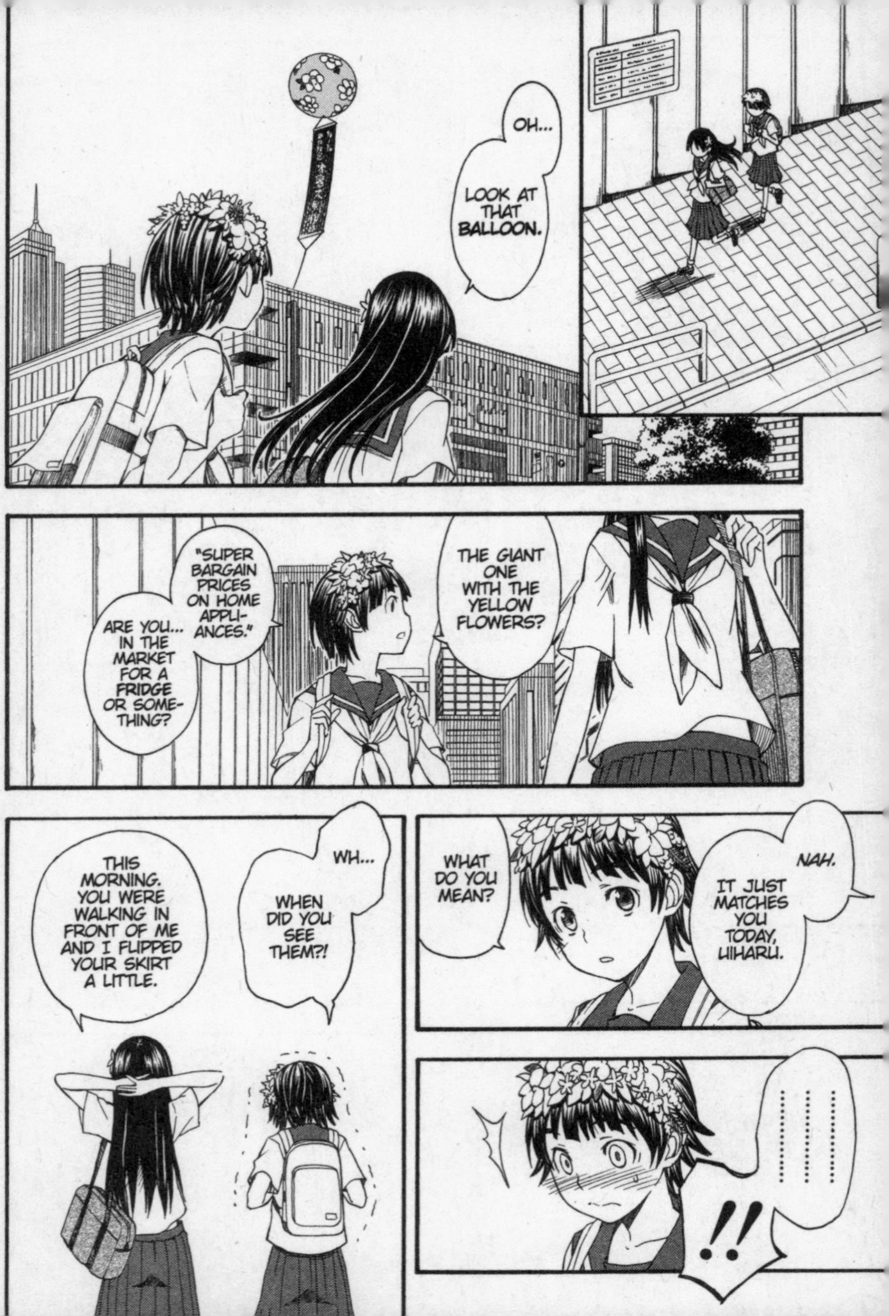
OH...
LOOK AT THAT BALLOON.
THE GIANT ONE WITH THE YELLOW FLOWERS?
"SUPER BARGAIN PRICES ON HOME APPLIANCES."
ARE YOU... IN THE MARKET FOR A FRIDGE OR SOMETHING?
NAH.
IT JUST MATCHES YOU TODAY, UIHARU.
WHAT DO YOU MEAN?
......
......
......
!!
WH...
WHEN DID YOU SEE THEM?!
THIS MORNING. YOU WERE WALKING IN FRONT OF ME AND I FLIPPED YOUR SKIRT A LITTLE.

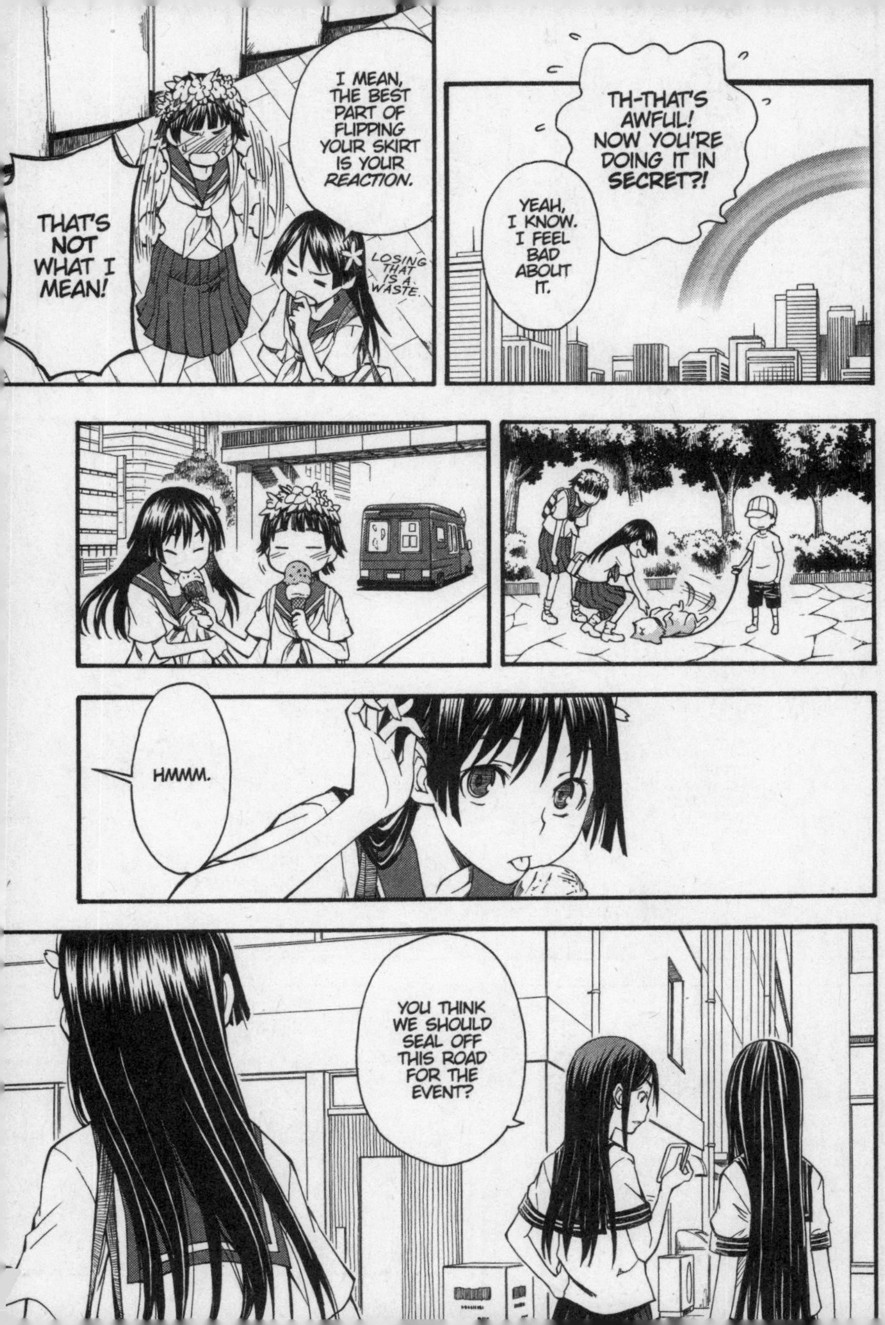
TH-THAT'S AWFUL! NOW YOU'RE DOING IT IN SECRET?!
YEAH, I KNOW. I FEEL BAD ABOUT IT.
I MEAN, THE BEST PART OF FLIPPING YOUR SKIRT IS YOUR *REACTION.*
LOSING THAT IS A WASTE.
THAT'S NOT WHAT I MEAN!
HMMM.
YOU THINK WE SHOULD SEAL OFF THIS ROAD FOR THE EVENT?

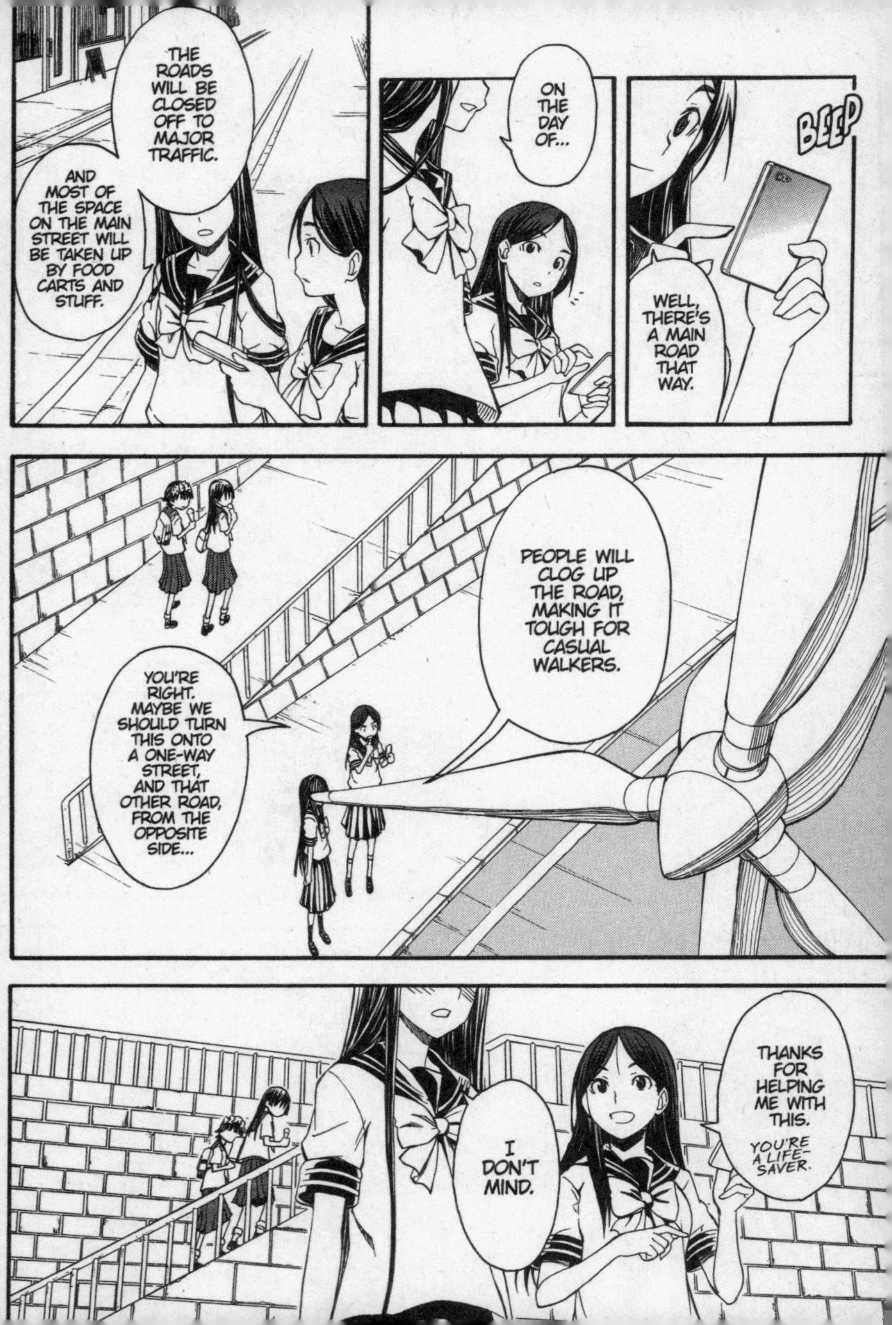
BEEP
WELL, THERE'S A MAIN ROAD THAT WAY.
ON THE DAY OF...
THE ROADS WILL BE CLOSED OFF TO MAJOR TRAFFIC.
AND MOST OF THE SPACE ON THE MAIN STREET WILL BE TAKEN UP BY FOOD CARTS AND STUFF.
PEOPLE WILL CLOG UP THE ROAD, MAKING IT TOUGH FOR CASUAL WALKERS.
YOU'RE RIGHT. MAYBE WE SHOULD TURN THIS ONTO A ONE-WAY STREET, AND THAT OTHER ROAD, FROM THE OPPOSITE SIDE...
THANKS FOR HELPING ME WITH THIS.
YOU'RE A LIFE-SAVER.
I DON'T MIND.

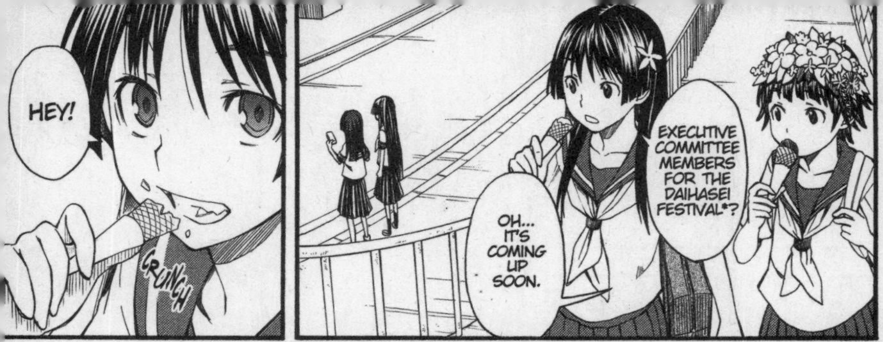
EXECUTIVE COMMITTEE MEMBERS FOR THE DAIHASEI FESTIVAL*?
OH... IT'S COMING UP SOON.
HEY!
CRUNCH

*Literally "Grand Champion Star Festival," a city-wide sports competition between the various schools in Academy City.

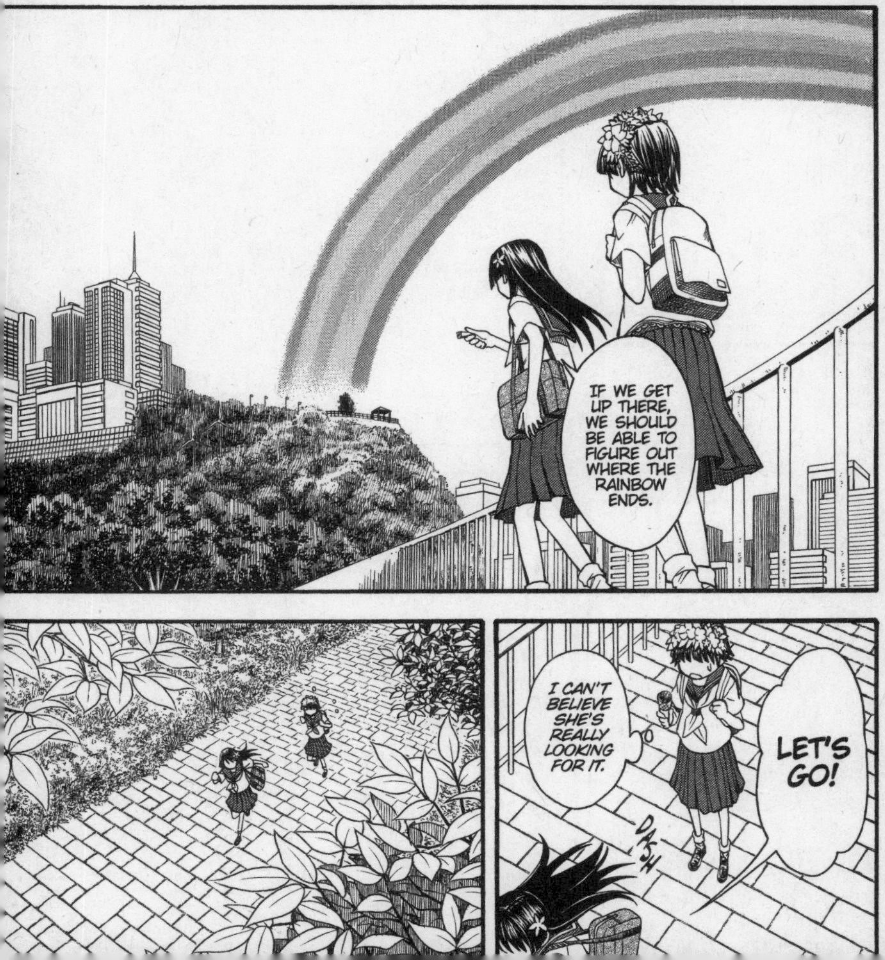
IF WE GET UP THERE, WE SHOULD BE ABLE TO FIGURE OUT WHERE THE RAINBOW ENDS.
LET'S GO!
I CAN'T BELIEVE SHE'S REALLY LOOKING FOR IT.
DASH

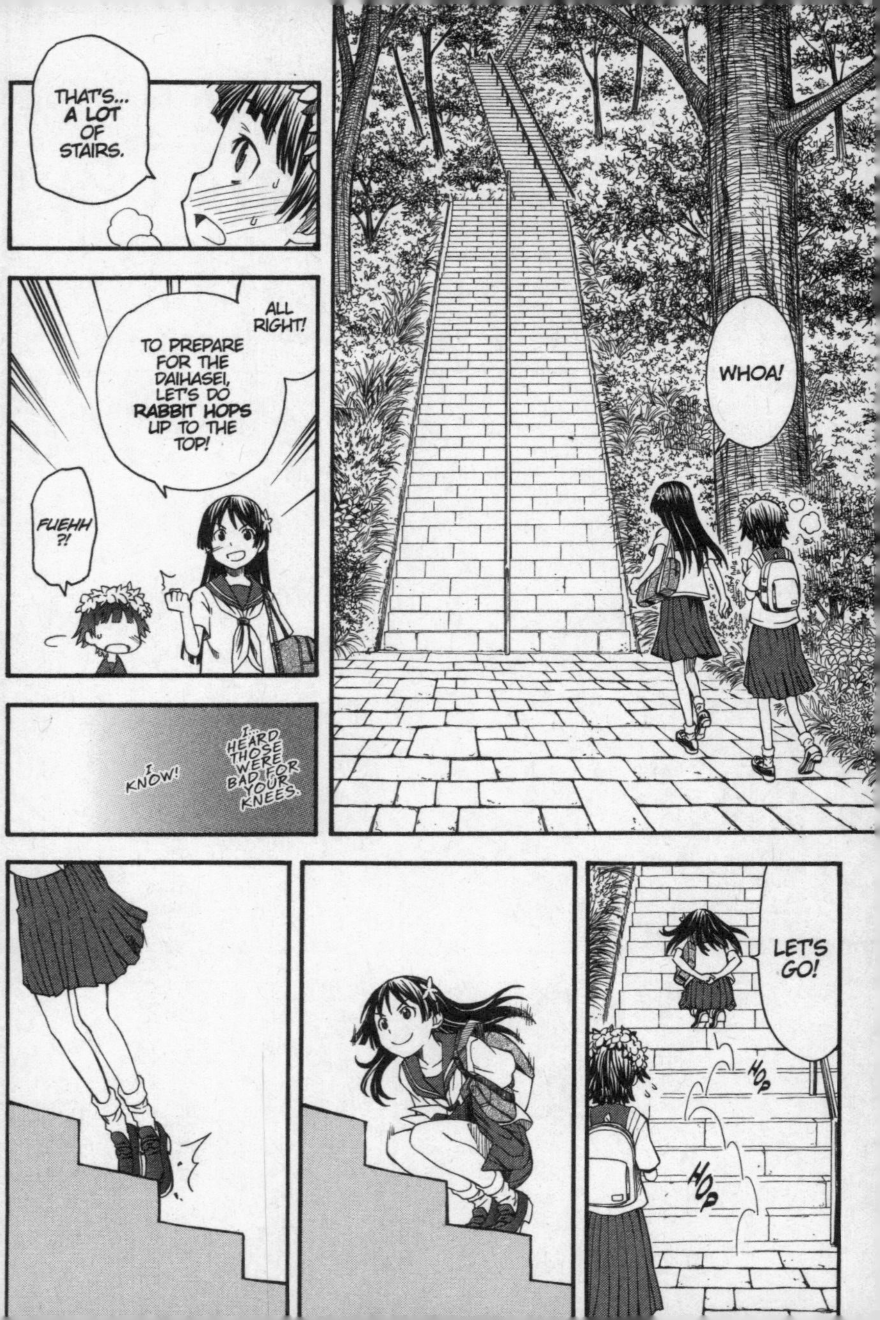
WHOA!
THAT'S... A LOT OF STAIRS.
ALL RIGHT!
TO PREPARE FOR THE DAIHASEI, LET'S DO RABBIT HOPS UP TO THE TOP!
FUEHH ?!
I... HEARD THOSE WERE BAD FOR YOUR KNEES.
I KNOW!
LET'S GO!
HOP
HOP

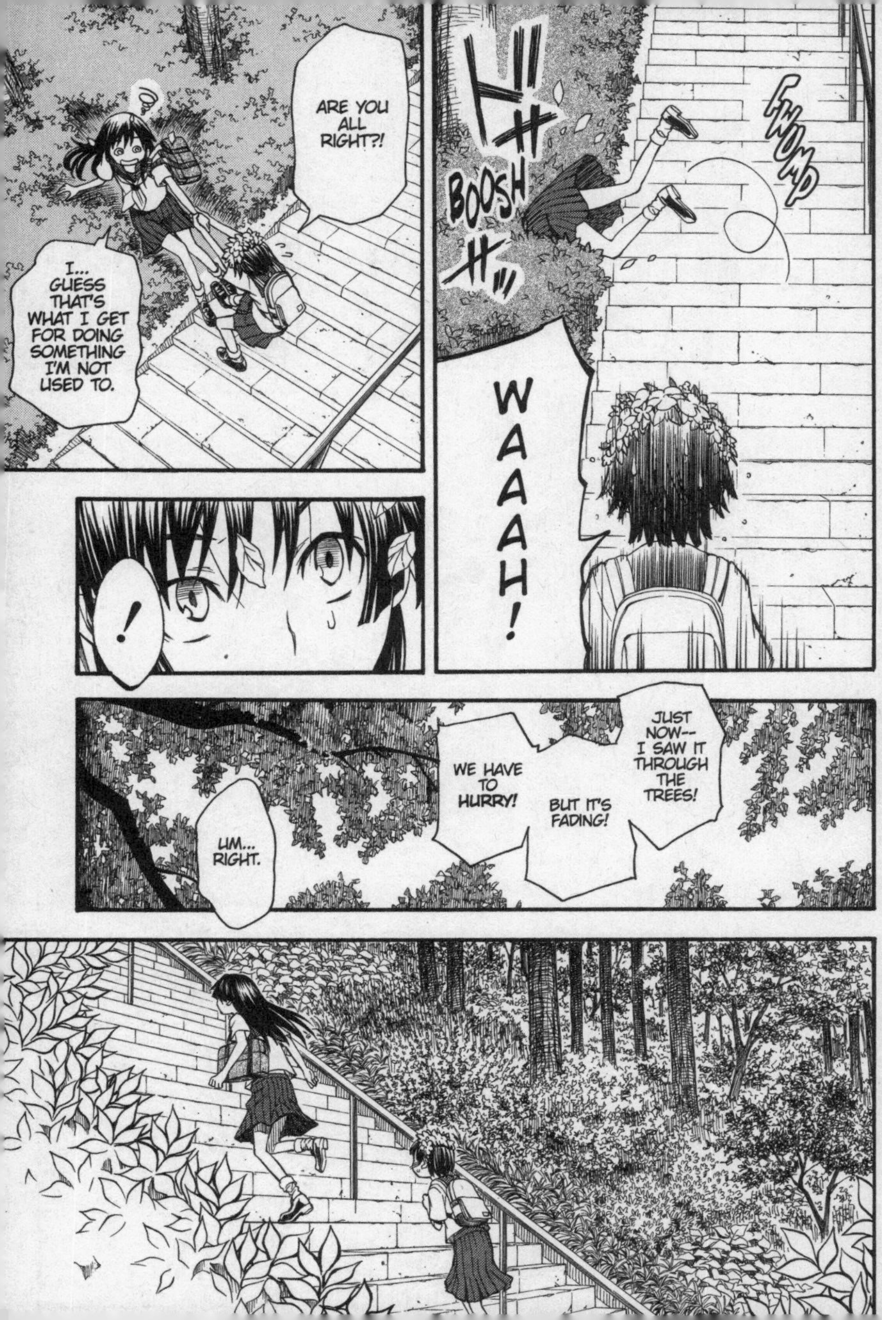
FWOMP
BOOSH
WAAAH!
ARE YOU ALL RIGHT?!
I... GUESS THAT'S WHAT I GET FOR DOING SOMETHING I'M NOT USED TO.
!
JUST NOW-- I SAW IT THROUGH THE TREES!
BUT IT'S FADING!
WE HAVE TO HURRY!
UM... RIGHT.

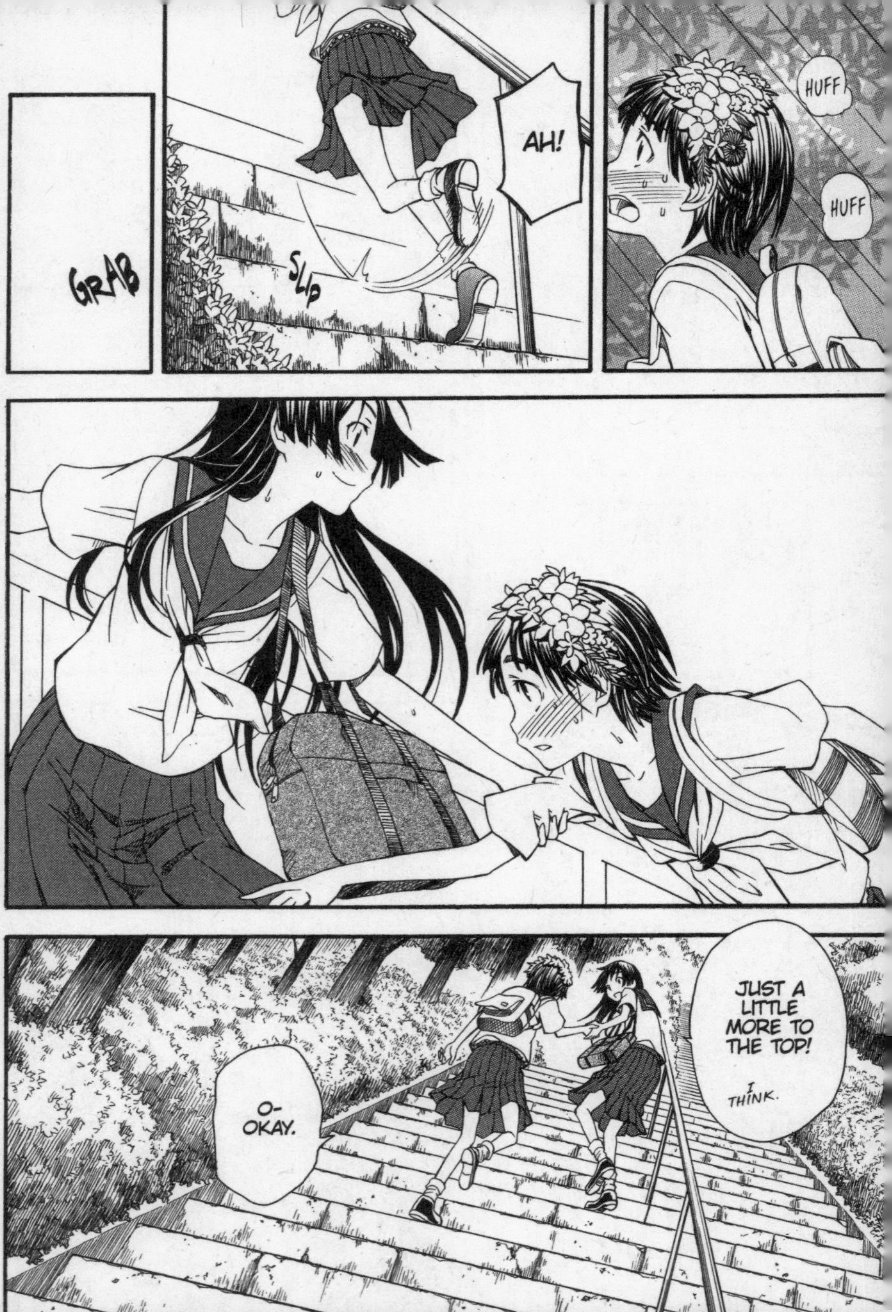
HUFF
HUFF
AH!
SLIP
GRAB
JUST A LITTLE MORE TO THE TOP!
I THINK.
O-OKAY.

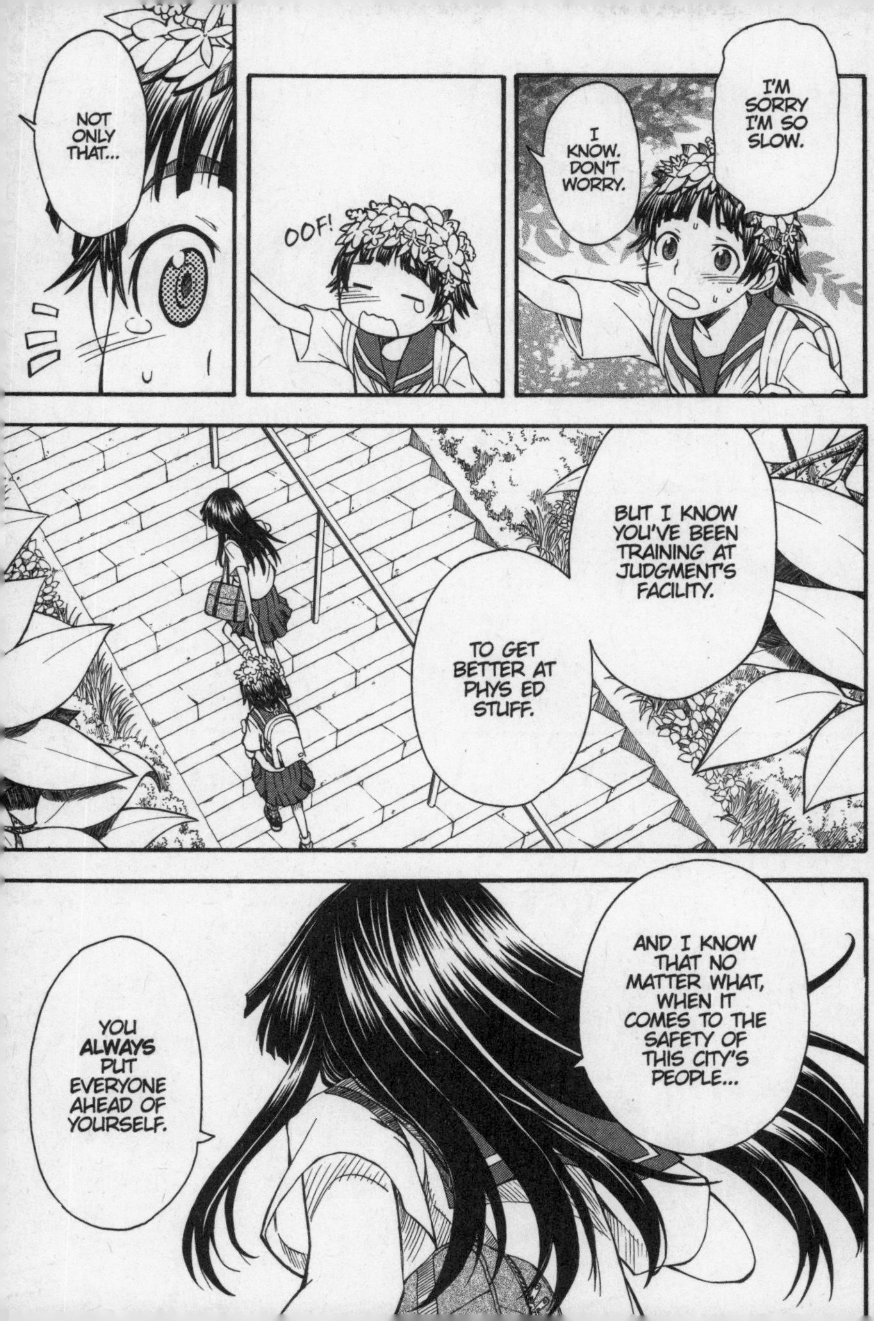
I'M SORRY I'M SO SLOW.
I KNOW. DON'T WORRY.
OOF!
NOT ONLY THAT...
BUT I KNOW YOU'VE BEEN TRAINING AT JUDGMENT'S FACILITY.
TO GET BETTER AT PHYS ED STUFF.
AND I KNOW THAT NO MATTER WHAT, WHEN IT COMES TO THE SAFETY OF THIS CITY'S PEOPLE...
YOU ALWAYS PUT EVERYONE AHEAD OF YOURSELF.

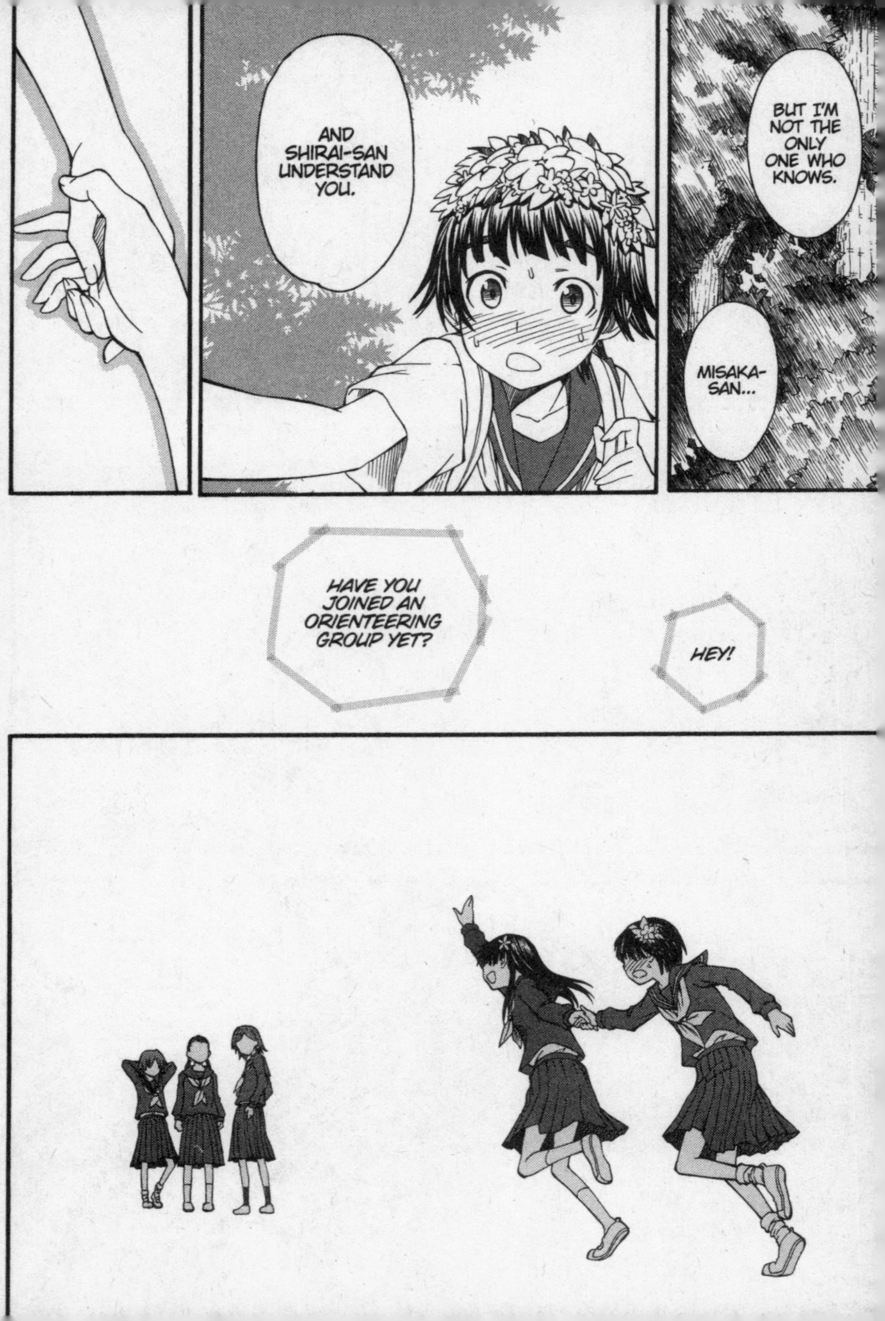
BUT I'M NOT THE ONLY ONE WHO KNOWS.
MISAKA-SAN...
AND SHIRAI-SAN UNDERSTAND YOU.
HEY!
HAVE YOU JOINED AN ORIENTEERING GROUP YET?

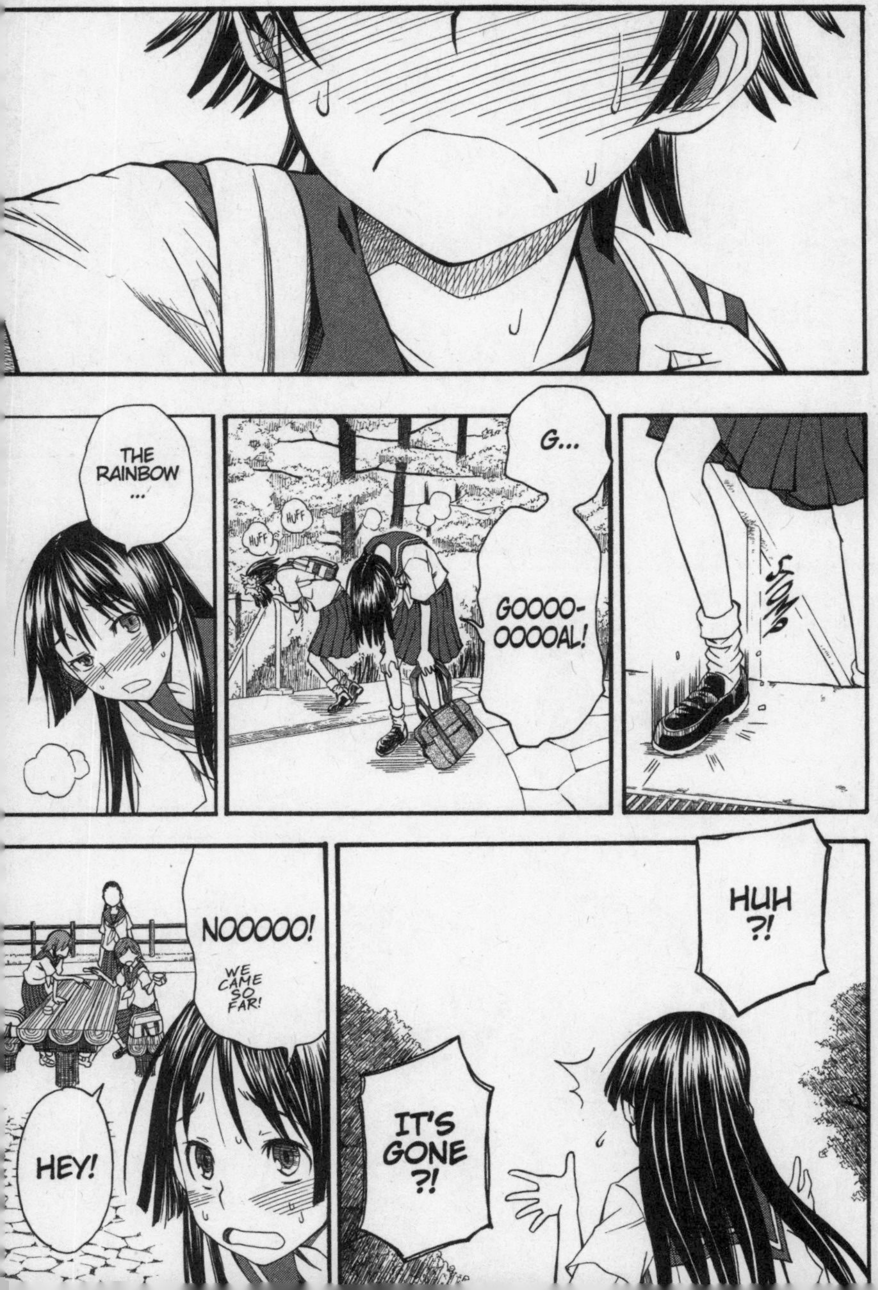
STOMP
G...
GOOOO-OOOOAL!
HUFF
HUFF
THE RAINBOW ...
HUH ?!
IT'S GONE ?!
NOOOOO!
WE CAME SO FAR!
HEY!

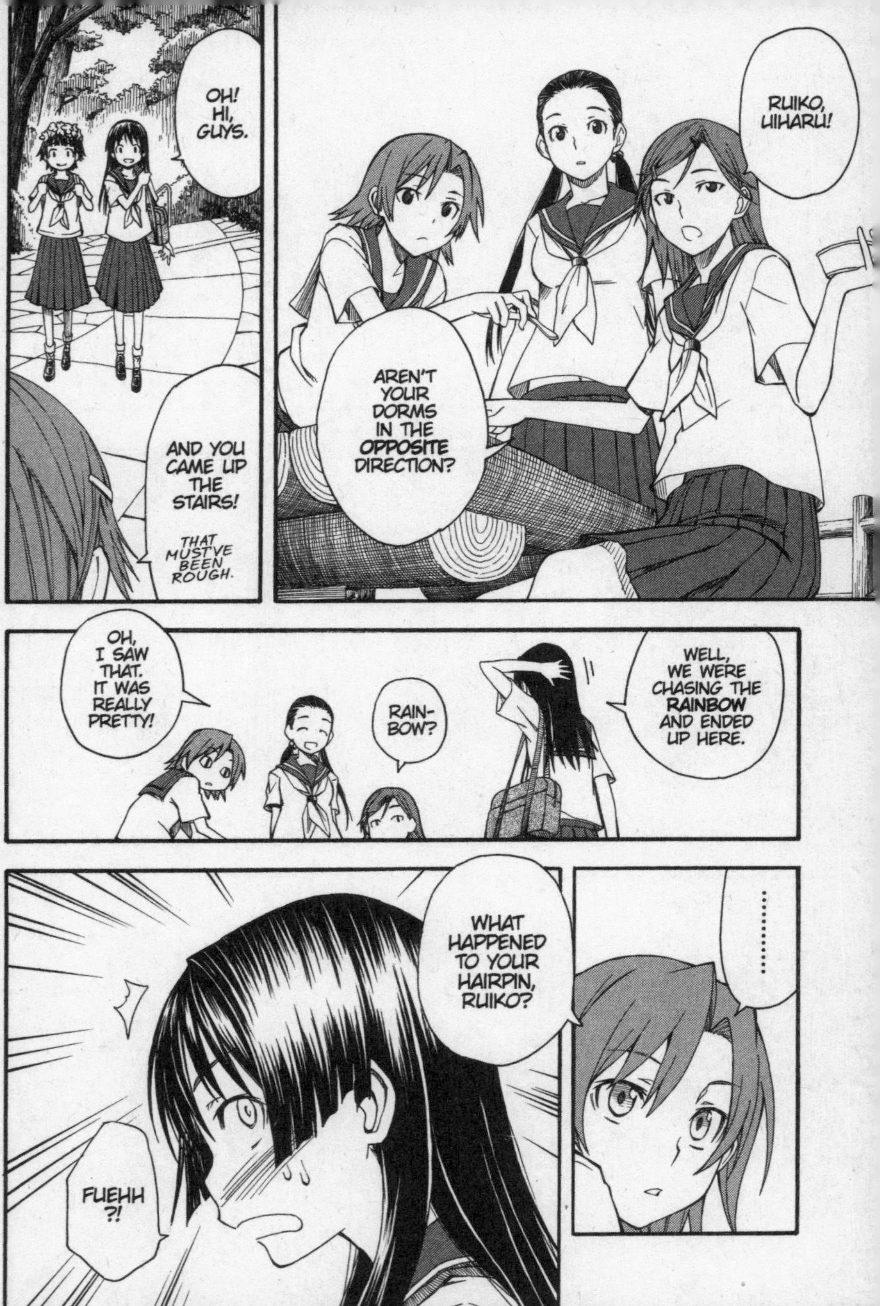
RUIKO, UIHARU!
AREN'T YOUR DORMS IN THE OPPOSITE DIRECTION?
OH! HI, GUYS.
AND YOU CAME UP THE STAIRS!
THAT MUSTVE BEEN ROUGH.
WELL, WE WERE CHASING THE RAINBOW AND ENDED UP HERE.
RAIN-BOW?
OH, I SAW THAT. IT WAS REALLY PRETTY!
......
WHAT HAPPENED TO YOUR HAIRPIN, RUIKO?
FUEHH ?!

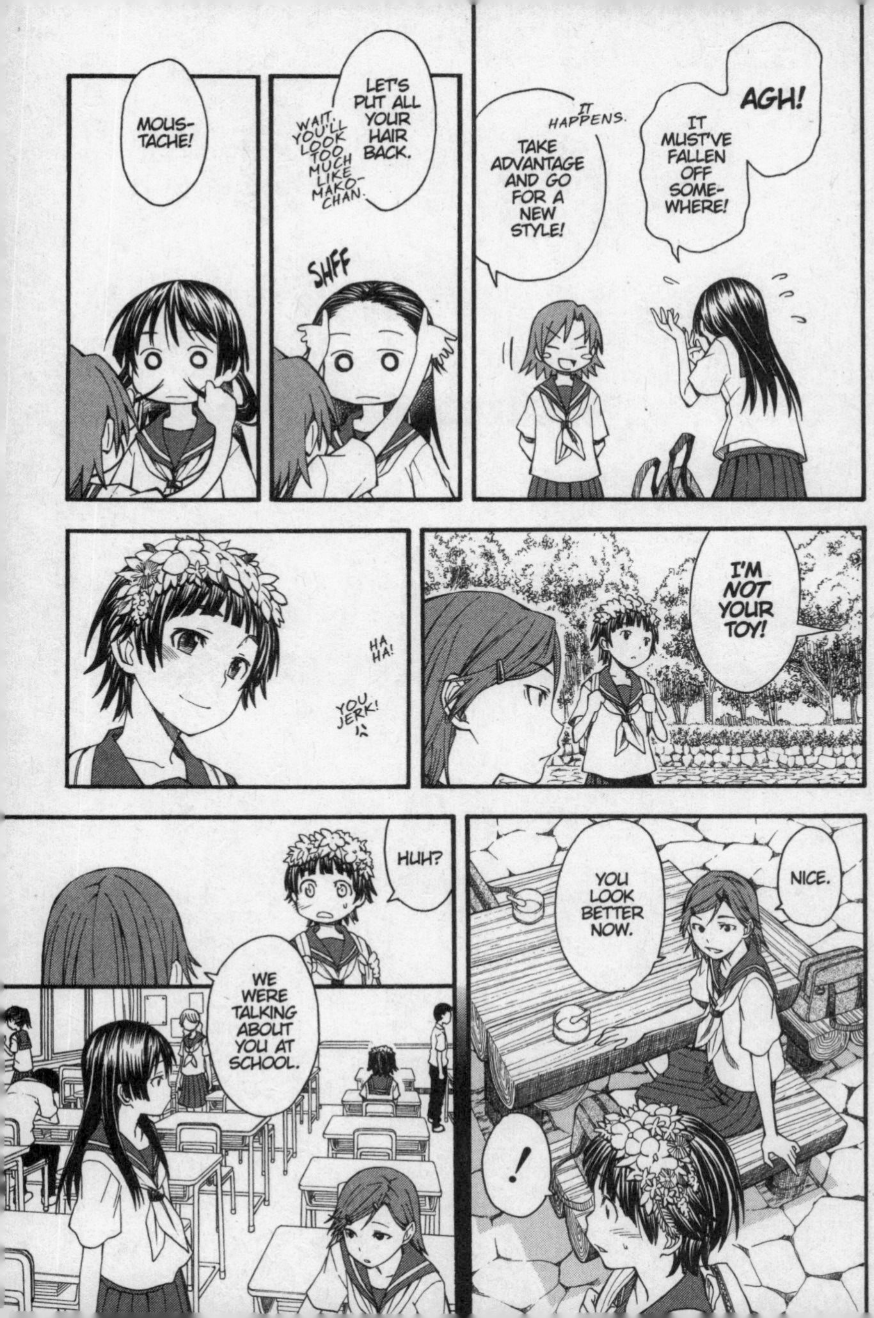
AGH!
IT MUST'VE FALLEN OFF SOMEWHERE!
IT HAPPENS.
TAKE ADVANTAGE AND GO FOR A NEW STYLE!
LET'S PUT ALL YOUR HAIR BACK.
WAIT, YOU'LL LOOK TOO MUCH LIKE MAKO-CHAN.
SHFF
MOUS-TACHE!
I'M NOT YOUR TOY!
HA HA!
YOU JERK!
NICE.
YOU LOOK BETTER NOW.
!
HUH?
WE WERE TALKING ABOUT YOU AT SCHOOL.

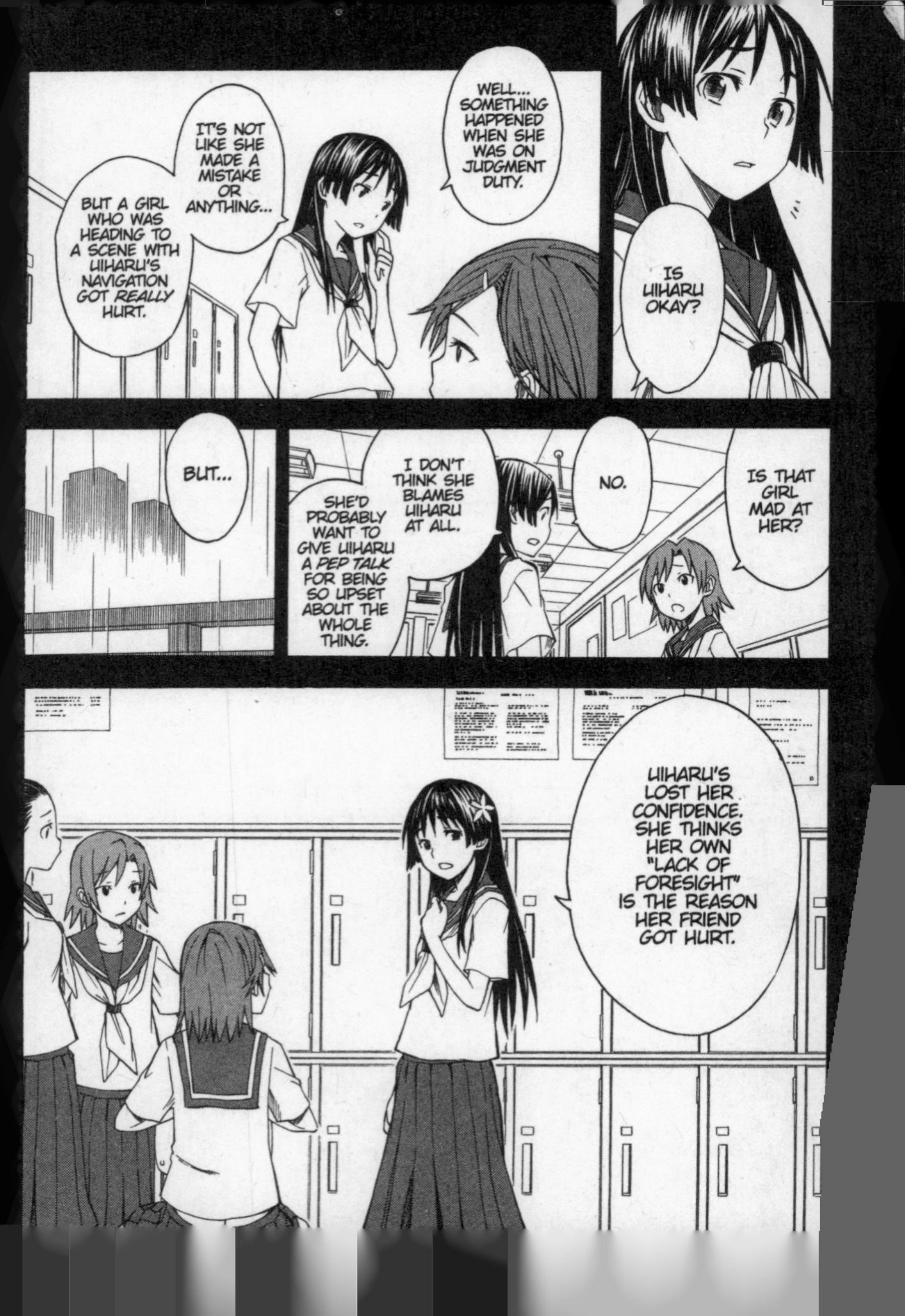
IS UIHARU OKAY?
WELL... SOMETHING HAPPENED WHEN SHE WAS ON JUDGMENT DUTY.
IT'S NOT LIKE SHE MADE A MISTAKE OR ANYTHING...
BUT A GIRL WHO WAS HEADING TO A SCENE WITH UIHARU'S NAVIGATION GOT *REALLY* HURT.
IS THAT GIRL MAD AT HER?
NO.
I DON'T THINK SHE BLAMES UIHARU AT ALL.
SHE'D PROBABLY WANT TO GIVE UIHARU A *PEP TALK* FOR BEING SO UPSET ABOUT THE WHOLE THING.
BUT...
UIHARU'S LOST HER CONFIDENCE. SHE THINKS HER OWN "LACK OF FORESIGHT" IS THE REASON HER FRIEND GOT HURT.

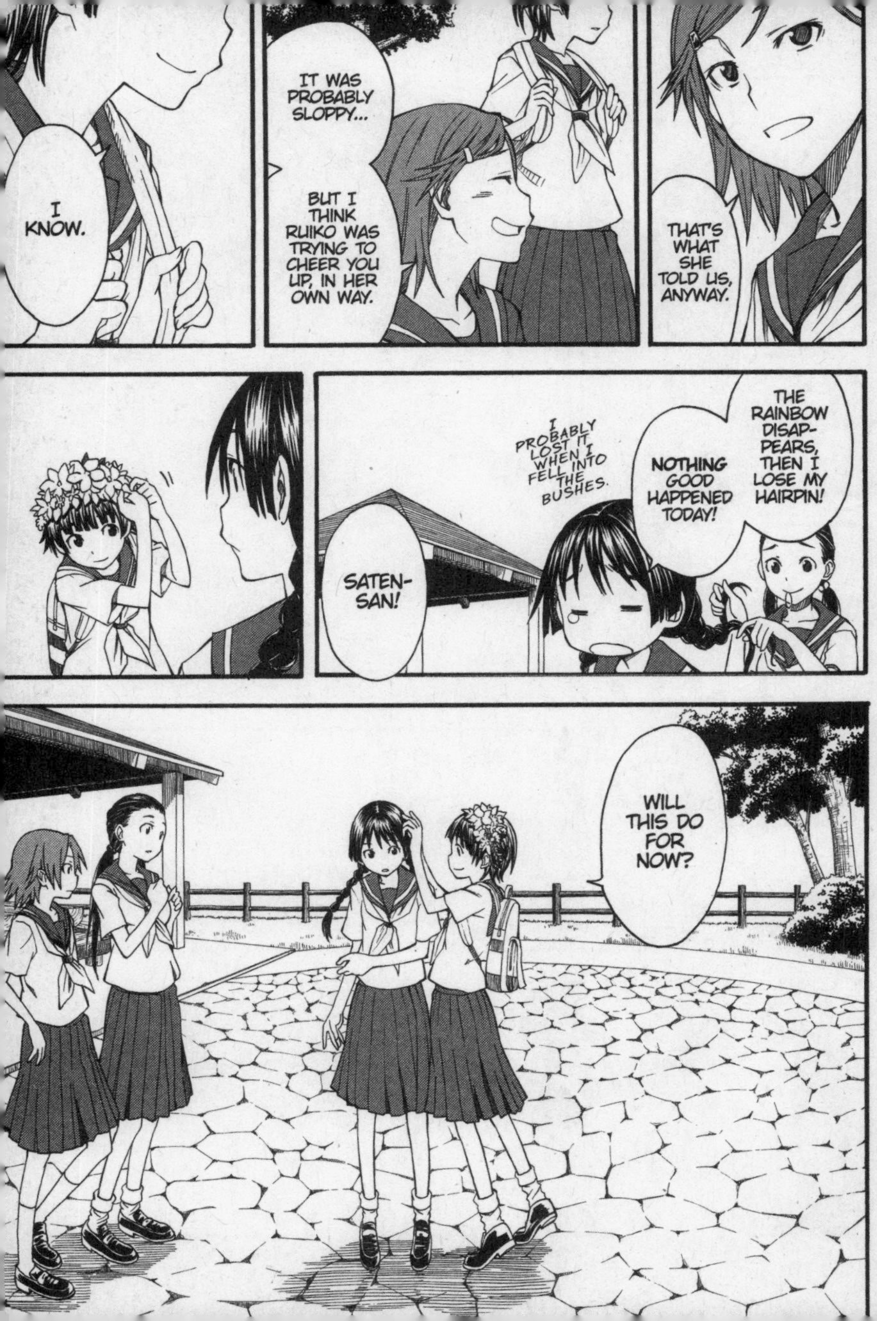
THAT'S WHAT SHE TOLD US, ANYWAY.
IT WAS PROBABLY SLOPPY...
BUT I THINK RUIKO WAS TRYING TO CHEER YOU UP, IN HER OWN WAY.
I KNOW.
THE RAINBOW DISAP-PEARS, THEN I LOSE MY HAIRPIN!
NOTHING GOOD HAPPENED TODAY!
I PROBABLY LOST IT WHEN I FELL INTO THE BUSHES.
SATEN-SAN!
WILL THIS DO FOR NOW?

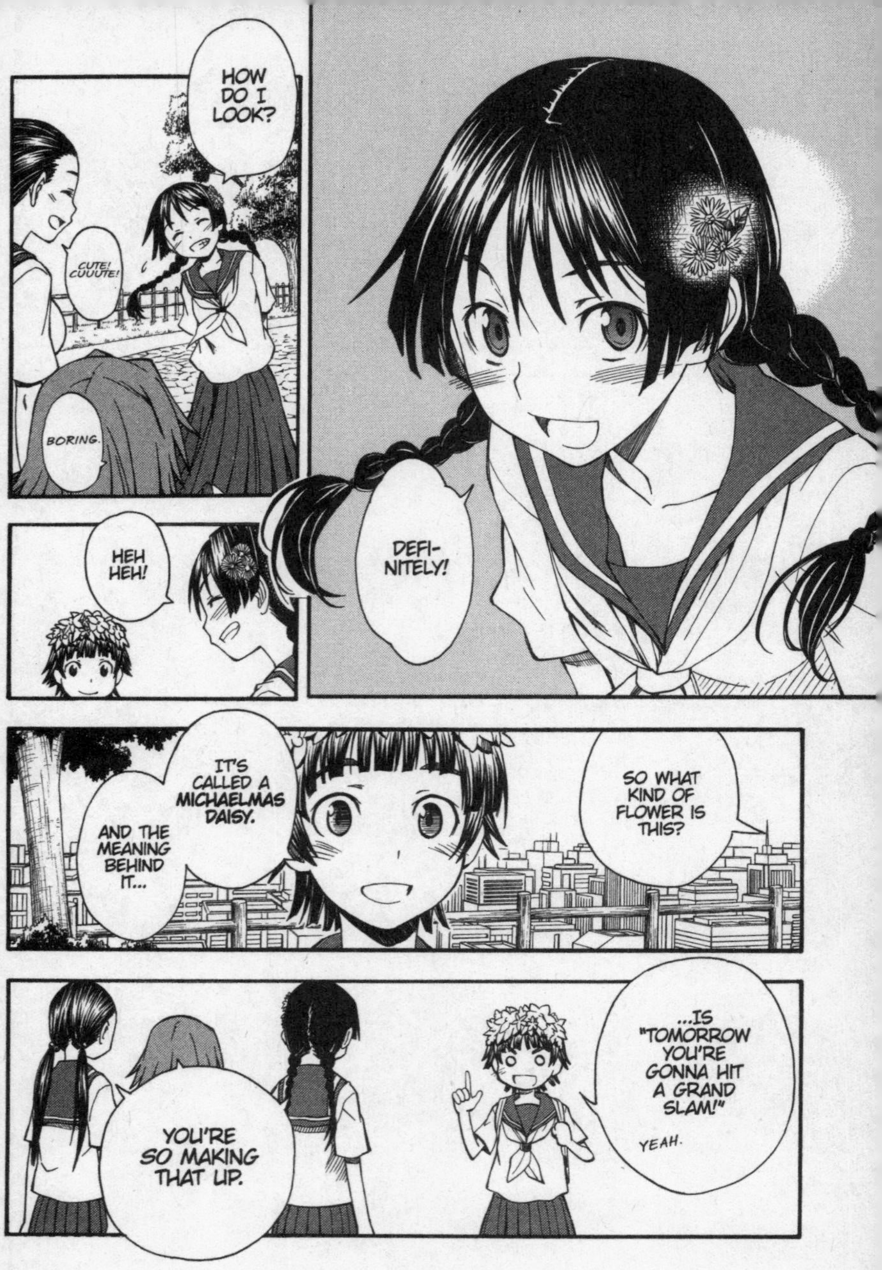
DEFI-NITELY!
HOW DO I LOOK?
CUTE! CUUUTE!
BORING.
HEH HEH!
SO WHAT KIND OF FLOWER IS THIS?
IT'S CALLED A MICHAELMAS DAISY.
AND THE MEANING BEHIND IT...
...IS "TOMORROW YOU'RE GONNA HIT A GRAND SLAM!"
YEAH.
YOU'RE SO MAKING THAT UP.

A Certain SCIENTIFIC Railgun

A Certain Lady's Paradise

I'M SO SORRY!
DEPRESSION
DON'T WORRY, UIHARU.
OH, PLEASE LEAVE JUDGMENT TO ME!
BRIGHTEN
AND IF THERE'S ANYTHING YOU NEED--
I ALREADY BROUGHT PLENTY FROM MY ROOM.
SMILE ♡
......
Oneesama Cuddle Pillow
Oneesama Doll
Oneesama Picture Album
STILL...
...YOU COULD BRING ME A PAIR OF ONEE-SAMA'S UNDER-WEAR.
SHE'S TERRIBLE. SOMEONE HAS TO STOP THIS.
OH HO HO HO HO HO!

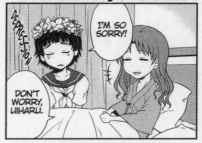

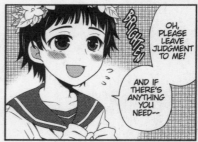

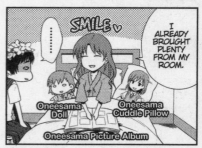

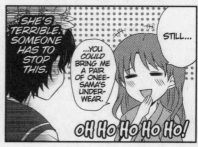

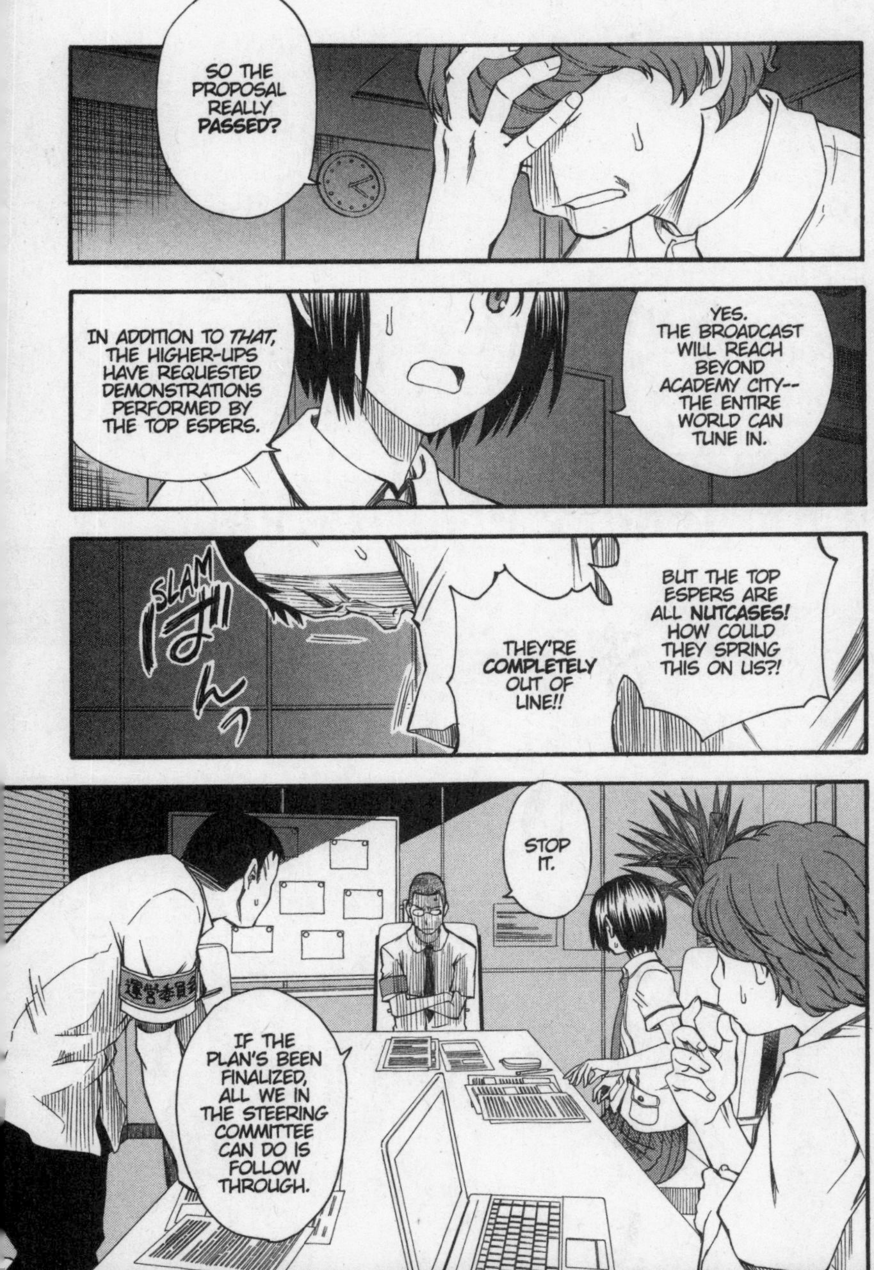
SO THE PROPOSAL REALLY PASSED?
YES. THE BROADCAST WILL REACH BEYOND ACADEMY CITY-- THE ENTIRE WORLD CAN TUNE IN.
IN ADDITION TO THAT, THE HIGHER-UPS HAVE REQUESTED DEMONSTRATIONS PERFORMED BY THE TOP ESPERS.
BUT THE TOP ESPERS ARE ALL NUTCASES! HOW COULD THEY SPRING THIS ON US?!
THEY'RE COMPLETELY OUT OF LINE!!
SLAM
ばんっ
STOP IT.
IF THE PLAN'S BEEN FINALIZED, ALL WE IN THE STEERING COMMITTEE CAN DO IS FOLLOW THROUGH.

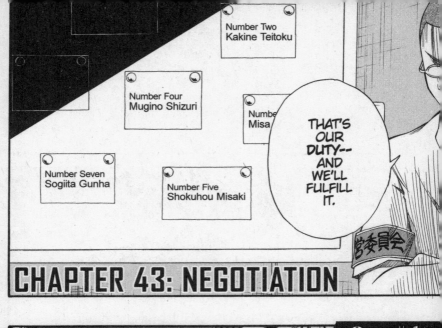

Number Two
Kakine Teitoku

Number Four
Mugino Shizuri

Numbe
Misa

Number Seven
Sogiita Gunha

Number Five
Shokuhou Misaki

THAT'S OUR DUTY-- AND WE'LL FULFILL IT.

CHAPTER 43: NEGOTIATION

Case # 1

LOOKIN' GOOD, ACCELER- ATOR.

TAP
TAP
TAP

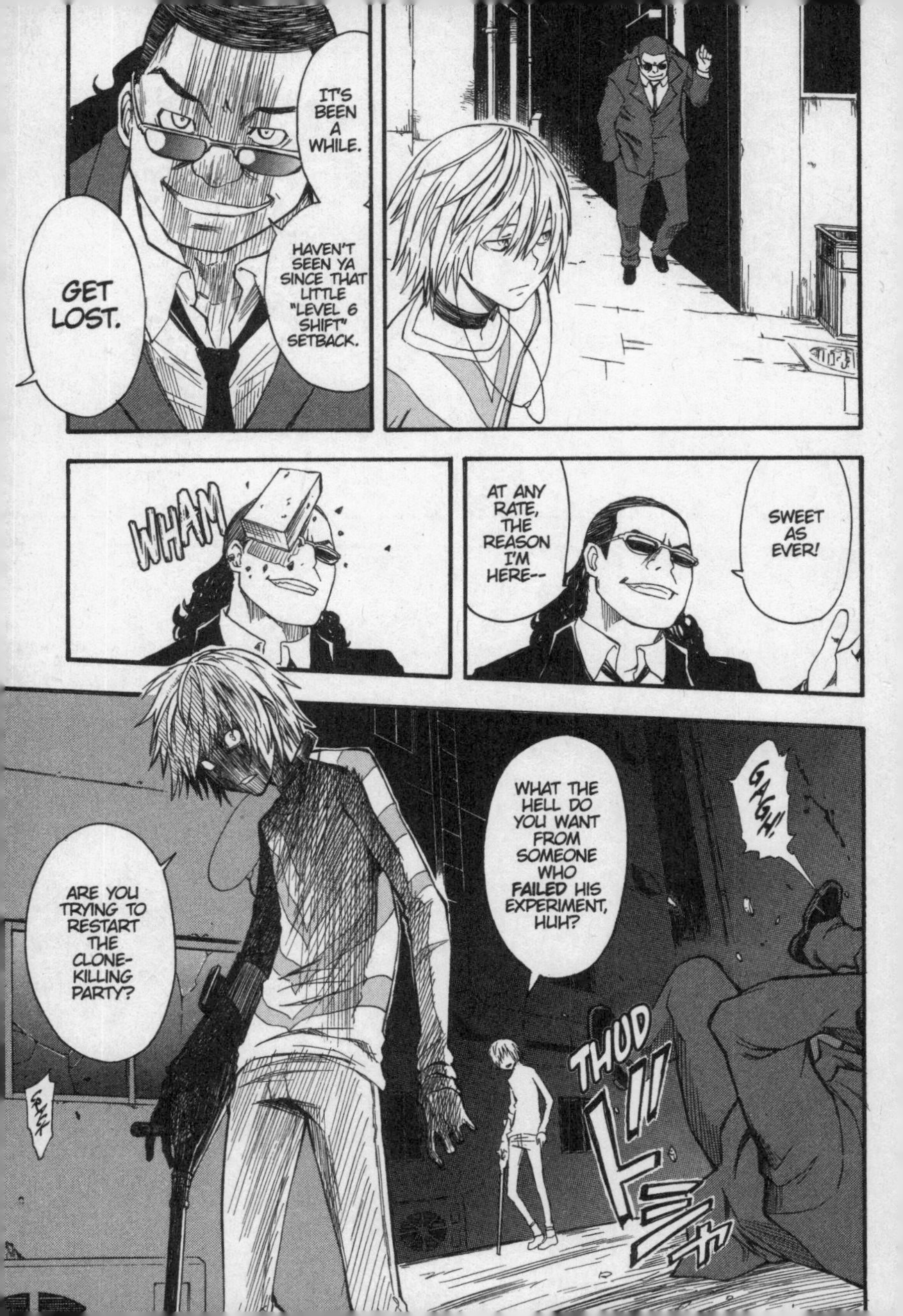
IT'S BEEN A WHILE.
HAVEN'T SEEN YA SINCE THAT LITTLE "LEVEL 6 SHIFT" SETBACK.
GET LOST.
SWEET AS EVER!
AT ANY RATE, THE REASON I'M HERE--
WHAM
GAGH!
THUD
WHAT THE HELL DO YOU WANT FROM SOMEONE WHO FAILED HIS EXPERIMENT, HUH?
ARE YOU TRYING TO RESTART THE CLONE-KILLING PARTY?

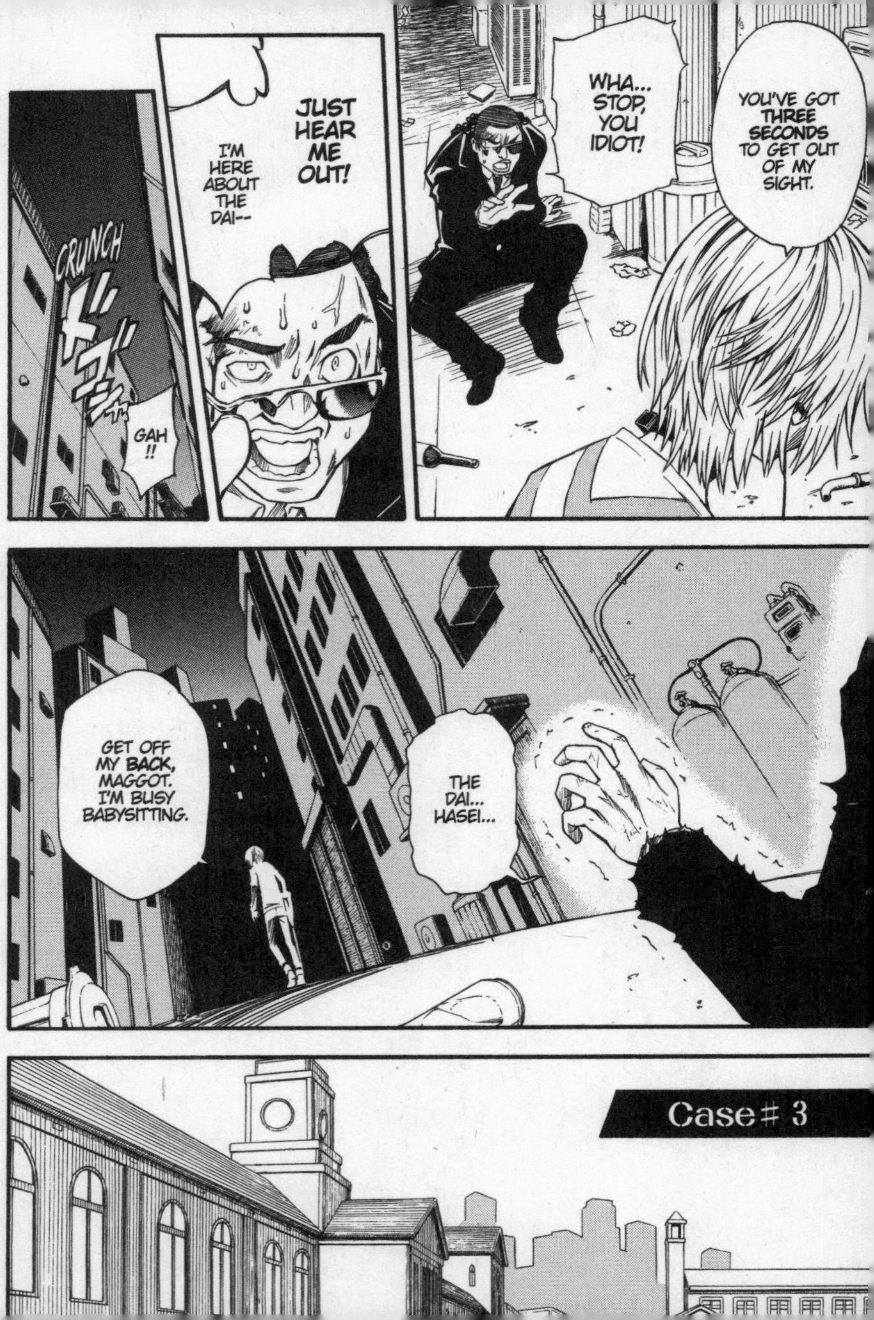
YOU'VE GOT THREE SECONDS TO GET OUT OF MY SIGHT.
WHA... STOP, YOU IDIOT!
JUST HEAR ME OUT!
I'M HERE ABOUT THE DAI--
CRUNCH
GAH !!
THE DAI... HASEI...
GET OFF MY BACK, MAGGOT. I'M BUSY BABYSITTING.
Case# 3

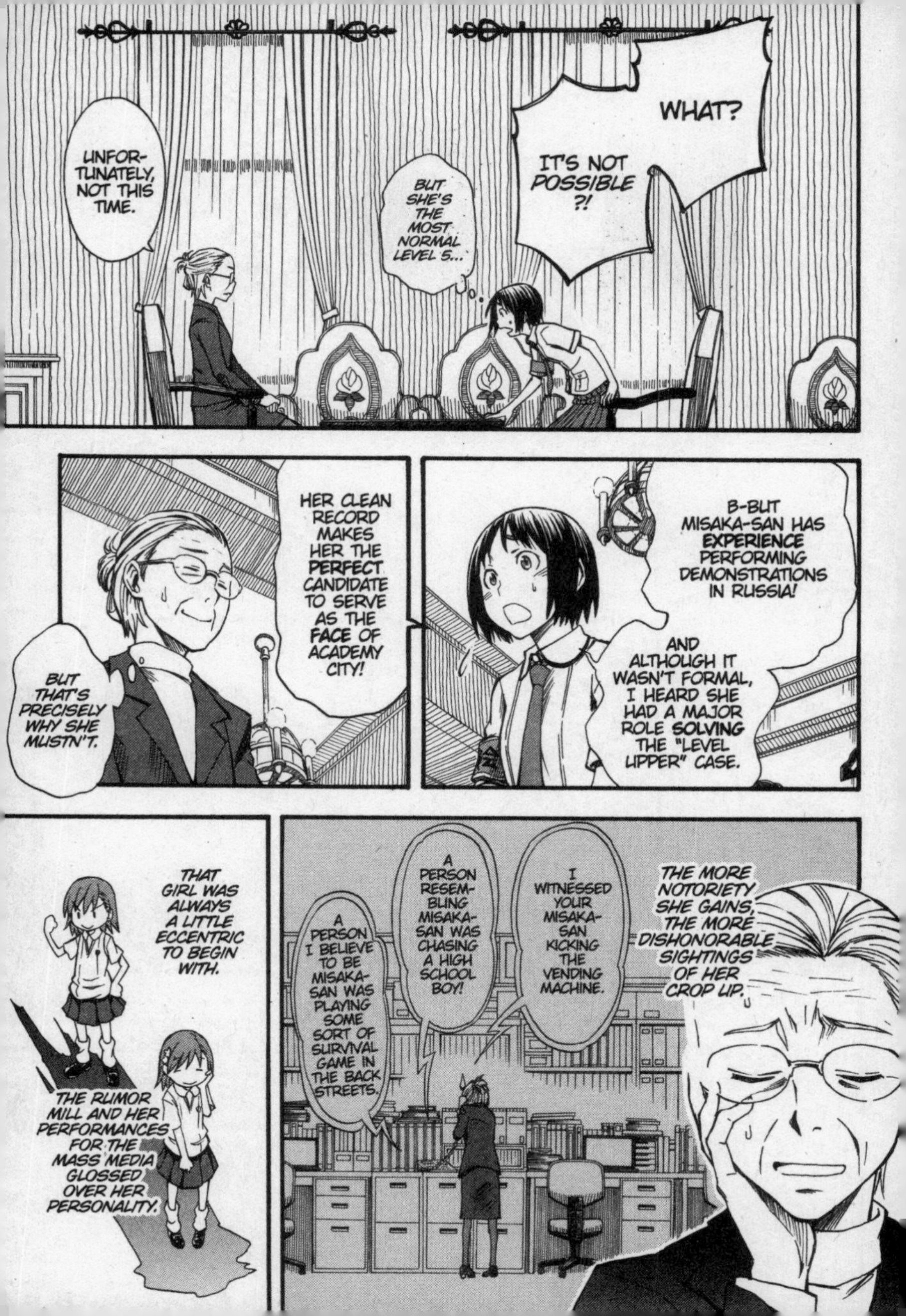
WHAT?
IT'S NOT POSSIBLE?!
BUT SHE'S THE MOST NORMAL LEVEL 5...
UNFORTUNATELY, NOT THIS TIME.
B-BUT MISAKA-SAN HAS EXPERIENCE PERFORMING DEMONSTRATIONS IN RUSSIA!
AND ALTHOUGH IT WASN'T FORMAL, I HEARD SHE HAD A MAJOR ROLE SOLVING THE "LEVEL UPPER" CASE.
HER CLEAN RECORD MAKES HER THE PERFECT CANDIDATE TO SERVE AS THE FACE OF ACADEMY CITY!
BUT THAT'S PRECISELY WHY SHE MUSTN'T.
THE MORE NOTORIETY SHE GAINS, THE MORE DISHONORABLE SIGHTINGS OF HER CROP UP.
I WITNESSED YOUR MISAKA-SAN KICKING THE VENDING MACHINE.
A PERSON RESEMBLING MISAKA-SAN WAS CHASING A HIGH SCHOOL BOY!
A PERSON I BELIEVE TO BE MISAKA-SAN WAS PLAYING SOME SORT OF SURVIVAL GAME IN THE BACK STREETS.
THAT GIRL WAS ALWAYS A LITTLE ECCENTRIC TO BEGIN WITH.
THE RUMOR MILL AND HER PERFORMANCES FOR THE MASS MEDIA GLOSSED OVER HER PERSONALITY.

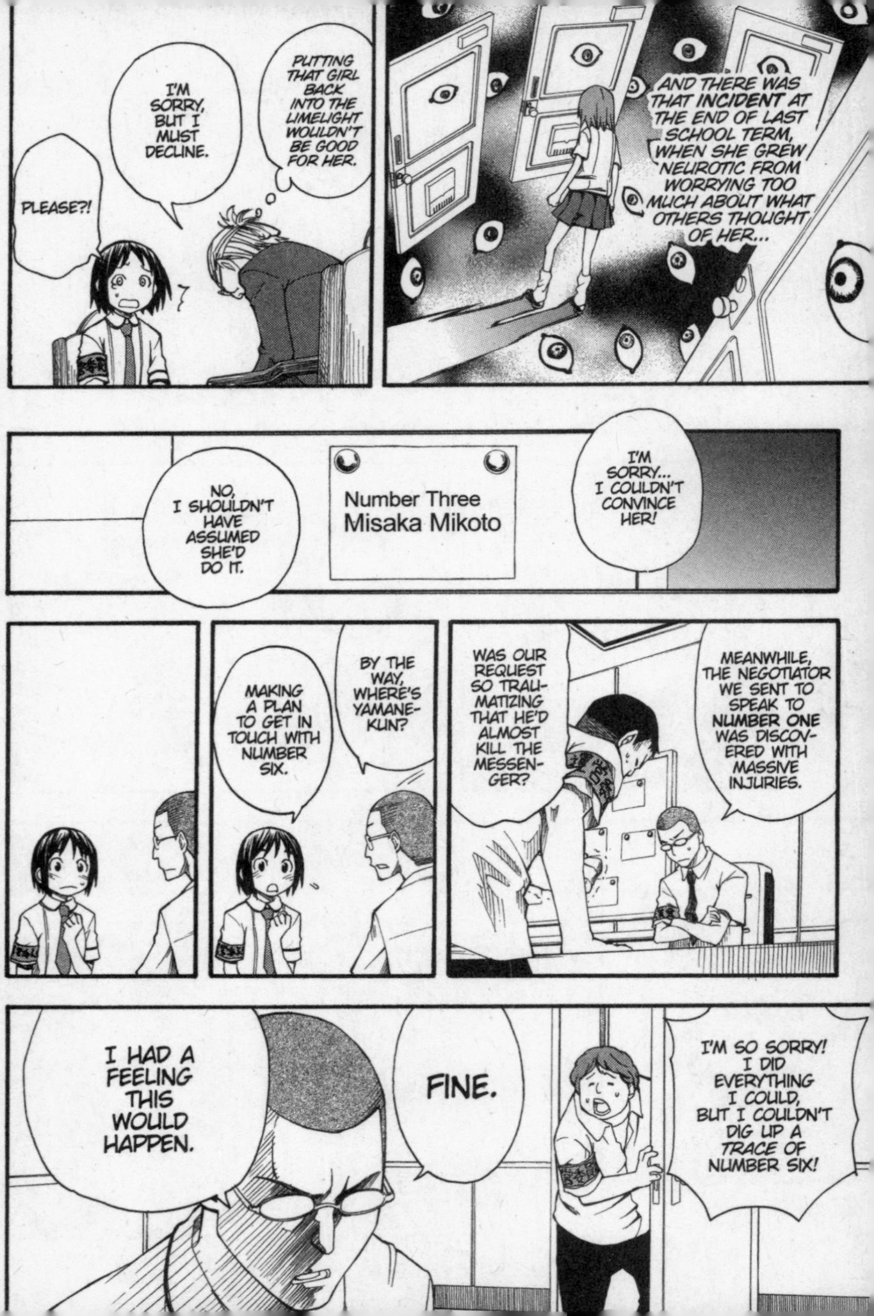
AND THERE WAS THAT INCIDENT AT THE END OF LAST SCHOOL TERM, WHEN SHE GREW NEUROTIC FROM WORRYING TOO MUCH ABOUT WHAT OTHERS THOUGHT OF HER...
PUTTING THAT GIRL BACK INTO THE LIMELIGHT WOULDN'T BE GOOD FOR HER.
I'M SORRY, BUT I MUST DECLINE.
PLEASE?!
I'M SORRY... I COULDN'T CONVINCE HER!
Number Three Misaka Mikoto
NO, I SHOULDN'T HAVE ASSUMED SHE'D DO IT.
MEANWHILE, THE NEGOTIATOR WE SENT TO SPEAK TO NUMBER ONE WAS DISCOVERED WITH MASSIVE INJURIES.
WAS OUR REQUEST SO TRAUMATIZING THAT HE'D ALMOST KILL THE MESSENGER?
BY THE WAY, WHERE'S YAMANE-KUN?
MAKING A PLAN TO GET IN TOUCH WITH NUMBER SIX.
I'M SO SORRY! I DID EVERYTHING I COULD, BUT I COULDN'T DIG UP A TRACE OF NUMBER SIX!
FINE.
I HAD A FEELING THIS WOULD HAPPEN.

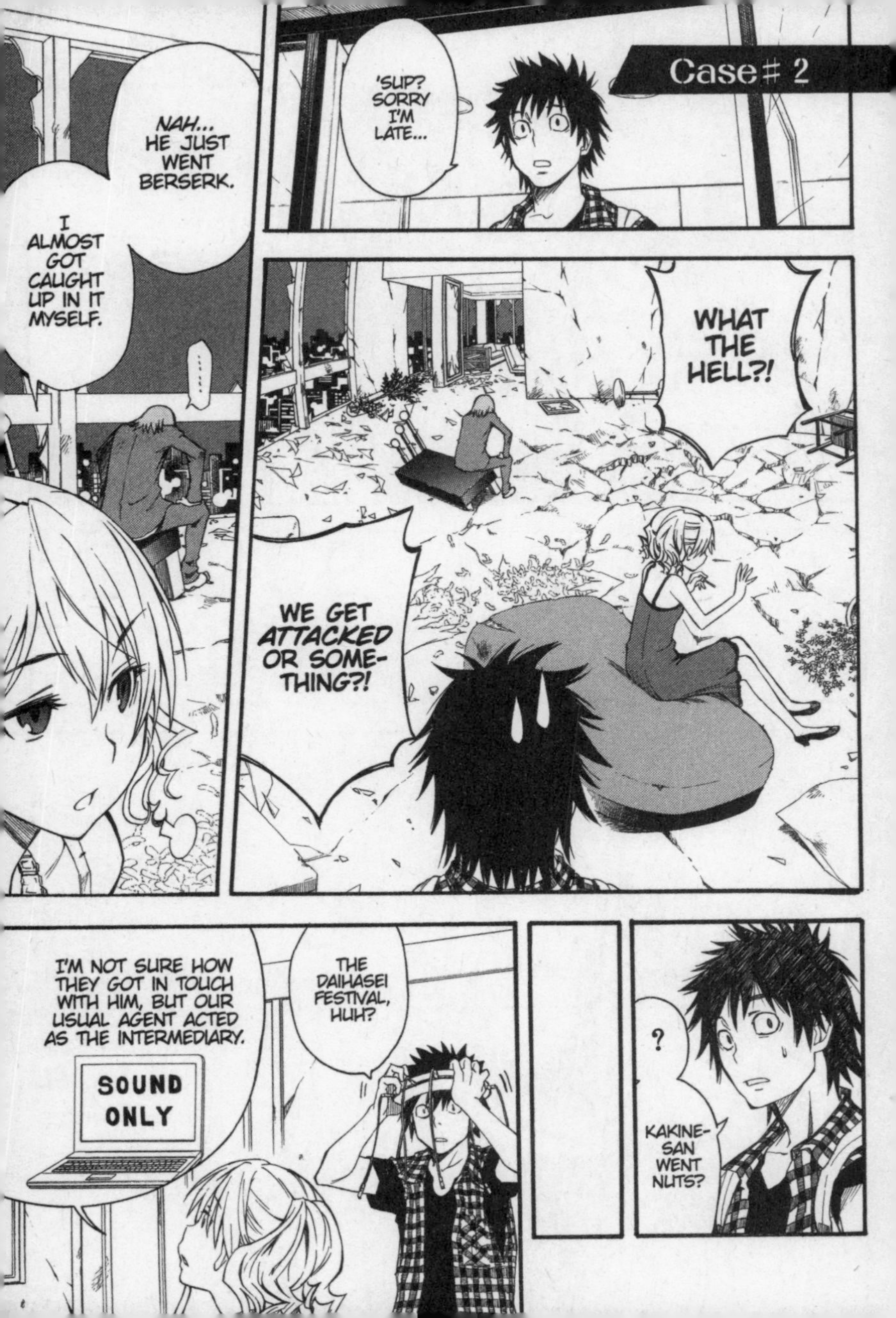
Case # 2
'SUP? SORRY I'M LATE...
WHAT THE HELL?!
WE GET ATTACKED OR SOME-THING?!
NAH... HE JUST WENT BERSERK.
I ALMOST GOT CAUGHT UP IN IT MYSELF.
......
?
KAKINE-SAN WENT NUTS?
THE DAIHASEI FESTIVAL, HUH?
I'M NOT SURE HOW THEY GOT IN TOUCH WITH HIM, BUT OUR USUAL AGENT ACTED AS THE INTERMEDIARY.
SOUND ONLY

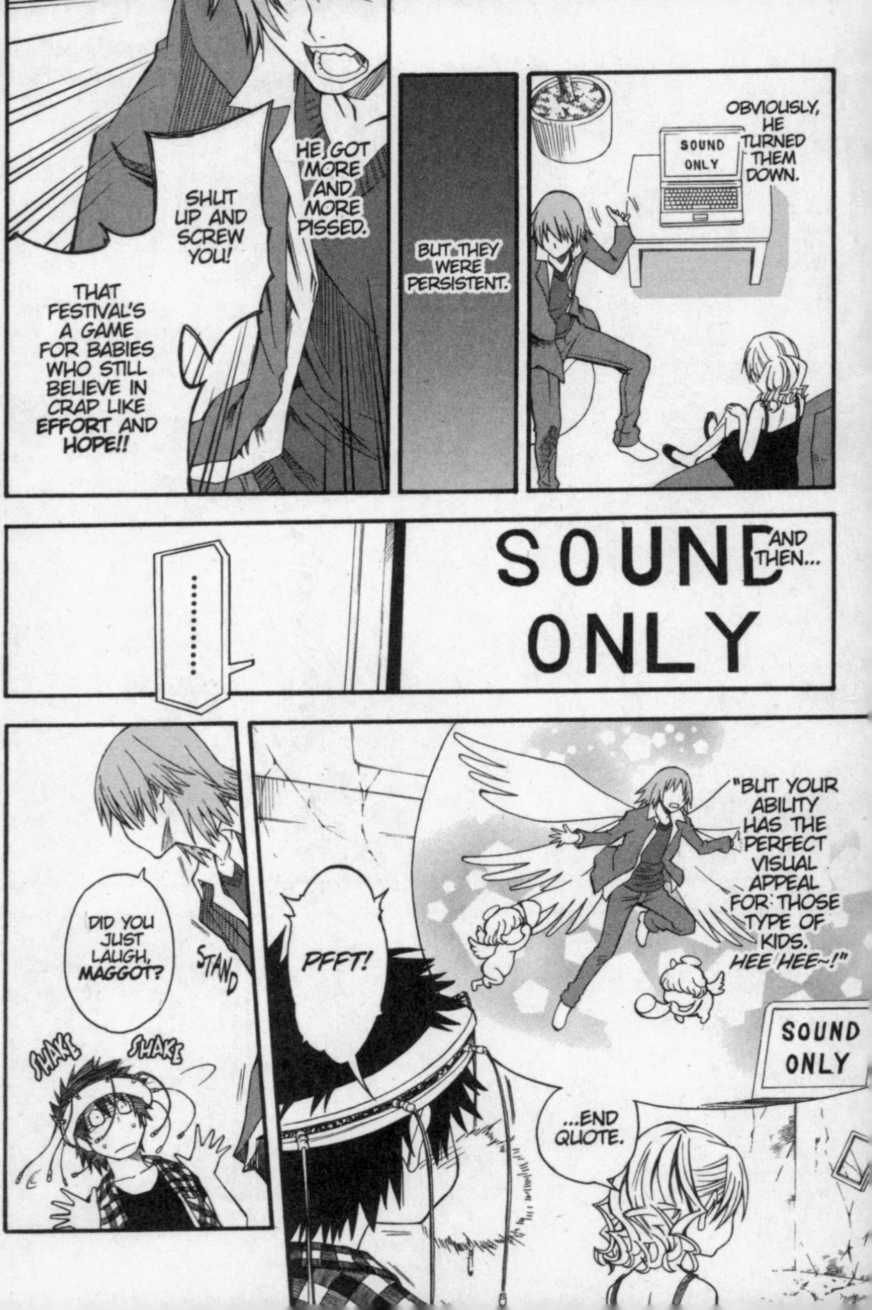
OBVIOUSLY, HE TURNED THEM DOWN.
SOUND ONLY
BUT THEY WERE PERSISTENT.
HE GOT MORE AND MORE PISSED.
SHUT UP AND SCREW YOU!
THAT FESTIVAL'S A GAME FOR BABIES WHO STILL BELIEVE IN CRAP LIKE EFFORT AND HOPE!!
AND THEN...
SOUND ONLY
....
"BUT YOUR ABILITY HAS THE PERFECT VISUAL APPEAL FOR THOSE TYPE OF KIDS. HEE HEE~!"
SOUND ONLY
...END QUOTE.
PFFT!
DID YOU JUST LAUGH, MAGGOT?
STAND
SHAKE SHAKE

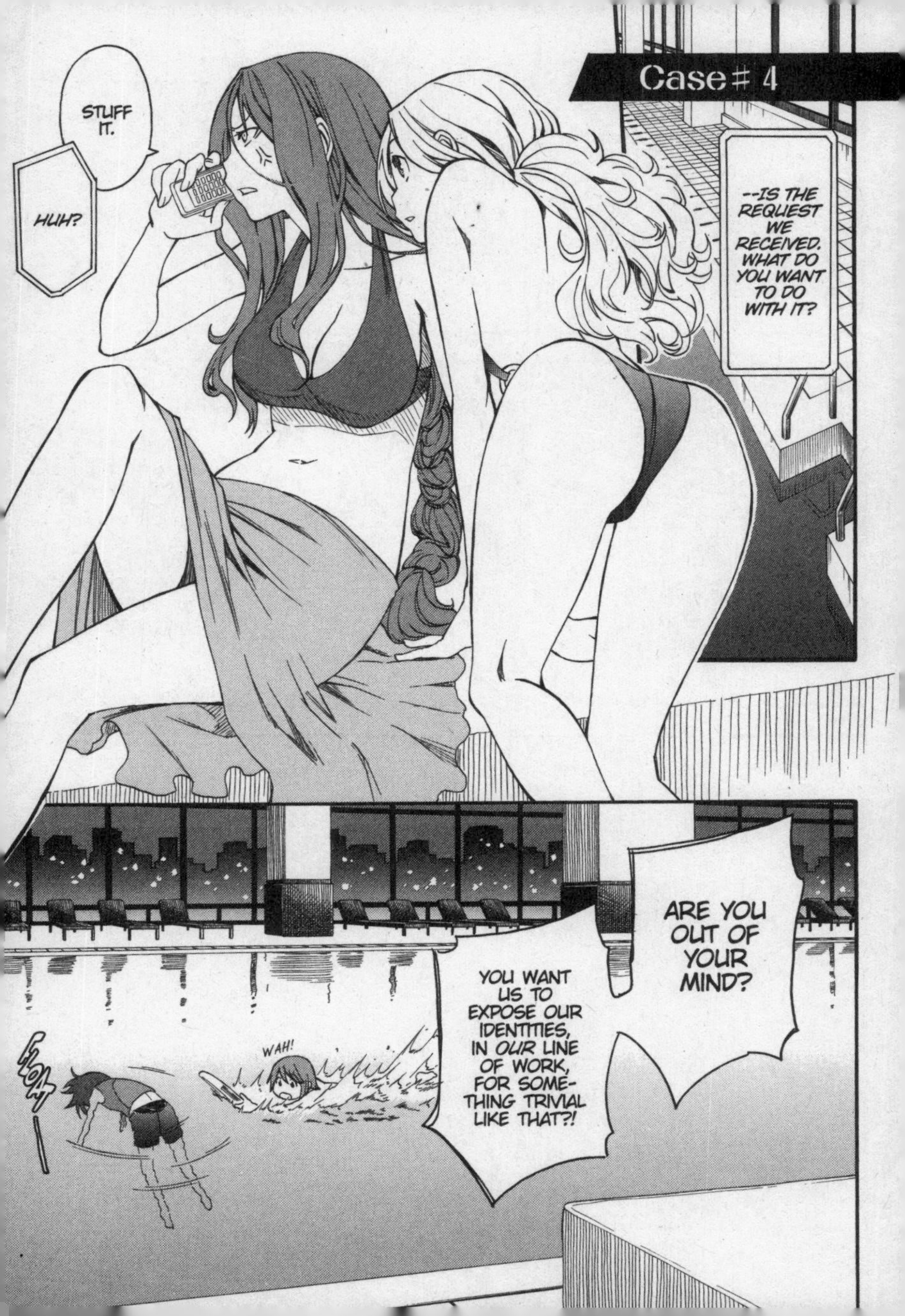
Case # 4
--IS THE REQUEST WE RECEIVED. WHAT DO YOU WANT TO DO WITH IT?
HUH?
STUFF IT.
ARE YOU OUT OF YOUR MIND?
YOU WANT US TO EXPOSE OUR IDENTITIES, IN *OUR* LINE OF WORK, FOR SOME-THING TRIVIAL LIKE THAT?!
WAH!

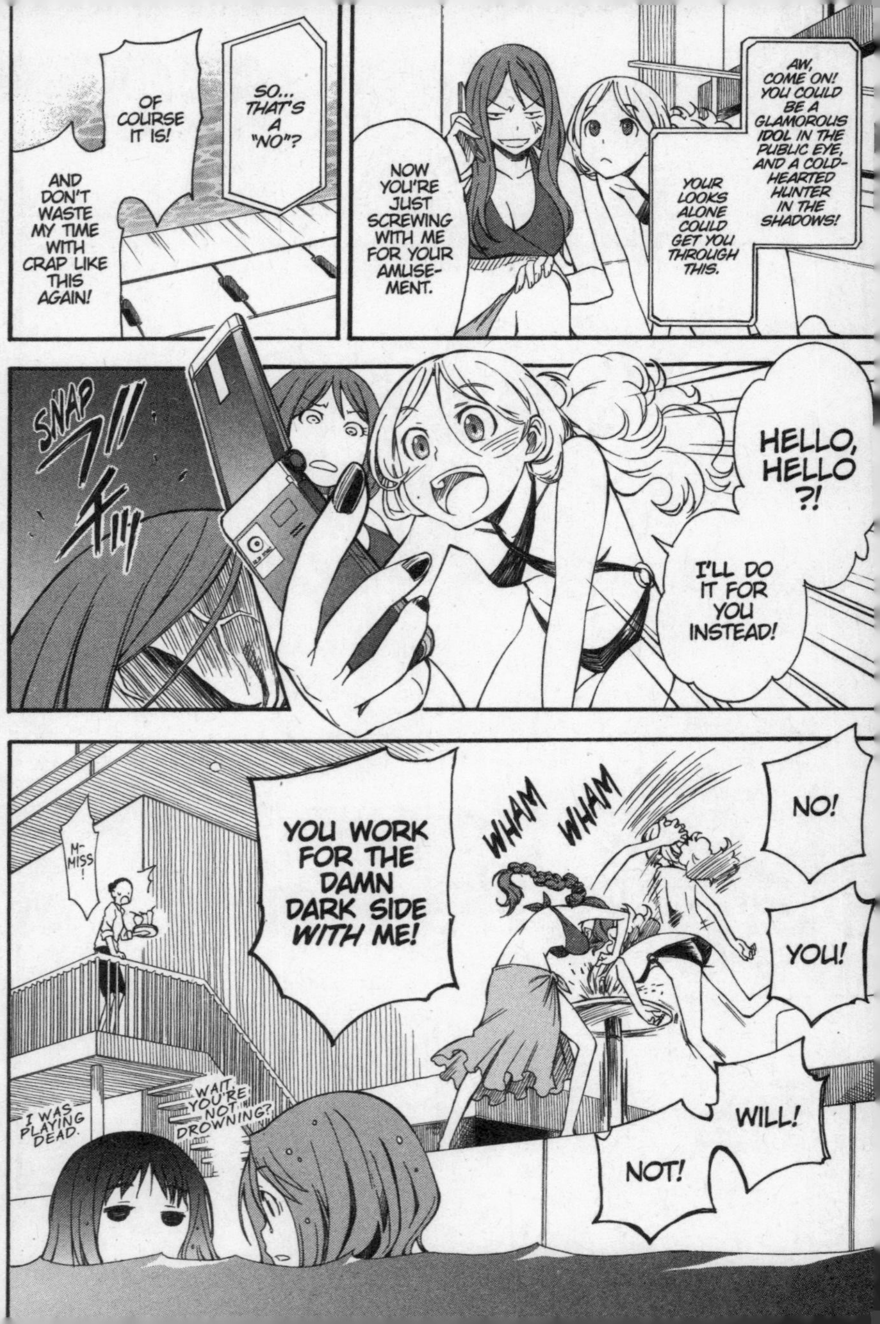
AW, COME ON! YOU COULD BE A GLAMOROUS IDOL IN THE PUBLIC EYE, AND A COLD-HEARTED HUNTER IN THE SHADOWS!
YOUR LOOKS ALONE COULD GET YOU THROUGH THIS.
NOW YOU'RE JUST SCREWING WITH ME FOR YOUR AMUSE-MENT.
SO... THAT'S A "NO"?
OF COURSE IT IS!
AND DON'T WASTE MY TIME WITH CRAP LIKE THIS AGAIN!
HELLO, HELLO ?!
I'LL DO IT FOR YOU INSTEAD!
SNAP
NO!
YOU!
WILL!
NOT!
WHAM
WHAM
YOU WORK FOR THE DAMN DARK SIDE WITH ME!
M-MISS!
WAIT. YOU'RE NOT DROWNING?
I WAS PLAYING DEAD.

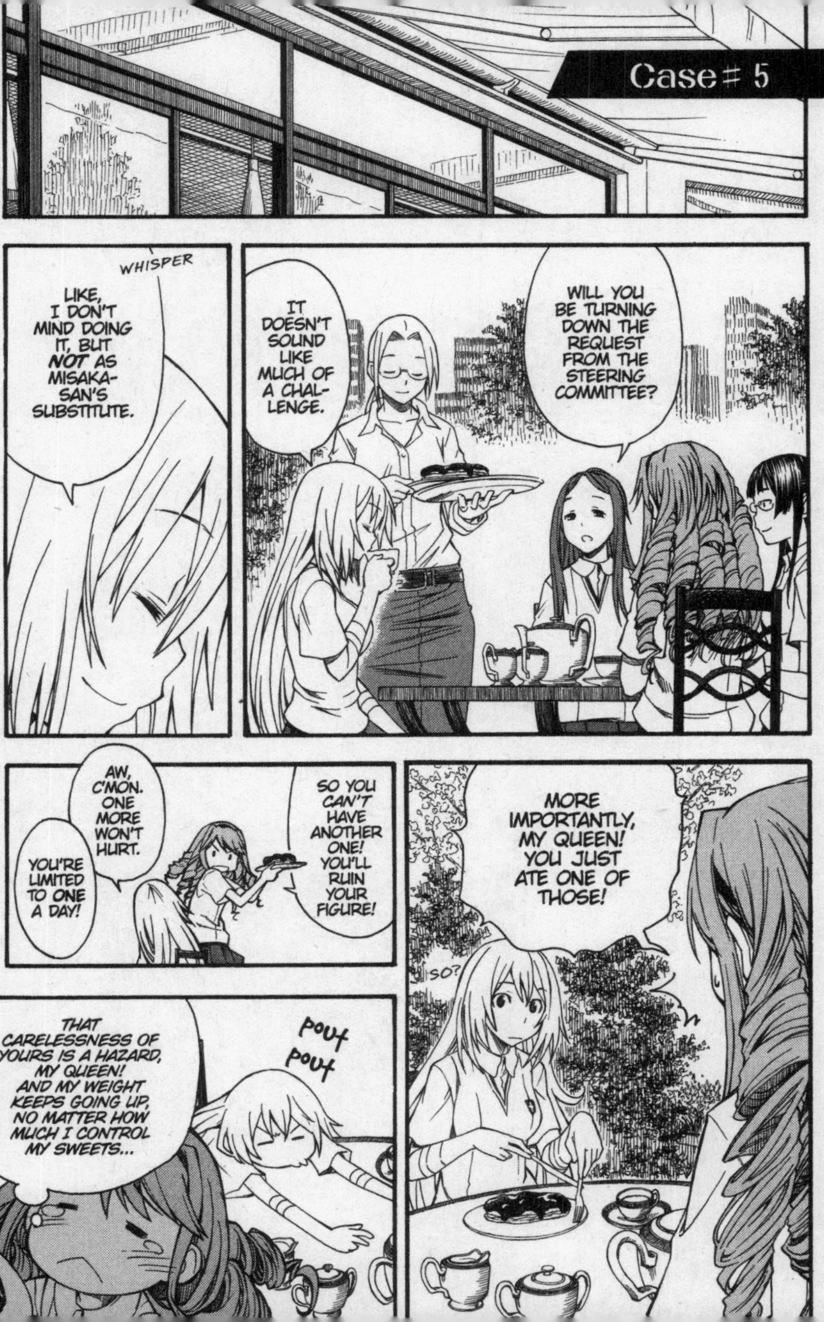
Case # 5
WILL YOU BE TURNING DOWN THE REQUEST FROM THE STEERING COMMITTEE?
IT DOESN'T SOUND LIKE MUCH OF A CHALLENGE.
WHISPER
LIKE, I DON'T MIND DOING IT, BUT NOT AS MISAKA-SAN'S SUBSTITUTE.
MORE IMPORTANTLY, MY QUEEN! YOU JUST ATE ONE OF THOSE!
SO?
SO YOU CAN'T HAVE ANOTHER ONE! YOU'LL RUIN YOUR FIGURE!
AW, C'MON. ONE MORE WON'T HURT.
YOU'RE LIMITED TO ONE A DAY!
POUT POUT
THAT CARELESSNESS OF YOURS IS A HAZARD, MY QUEEN! AND MY WEIGHT KEEPS GOING UP, NO MATTER HOW MUCH I CONTROL MY SWEETS...

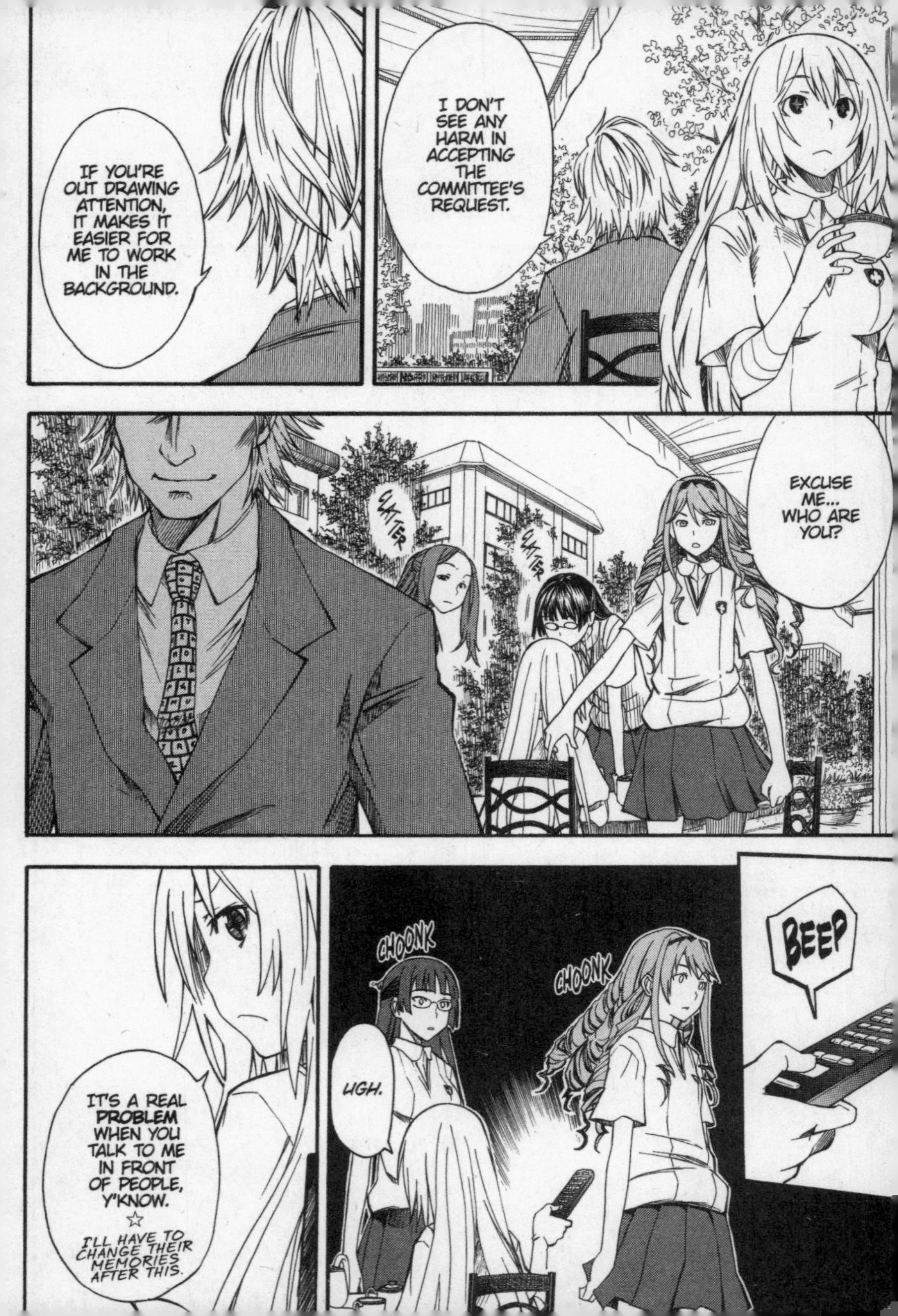
I DON'T SEE ANY HARM IN ACCEPTING THE COMMITTEE'S REQUEST.
IF YOU'RE OUT DRAWING ATTENTION, IT MAKES IT EASIER FOR ME TO WORK IN THE BACKGROUND.
EXCUSE ME... WHO ARE YOU?
CLATTER
CLATTER
BEEP
CHOONK
CHOONK
UGH.
IT'S A REAL PROBLEM WHEN YOU TALK TO ME IN FRONT OF PEOPLE, Y'KNOW. ☆
I'LL HAVE TO CHANGE THEIR MEMORIES AFTER THIS.

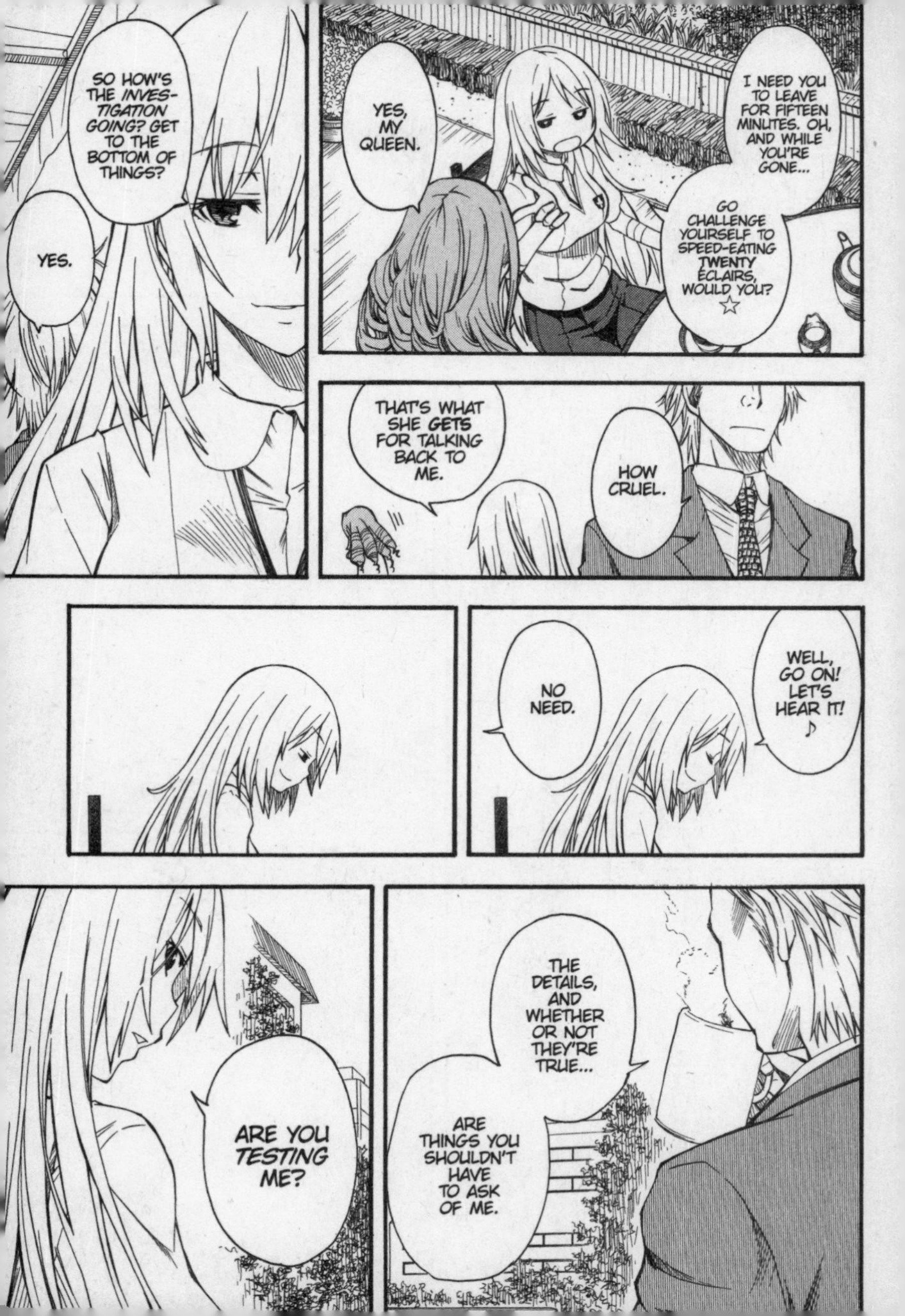
I NEED YOU TO LEAVE FOR FIFTEEN MINUTES. OH, AND WHILE YOU'RE GONE...
GO CHALLENGE YOURSELF TO SPEED-EATING TWENTY ÉCLAIRS, WOULD YOU? ☆
YES, MY QUEEN.
HOW CRUEL.
THAT'S WHAT SHE GETS FOR TALKING BACK TO ME.
SO HOW'S THE *INVESTIGATION* GOING? GET TO THE BOTTOM OF THINGS?
YES.
WELL, GO ON! LET'S HEAR IT! ♪
NO NEED.
THE DETAILS, AND WHETHER OR NOT THEY'RE TRUE...
ARE THINGS YOU SHOULDN'T HAVE TO ASK OF ME.
ARE YOU *TESTING* ME?

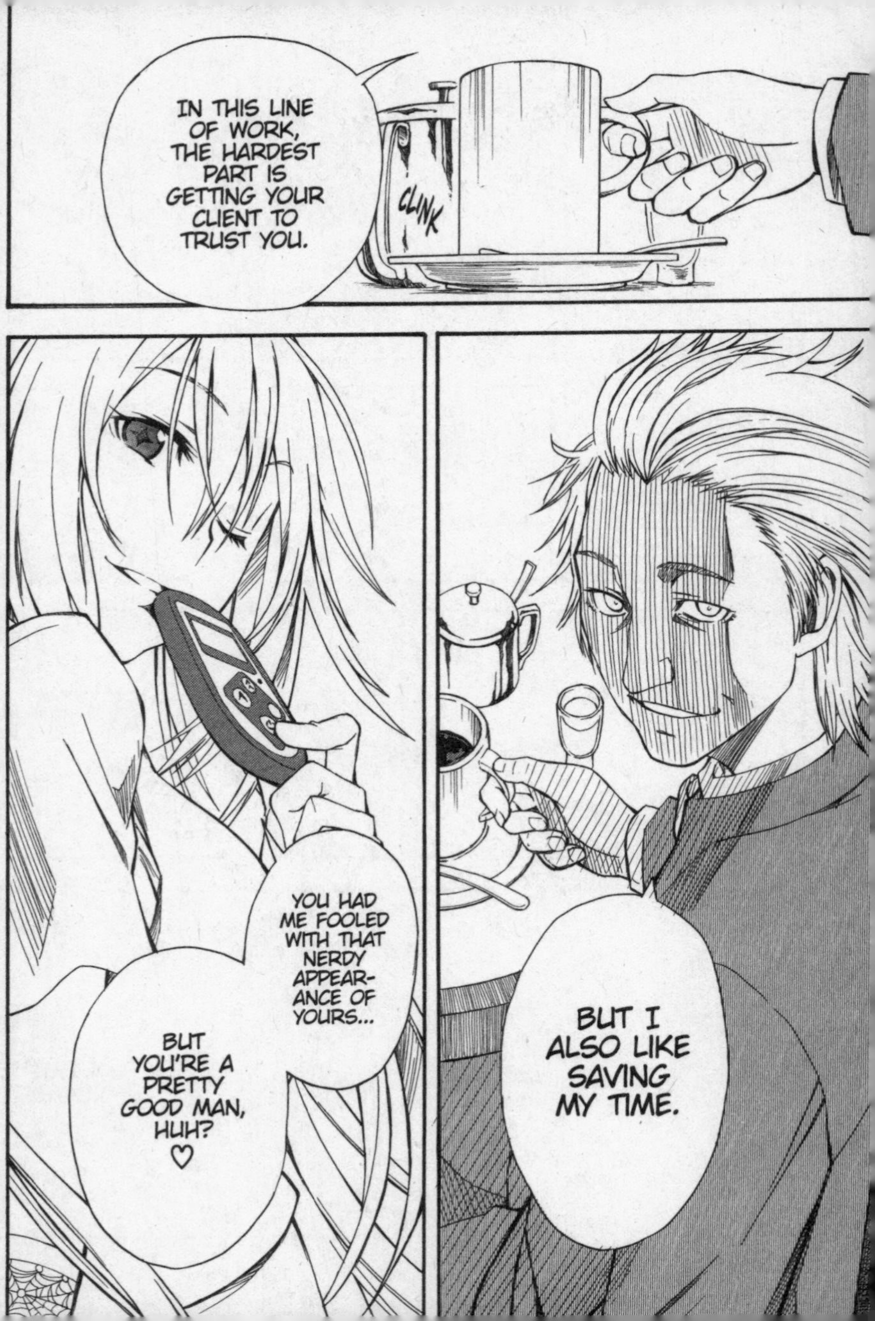
IN THIS LINE OF WORK, THE HARDEST PART IS GETTING YOUR CLIENT TO TRUST YOU.
CLINK
BUT I ALSO LIKE SAVING MY TIME.
YOU HAD ME FOOLED WITH THAT NERDY APPEARANCE OF YOURS...
BUT YOU'RE A PRETTY GOOD MAN, HUH? ♡

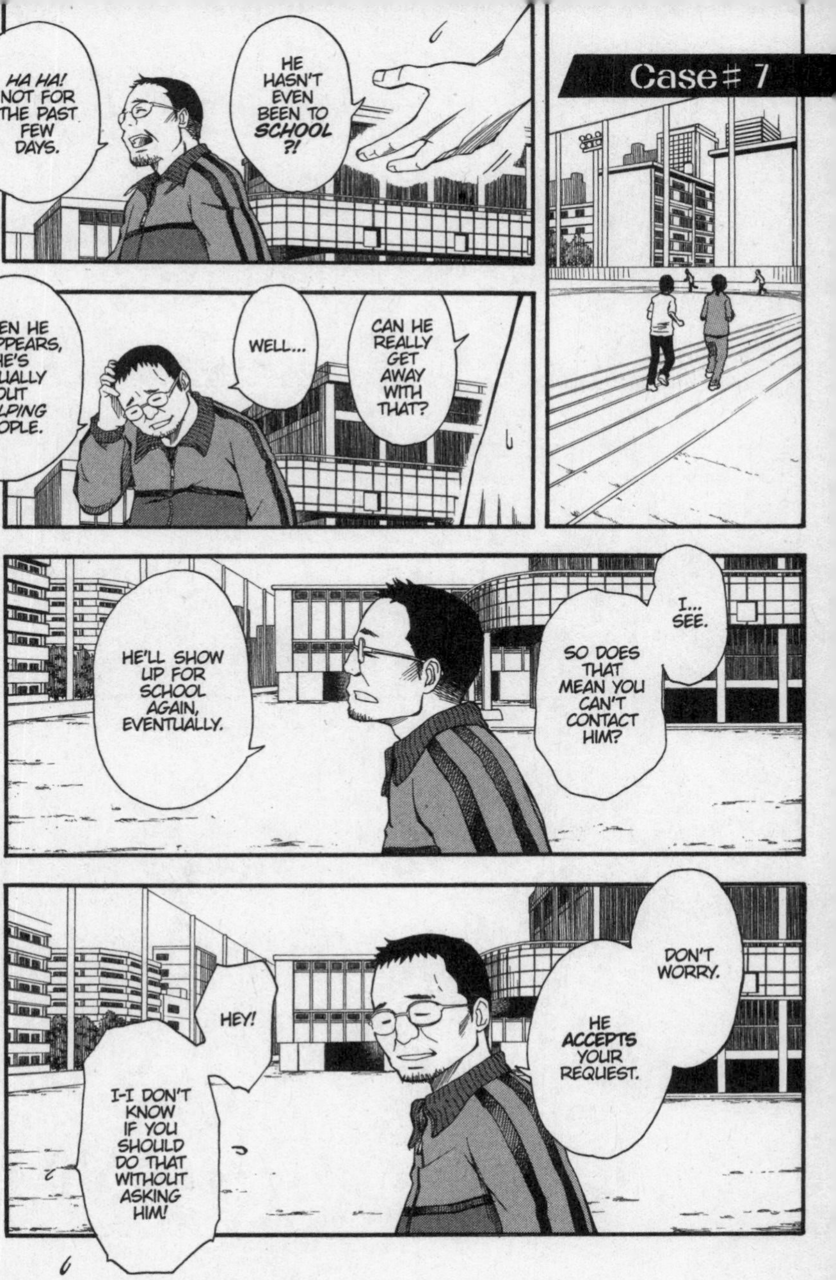
Case # 7
HE HASN'T EVEN BEEN TO SCHOOL?!
HA HA! NOT FOR THE PAST FEW DAYS.
CAN HE REALLY GET AWAY WITH THAT?
WELL...
WHEN HE DISAPPEARS, HE'S USUALLY OUT HELPING PEOPLE.
I... SEE.
SO DOES THAT MEAN YOU CAN'T CONTACT HIM?
HE'LL SHOW UP FOR SCHOOL AGAIN, EVENTUALLY.
DON'T WORRY.
HE ACCEPTS YOUR REQUEST.
HEY!
I-I DON'T KNOW IF YOU SHOULD DO THAT WITHOUT ASKING HIM!

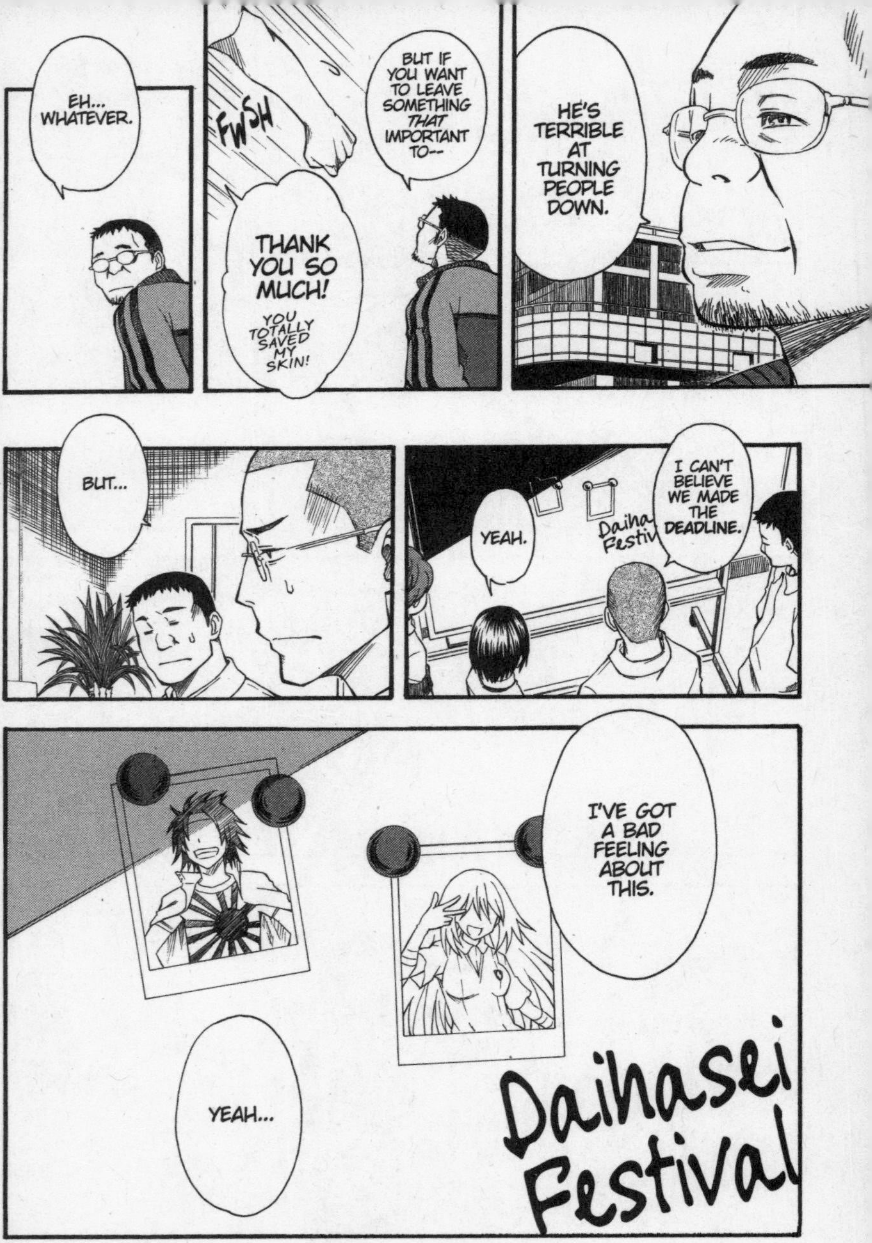
HE'S TERRIBLE AT TURNING PEOPLE DOWN.
BUT IF YOU WANT TO LEAVE SOMETHING *THAT* IMPORTANT TO--
FWSH
THANK YOU SO MUCH!
YOU TOTALLY SAVED MY SKIN!
EH... WHATEVER.
I CAN'T BELIEVE WE MADE THE DEADLINE.
YEAH.
BUT...
I'VE GOT A BAD FEELING ABOUT THIS.
Daihasei Festival
YEAH...

A Certain
SCIENTIFIC
Railgun

A Certain New Story Arc's Standbys

WE'RE FINALLY STARTING A BRAND NEW STORY ARC!
ARE WE?
IT'S NOT THAT EXCITING.
WHAT ARE YOU TALKING ABOUT?!
IT'S TIME TO PUT YOURSELF OUT THERE! YOU DON'T WANT TO LOSE YOUR PLACE IN THE SERIES!
KEEP YOUR VOICE DOWN, UIHARU!
OR END UP WITH ZERO APPEAR-ANCES!
HMM? WHAT WAS THAT?
CRUSH
ZERO APPEAR-ANCES LATELY.

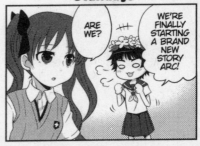

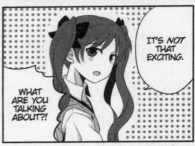

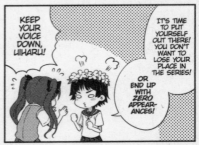

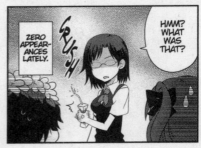

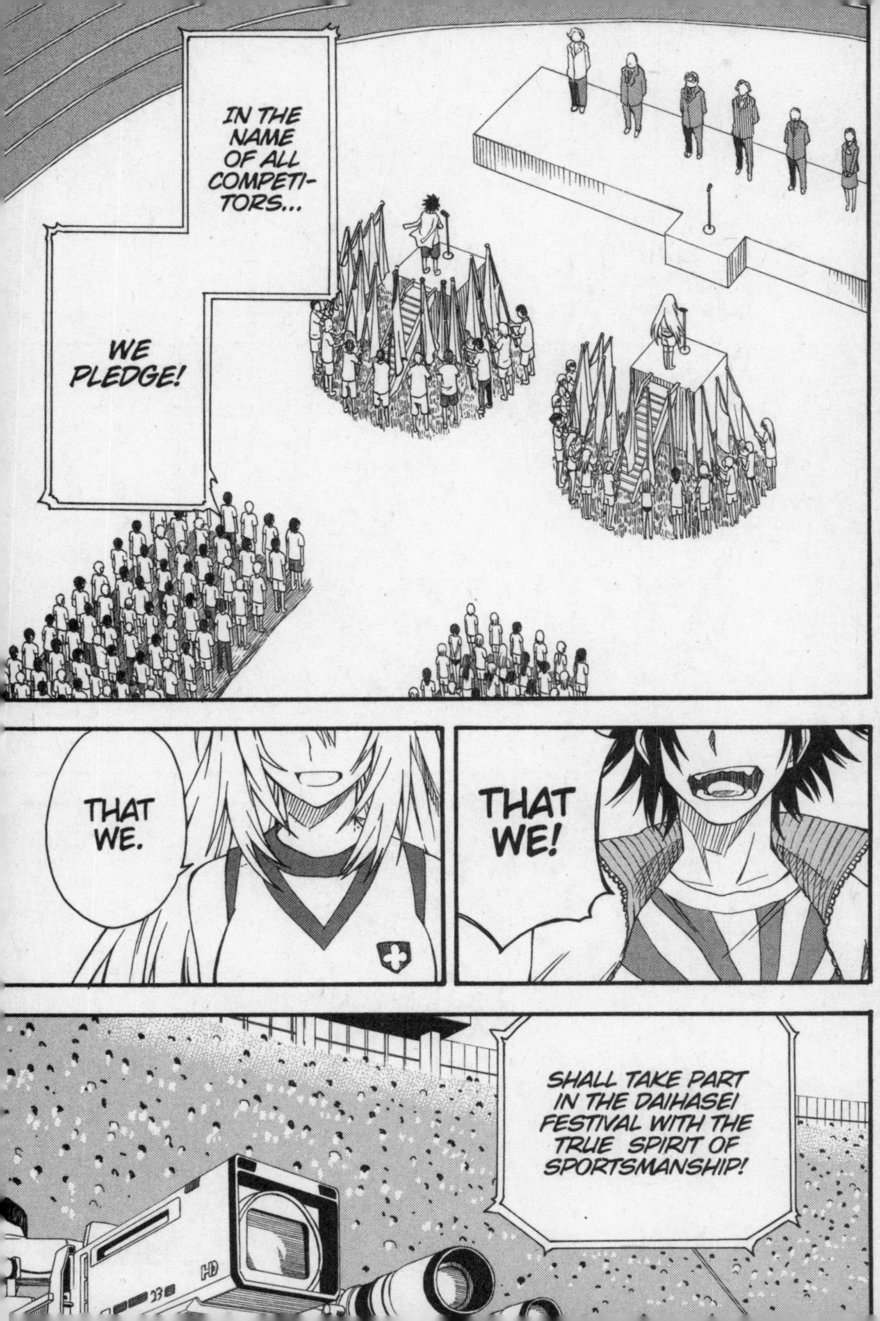
IN THE NAME OF ALL COMPETI-TORS...
WE PLEDGE!
THAT WE!
THAT WE.
SHALL TAKE PART IN THE DAIHASEI FESTIVAL WITH THE TRUE SPIRIT OF SPORTSMANSHIP!

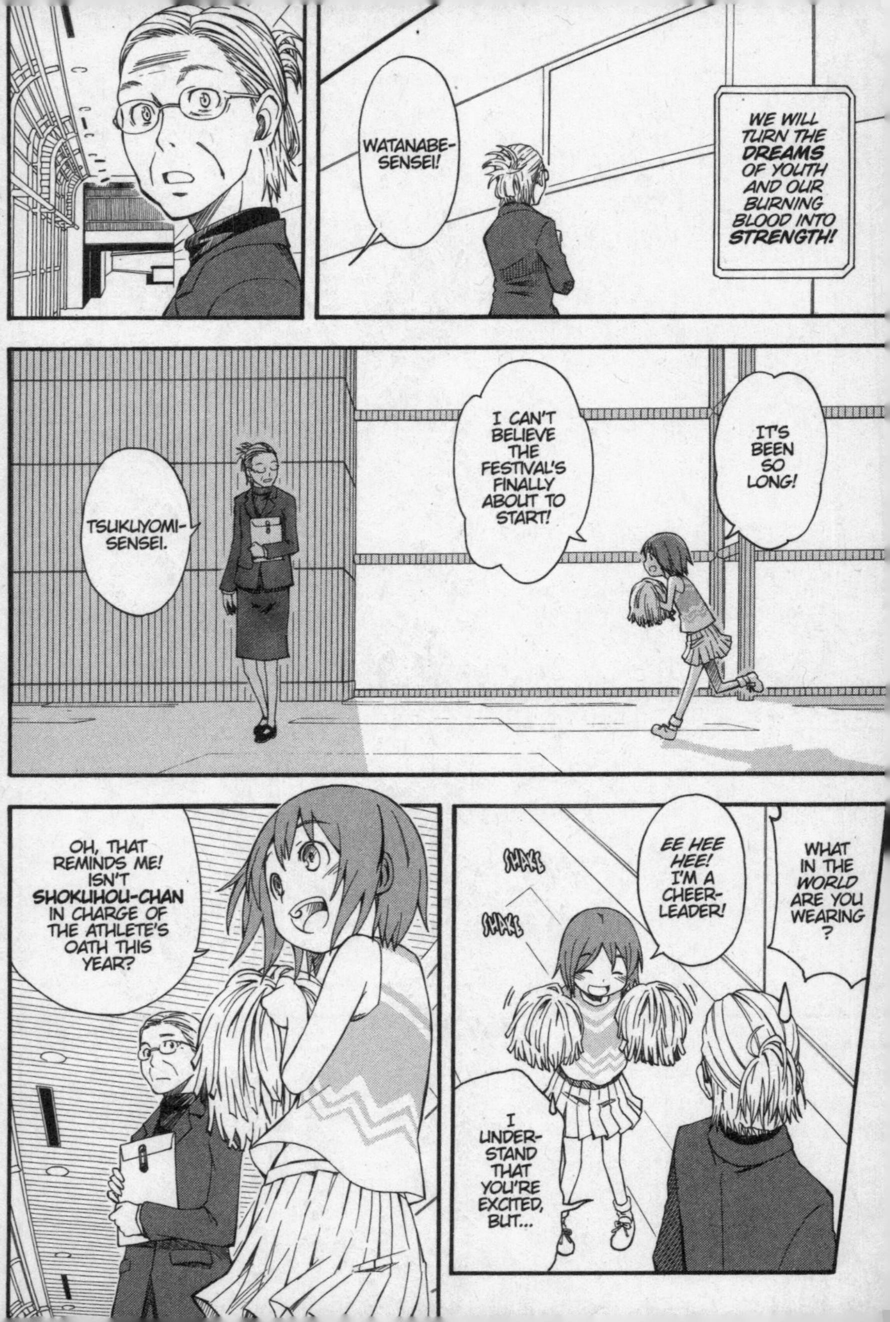
WE WILL TURN THE DREAMS OF YOUTH AND OUR BURNING BLOOD INTO STRENGTH!
WATANABE-SENSEI!
IT'S BEEN SO LONG!
I CAN'T BELIEVE THE FESTIVAL'S FINALLY ABOUT TO START!
TSUKUYOMI-SENSEI.
WHAT IN THE WORLD ARE YOU WEARING?
EE HEE HEE! I'M A CHEER-LEADER!
SHAKE
SHAKE
I UNDER-STAND THAT YOU'RE EXCITED, BUT...
OH, THAT REMINDS ME! ISN'T SHOKUHOU-CHAN IN CHARGE OF THE ATHLETE'S OATH THIS YEAR?

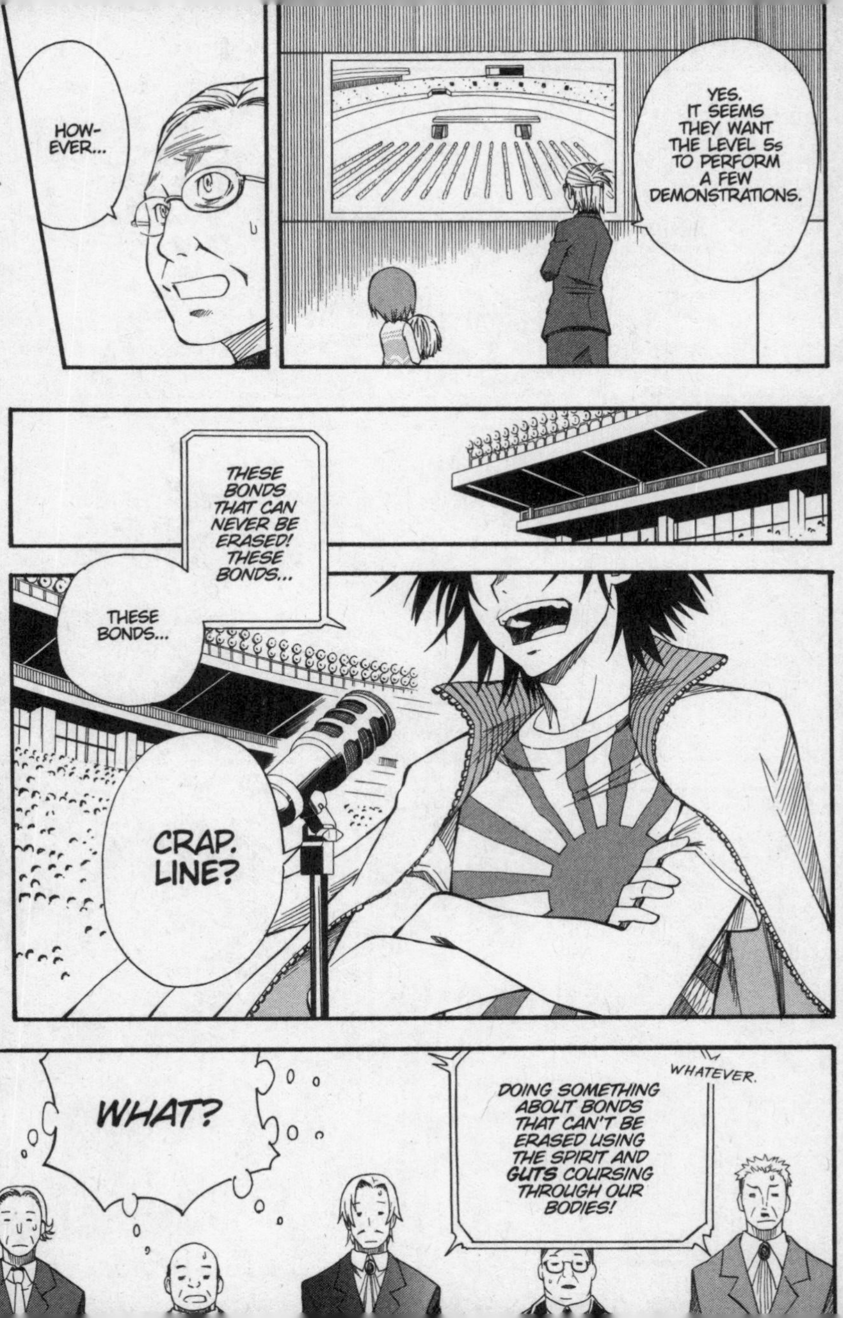
YES. IT SEEMS THEY WANT THE LEVEL 5s TO PERFORM A FEW DEMONSTRATIONS.
HOW-EVER...
THESE BONDS THAT CAN NEVER BE ERASED! THESE BONDS...
THESE BONDS...
CRAP. LINE?
WHATEVER.
DOING SOMETHING ABOUT BONDS THAT CAN'T BE ERASED USING THE SPIRIT AND **GUTS** COURSING THROUGH OUR BODIES!
WHAT?

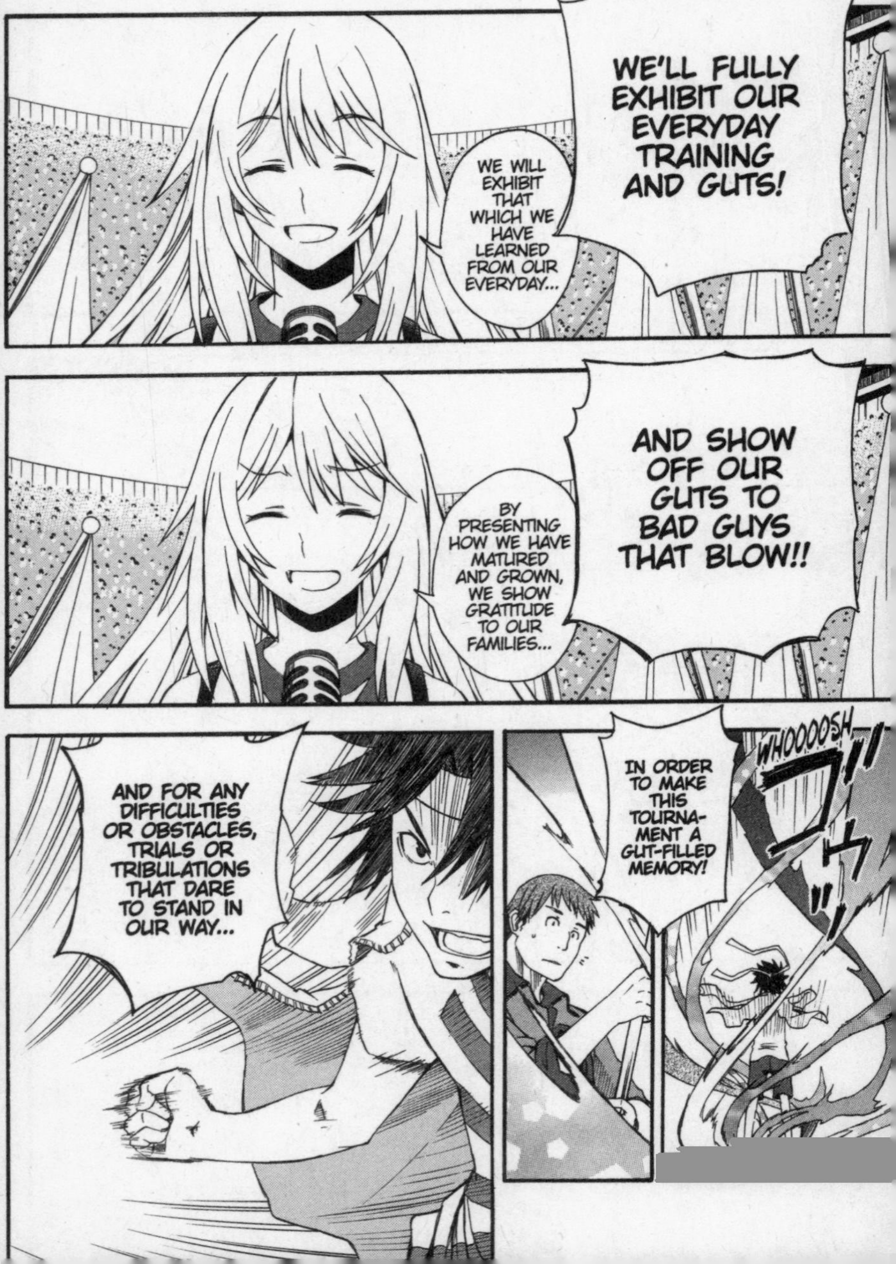
WE'LL FULLY EXHIBIT OUR EVERYDAY TRAINING AND GUTS!
WE WILL EXHIBIT THAT WHICH WE HAVE LEARNED FROM OUR EVERYDAY...
AND SHOW OFF OUR GUTS TO BAD GUYS THAT BLOW!!
BY PRESENTING HOW WE HAVE MATURED AND GROWN, WE SHOW GRATITUDE TO OUR FAMILIES...
IN ORDER TO MAKE THIS TOURNA-MENT A GUT-FILLED MEMORY!
WHOOOOSH
AND FOR ANY DIFFICULTIES OR OBSTACLES, TRIALS OR TRIBULATIONS THAT DARE TO STAND IN OUR WAY...

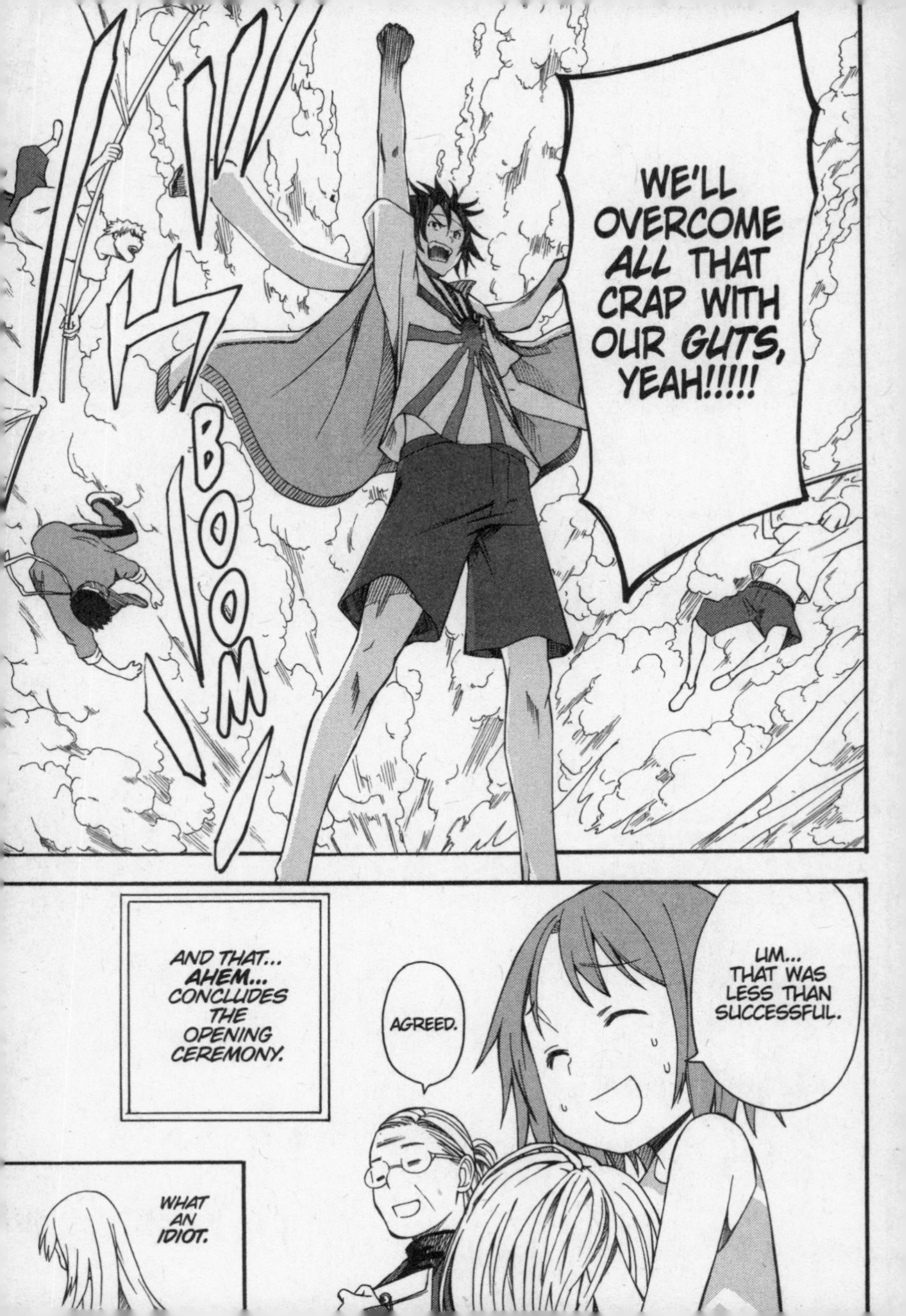
WE'LL OVERCOME ALL THAT CRAP WITH OUR GUTS, YEAH!!!!!
BOOM
UM... THAT WAS LESS THAN SUCCESSFUL.
AGREED.
AND THAT... AHEM... CONCLUDES THE OPENING CEREMONY.
WHAT AN IDIOT.

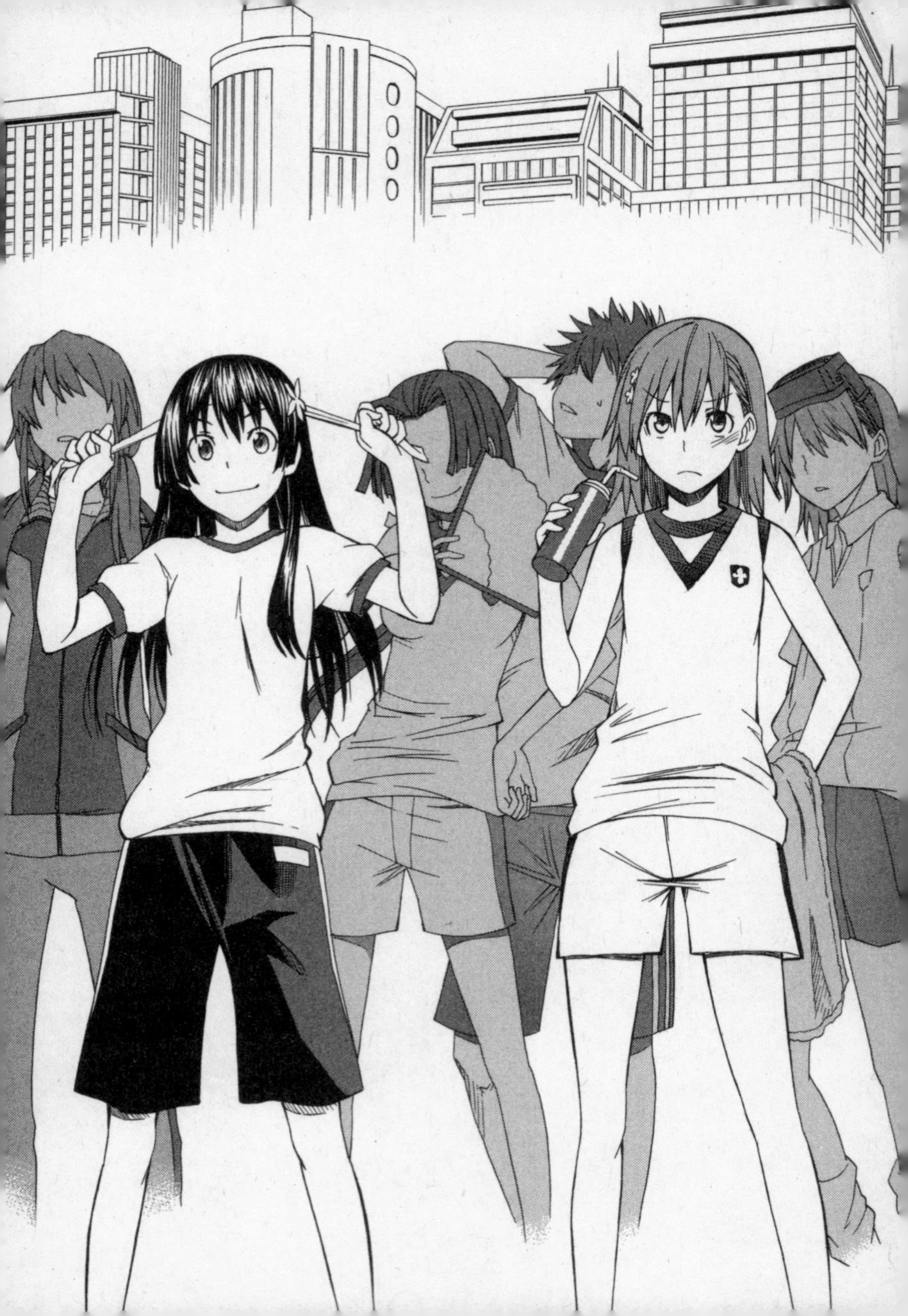

CHAPTER 44: COMMENCEMENT

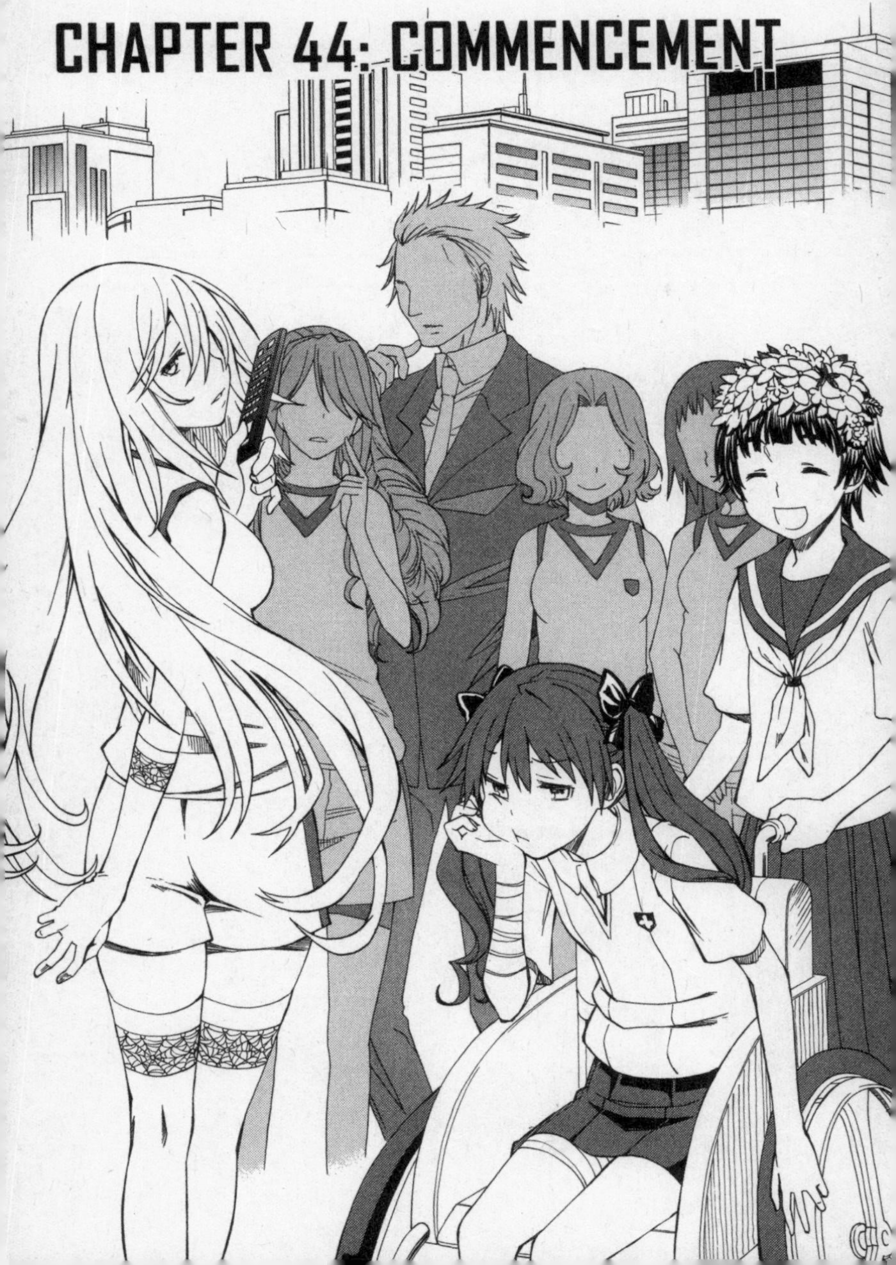

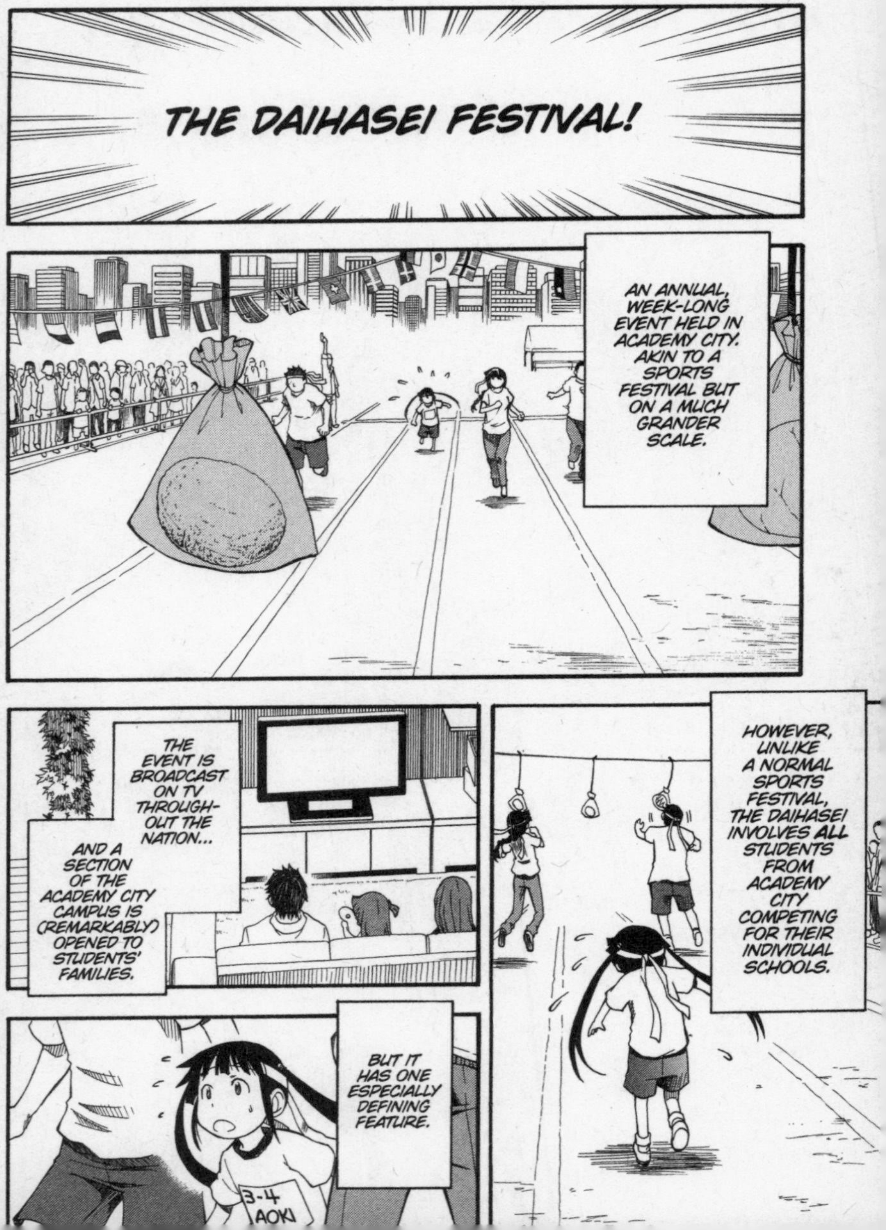
THE DAIHASEI FESTIVAL!
AN ANNUAL, WEEK-LONG EVENT HELD IN ACADEMY CITY. AKIN TO A SPORTS FESTIVAL BUT ON A MUCH GRANDER SCALE.
HOWEVER, UNLIKE A NORMAL SPORTS FESTIVAL, THE DAIHASEI INVOLVES ALL STUDENTS FROM ACADEMY CITY COMPETING FOR THEIR INDIVIDUAL SCHOOLS.
THE EVENT IS BROADCAST ON TV THROUGH-OUT THE NATION...
AND A SECTION OF THE ACADEMY CITY CAMPUS IS (REMARKABLY) OPENED TO STUDENTS' FAMILIES.
BUT IT HAS ONE ESPECIALLY DEFINING FEATURE.
3-4
AOKI

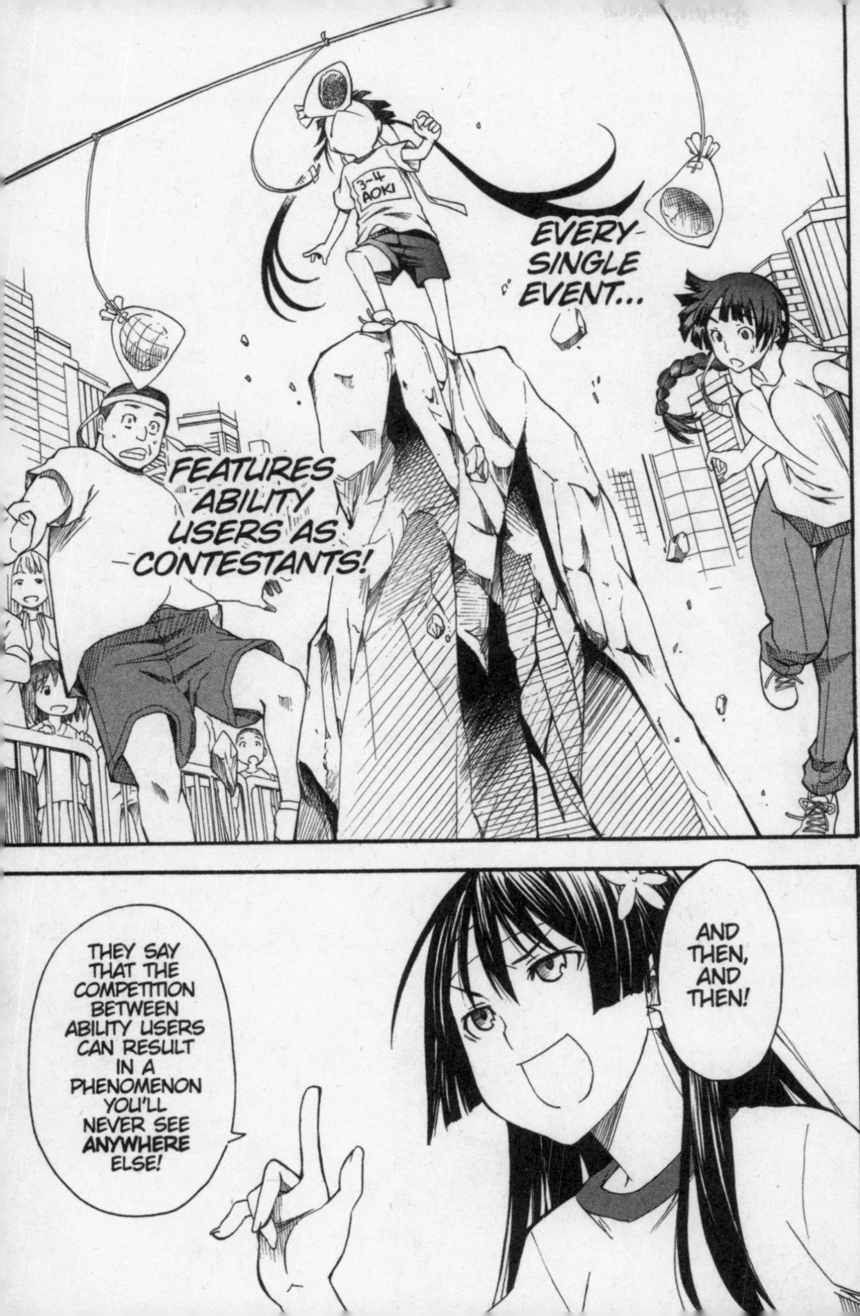
3-4
AOKI
EVERY SINGLE EVENT...
FEATURES ABILITY USERS AS CONTESTANTS!
AND THEN, AND THEN!
THEY SAY THAT THE COMPETITION BETWEEN ABILITY USERS CAN RESULT IN A PHENOMENON YOU'LL NEVER SEE ANYWHERE ELSE!

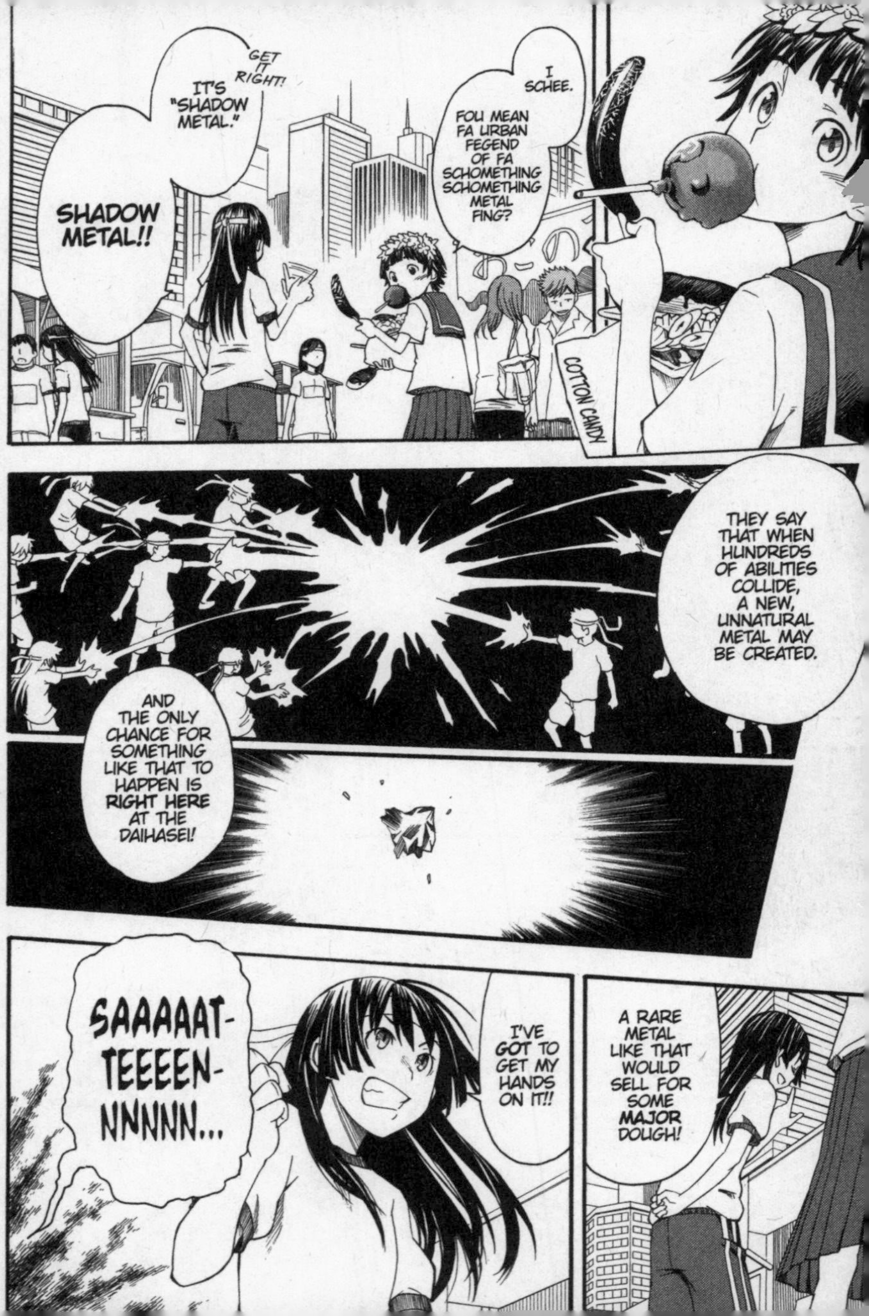

I SCHEE.
FOU MEAN FA URBAN FEGEND OF FA SCHOMETHING SCHOMETHING METAL FING?
COTTON CANDY
IT'S "SHADOW METAL."
GET IT RIGHT!
SHADOW METAL!!
THEY SAY THAT WHEN HUNDREDS OF ABILITIES COLLIDE, A NEW, UNNATURAL METAL MAY BE CREATED.
AND THE ONLY CHANCE FOR SOMETHING LIKE THAT TO HAPPEN IS RIGHT HERE AT THE DAIHASEI!
A RARE METAL LIKE THAT WOULD SELL FOR SOME MAJOR DOUGH!
I'VE GOT TO GET MY HANDS ON IT!!
SAAAAAT-TEEEEEN-NNNNN...

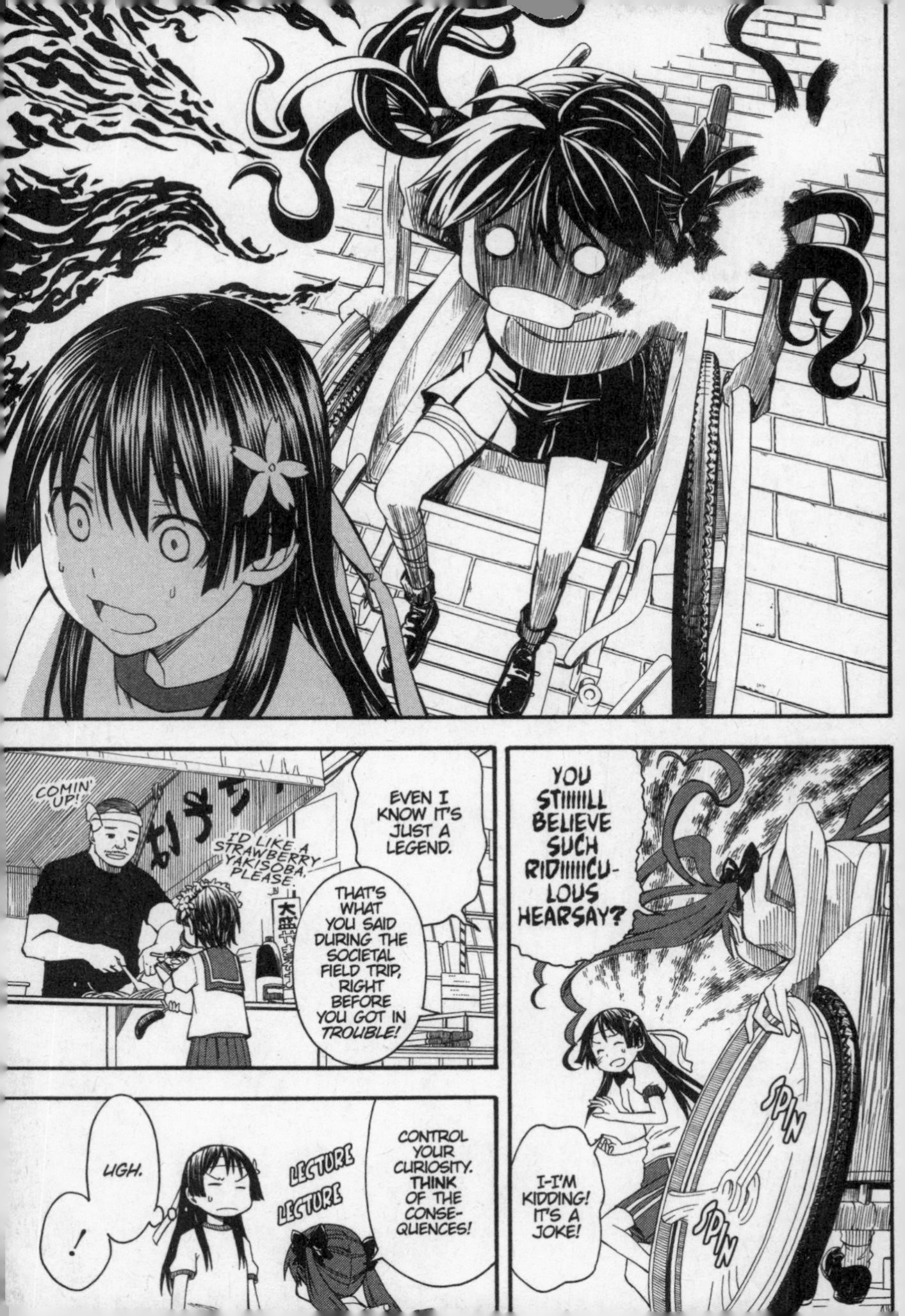
YOU STIIIIILL BELIEVE SUCH RIDIIIIICU-LOUS HEARSAY?
SPIN
SPIN
I-I'M KIDDING! IT'S A JOKE!
EVEN I KNOW IT'S JUST A LEGEND.
THAT'S WHAT YOU SAID DURING THE SOCIETAL FIELD TRIP, RIGHT BEFORE YOU GOT IN *TROUBLE!*
I'D LIKE A STRAWBERRY YAKISOBA, PLEASE.
COMIN' UP!
CONTROL YOUR CURIOSITY. THINK OF THE CONSE-QUENCES!
LECTURE
LECTURE
UGH.
!

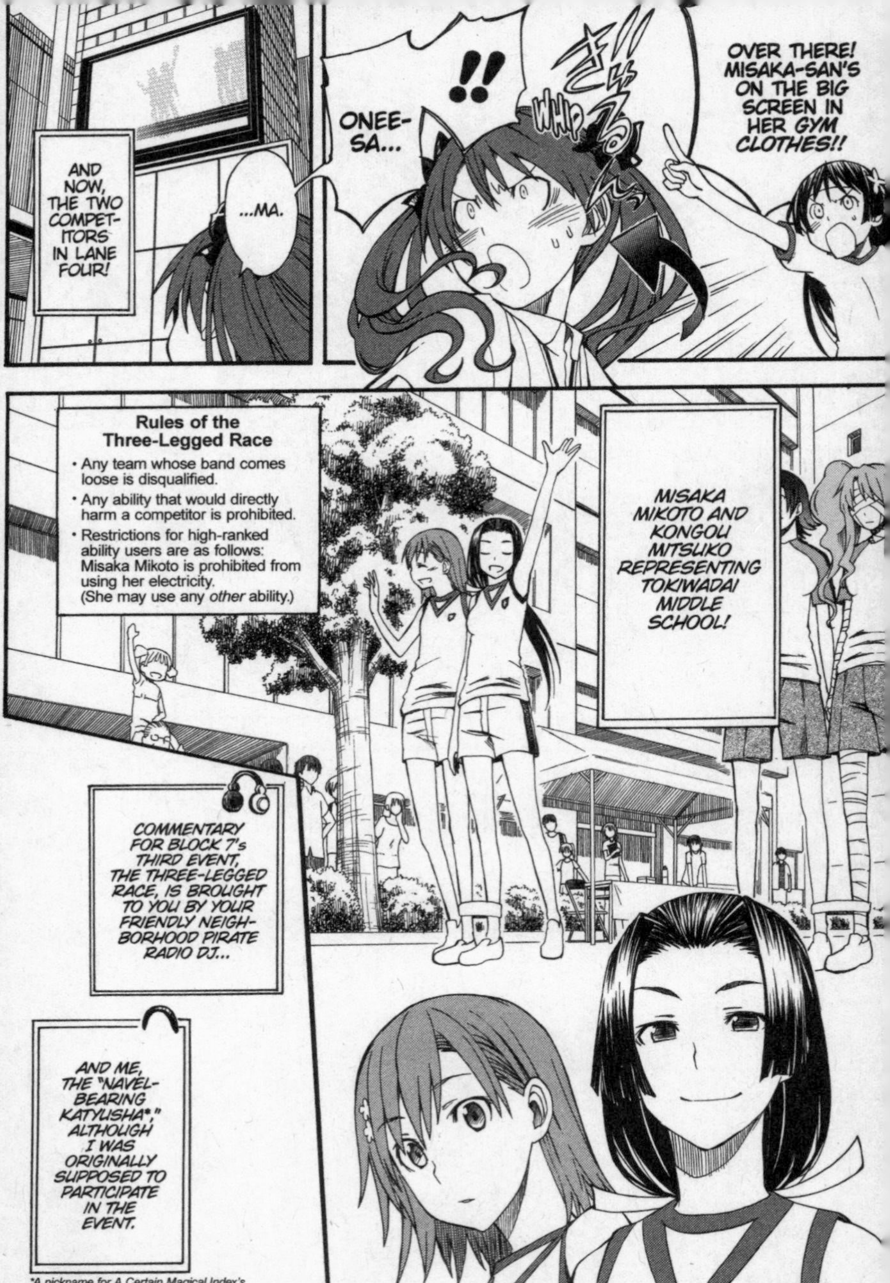
OVER THERE! MISAKA-SAN'S ON THE BIG SCREEN IN HER GYM CLOTHES!!
WHIP
!!
ONEE-SA...
...MA.
AND NOW, THE TWO COMPETITORS IN LANE FOUR!
MISAKA MIKOTO AND KONGOU MITSUKO REPRESENTING TOKIWADAI MIDDLE SCHOOL!
Rules of the Three-Legged Race
· Any team whose band comes loose is disqualified.
· Any ability that would directly harm a competitor is prohibited.
· Restrictions for high-ranked ability users are as follows: Misaka Mikoto is prohibited from using her electricity. (She may use any *other* ability.)
COMMENTARY FOR BLOCK 7's THIRD EVENT, THE THREE-LEGGED RACE, IS BROUGHT TO YOU BY YOUR FRIENDLY NEIGHBORHOOD PIRATE RADIO DJ...
AND ME, THE "NAVEL-BEARING KATYUSHA*," ALTHOUGH I WAS ORIGINALLY SUPPOSED TO PARTICIPATE IN THE EVENT.

*A nickname for *A Certain Magical Index*'s Kumokawa Seria.

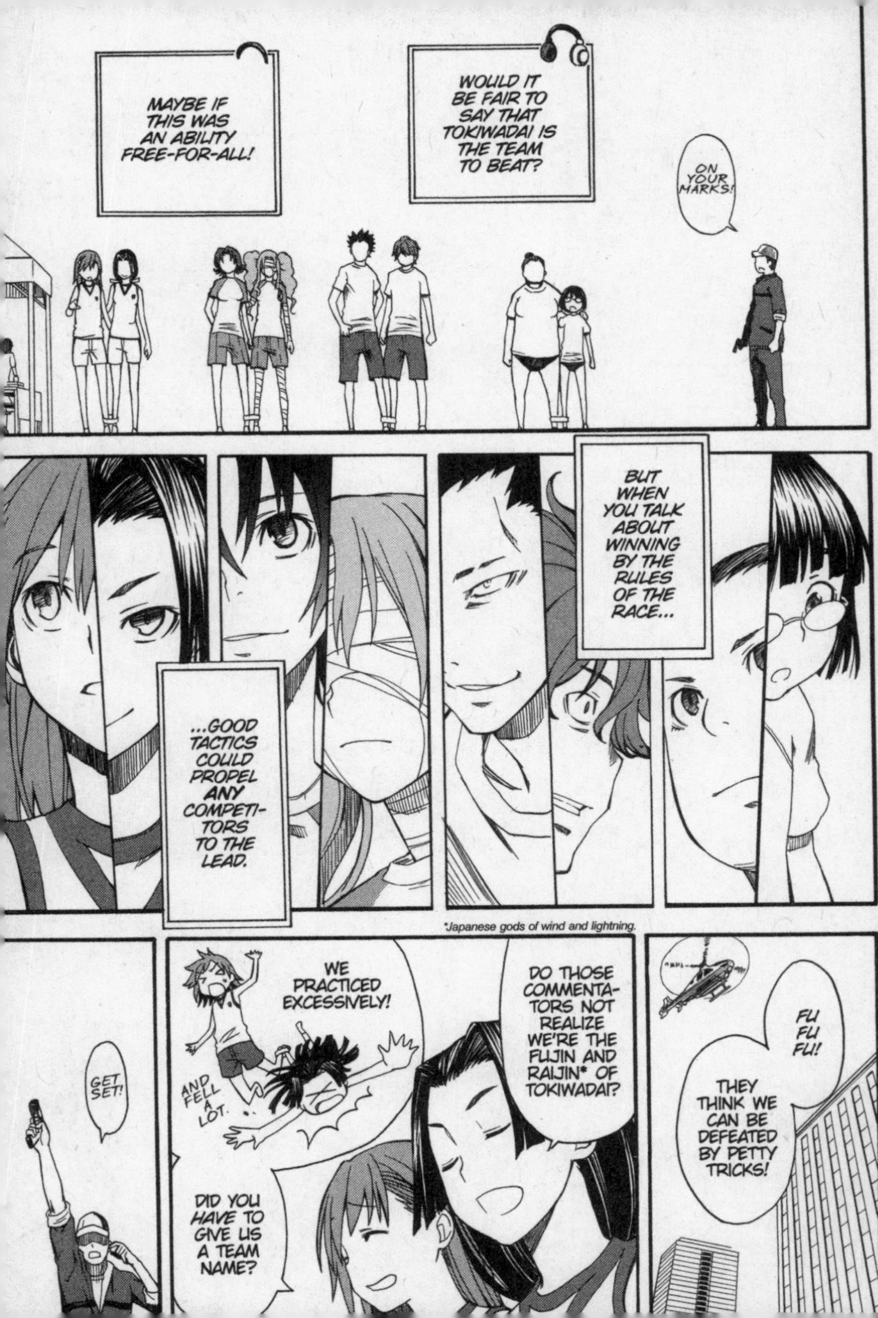
ON YOUR MARKS!
WOULD IT BE FAIR TO SAY THAT TOKIWADAI IS THE TEAM TO BEAT?
MAYBE IF THIS WAS AN ABILITY FREE-FOR-ALL!
BUT WHEN YOU TALK ABOUT WINNING BY THE RULES OF THE RACE...
...GOOD TACTICS COULD PROPEL ANY COMPETITORS TO THE LEAD.
FU FU FU!
THEY THINK WE CAN BE DEFEATED BY PETTY TRICKS!
DO THOSE COMMENTATORS NOT REALIZE WE'RE THE FUJIN AND RAIJIN* OF TOKIWADAI?
WE PRACTICED EXCESSIVELY!
AND FELL A LOT.
DID YOU HAVE TO GIVE US A TEAM NAME?
GET SET!
*Japanese gods of wind and lightning.

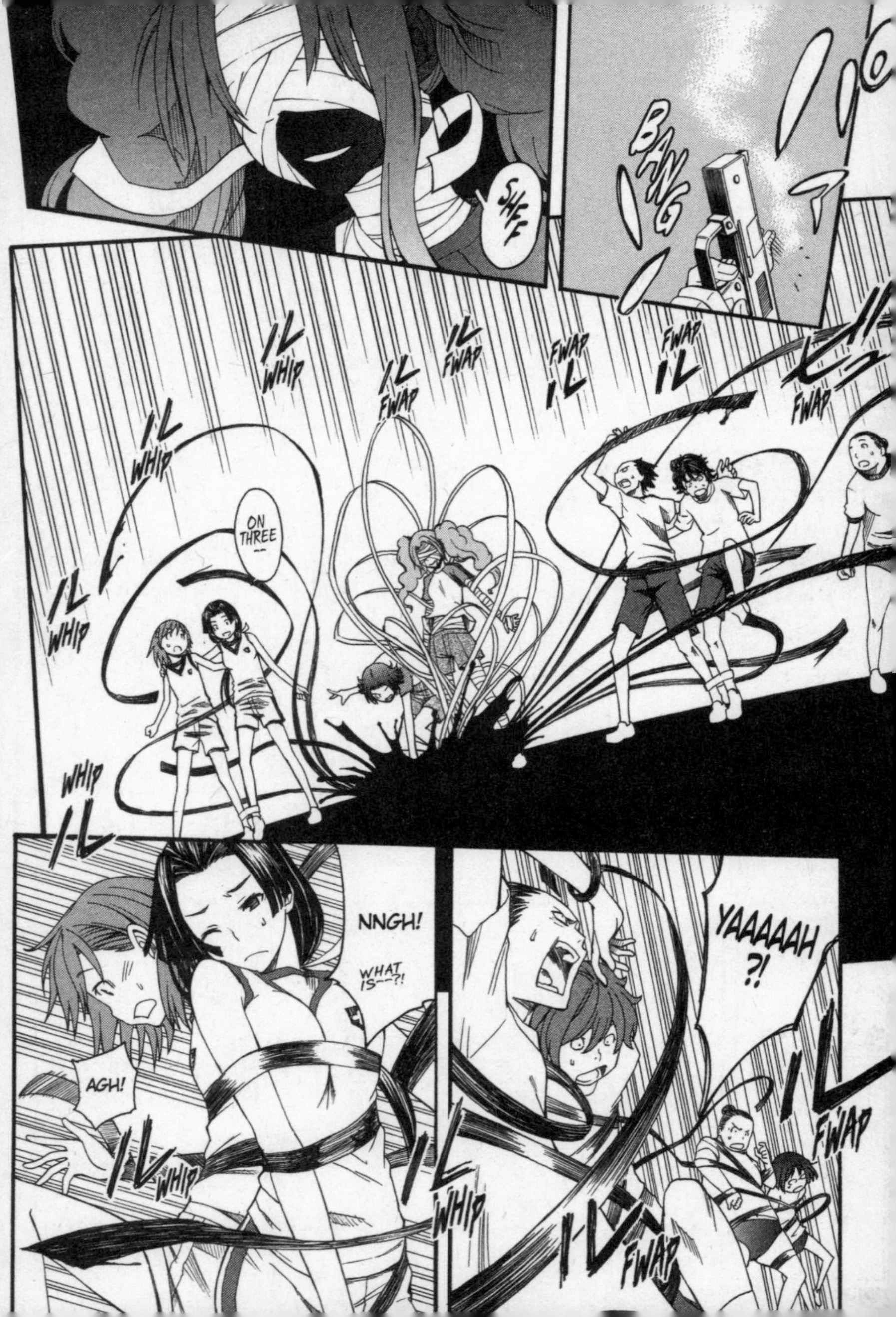

BANG
SHF
FWAP
FWAP
FWAP
FWAP
FWAP
WHIP
WHIP
ON THREE --
WHIP
WHIP
YAAAAAH?!
FWAP
FWAP
WHIP
NNGH!
WHAT IS--?!
AGH!
WHIP

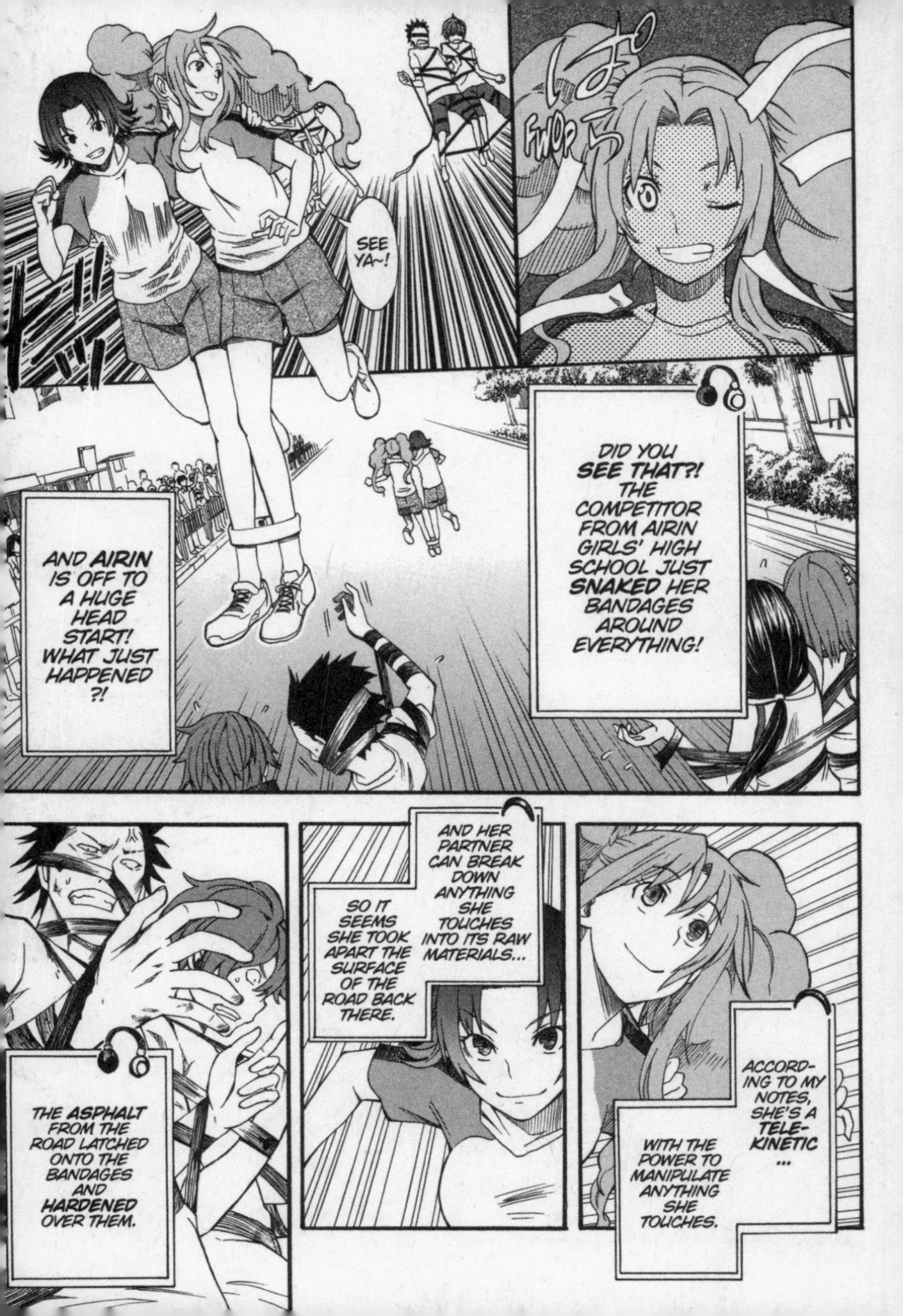
FWOP
SEE YA~!
DID YOU **SEE THAT?!** THE COMPETITOR FROM AIRIN GIRLS' HIGH SCHOOL JUST **SNAKED** HER BANDAGES AROUND EVERYTHING!
AND **AIRIN** IS OFF TO A HUGE HEAD START! WHAT JUST HAPPENED ?!
ACCORD-ING TO MY NOTES, SHE'S A **TELE-KINETIC** ...
WITH THE POWER TO MANIPULATE ANYTHING SHE TOUCHES.
AND HER PARTNER CAN BREAK DOWN ANYTHING SHE TOUCHES INTO ITS RAW MATERIALS...
SO IT SEEMS SHE TOOK APART THE SURFACE OF THE ROAD BACK THERE.
THE **ASPHALT** FROM THE ROAD LATCHED ONTO THE BANDAGES AND **HARDENED** OVER THEM.

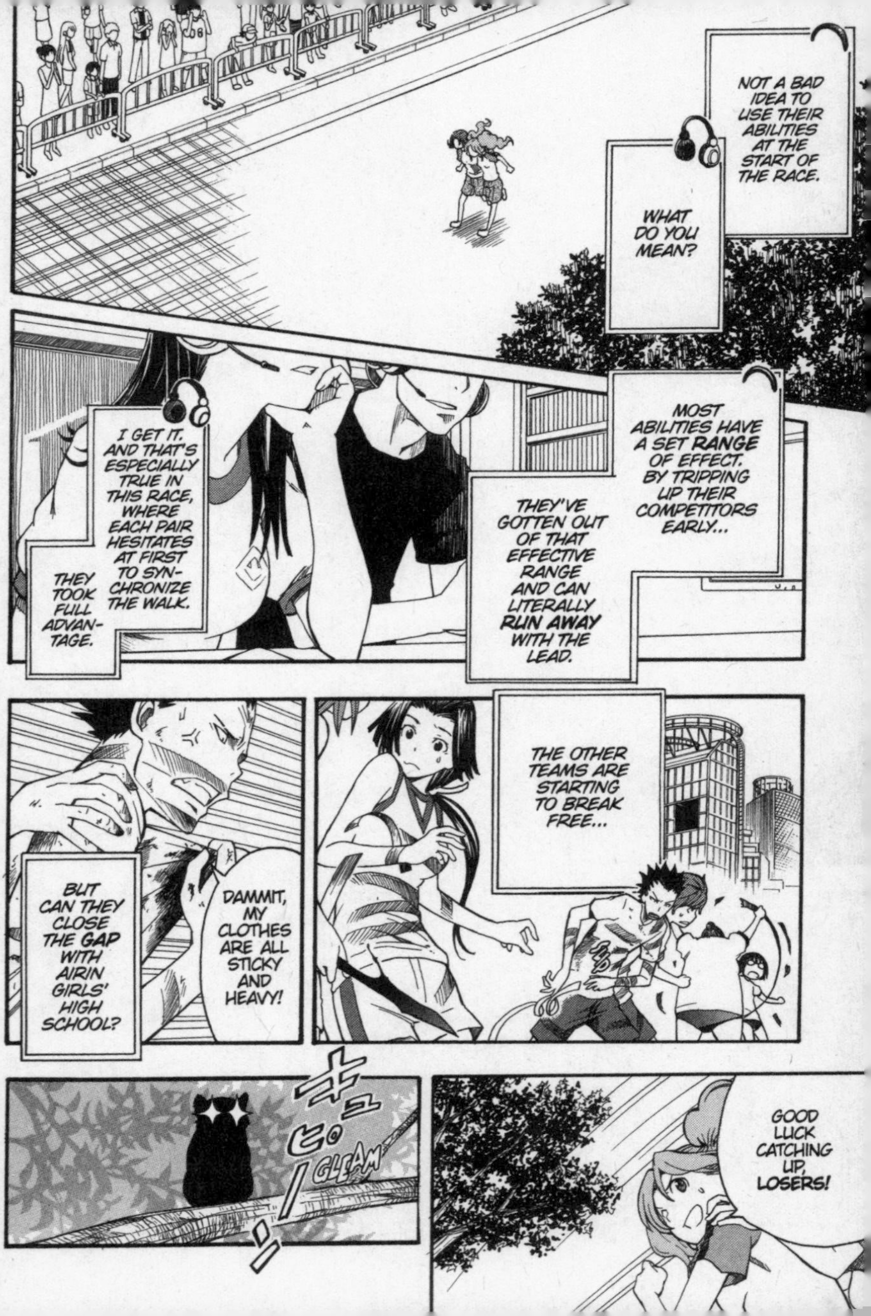
NOT A BAD IDEA TO USE THEIR ABILITIES AT THE START OF THE RACE.
WHAT DO YOU MEAN?
MOST ABILITIES HAVE A SET RANGE OF EFFECT. BY TRIPPING UP THEIR COMPETITORS EARLY...
THEY'VE GOTTEN OUT OF THAT EFFECTIVE RANGE AND CAN LITERALLY RUN AWAY WITH THE LEAD.
I GET IT. AND THAT'S ESPECIALLY TRUE IN THIS RACE, WHERE EACH PAIR HESITATES AT FIRST TO SYNCHRONIZE THE WALK.
THEY TOOK FULL ADVANTAGE.
THE OTHER TEAMS ARE STARTING TO BREAK FREE...
DAMMIT, MY CLOTHES ARE ALL STICKY AND HEAVY!
BUT CAN THEY CLOSE THE GAP WITH AIRIN GIRLS' HIGH SCHOOL?
GOOD LUCK CATCHING UP, LOSERS!
GLEAM

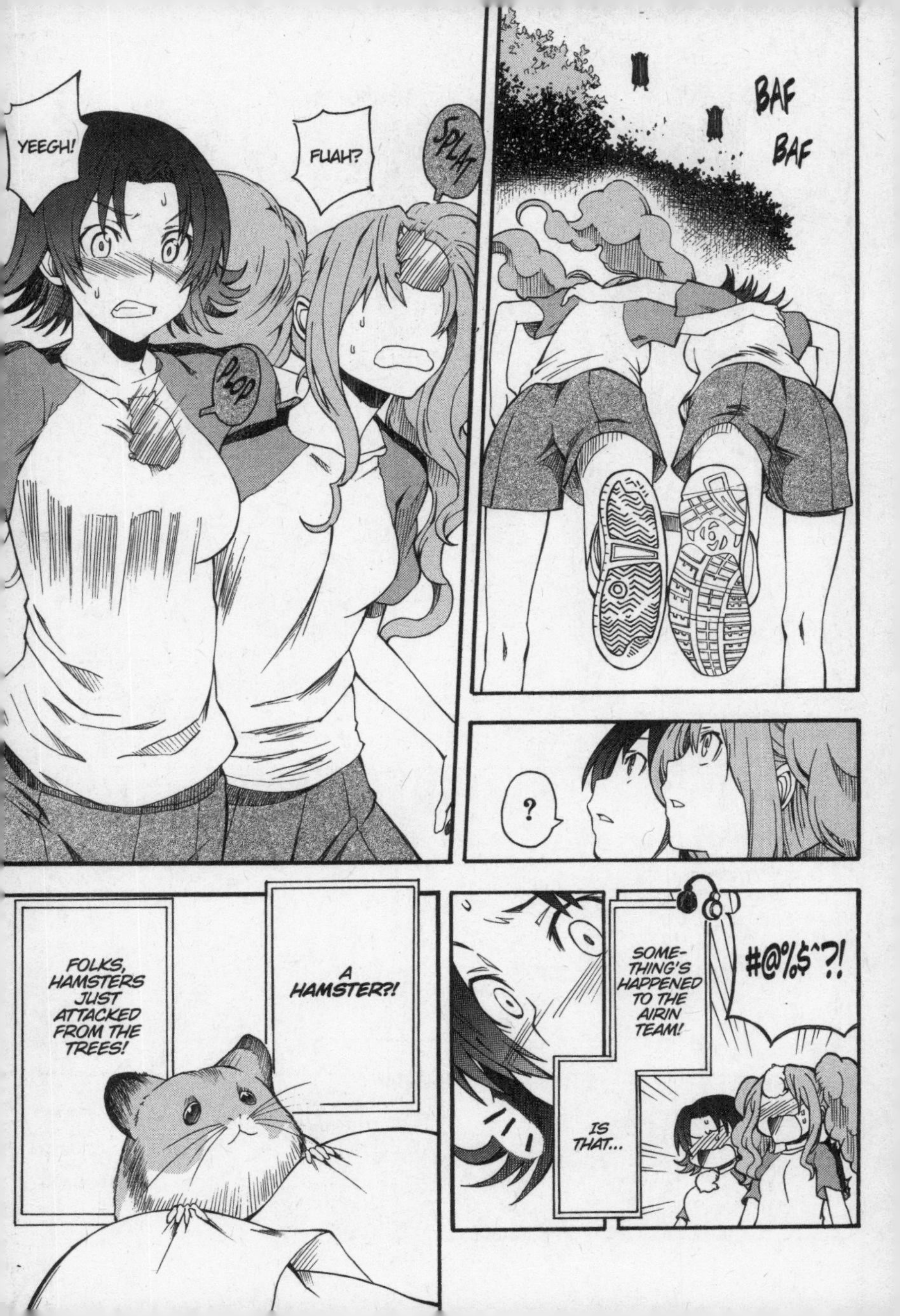
BAF
BAF
?
SPLAT
FUAH?
YEEGH!
PLOP
#@%$^?!
SOME-THING'S HAPPENED TO THE AIRIN TEAM!
IS THAT...
A HAMSTER?!
FOLKS, HAMSTERS JUST ATTACKED FROM THE TREES!

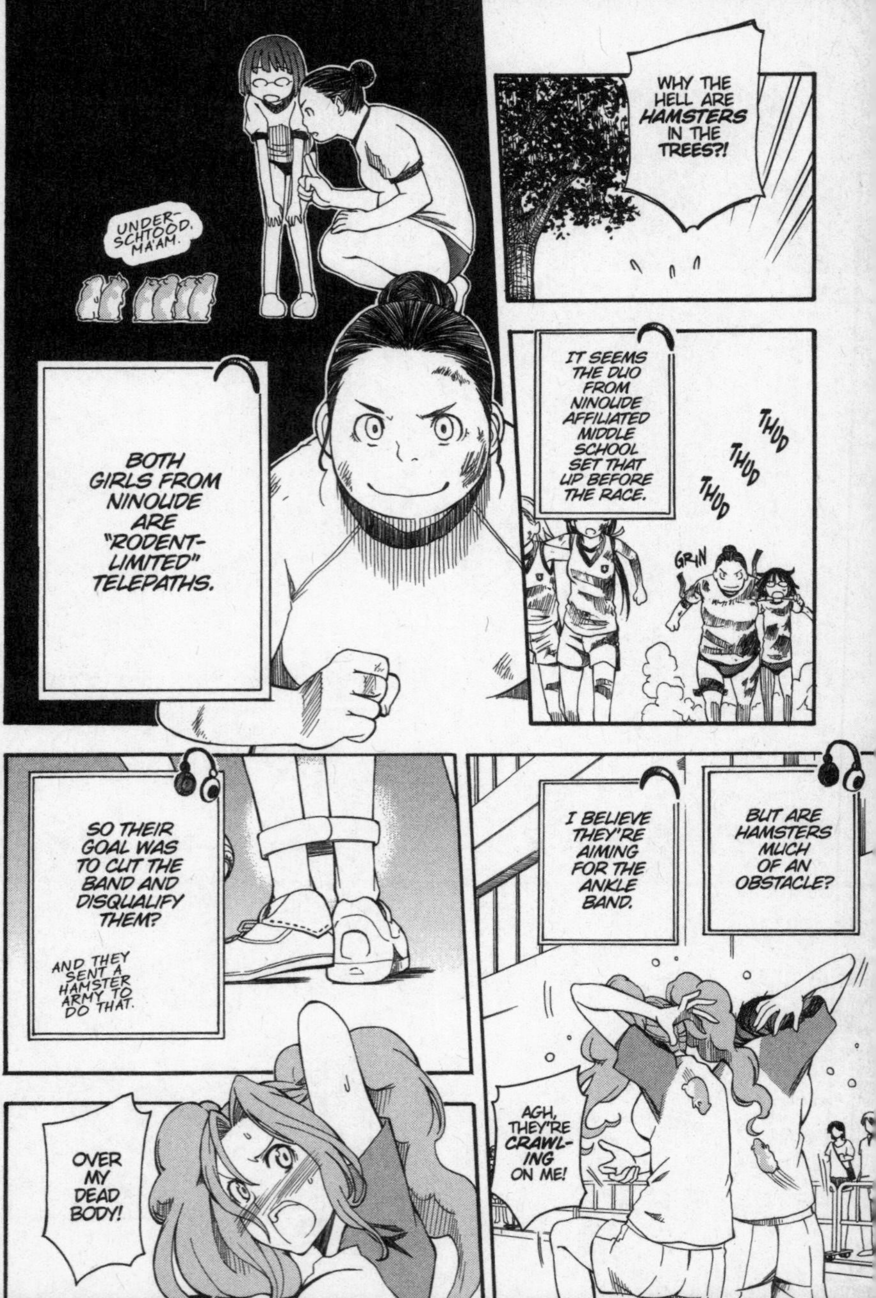
WHY THE HELL ARE HAMSTERS IN THE TREES?!
IT SEEMS THE DUO FROM NINOUDE AFFILIATED MIDDLE SCHOOL SET THAT UP BEFORE THE RACE.
THUD THUD THUD
GRIN
UNDER-SCHTOOD, MA'AM.
BOTH GIRLS FROM NINOUDE ARE "RODENT-LIMITED" TELEPATHS.
BUT ARE HAMSTERS MUCH OF AN OBSTACLE?
I BELIEVE THEY'RE AIMING FOR THE ANKLE BAND.
AGH, THEY'RE CRAWL-ING ON ME!
SO THEIR GOAL WAS TO CUT THE BAND AND DISQUALIFY THEM?
AND THEY SENT A HAMSTER ARMY TO DO THAT.
OVER MY DEAD BODY!

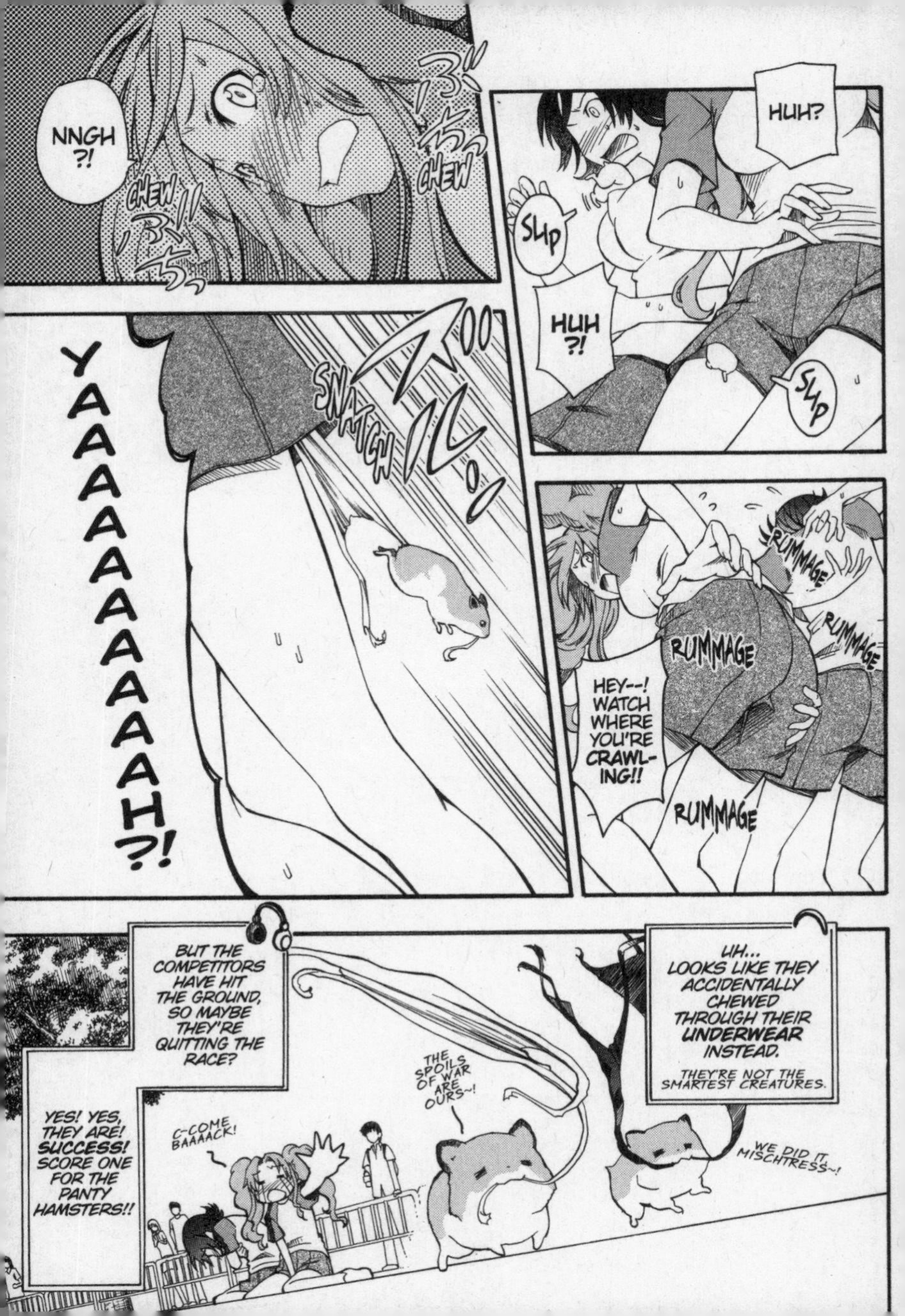
HUH?
SLIP
HUH?!
SLIP
NNGH?!
CHEW
CHEW
HEY--! WATCH WHERE YOU'RE CRAWLING!!
RUMMAGE
RUMMAGE
RUMMAGE
RUMMAGE
SNATCH
YAAAAAAAAAAH?!
UH... LOOKS LIKE THEY ACCIDENTALLY CHEWED THROUGH THEIR UNDERWEAR INSTEAD.
THEY'RE NOT THE SMARTEST CREATURES.
BUT THE COMPETITORS HAVE HIT THE GROUND, SO MAYBE THEY'RE QUITTING THE RACE?
WE DID IT, MISCHTRESS~!
THE SPOILS OF WAR ARE OURS~!
C-COME BAAAACK!
YES! YES, THEY ARE! SUCCESS! SCORE ONE FOR THE PANTY HAMSTERS!!

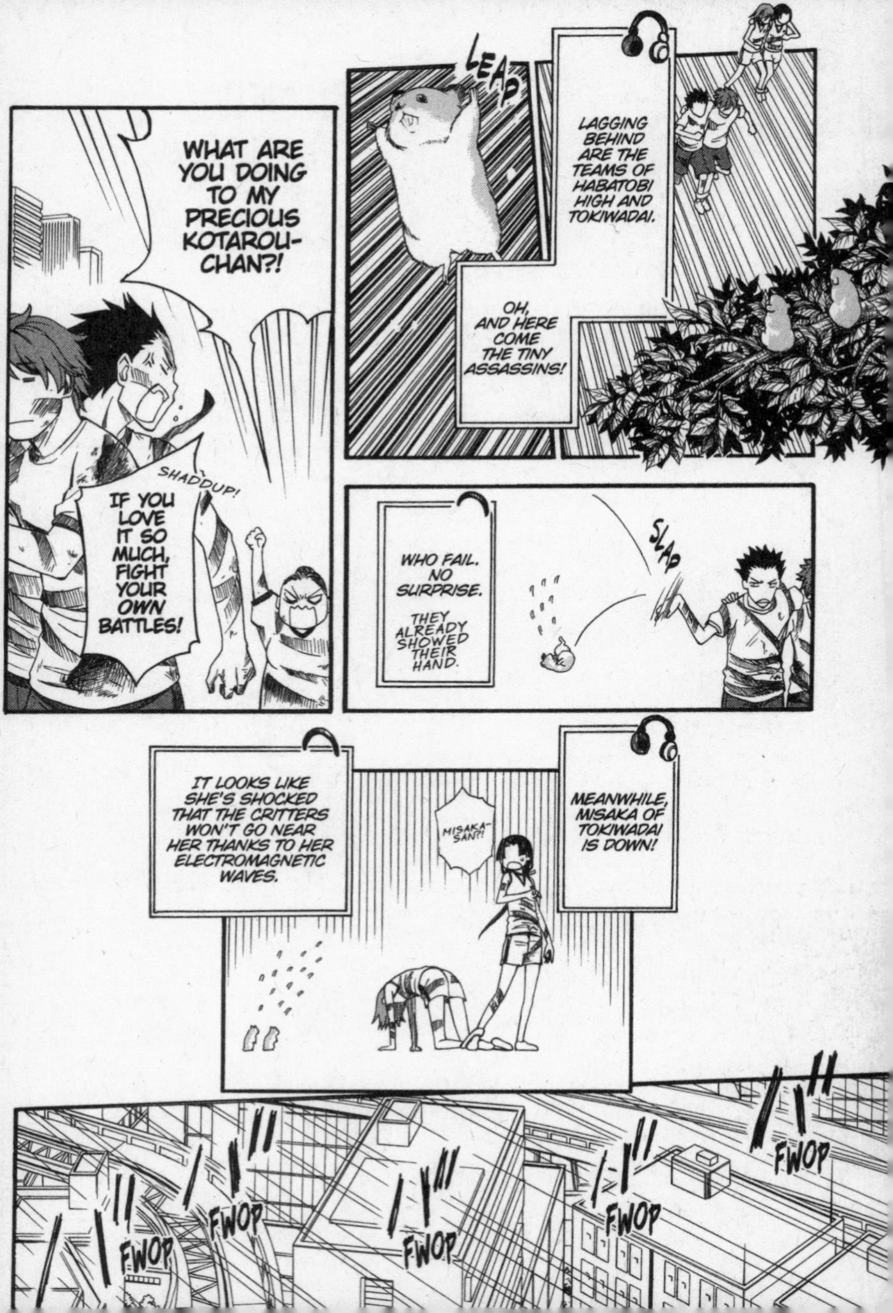
LAGGING BEHIND ARE THE TEAMS OF HABATOBI HIGH AND TOKIWADAI.
OH, AND HERE COME THE TINY ASSASSINS!
LEAP
WHO FAIL. NO SURPRISE.
THEY ALREADY SHOWED THEIR HAND.
SLAP
WHAT ARE YOU DOING TO MY PRECIOUS KOTAROU-CHAN?!
SHADDUP!
IF YOU LOVE IT SO MUCH, FIGHT YOUR OWN BATTLES!
MEANWHILE, MISAKA OF TOKIWADAI IS DOWN!
MISAKA-SAN?!
IT LOOKS LIKE SHE'S SHOCKED THAT THE CRITTERS WON'T GO NEAR HER THANKS TO HER ELECTROMAGNETIC WAVES.
FWOP
FWOP
FWOP
FWOP
FWOP

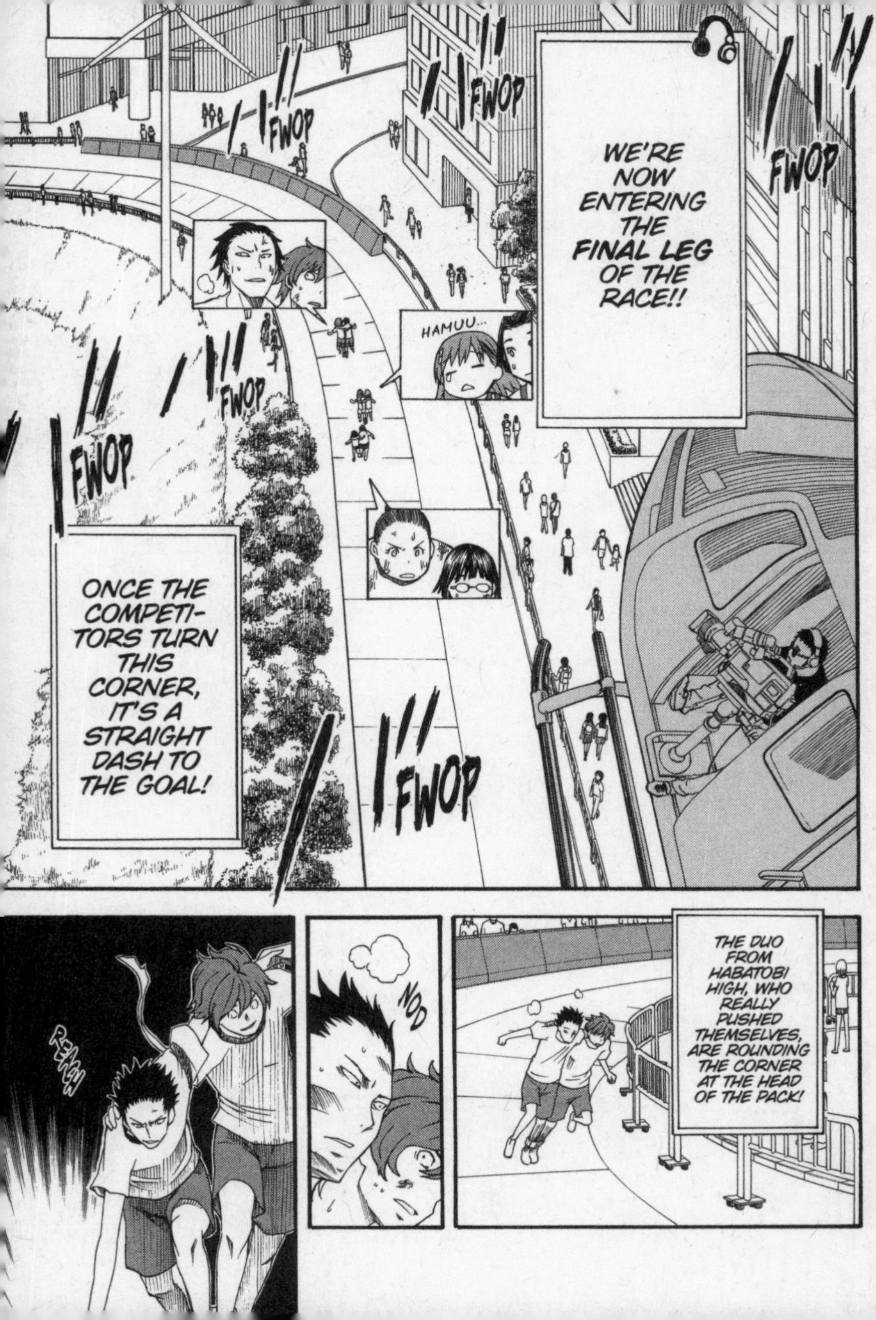
FWOP
WE'RE NOW ENTERING THE FINAL LEG OF THE RACE!!
FWOP
FWOP
FWOP
HAMUU...
FWOP
FWOP
ONCE THE COMPETITORS TURN THIS CORNER, IT'S A STRAIGHT DASH TO THE GOAL!
FWOP
THE DUO FROM HABATOBI HIGH, WHO REALLY PUSHED THEMSELVES, ARE ROUNDING THE CORNER AT THE HEAD OF THE PACK!
NOD
REACH

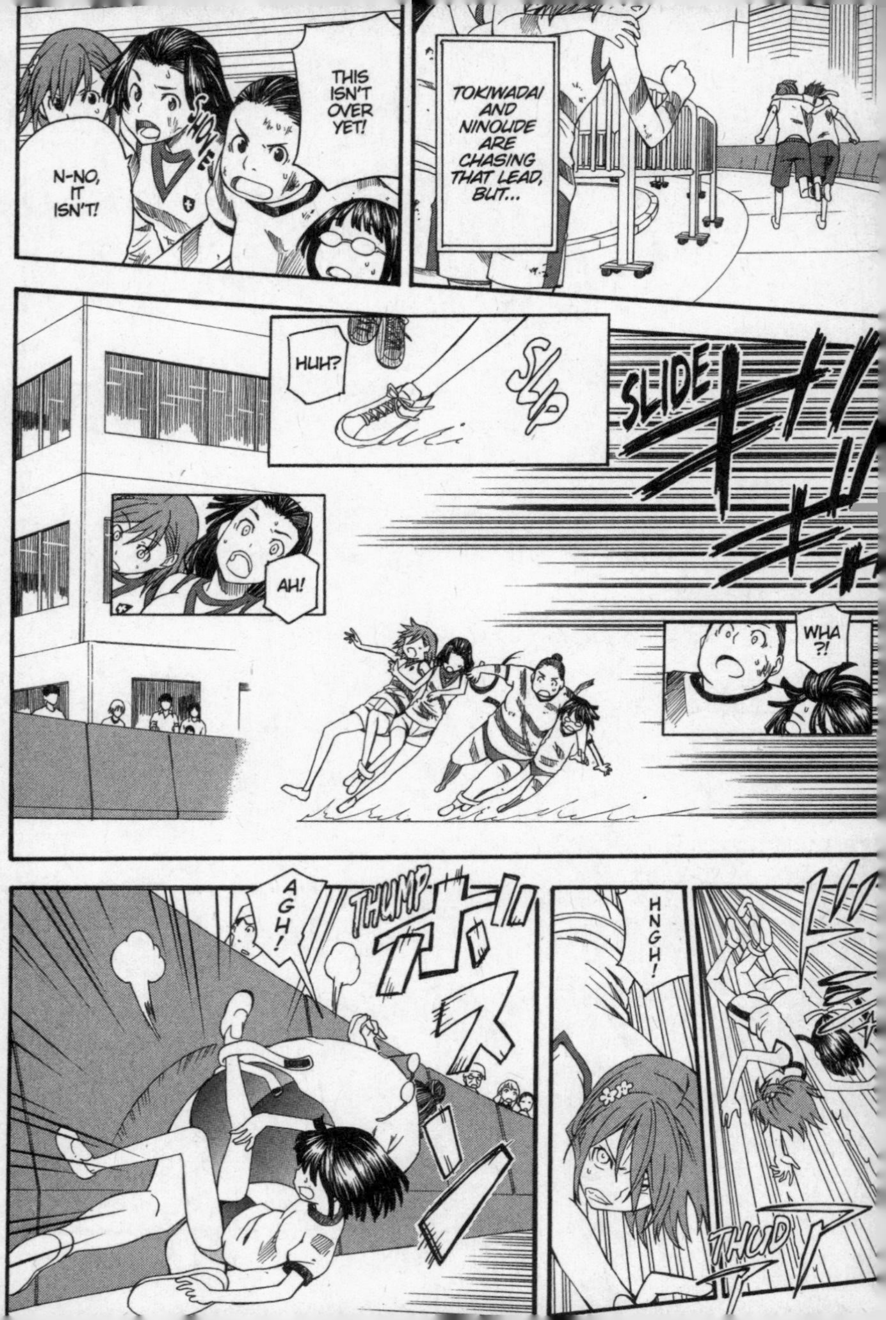

TOKIWADAI AND NINOUDE ARE CHASING THAT LEAD, BUT...
THIS ISN'T OVER YET!
N-NO, IT ISN'T!
SLIDE
WHA ?!
HUH?
SLIP
AH!
HNGH!
THUD
AGH!
THUMP

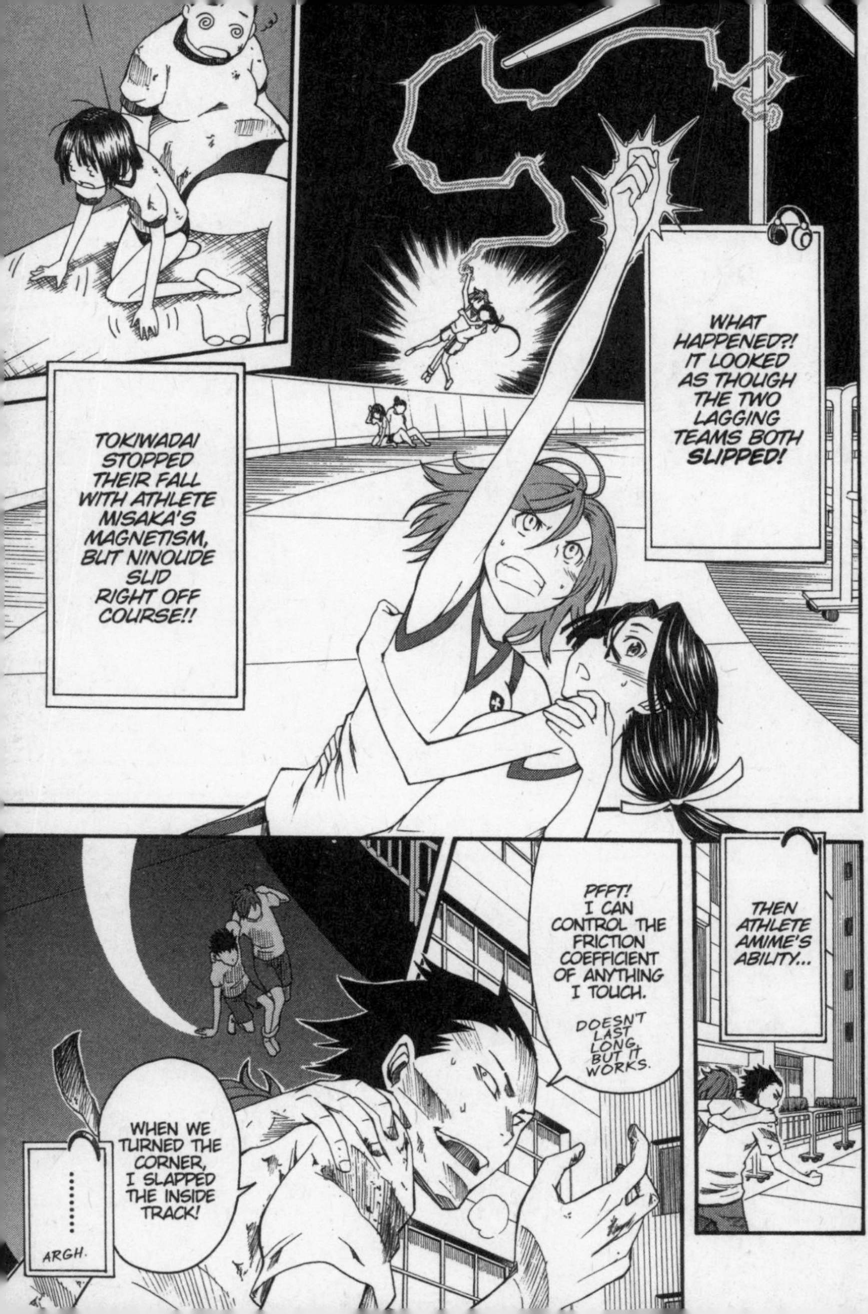
WHAT HAPPENED?! IT LOOKED AS THOUGH THE TWO LAGGING TEAMS BOTH SLIPPED!
TOKIWADAI STOPPED THEIR FALL WITH ATHLETE MISAKA'S MAGNETISM, BUT NINOUDE SLID RIGHT OFF COURSE!!
THEN ATHLETE AMIME'S ABILITY...
PFFT! I CAN CONTROL THE FRICTION COEFFICIENT OF ANYTHING I TOUCH.
DOESN'T LAST LONG, BUT IT WORKS.
WHEN WE TURNED THE CORNER, I SLAPPED THE INSIDE TRACK!
....
ARGH.

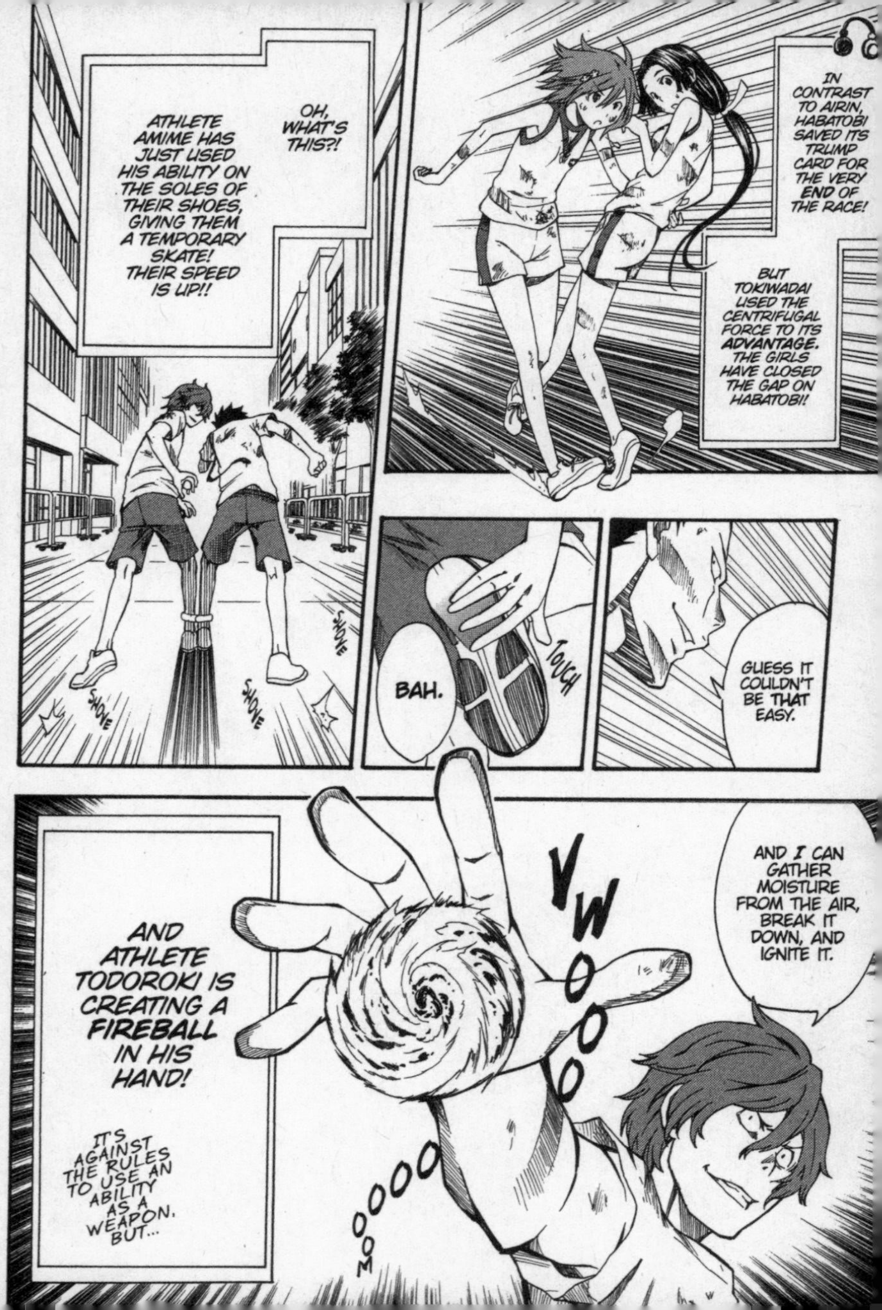
IN CONTRAST TO AIRIN, HABATOBI SAVED ITS TRUMP CARD FOR THE VERY END OF THE RACE!
BUT TOKIWADAI USED THE CENTRIFUGAL FORCE TO ITS ADVANTAGE. THE GIRLS HAVE CLOSED THE GAP ON HABATOBI!
GUESS IT COULDN'T BE THAT EASY.
TOUCH
BAH.
OH, WHAT'S THIS?!
ATHLETE AMIME HAS JUST USED HIS ABILITY ON THE SOLES OF THEIR SHOES, GIVING THEM A TEMPORARY SKATE! THEIR SPEED IS UP!!
SHOVE
SHOVE
SHOVE
AND I CAN GATHER MOISTURE FROM THE AIR, BREAK IT DOWN, AND IGNITE IT.
VWOOOOOOOOOOM
AND ATHLETE TODOROKI IS CREATING A FIREBALL IN HIS HAND!
IT'S AGAINST THE RULES TO USE AN ABILITY AS A WEAPON. BUT...

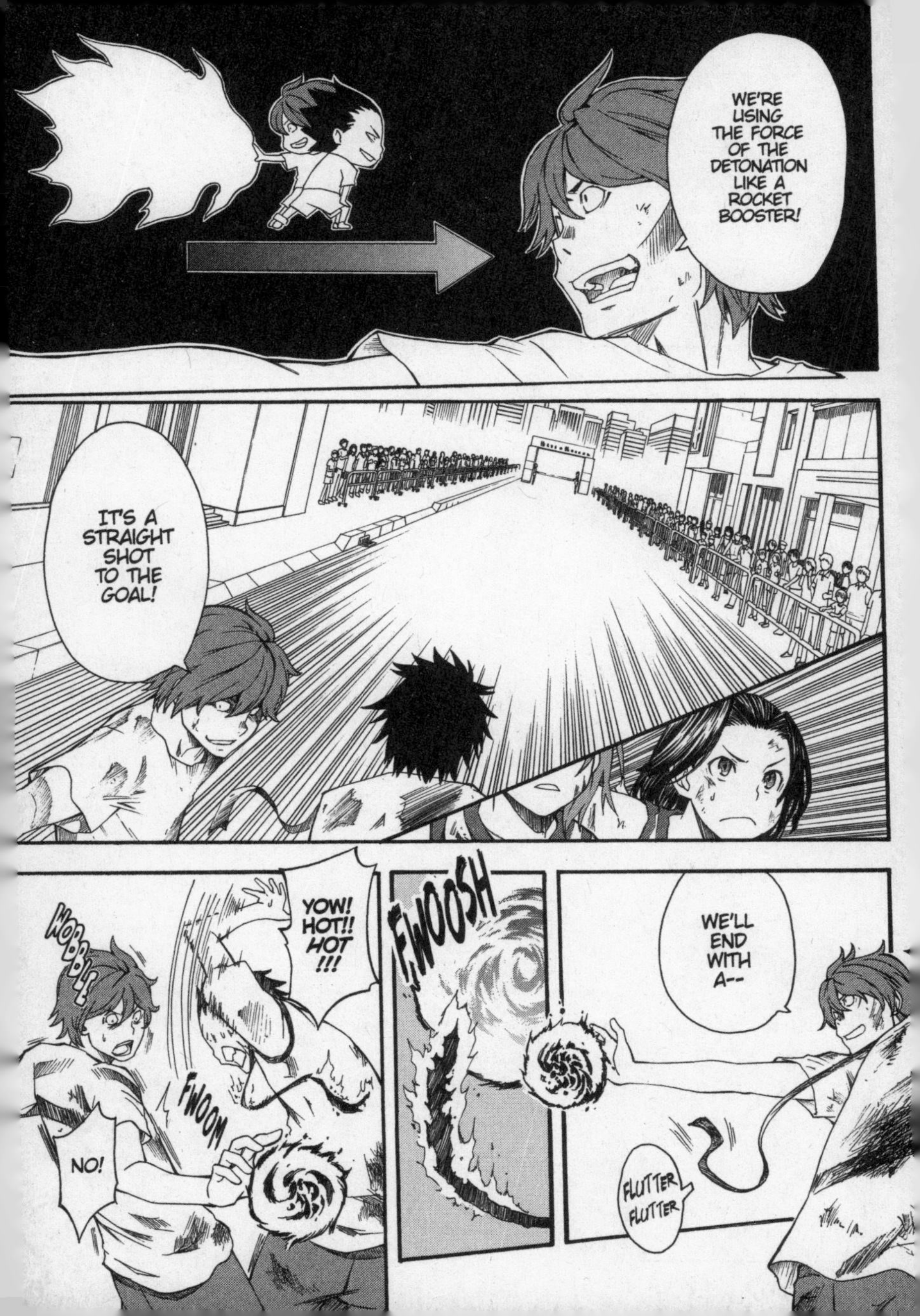
WE'RE USING THE FORCE OF THE DETONATION LIKE A ROCKET BOOSTER!
IT'S A STRAIGHT SHOT TO THE GOAL!
WE'LL END WITH A--
FLUTTER FLUTTER
FWOOSH
YOW! HOT!! HOT !!!
WOBBLE
FWOOM
NO!

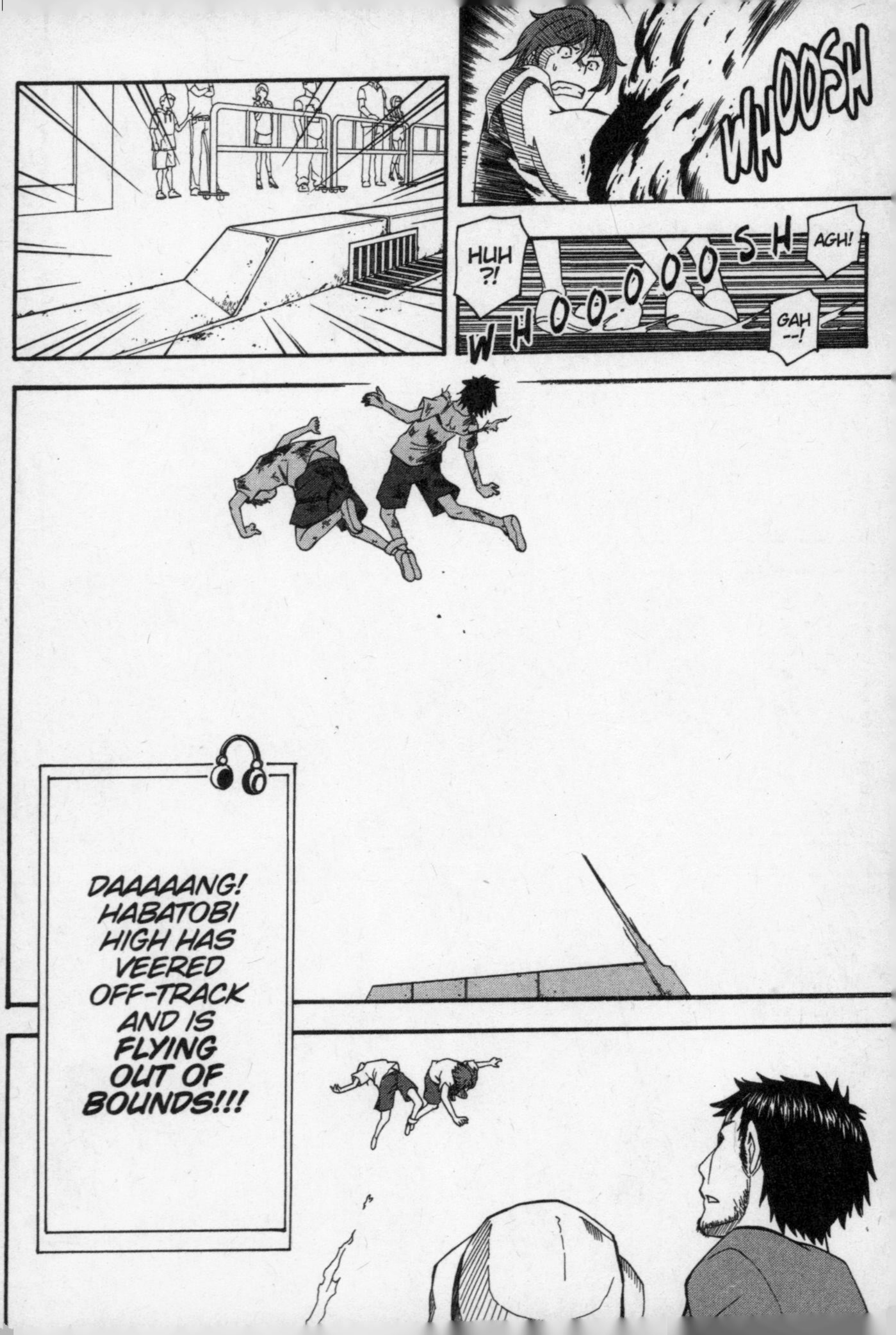
WHOOSH
AGH!
WHOOOOOOSH
HUH?!
GAH--!
DAAAAANG! HABATOBI HIGH HAS VEERED OFF-TRACK AND IS FLYING OUT OF BOUNDS!!!

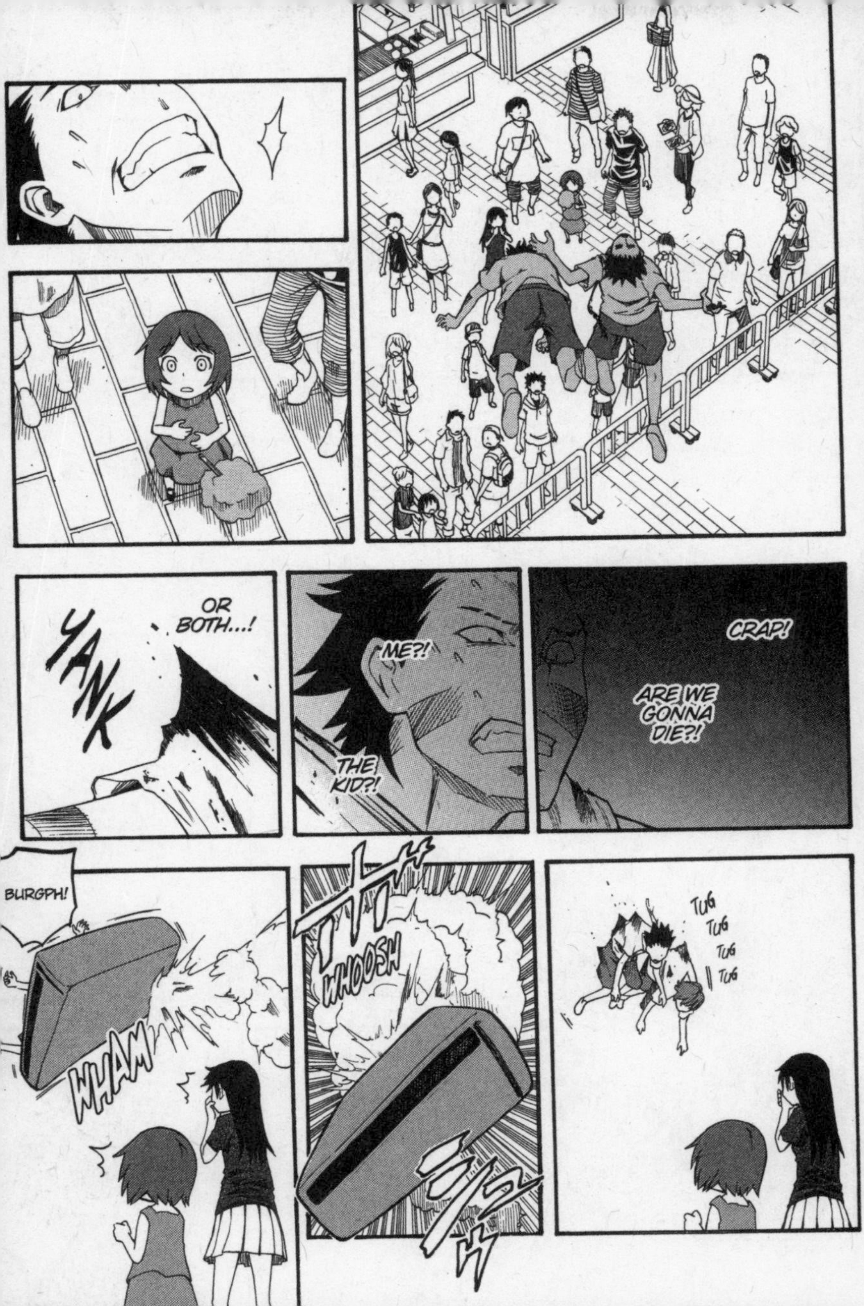
CRAP!
ARE WE GONNA DIE?!
ME?!
THE KID?!
OR BOTH...!
YANK
TUG
TUG
TUG
TUG
WHOOSH
BURGPH!
WHAM

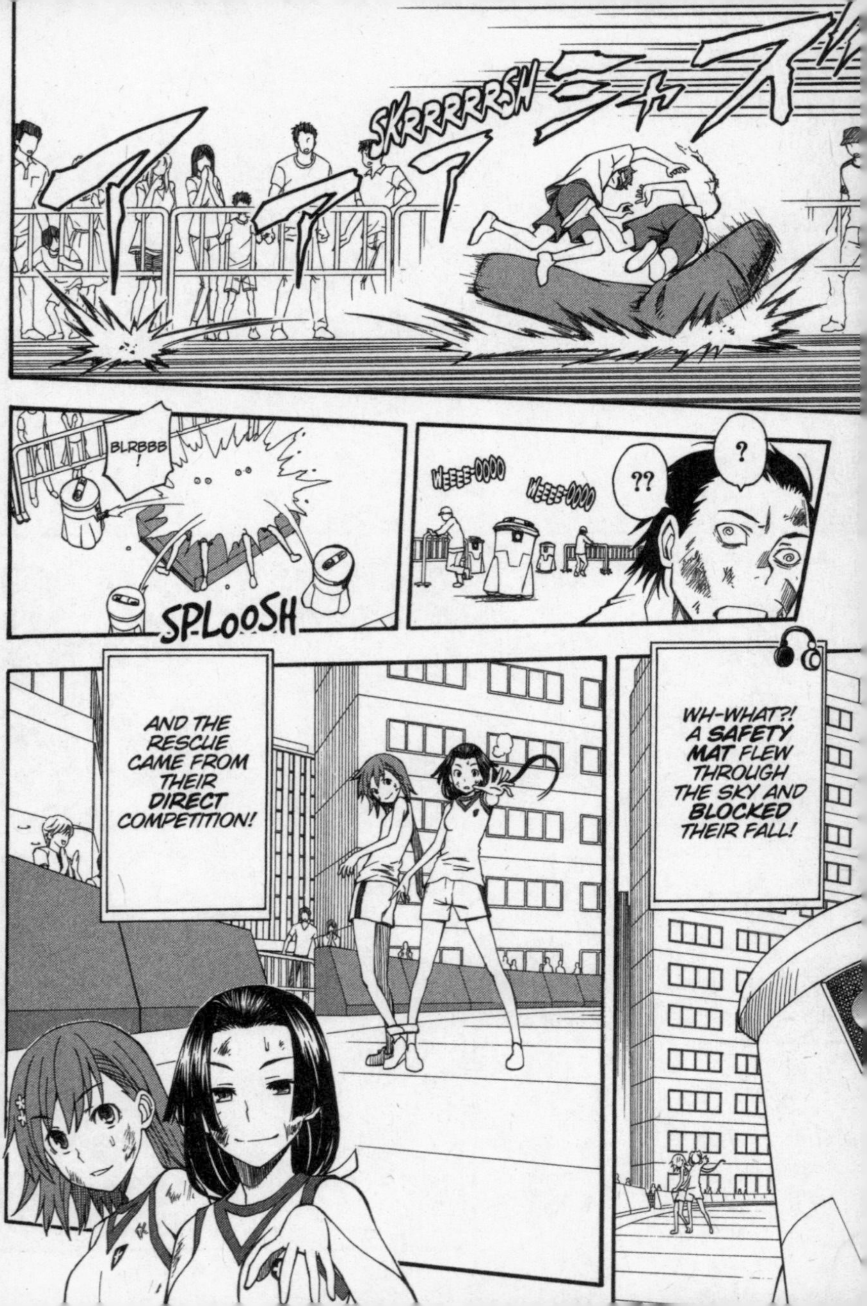
SKRRRRSH
?
??
WEEE-OOOO
WEEE-OOOO
BLRBBB!
SP-LOOSH
WH-WHAT?! A SAFETY MAT FLEW THROUGH THE SKY AND BLOCKED THEIR FALL!
AND THE RESCUE CAME FROM THEIR DIRECT COMPETITION!

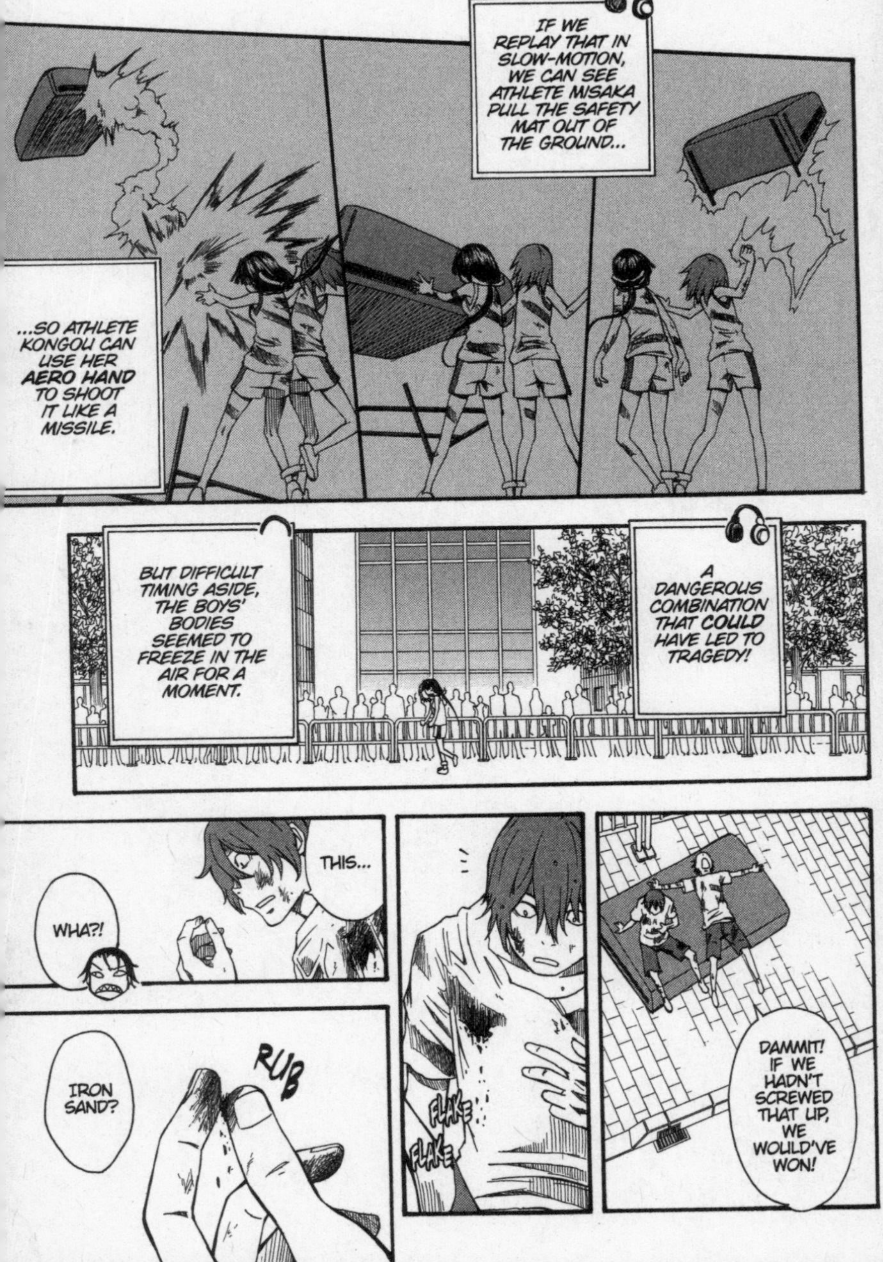
IF WE REPLAY THAT IN SLOW-MOTION, WE CAN SEE ATHLETE MISAKA PULL THE SAFETY MAT OUT OF THE GROUND...
...SO ATHLETE KONGOU CAN USE HER AERO HAND TO SHOOT IT LIKE A MISSILE.
A DANGEROUS COMBINATION THAT COULD HAVE LED TO TRAGEDY!
BUT DIFFICULT TIMING ASIDE, THE BOYS' BODIES SEEMED TO FREEZE IN THE AIR FOR A MOMENT.
DAMMIT! IF WE HADN'T SCREWED THAT UP, WE WOULD'VE WON!
FLAKE
FLAKE
THIS...
WHA?!
RUB
IRON SAND?

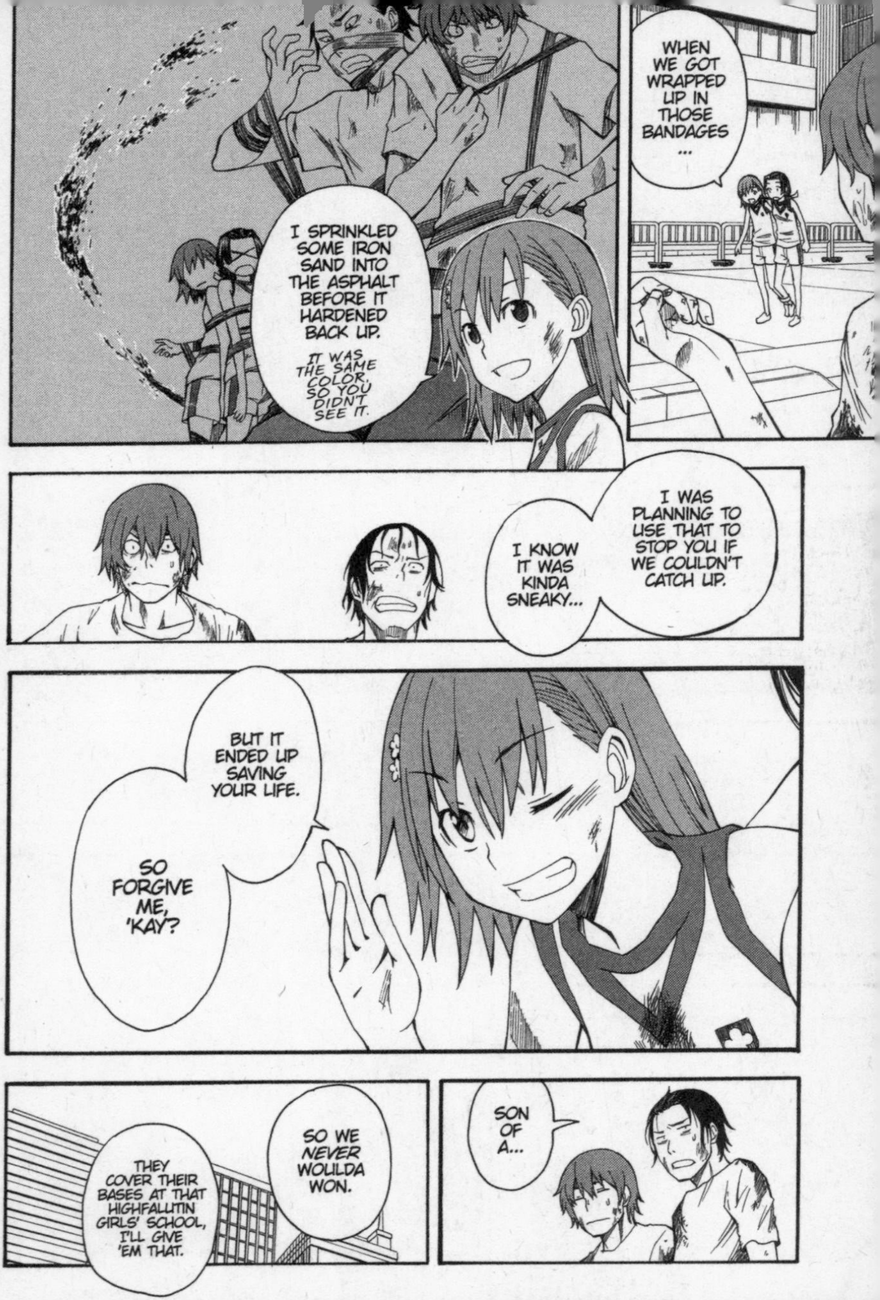
WHEN WE GOT WRAPPED UP IN THOSE BANDAGES ...
I SPRINKLED SOME IRON SAND INTO THE ASPHALT BEFORE IT HARDENED BACK UP.
IT WAS THE SAME COLOR, SO YOU DIDN'T SEE IT.
I WAS PLANNING TO USE THAT TO STOP YOU IF WE COULDN'T CATCH UP.
I KNOW IT WAS KINDA SNEAKY...
BUT IT ENDED UP SAVING YOUR LIFE.
SO FORGIVE ME, 'KAY?
SON OF A...
SO WE *NEVER* WOULDA WON.
THEY COVER THEIR BASES AT THAT HIGHFALUTIN GIRLS' SCHOOL, I'LL GIVE 'EM THAT.

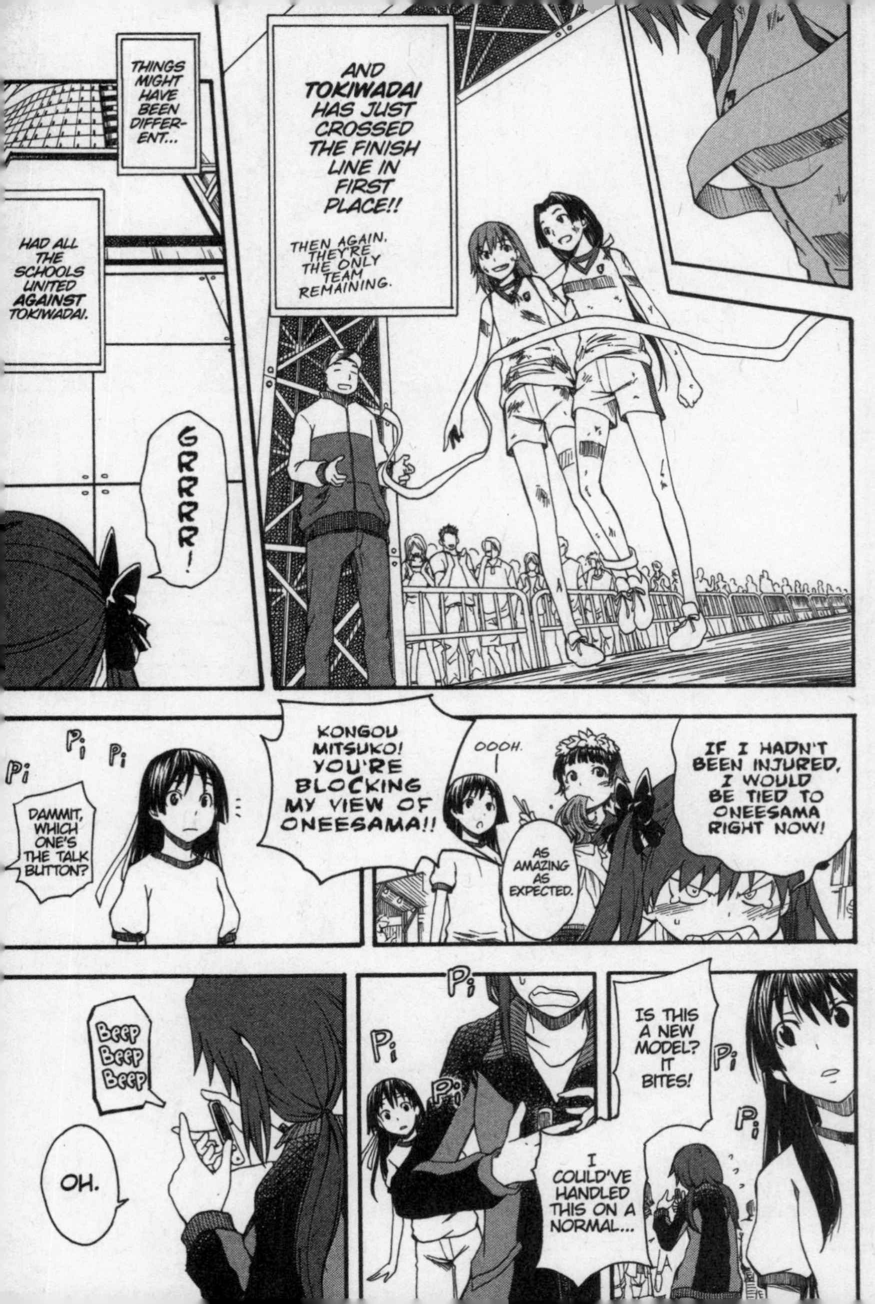
AND TOKIWADAI HAS JUST CROSSED THE FINISH LINE IN FIRST PLACE!!
THEN AGAIN, THEY'RE THE ONLY TEAM REMAINING.
THINGS MIGHT HAVE BEEN DIFFERENT...
HAD ALL THE SCHOOLS UNITED AGAINST TOKIWADAI.
GRRRR!
IF I HADN'T BEEN INJURED, I WOULD BE TIED TO ONEESAMA RIGHT NOW!
KONGOU MITSUKO! YOU'RE BLOCKING MY VIEW OF ONEESAMA!!
OOOH.
AS AMAZING AS EXPECTED.
Pi Pi
Pi
DAMMIT, WHICH ONE'S THE TALK BUTTON?
IS THIS A NEW MODEL? IT BITES!
Pi
Pi
I COULD'VE HANDLED THIS ON A NORMAL...
Pi
Pi
Pi
Beep Beep Beep
OH.

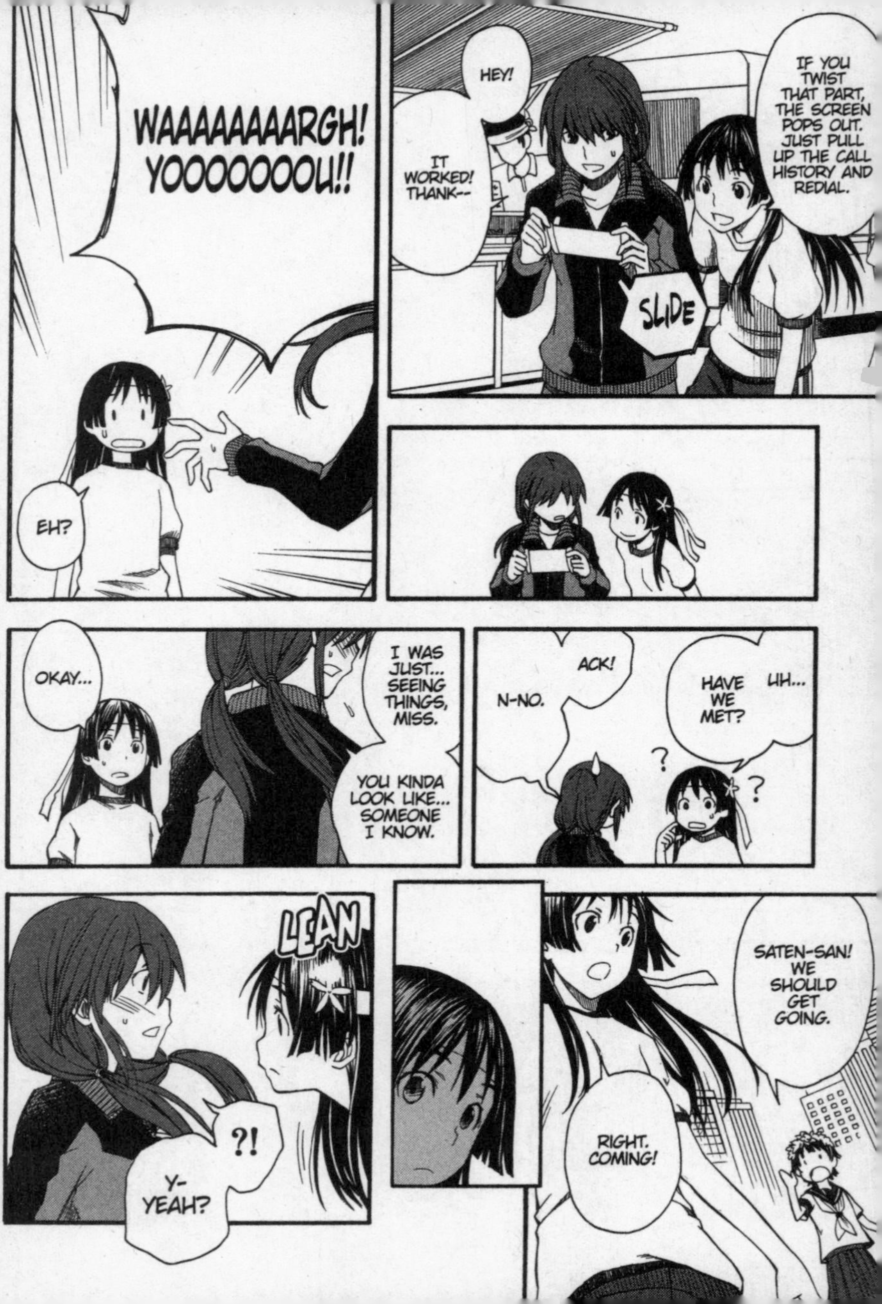
IF YOU TWIST THAT PART, THE SCREEN POPS OUT. JUST PULL UP THE CALL HISTORY AND REDIAL.
HEY!
IT WORKED! THANK--
SLIDE
WAAAAAAAARGH! YOOOOOOOU!!
EH?
UH... HAVE WE MET?
ACK!
N-NO.
I WAS JUST... SEEING THINGS, MISS.
YOU KINDA LOOK LIKE... SOMEONE I KNOW.
OKAY...
SATEN-SAN! WE SHOULD GET GOING.
RIGHT. COMING!
LEAN
?!
Y-YEAH?

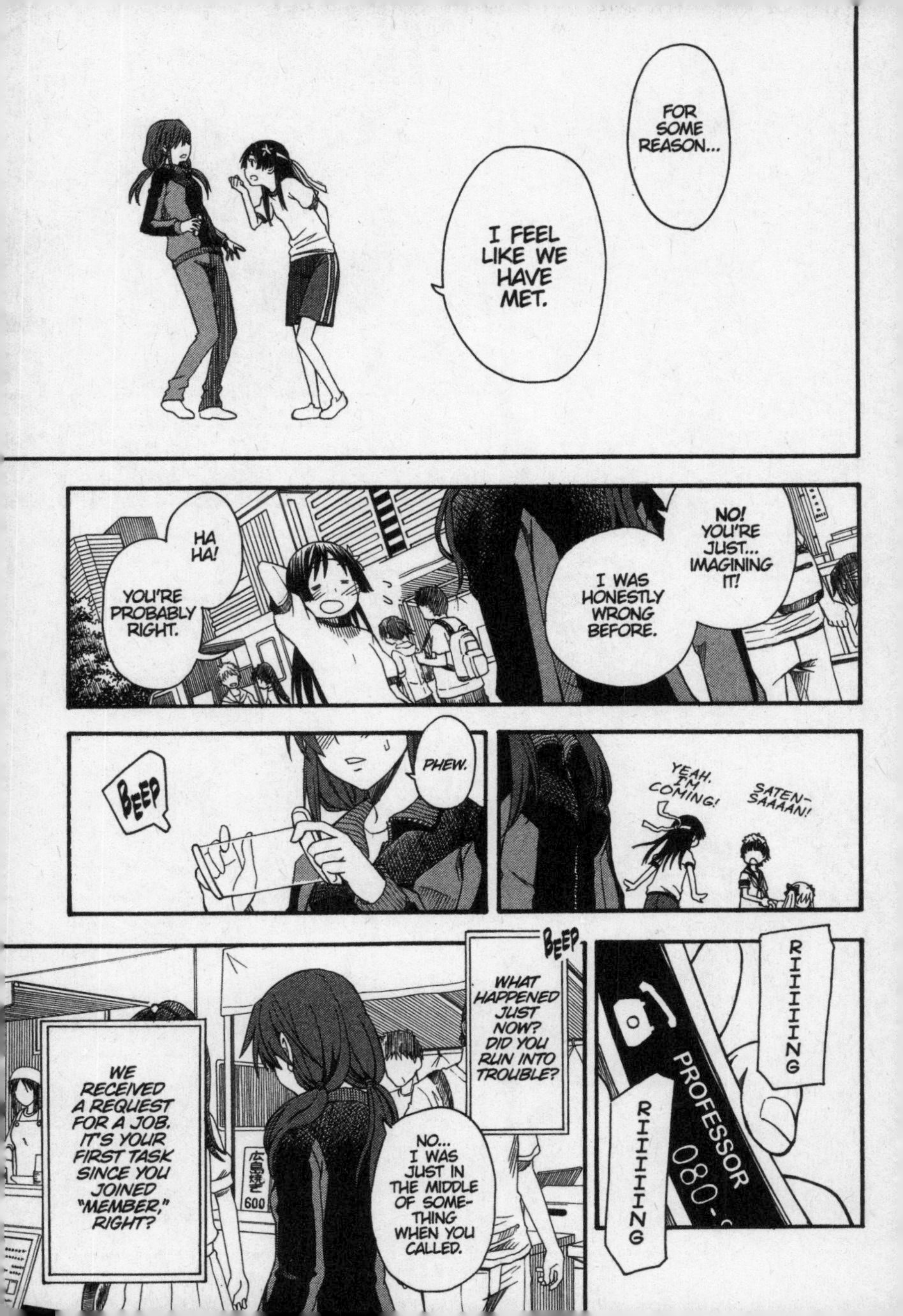
FOR SOME REASON...
I FEEL LIKE WE HAVE MET.
NO! YOU'RE JUST... IMAGINING IT!
I WAS HONESTLY WRONG BEFORE.
HA HA! YOU'RE PROBABLY RIGHT.
SATEN-SAAAAN!
YEAH, I'M COMING!
PHEW.
BEEP
RIIIIING
PROFESSOR 080-
RIIIIING
BEEP
WHAT HAPPENED JUST NOW? DID YOU RUN INTO TROUBLE?
NO... I WAS JUST IN THE MIDDLE OF SOME-THING WHEN YOU CALLED.
WE RECEIVED A REQUEST FOR A JOB. IT'S YOUR FIRST TASK SINCE YOU JOINED "MEMBER," RIGHT?

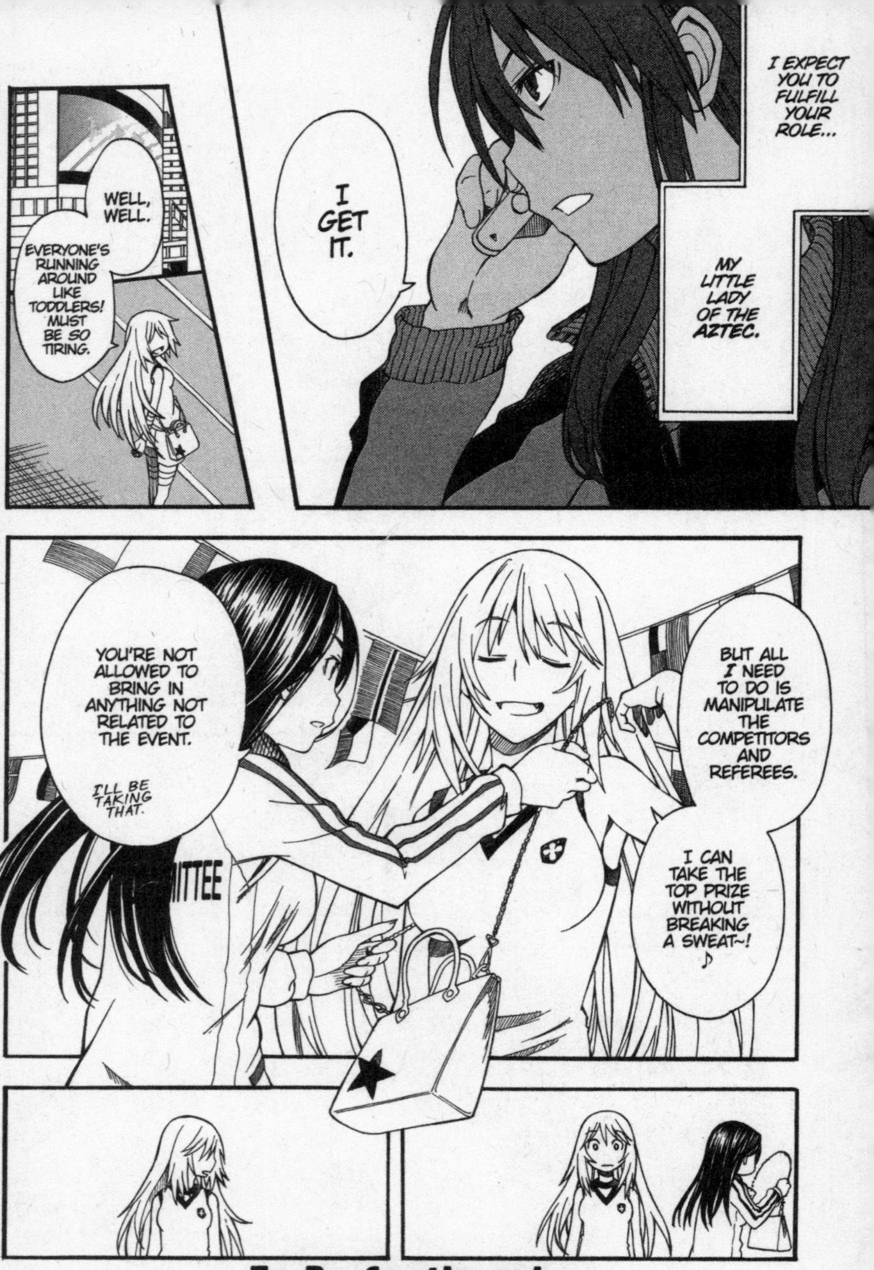
I EXPECT YOU TO FULFILL YOUR ROLE...
MY LITTLE LADY OF THE AZTEC.
I GET IT.
WELL, WELL.
EVERYONE'S RUNNING AROUND LIKE TODDLERS! MUST BE SO TIRING.
BUT ALL I NEED TO DO IS MANIPULATE THE COMPETITORS AND REFEREES.
I CAN TAKE THE TOP PRIZE WITHOUT BREAKING A SWEAT~! ♪
YOU'RE NOT ALLOWED TO BRING IN ANYTHING NOT RELATED TO THE EVENT.
I'LL BE TAKING THAT.

To Be Continued...

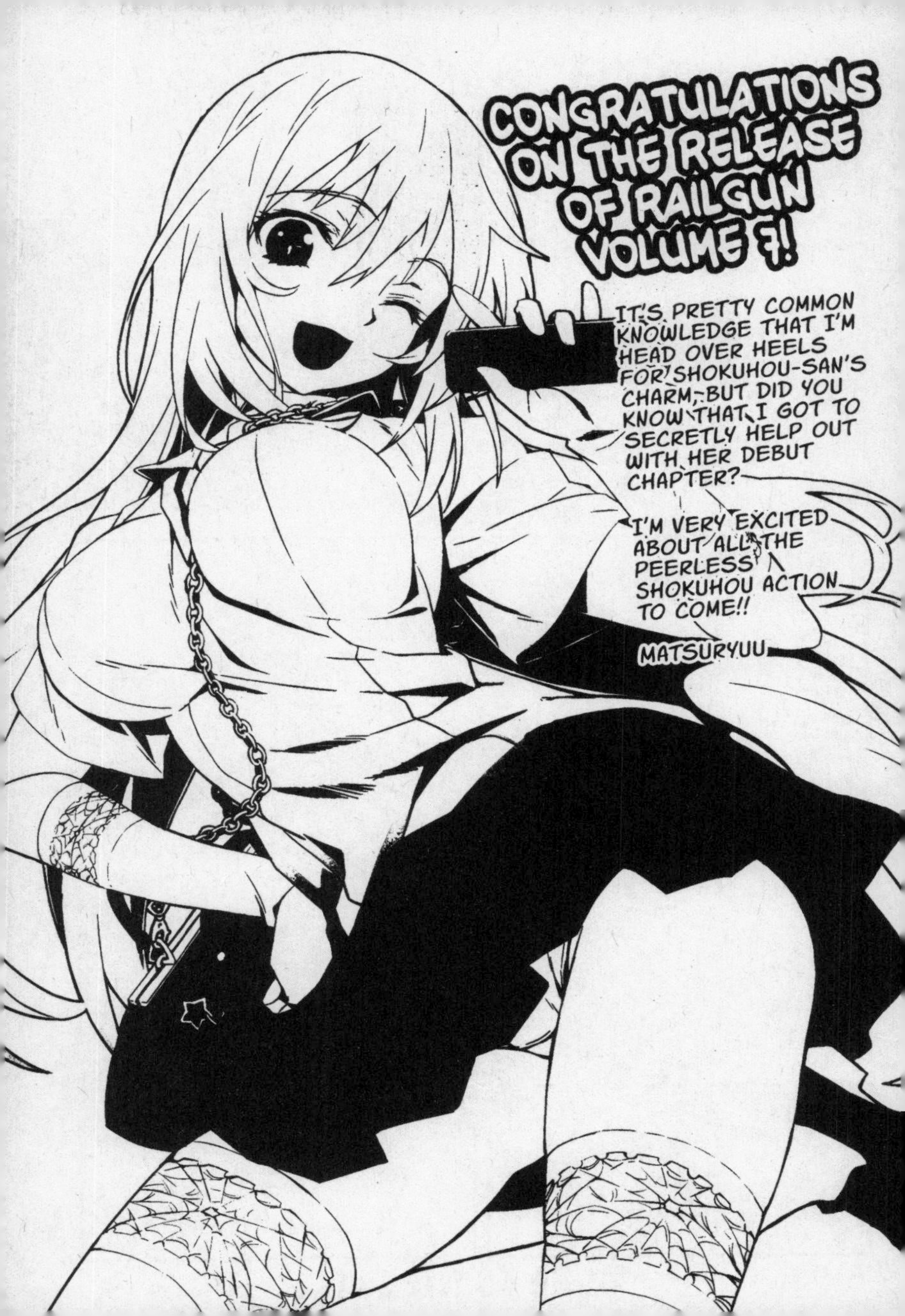
CONGRATULATIONS ON THE RELEASE OF RAILGUN VOLUME 7!
IT'S PRETTY COMMON KNOWLEDGE THAT I'M HEAD OVER HEELS FOR SHOKUHOU-SAN'S CHARM, BUT DID YOU KNOW THAT I GOT TO SECRETLY HELP OUT WITH HER DEBUT CHAPTER?
I'M VERY EXCITED ABOUT ALL THE PEERLESS SHOKUHOU ACTION TO COME!!
MATSURYUU

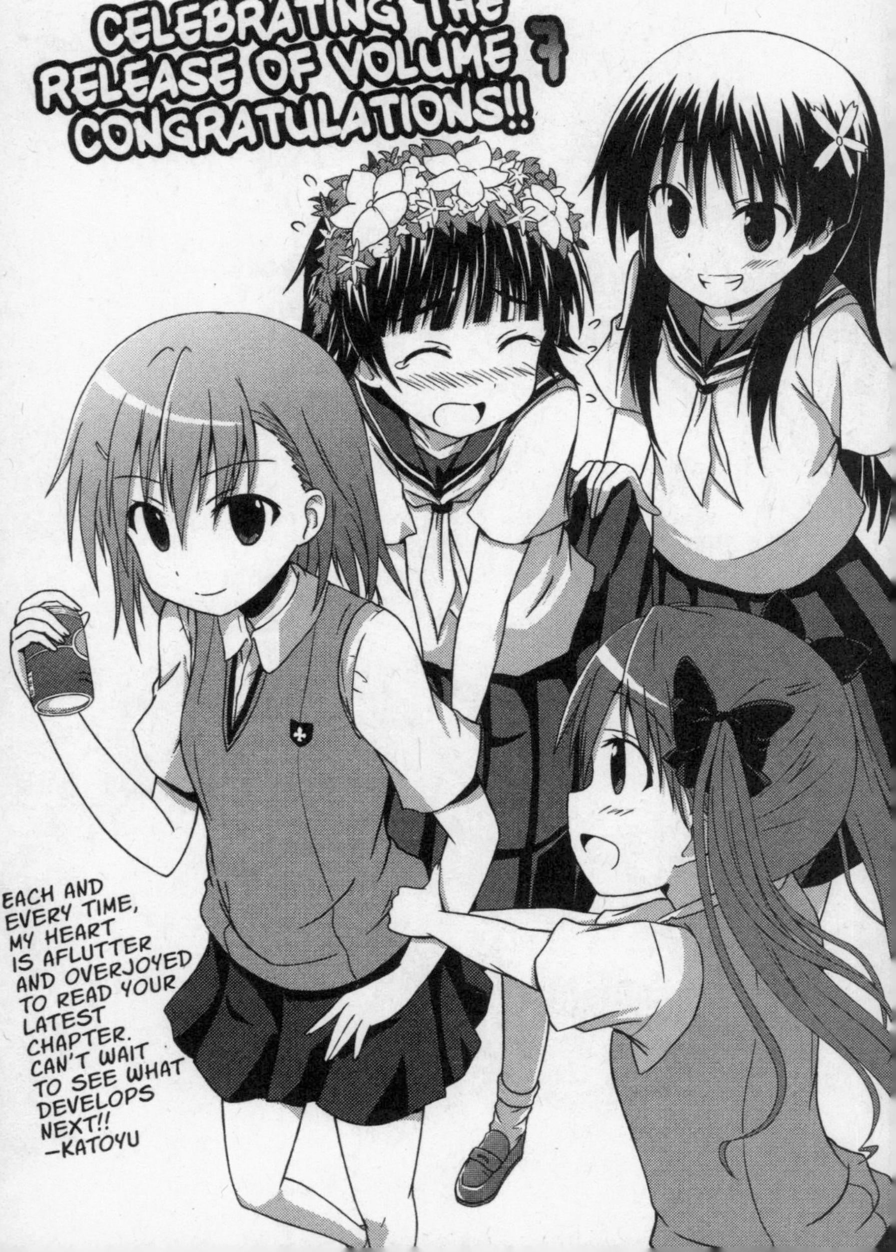
CELEBRATING THE RELEASE OF VOLUME 7 CONGRATULATIONS!!
EACH AND EVERY TIME, MY HEART IS AFLUTTER AND OVERJOYED TO READ YOUR LATEST CHAPTER. CAN'T WAIT TO SEE WHAT DEVELOPS NEXT!! –KATOYU

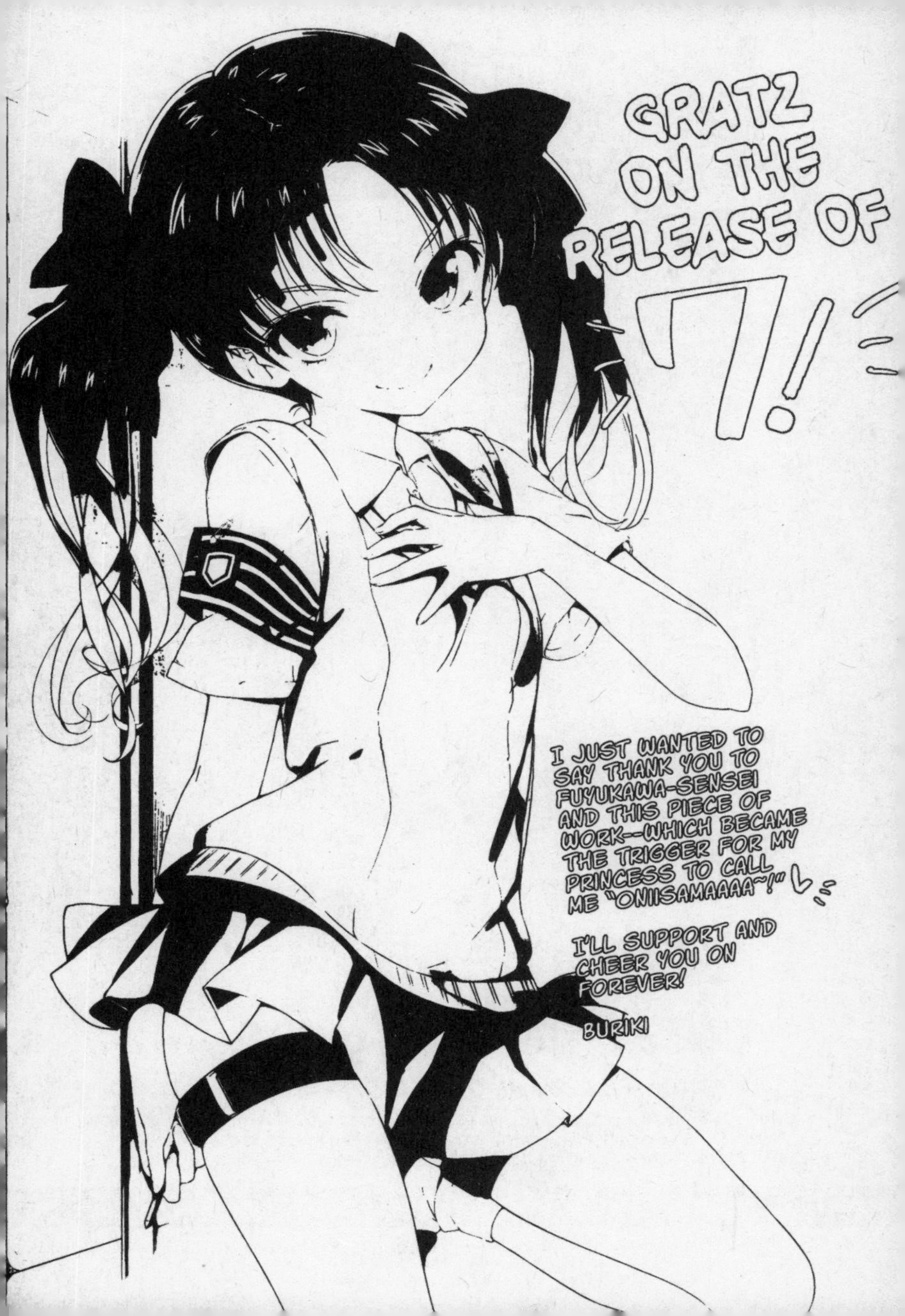
GRATZ ON THE RELEASE OF 7!
I JUST WANTED TO SAY THANK YOU TO FUYUKAWA-SENSEI AND THIS PIECE OF WORK--WHICH BECAME THE TRIGGER FOR MY PRINCESS TO CALL ME "ONIISAMAAAA~!"
I'LL SUPPORT AND CHEER YOU ON FOREVER!
BURIKI

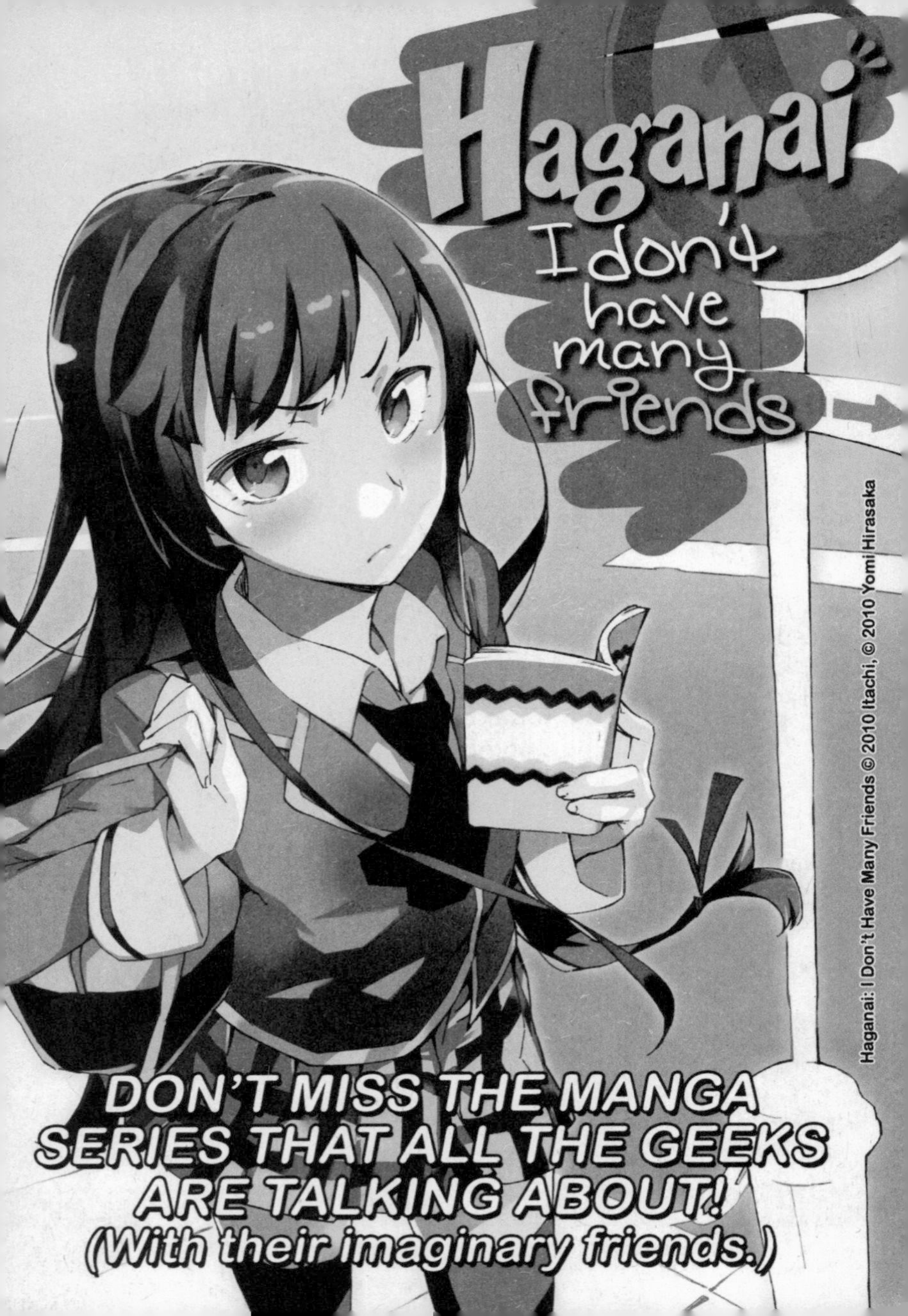
Haganai
I don't have many friends
DON'T MISS THE MANGA SERIES THAT ALL THE GEEKS ARE TALKING ABOUT!
(With their imaginary friends.)
Haganai: I Don't Have Many Friends © 2010 Itachi, © 2010 Yomi Hirasaka

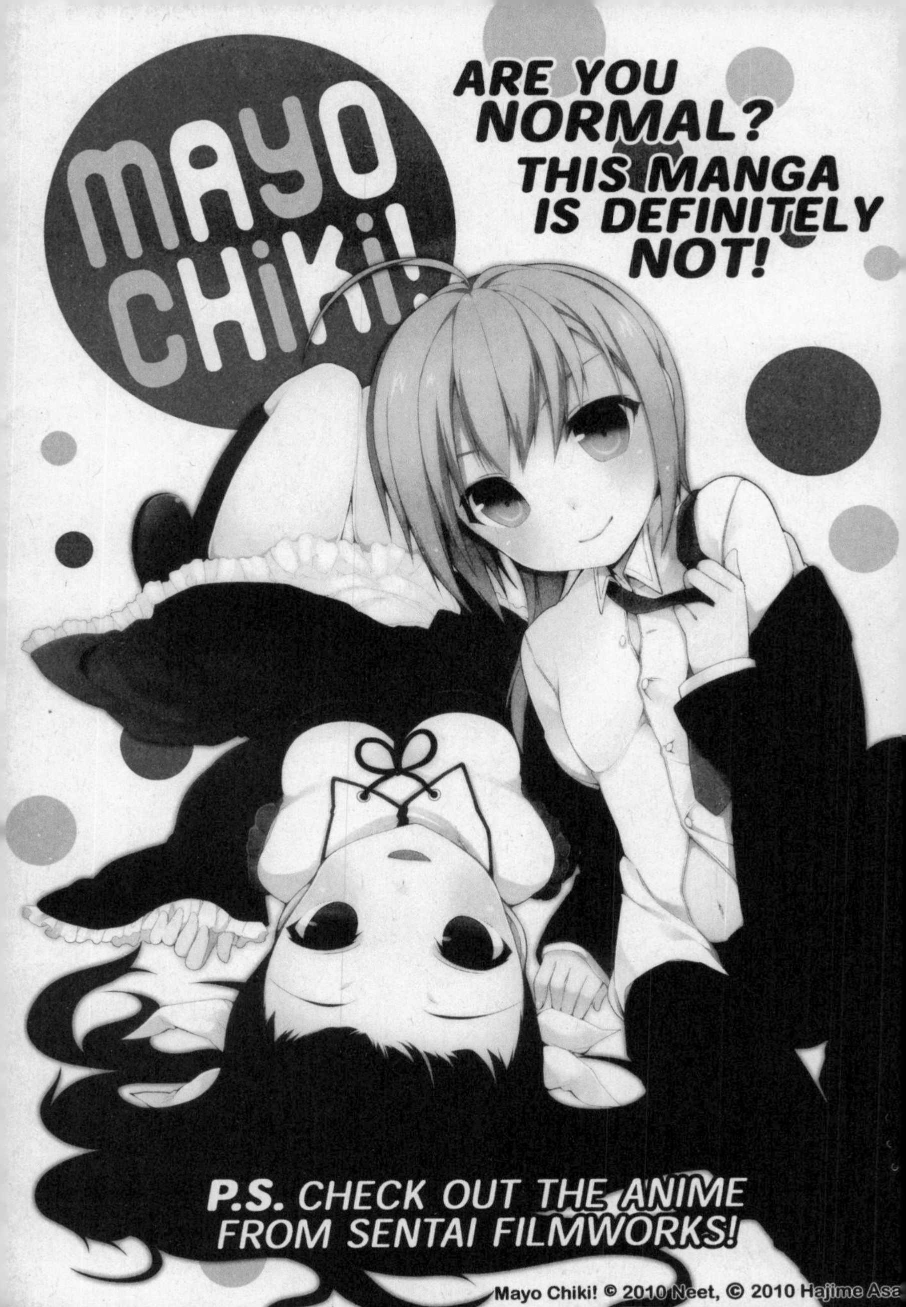
MAYO CHIKI!
ARE YOU NORMAL? THIS MANGA IS DEFINITELY NOT!
P.S. CHECK OUT THE ANIME FROM SENTAI FILMWORKS!

Yuri at its finest...

GIRL FRIENDS: The Complete Collection 1 & 2
Own the whole series today!

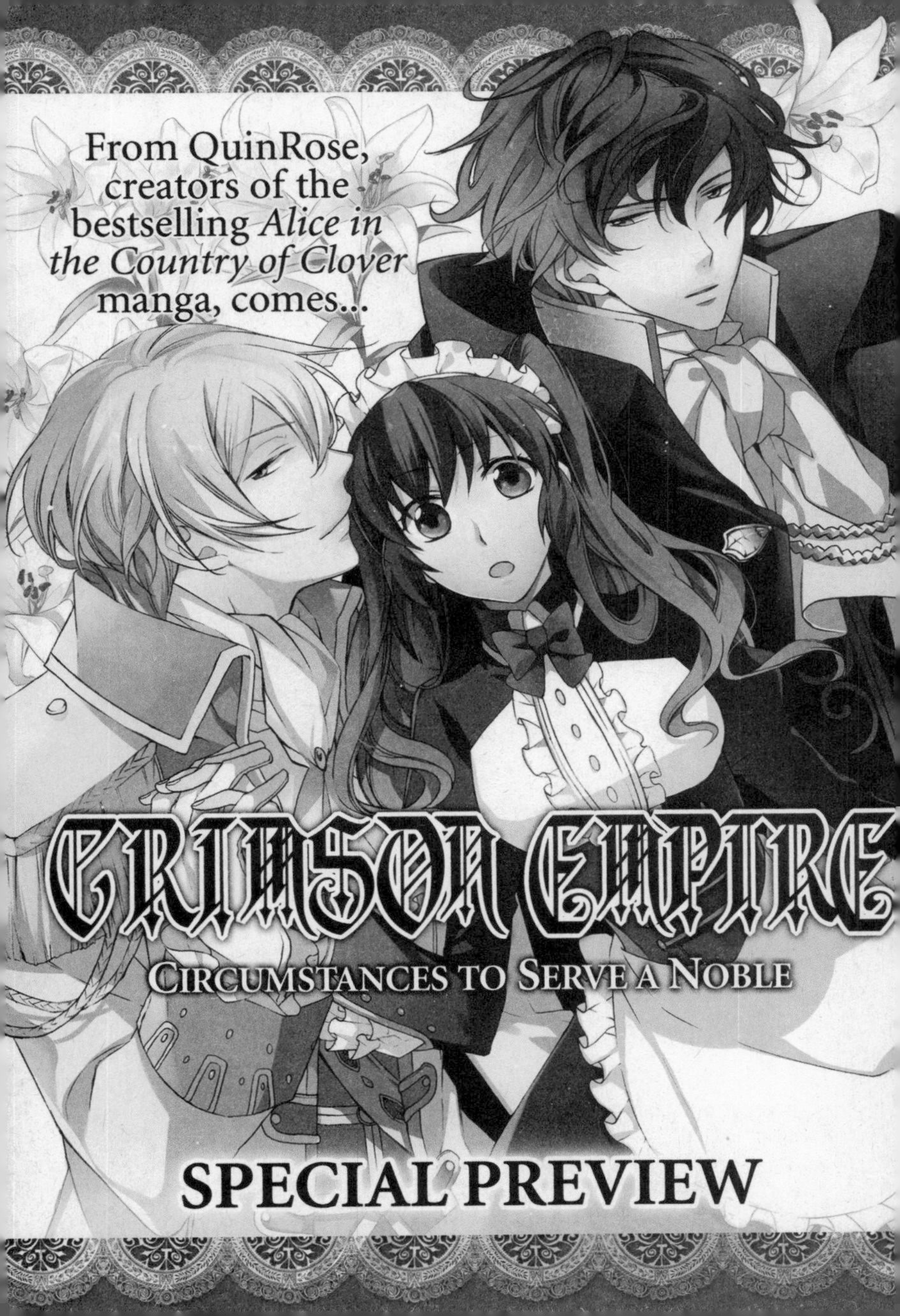
From QuinRose, creators of the bestselling *Alice in the Country of Clover* manga, comes...
CRIMSON EMPIRE
CIRCUMSTANCES TO SERVE A NOBLE
SPECIAL PREVIEW

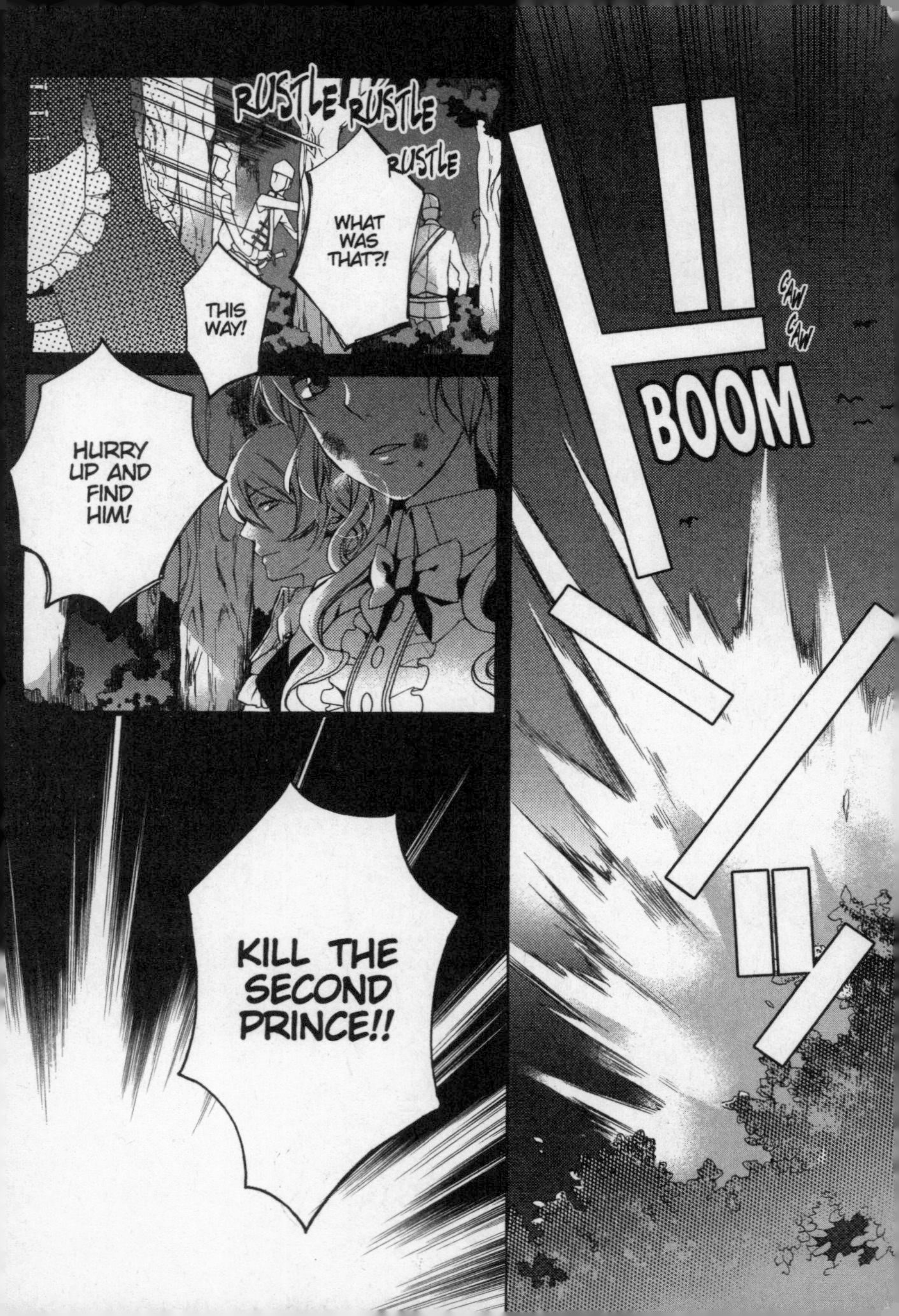
BOOM
CAW CAW
RUSTLE RUSTLE
RUSTLE
WHAT WAS THAT?!
THIS WAY!
HURRY UP AND FIND HIM!
KILL THE SECOND PRINCE!!

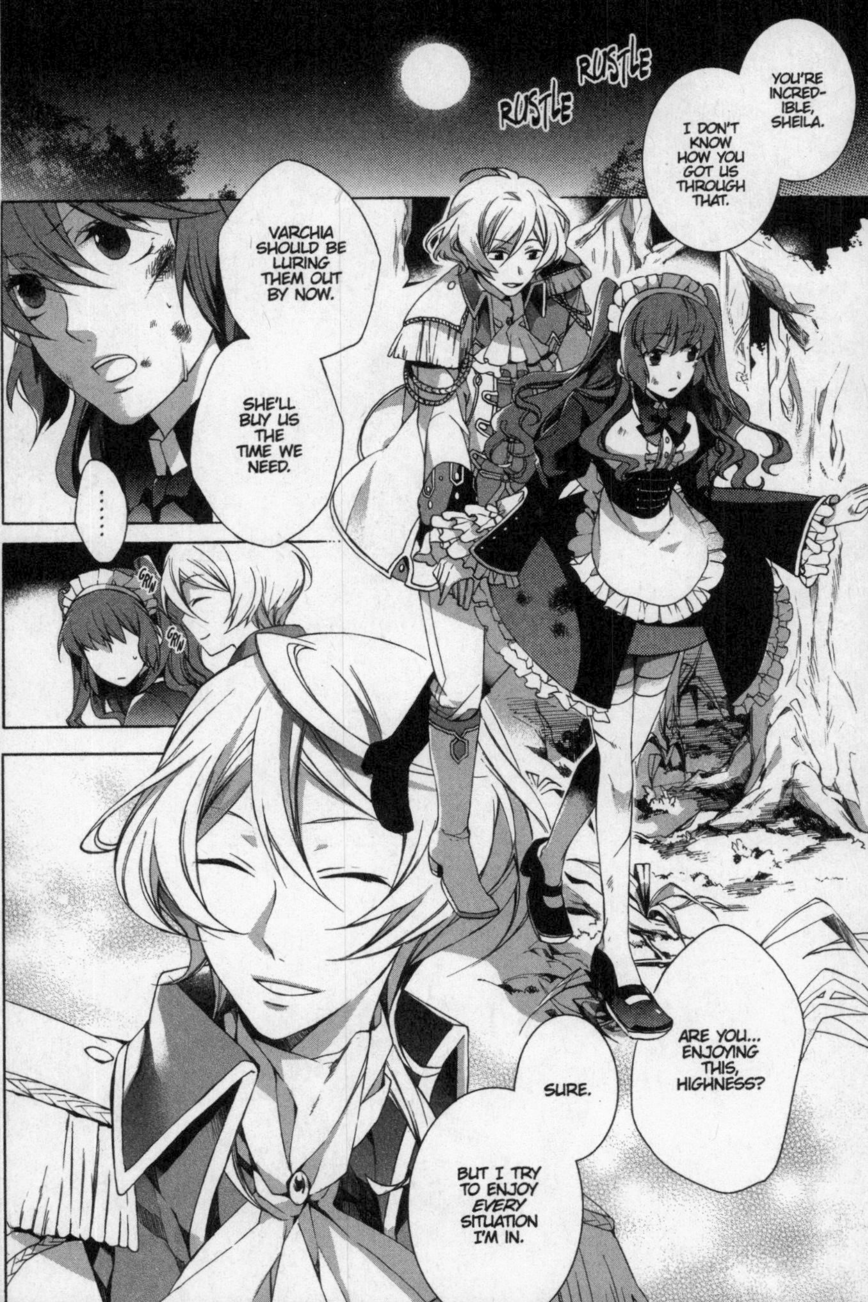
RUSTLE RUSTLE
YOU'RE INCRED-IBLE, SHEILA.
I DON'T KNOW HOW YOU GOT US THROUGH THAT.
VARCHIA SHOULD BE LURING THEM OUT BY NOW.
SHE'LL BUY US THE TIME WE NEED.
......
GRIN GRIN
ARE YOU... ENJOYING THIS, HIGHNESS?
SURE.
BUT I TRY TO ENJOY *EVERY* SITUATION I'M IN.

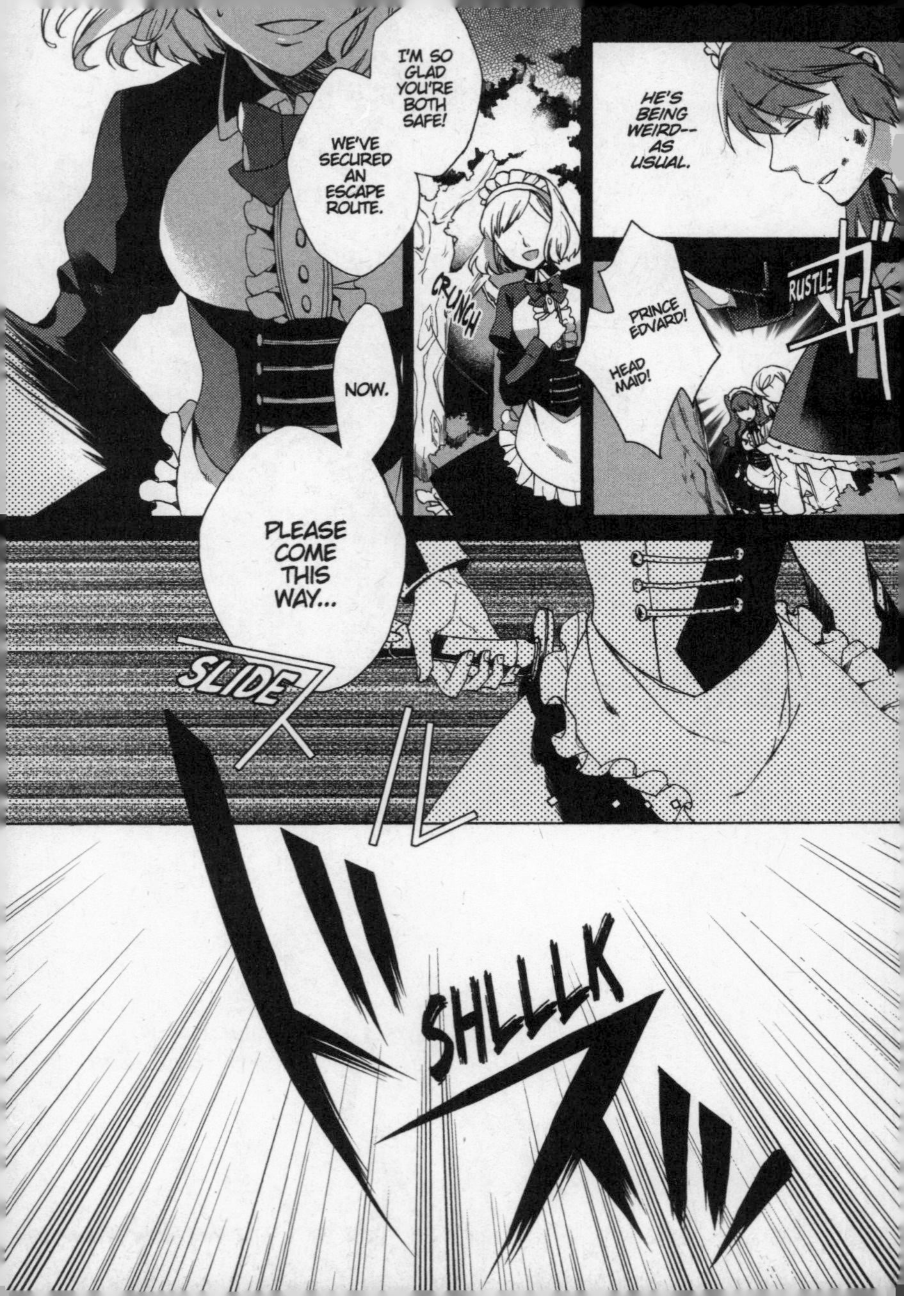
HE'S BEING WEIRD-- AS USUAL.
RUSTLE
PRINCE EDVARD!
HEAD MAID!
I'M SO GLAD YOU'RE BOTH SAFE!
WE'VE SECURED AN ESCAPE ROUTE.
CRUNCH
NOW.
PLEASE COME THIS WAY...
SLIDE
SHLLLK

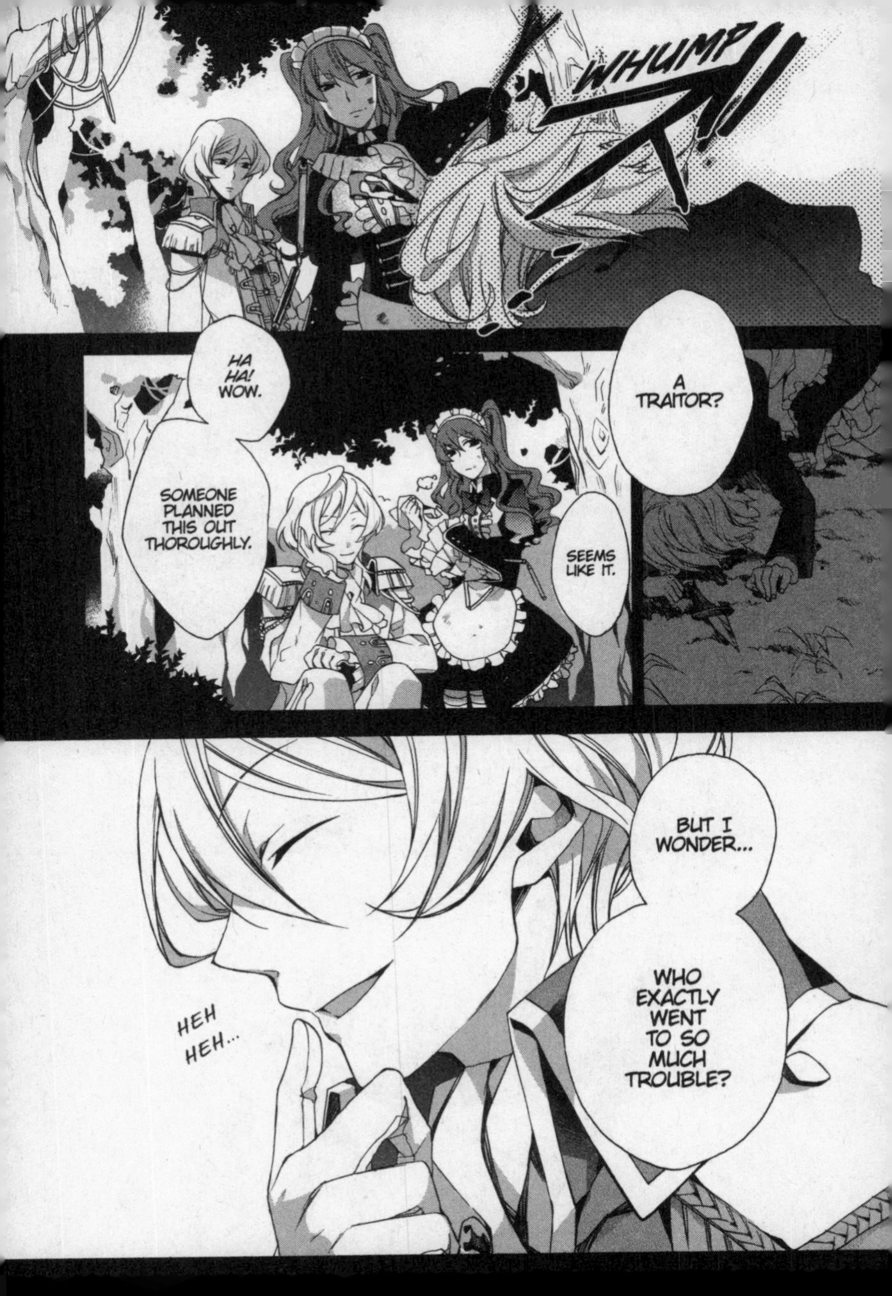
WHUMP!!
A TRAITOR?
SEEMS LIKE IT.
HA HA! WOW.
SOMEONE PLANNED THIS OUT THOROUGHLY.
BUT I WONDER...
WHO EXACTLY WENT TO SO MUCH TROUBLE?
HEH HEH...

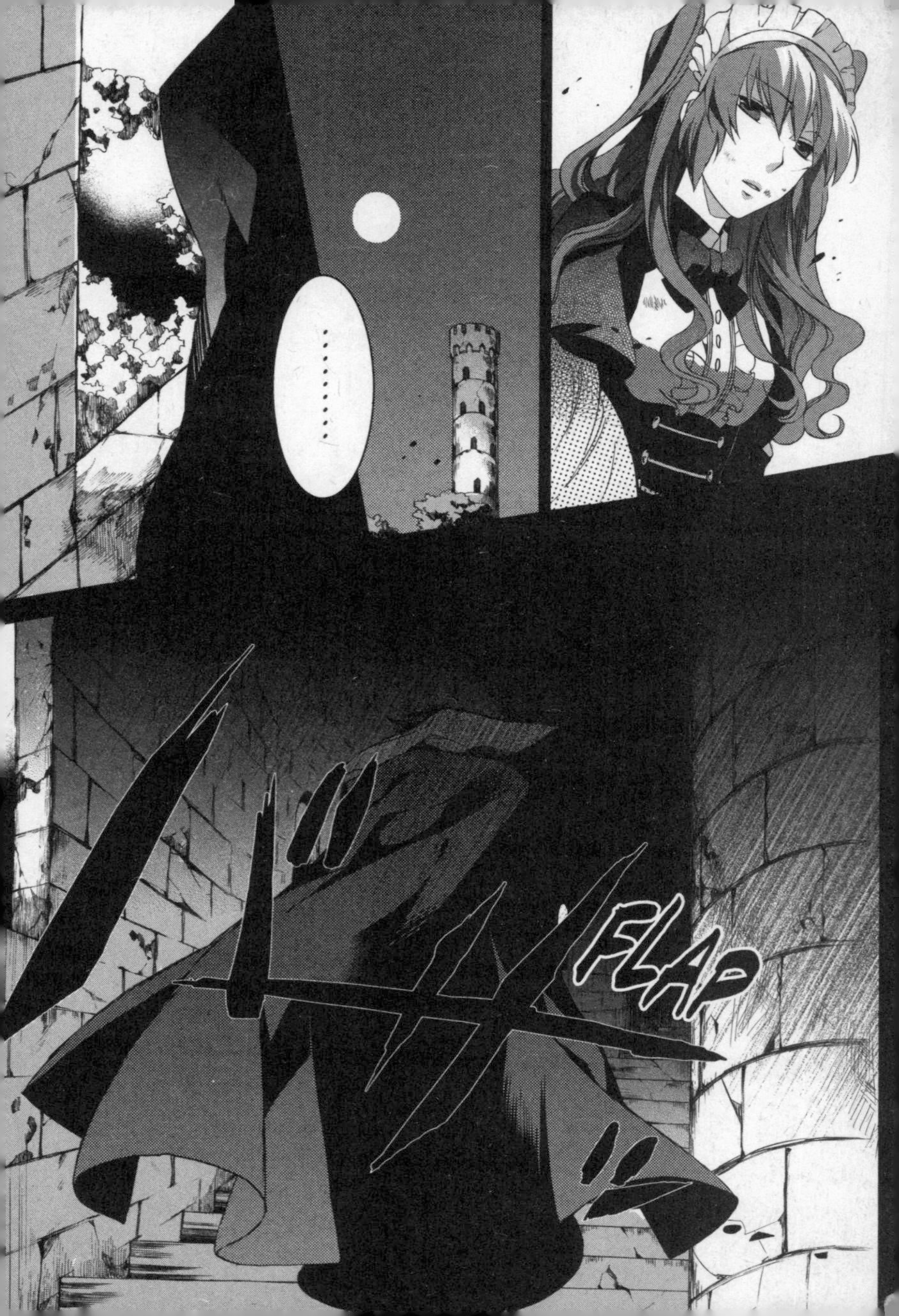

....
FLAP

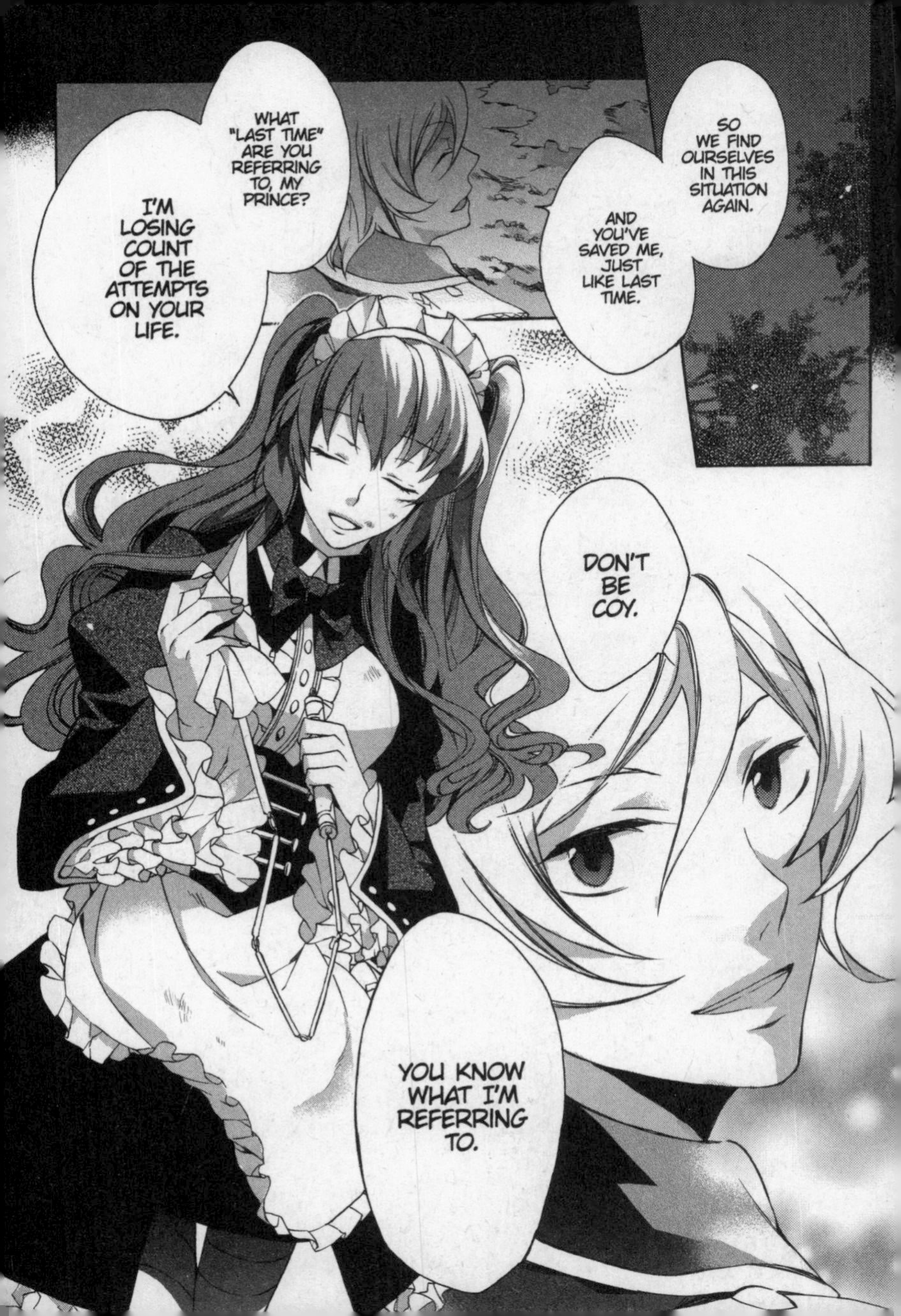
SO WE FIND OURSELVES IN THIS SITUATION AGAIN.
AND YOU'VE SAVED ME, JUST LIKE LAST TIME.
WHAT "LAST TIME" ARE YOU REFERRING TO, MY PRINCE?
I'M LOSING COUNT OF THE ATTEMPTS ON YOUR LIFE.
DON'T BE COY.
YOU KNOW WHAT I'M REFERRING TO.

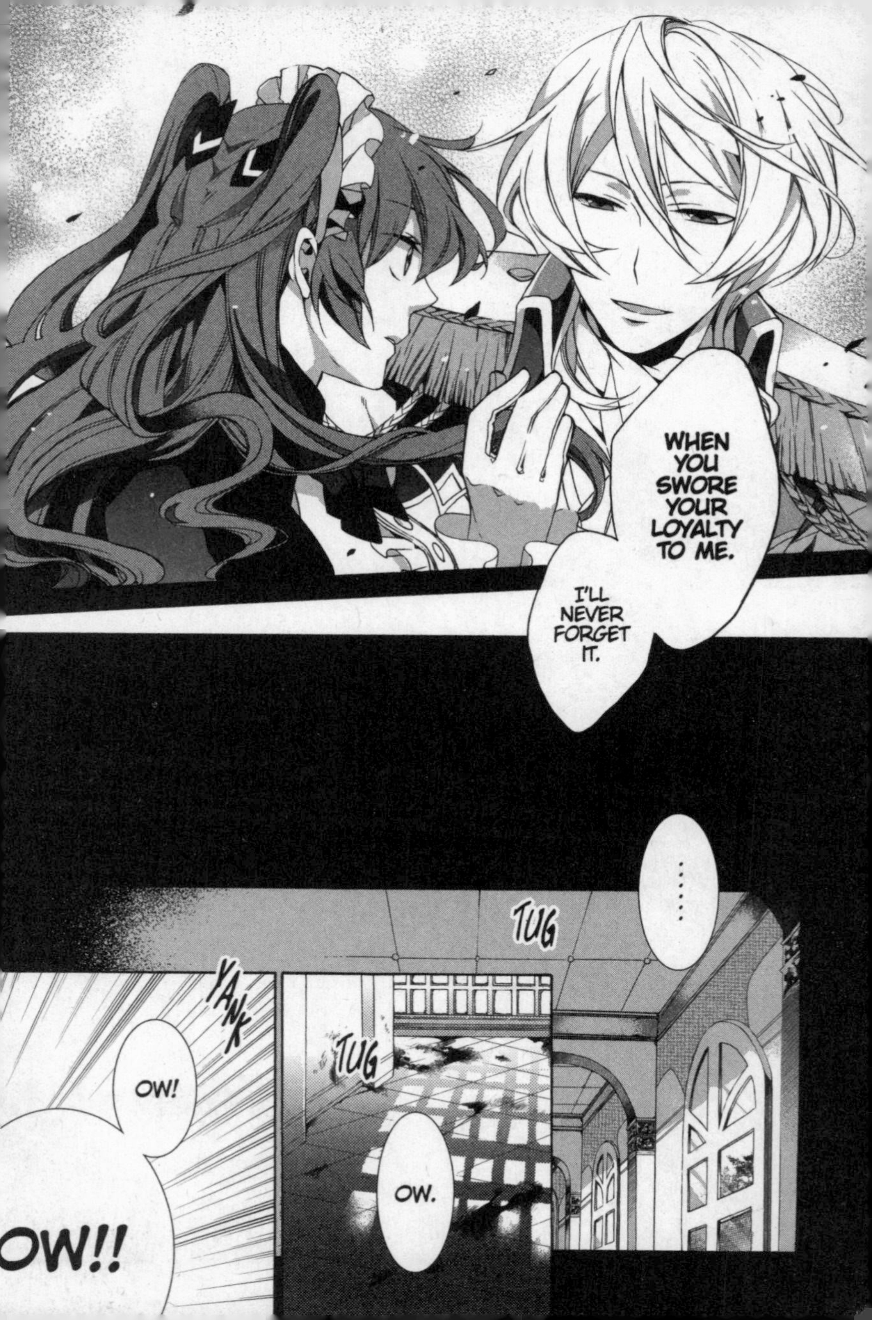
WHEN YOU SWORE YOUR LOYALTY TO ME.
I'LL NEVER FORGET IT.
......
TUG
TUG
OW.
YANK
OW!
OW!!

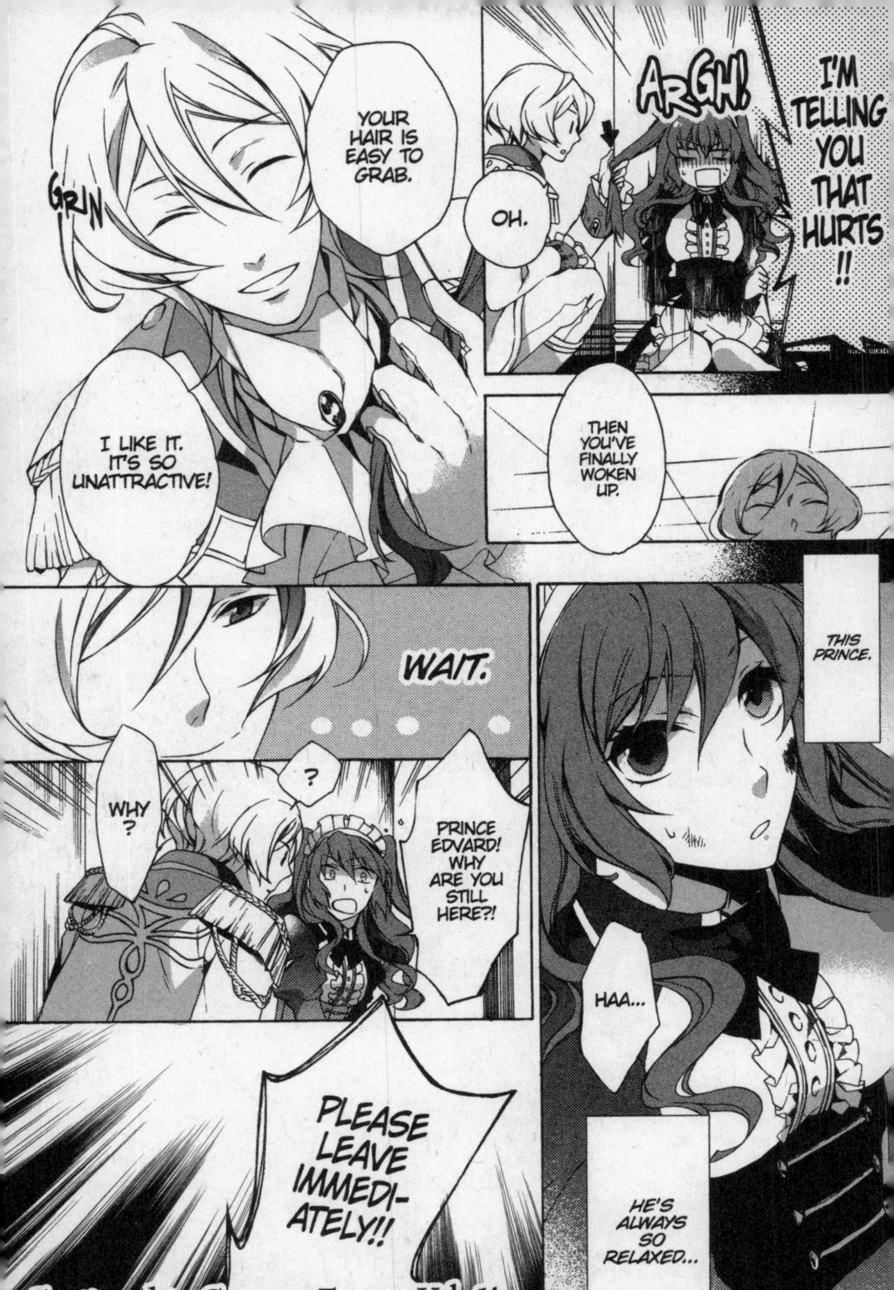

ARGH!
I'M TELLING YOU THAT HURTS!!
OH.
THEN YOU'VE FINALLY WOKEN UP.
YOUR HAIR IS EASY TO GRAB.
GRIN
I LIKE IT. IT'S SO UNATTRACTIVE!
THIS PRINCE.
HAA...
HE'S ALWAYS SO RELAXED...
WAIT.
• • • •
?
PRINCE EDVARD! WHY ARE YOU STILL HERE?!
WHY?
PLEASE LEAVE IMMEDI-ATELY!!

Continued in Crimson Empire Vol. 1!